Proceedings of the American Catholic Philosophical Association

Justice: Then and Now

Volume 90, 2016

Edited by:
Mirela Oliva and Mary Catherine Sommers
Center for Thomistic Studies
University of Saint Thomas

Editorial Assistants:
Andrew Grimes and Joseph Grossheim

Papers for the regular sessions were selected by the Program Committee:
Karen Chan
Chad Engelland
Hans Feichtinger
John Hittinger
Peter Koritansky
Turner Nevitt

Issued by the National Office of the American Catholic Philosophical Association
University of Saint Thomas
Houston, TX 77006

Since 1926 the *Proceedings of the American Catholic Philosophical Association* have published annual volumes that contain papers originally prepared for the Association's annual meeting. This volume contains a selection of papers from the Association's 2016 meeting. The acceptance rate for this volume was 21 percent.

These *Proceedings* are indexed in Academic Search Premier, American Humanities Index, Catholic Periodical and Literature Index, Current Abstracts, Expanded Academic ASAP, Google Scholar, Index Philosophicus, Index to Social Science & Humanities Proceedings, InfoTrac OneFile, International Bibliography of Periodical Literature (IBZ), International Philosophical Bibliography, ISI Alerting Services, Periodicals Index Online, The Philosopher's Index, PhilPapers, and Religious & Theological Abstracts.

For information regarding print copies, subscriptions, online access, and ACPA membership please contact:

Philosophy Documentation Center
P.O. Box 7147
Charlottesville, VA 22906-7147
Phone: 434-220-3300
Fax: 434-220-3301
order@pdcnet.org
www.pdcnet.org

ISBN: 978-1-63435-042-6
ISSN: 0065-7638 (print)
ISSN: 2153-7925 (online)

Published on behalf of the American Catholic Philosophical Association by the Philosophy Documentation Center, Charlottesville, Virginia.

Proceedings of the American Catholic Philosophical Association

Justice: Then and Now

Volume 90, 2016

TABLE OF CONTENTS

Rule of Law and the Virtue of Justice: The Socrates of Plato's *Crito* and a Pair of Later Moral Issues

Kevin L. Flannery, S.J.

Abstract: The author considers, first of all, recent and fairly recent interpretations of Plato's dialogue the *Crito*, arguing that the character Socrates, whose expressed ideas probably correspond in major detail to the convictions of the historical Socrates, is not saying that the laws of Athens demand unquestioning obedience. The dialogue is rather an account of the debate that goes on in Socrates's mind itself. A strong consideration in this debate is clearly the rule of law; but equally strong is Socrates's lifelong commitment to carry out what, in the end, he regards as the most reasonable course of action. The author then considers two contemporary ethical issues: our way of coming to know the natural law and the proper understanding of laws that allow of exceptions. Regarding the first, he argues—consistently with what we find not only in the *Crito* but also in Aristotle and Thomas Aquinas—that we come to know the natural law through being immersed in the laws and customs of a particular society: the more just the society, the better access to the natural law it provides. Regarding the second, he argues that an article in Aquinas is sometimes interpreted as suggesting that the realm of concrete human experience is beyond the reach of law. He argues, in the spirit of the historical Socrates, that the rule of law is equivalent to the rule of reason and that this does reach into the realm of concrete human experience, where exceptions are sometimes recognized as contained in the law.

I. Introduction[1]

Plato's early dialogue *Crito* has often elicited negative reactions because of the main reason Socrates gives in the dialogue for not leaving Athens and so consenting to the sentence of death issued against him by a jury of his fellow citizens. For he says there that he will not leave because that would be to disobey the laws of Athens. Writes George Grote in the nineteenth century:

This dialogue puts into the mouth of Socrates a rhetorical harangue forcible and impressive, which he supposes himself to hear from personified Nomos [law] or Athens, claiming for herself and her laws plenary and

unmeasured obedience from all her citizens, as covenant due to her from
each. He [Socrates] declares his own heartfelt adhesion to the claim.[2]

More recently (that is, in 1979), A. D. Woozley criticizes what he calls "the parental
authority argument" in the *Crito*. He writes: "But to allow that the state's right to
obedience from its subjects is such [as the parental authority argument suggests] is
to concede to the state a metaphysical status which belongs to myth rather than to
reason."[3] Largely owing to Richard Kraut's masterful study *Socrates and the State*,
which appeared in 1984, interpretations of the *Crito* tend now to be more sensitive
to the subtle juggling of ideas that occurs there.[4] But there is still little agreement
on the role the rule of law plays in the dialogue.

What we have, I believe, in the *Crito* is Plato's account of how Socrates's
conscience habitually operated and, in particular, how it operated in the face of
his sentencing to death. The *Crito* depicts the operations of the *virtue* of justice:
not—or not simply—the arithmetical and geometrical operations of the fifth book
of Aristotle's *Nicomachean Ethics*—but the operations of that moral virtue, justice,
in a just soul. Aristotle himself speaks of any virtue as an "aiming": like the aiming
of an archer.[5] An archer's skill comes down ultimately to his having "a feel" for how
to strike a target: possibly a moving target. This feel certainly grows out of what he
has learned in his training as an archer: how a bow works, the differences among
arrows, how accurate a shot can be at what distance, in what conditions, and so on.
But, given these basic principles, the skilled archer still, at the moment of releas-
ing the arrow, must rely on his "sense" that that is the angle, the direction, and the
moment to let it fly.

In what follows, I expound, first of all, how I understand the *Crito*. By most
accounts, the Socrates as portrayed in that dialogue is very close to the historical
Socrates. Since the dialogue was written and rendered public not long after the
death of Socrates, any misrepresentation of Socrates's well-known beliefs and attitudes would have been spurned out of hand. The historical Socrates maintained
that he was incapable of definitive answers in the practical sphere. The Socrates of
the *Crito* is this same Socrates. This does not mean, however, that he regards the
sphere of concrete human actions as ultimately unintelligible, as does the Socrates
in Plato's *Republic* (see 331c1–9). He is committed to seeking always reasonable
answers to moral questions—which is to say answers that are consistent with the
moral truths of which he is quite sure.[6] Having set out these ideas from the *Crito*,
I then bring them to bear upon a pair of issues, arising especially in Aristotle and
Thomas Aquinas, who find rather more intelligibility in the practical sphere than
either Plato or the Socrates of the *Crito*, but whose insights have often been missed
by contemporary authors, even by some who regard themselves as continuing the
Aristotelian-Thomistic tradition.

II. The Socrates of the *Crito*

The basic story line of the *Crito* is familiar to us all. Socrates has already been
condemned to death—ordered by the jury to drink the hemlock—although there

has been a delay of some weeks because of a custom in Athens that no one could be executed until the ship sent every year to Delos to honor Apollo returned. It appears that Socrates has yet a day or two to decide whether to accept the sentence and take the poison or to escape to another city, which would be easy enough. His old and good friend Crito comes to the prison and attempts to persuade Socrates to escape, arguing that both his friends and family would be better off and, indeed, that it would be unjust for him to remain. Socrates presents some of his reasons for not escaping, and then he introduces a chorus of characters of his own who present yet more reasons. "What if," he suggests to Crito, as we were making our escape, "the laws and the commonwealth" should present themselves and ask, "O Socrates, what is it you have in mind to do?"[7] The laws then argue, in tones of authority, that Socrates ought to accept the sentence—which he decides to do. There the dialogue ends.

That the situation is not one in which the correct choice is immediately apparent is indicated by Plato right from the beginning of the dialogue. Crito arrives in the morning and is present as Socrates awakes, who tells him that he has had a dream of a beautiful woman who quotes Homer to him: "On the third day, you would come to fertile Phthia" (44b3). This oracle is ambiguous. On the one hand, Phthia is a city in Thessaly, from which area Crito hails; so the oracle could mean that Socrates is to go off with Crito to Thessaly. On the other hand, the words of the oracle are the words of Achilles in the *Iliad*, who chooses not to go the Phthia (also *his* home) but back into battle where (apparently) he dies for the honor of Athens.[8]

The beautiful woman has indicated to Socrates nothing definitive. Nor does Socrates find Crito's arguments wholly persuasive; and so, having heard him out, he says to him, "We must investigate whether one ought to act in that manner or not, for I—not just at the moment but always—am one who is persuaded by no other of my own reasonings than that one which seems to me, on thinking it through, the best" (46b3–6). Appearing in this remark is a word that occurs in one form or another repeatedly and conspicuously throughout the dialogue: πείθεσθαι (or πείθειν), "to be persuaded." The word itself has been an object of controversy, for one way of avoiding the conclusion that Plato is arguing in the *Crito* that, in the end, we must all simply obey the law, has to do with the meaning of that word as it appears in the argument that Socrates assigns to the voice of the laws. At one point, the laws speak of themselves as "fatherland" [πατρίς—51a9], more holy and estimable even than one's own mother and father, and then tell Socrates that he ought "either to persuade it [the fatherland] or do whatever it commands and suffer in silence whatever it orders one to suffer" (51b3–5). That refrain, "persuade [πείθειν] or obey," occurs a number of times (51b9–c1 and 51e7) in the subsequent discourse—where it certainly sounds like the ultimatum that (I believe) it is. But it has been pointed out that the key word πείθειν might be translated as "to try to persuade." Understanding the situation thus would allow for disobedience, as long as a sincere effort is made to persuade the commonwealth that its judgment is wrong.

This solution strikes me (and several others commentators) as implausible. If all Socrates has to do in order to leave Athens with ethical consistency is to *attempt* to persuade the fatherland, why does he not just do that and be done with it? The fact is, however, that the persuasion of which Plato speaks is not the hit-or-miss persuasion that occurs in forensic situations, where orators or sophists attempt to win over other minds; it is occurring in the mind of Socrates himself, who is persuaded (as we have seen) by "no other of [his] own reasonings than that one which seems to [him], on thinking it through, the best." Socrates cannot bring himself to consent to Crito's solution of an escape because to do so would be to consent to there remaining in his practical reasoning—in his conscience—an inconsistency. Such a situation is unlike failing to persuade a jury—which one can do (that is, fail to persuade) and still maintain one's intellectual self-respect. The point of this (internal) debate is to overcome any such internal conflict.

The laws speaking within Socrates present strong arguments which conflict with the arguments presented by Crito. They argue, for instance, that Socrates's friends and children would probably be worse off if he flees (53a8–b3, 54a5–b1) and (most prominently) that by remaining in Athens for so long without rejecting its laws he has, in effect, accepted them as binding—if not upon all living there—then upon him. The laws themselves acknowledge that their arguments are not "compelling" in either sense of that word. "We propose things," they say; "we do not churlishly give orders to do whatever we command."[9] So, it may indeed be that there is no hard and fast principle telling Socrates to accept the sentence of death rather than to flee. Nonetheless, the arguments adduced by the laws are strong. As he says, he will go with the piece of reasoning that seems to him, "on thinking it through, the best." By sticking to this methodology—and rejecting the argument that seems to him not the best—he eliminates from his practical reasoning the unease of serious doubt.

That this is what is going on in the *Crito* is an aid in understanding a puzzling remark that Socrates makes as he is introducing the voice of the laws into his conversation with Crito. As we have seen, Socrates raises at one point the prospect that the laws might present themselves and ask, "O Socrates, what is it you have in mind to do?"—that is, by fleeing, as Crito suggests he should. And then the laws add:

> Do you conceive of that which you propose to do as anything other than to destroy us and the entire city in as much as in you lies? Or does it seem to you that the city can exist and not be overthrown in which judgments issued have no force but are rendered moot by private persons and so destroyed?[10]

But how is it that this one instance of defying a judgment—which the laws themselves (later in this same discourse) recognize as unjust (54b8–c3)—would destroy the laws and "the entire city"?[11] Might not such defiance even cause the city to reconsider its way of selecting juries, its rules for the admission of evidence, and so on? But, again, this argument is not really about winning and losing arguments in tribunals or assemblies or about changing legal procedures. It is about taking seriously strong arguments and being consistent in one's own thinking. If such considerations in fact do not matter—if consistency itself does not matter—, how can law survive? How can civilization survive?

III. Natural Law

I would like now to discuss two issues of contemporary interest in ethics. They correspond to the two sides of the Socratic coin: the one side imaging the fundamental role of law in ethical decision making; the other, law's reasonability. The first issue concerns our way of coming to know the natural law; the second, the proper understanding of laws that allow of exceptions. The intellectual structure within which these issues arise is a Thomistic one. I do not claim, of course, that Thomas Aquinas knew the *Crito*—in all likelihood he had never heard of it—but the foundations of his ethical theory are Aristotelian, and Aristotle, I would argue, shared two things with the Socrates of the *Crito*: the belief that the basis of ethics is to be found in law (or laws)—both written and unwritten—and the conviction that genuine law is reasonable.[12]

This concept, "genuine law," *pace* the authors mentioned earlier, is present throughout Plato's early works. The way that Plato, in the *Crito* but also in other dialogues, understands the various levels of law bears a marked resemblance to the hierarchy of laws that Thomas inherited from Augustine, according to which human (temporal) law falls under natural law and natural law under eternal law (or God himself).[13] The *Apology of Socrates* belongs to the same period in Plato's career as the *Crito*, during which he was primarily interested in passing on his master's teaching. In the work (it is not really a dialogue), Socrates recounts how he defied the "unjust" [ἄδικον] and "unholy" [ἀνόσιον] order of the Thirty Tyrants to him and to four others to bring in the innocent Leon of Salamis to be executed.[14] "For that regime [ἀρχή], however strong it was, did not frighten me into doing something unjust [ἄδικόν τι]," he says; "but, when we left the Rotunda, the four went to Salamis and fetched Leon; I, however, walked away homewards" (32c8–d7). Just prior to this remark, Socrates also recounts that he voted, when Athens was still a democracy, against the condemnation of certain generals who had failed to gather up the dead after the battle of Arginusae. He describes that condemnation as illegal.[15]

It is apparent that Plato considered both condemnations—not only that of the generals but also that of Leon—to be illegal; both the decisions of democratic assemblies and "executive actions" are for him, therefore, answerable to a law of a higher rank. We find, of course, a somewhat different situation in the *Crito*—and yet a certain hierarchy of laws is also there in evidence. The laws, as we have seen, recognize that the condemnation of Socrates was unjust, and yet they maintain that the jury followed proper procedure, according to what we would call positive law. The personified laws also speak of a law (or laws) above themselves. They tell Socrates that, should he leave Athens, they will be angry with him while he lives but, "also in the netherworld, our brothers, the laws in Hades, will not receive you kindly, knowing that you undertook to destroy us, in as much as in you lies" (54d6–8). So, it is clear that Socrates (along with Plato) recognizes levels of law, not unlike what we find in Thomas.

But the crucial question is, how does Socrates—or anyone, for that matter—come to know the higher laws? As I have been arguing, Plato's *Crito* is about conscience: the operations of Socrates's conscience; but it is clearly not about what is sometimes called "personal conscience." Near the end of the dialogue, Socrates compares the various voices—or arguments—in the dialogue to persons afflicted by a corybantic frenzy who are finally tamed by the music of flutes:[16] the voices in his mind agree in the end that the option most consistent with the moral convictions already established there is to remain in Athens.[17] But these voices correspond to realities outside his mind: to the arguments of his friend Crito and, most especially, to the rule of law as discoverable by honest and open immersion in the political culture of Athens. Socrates's frenzy ultimately comes to rest, then, in genuine law such as is consistent with a higher law. How then do we come to know the higher law? By a similar—but always critical—immersion.

One very common contemporary answer to the question "How do we come to know the higher laws?" is that we recognize that law which is above human law—that is to say, the natural law—in the basic human goods such as life, knowledge, self-integration, and practical reasonableness.[18] According to this approach, the first precept of practical reason directs us towards good ("good is to be done and pursued"), this precept being specified (or "determined") with respect to the basic human goods. Reference to these goods constitutes the entire sense of these "determinations" of the first principle, which are the basic precepts of the natural law.[19] This approach has the advantage of providing an explanation of how the natural law can be said to be known, at least in its most general contours, by everyone. The precepts of natural law, in that they direct one's thinking toward life, knowledge, etc., are "self-evident."[20] This quality, self-evidence, is to be associated—or so the argument goes—with the expression, *per se notum quoad nos*, as employed in the much studied article of the *Summa theologiae* on the number of the precepts of the natural law: *Summa theologiae* 1-2.94.2.[21]

But the same approach is very different from what we find in Plato—and, as I would argue, from what we find in Thomas Aquinas. Basic in Plato are not goods but laws. The laws in the *Crito* insist with Socrates that he has in effect made an agreement to obey them in so far as he has never rejected them, by whom he has been formed.[22] They make also an allusion to the "right of passage" in the education of young men in ancient Athens, at which point one "has been deemed worthy [δοκιμασθῇ] and has beheld both the way things are done in the city and us the laws."[23]

This set of presuppositions comes into the Thomistic tradition. Aristotle speaks of the requisite period of formation in the first book of the *Nicomachean Ethics*, where he says that, in ethics, we must begin with the things intelligible to us, either composites or *sensibilia*, as opposed to things (such as the first principles of geometry) that are intelligible *simpliciter*.[24] "For this reason," he says, "it is necessary that one, who would assist competently at lectures regarding things that are noble, just and (generally) political, be brought up well in the customs."[25] In Thomas's commentary he identifies what is learned in this ethical novitiate as the things that are *magis nota quoad nos*.[26]

Not insignificant here is the idea that a young person comes only gradually to understand the bases of ethics; but also important for present purposes is the idea that what one comes to understand are not, strictly speaking, self-evident precepts about human goods but rather laws and customs with determinate content—which are, however, consonant with our basic inclinations such as are indeed oriented towards goods. These are what Thomas says, in the article on the precepts of natural law (*ST* 1-2.94.2), are *per se nota quoad nos*: "intelligible in themselves" not *solis sapientibus* (not solely to the wise) but "even to us." Plato acknowledges in the *Crito* that the various systems of law are not equally suited to this task of instilling in youth the first principles of justice. The personified laws of Athens describe Thessaly—which certainly had a legal system—as "full of disorder and licentiousness" (53d3–4) and so as relatively unsuitable for bringing up children. Nonetheless, it is within a system of laws that a young person arrives at a grasp of the precepts that correspond to the higher law. The better the system, the more access it provides.

It might be argued that, in the passages in the commentary on the *Ethics* here cited, Thomas speaks not of things that are *per se nota quoad nos* (as in *ST* 1-2.94.2) but of things that are *magis nota quoad nos*. In this same section of his commentary, however, he makes the same distinction that we find in *ST* 1-2.94.2 between the sort of knowledge a mathematician has and that which is required for ethical thought or practice—and there can be little doubt that he would put that in ethics which is known *per se quoad nos* (as in *ST* 1-2.94.2) on the *magis nota quoad nos* side of the distinction drawn in the commentary, that is, among the things that one knows not qua theoretician but at the level of moral perception.[27] Such things are learned, especially in our day, in good families and good schools. He also says in this section of the commentary, as part of his remarks on the things that are *magis nota quoad nos*, that a man who is an expert in human matters "can be possessed of these principles of actions either on his own as one who considers them *per se*, or he can easily pick them up from another."[28]

Locating the bases of ethics in propositions simply about self-evident goods makes it very difficult to defend a number of distinctions that are part of the natural law tradition. According to this approach to natural law, performing an immoral action is a matter of intending and choosing contrary to the goods mentioned in the first precepts rather than a matter of acting not in accordance with precepts having explicitly to do with the type of actions at issue.

At the beginning of the corpus of *ST* 2-2.64.7 on killing in self-defense, Thomas Aquinas says that, in the case of self-defense by a private individual, where the death of the assailant is beside the agent's intention [*praeter intentionem*], such an act can be moral (given proportionality of the means employed).[29] Those who understand the first precepts of natural law as simply about self-evident goods interpret Thomas as saying here (with his talk of intention) that what makes such acts moral is the fact that the agent makes no choice going contrary to the good of (human) life. But there's a problem with this. Later in the same corpus Thomas acknowledges that killing in war and capital punishment *are* intended but he also says that they are permissible (provided no other factors such as private animosity enter in).[30]

If one holds that a choice against a basic good (as mentioned in the appropriate first precept) is decisive in natural law ethics, this is inexplicable—or, at least, inexplicable in a convincing manner. But that is not the basis upon which Thomas makes the two affirmations. The first (that private self-defense can be moral) mentions as a preliminary point that any action gets its species from what is intended, not from what is beside the intention. A species of acts, however, can contain either good acts or bad acts. Thomas's point about what is within or outside of one's intention has nothing directly to do with whether the acts are good or bad: for or against the natural law. And so that preliminary point cannot be the basis of Thomas's assertion that private self-defense is not immoral.[31]

The primary component in that basis is rather the principle that "it is natural for anything to maintain itself in being, as far as that is possible." In invoking this principle Thomas does not mean to suggest that even this principle is morally determinative with respect to all cases in which a private citizen kills an attacker, for in the same breath he says that such a killing, if it involves disproportionate means, is immoral. The idea is rather that, given the larger moral and legal complex in which it is situated, which includes the various species of acts, this particular species is permissible as an instance of maintaining oneself in being, as far as that is possible.

The second affirmation (that those with the appropriate public authority are permitted to intend to kill) depends upon a different set of concrete moral and legal factors and (to repeat) not upon whether the choice goes—or does not go—contrary to a precept whose whole sense is the idea that human life is good. Thomas mentions in this regard "the case of the soldier fighting against the foe and of the minister of a judge struggling with robbers." Such "intendings to kill" are permissible because "the public good" requires it. Or, as Thomas puts it, "it is not lawful for a man to intend killing a man in self-defense, except for such as have public authority, who while intending to kill a man in self-defense, refer this to the public good." Such acts are of a different species from acts of private self-defense.

A similar problem confronts those who, by invoking the basic human goods, wish to defend the Church's distinction between (immoral) artificial contraception and (moral) natural family planning (NFP). For it is apparent that couples who practice the latter intend and choose not to have a child—that is why its called family *planning*—and yet that is also the reason why artificial contraception would be immoral: that is, because its intention is to impede the good of a prospective life.

In contrast then to approaches to the natural law that look primarily to precepts regarding the basic human goods, it is much easier and more plausible to say that the moral difference between these various types of acts depends upon what is reasonable and so recognized in sound law, whether written or unwritten. It is reasonable, that is, on such a basis to maintain that a soldier's deliberate killing in battle or a young couple's choice to begin a family a year or two later is acceptable human behavior but that intentionally killing even a threatening neighbor or deliberately thwarting the inherent purpose of the marital act is not.

There are wholly understandable reasons why a scholar might want to disassociate natural law from "law"—that word rumbling with the appropriately ominous timbre—by associating it rather with intended good (or goods): they are the same reasons that have prompted negative reactions, especially in fairly recent years, to the *Crito* and to Socrates's decision to remain in Athens because the laws call for that.

The desire to avoid, when expounding one's preferred ethical theory, denunciation as "legalistic" is not without sense. But, as argued above, the position advocated in the *Crito* cannot be described as legalistic. Not only is it recognized there that some cities are governed by bad laws but, as we know, the Socrates who speaks there was prepared in certain cases to disobey even the laws of Athens, which system of laws he regarded as good. The just person is the person, formed by the laws in upright behavior, who seeks to determine honestly and with logical rigor what is the best thing to do in whatever situation.

IV. Laws that Allow of Exceptions

We find this same combination of high regard for laws and virtuous commitment to justice as distinct from the legalistic in Aristotle—and, by derivation, also in Thomas Aquinas. In the first five chapters of book five of the *Nicomachean Ethics*, Aristotle sets out what were described above as the "arithmetical and geometrical operations" of justice; that is to say, his account of the types of "universal" justice: distributive and corrective (or commutative) justice.[32] In the succeeding six chapters, he addresses a number of connected issues, explaining more fully and precisely what he understands by justice. In chapter 7, he divides political justice into natural political justice and legal political justice. Legal political justice is conventional, he says, and so "not by nature" [οὐ φύσει—1134b30], although even natural political justice is "moveable" or "changeable."[33] And then in chapter 10, he considers ἐπιείκεια (reasonableness) and τὸ ἐπιεικὲς (the reasonable). These words—ἐπιείκεια and τὸ ἐπιεικὲς—could be translated 'equity' and 'the equitable'; but, since those terms are today instinctively understood as legal terms, in the present context it is best to avoid those translations, so as to obviate any suggestion that ἐπιείκεια and τὸ ἐπιεικὲς have to do with the "merely legal." In the Liddell-Scott-Jones *Greek-English Lexicon*, the primary—and more literal—meaning given for ἐπιείκεια is 'reasonableness.' Some recent translations of the *Nicomachean Ethics* render the word as 'decency.'

Regarding the reasonable, Aristotle remarks rather paradoxically—but quite accurately—that:

> 'Just' and 'reasonable' are the same thing and both are good but the reasonable is better. This, however, brings to the fore the aporia that the reasonable is just—not, however, the just according to the law but rather a correction of the legally just.[34]

He goes on to explain. A lawmaker must frame a law in general terms, knowing from the beginning [εὐθὺς] that it will sometimes miss its mark since that is the nature of the matter [ἡ ὕλη] he is dealing with: human affairs (1137b19). "[T]he defect [ἁμάρτημα]," he says, "is not in the law or in the lawmaker but in the nature of the affair" (1137b17–19). Were the lawmaker on the scene when the law actually misses its mark, he would certainly correct the shortcoming and legislate accordingly (1137b22–24). In the chapter's concluding remarks, Aristotle says that "he who is inclined to prefer and to do such [reasonable] things and whose precision with respect to justice is directed not toward the worse but who diminishes the difficulties, even while having the law as his aid, is reasonable [ἐπιεικής]."[35] Aristotle's saying that the person he has in mind "is inclined to prefer and to do" [προαιρετικὸς καὶ πρακτικός] the right and reasonable thing is clear indication that he is referring now to a character trait: a moral virtue in the strict sense.

Plato is depicting this same virtue in his portrayal of the Socrates of the *Crito*: a man who takes the law seriously—to the point of dying in obedience to it—but is also committed to the exercise of reason, the very essence of law. This same virtue comes into Thomas Aquinas, who, in a frequently cited article of the *Summa*, basically repeats the Aristotelian position on reasonableness (ἐπιείκεια) and its relationship to law. Thomas says in *ST* 1-2.94.4—that is, just two articles after the article about the precepts of the natural law—that, although the common principles of practical reason enjoy "a certain necessity" [*aliqua necessitas*], "the more one goes down into proper principles, the more one encounters defect [*defectus*]."[36] And then: "In matters of action, there is not the same truth or practical rectitude for all with respect to the proper [principles], but only with respect to the common [principles]."[37]

The *defectus* of which Thomas speaks here is not a characteristic of the moral situation to which a lower proper principle (or precept) of practical reason pertains—or, more precisely, fails to pertain. It has to do rather with the relationship between a lower "proper" principle and the situation under consideration. There is a disparity. The principle speaks of something that does not apply to the situation at hand. So, the *defectus* has nothing immediately to do with either the proper principle itself or with the situation to which it refers. The word *defectus* refers only to the mismatch between the two. There is a disparity between law as formulated and law as it should be applied.[38] This is not to deny that in a sense there is something inadequate about the principle in as much as it "fails" to apply to the situation; the point is rather that (as we shall see more clearly shortly) the principle was never meant so to apply to such situations.

It is also important to acknowledge that there is nothing negative or lacking in that to which the proper principle "fails" to refer. Thomas's position is not that these states of affair are somehow defective or unintelligible. This point has been missed in a couple of recent ecclesial documents: to wit, the International Theological Commission's "In search of a universal ethic: a new look at the natural law" (2009) and Pope Francis's apostolic exhortation *Amoris laetitia* (2016). Both of these documents translate the remark about encountering disparity between proper principle and concrete situation in a way that suggests that, as we enter into the realm of concrete moral situations, the situations themselves become indeterminate.

The Theological Commission's document translates the relevant piece in the following manner:

> although there is some necessity in the general principles, the more we descend to particular matters, the more we encounter indeterminacy. . . .
> In matters of action, truth or practical rectitude is not the same for all in its particular applications, but only in its general principles.[39]

Amoris laetitia has a similar rendering of the same passage, speaking, however, at least in the English translation, not (as in the Theological Commission's translation) of "particular matters" and "particular applications" but (in both cases) of "matters of detail."[40] But both translations simply ignore the word twice repeated here: *propria*, which clearly makes reference not to "particular matters" or "matters of detail" but to proper principles—which (again) occasionally fail to apply to particular cases.[41]

The relevant section of *Amoris laetitia* has to do with the application of "rules" to possibly irregular marriage situations. Such an interpretation of Thomas's words can easily be used to argue that, in particular cases, there is no way that we can ever say whether a valid marriage was ever contracted, for such matters are inherently indeterminate. The document speaks in this section of having recourse to "discernment"—which is fine, as long as the discernment is conducted with the assistance of the rationality embodied in law or (as Aristotle puts it) "even while having the law as [one's] aid" (*EN* 5.10.1138a1–2). The problem is that, once reason and the rule of law have been excluded, all that is left is things like personal preference, self-deception, and ideology.

It is not impossible to mount a defense of such translations (or, actually, interpretations) of *ST* 1-2.94.4. In Thomas's own commentary on Aristotle's chapter on reasonableness (*EN* 5.10), he writes: "Because the matter of human actions is indeterminate, thus it is that their measure—which is the law—must be indeterminate, as if not always being in the same state."[42] He also occasionally speaks as if there were something defective in the situations to which a law would—but ultimately does not—apply, thereby giving the impression that there is a realm in human experience beyond the reach of reason and so of law.[43] But those remarks are more plausibly understood as his saying that, because in human affairs one intelligible state can easily change into another—when, that is, in a particular situation, a morally relevant "circumstance" is present—human affairs are such that possibly qualifying factors cannot be put into laws.[44]

In other words, Thomas is not saying in *ST* 1-2.94.4 that the realm of human experience is beyond the reach of practical reason: quite the contrary. He cites there an example that occurs also in Plato.[45] A "proper conclusion," he says, from the common principle "act according to reason" is that "deposits are to be returned." This proper conclusion (or principle) is in general true, he says, but "it can happen that to do so would be harmful and, as a consequence, irrational." Suppose that the deposit left with one is a weapon and that its owner demands its return so that he might fight against the commonwealth (the *patria*).[46] Thomas finds absolutely no indeterminacy here. It would be irrational, he says—and, therefore, contrary to the common principle that he cites ("act according to reason")—to return the weapon.[47]

He cites this same example in his commentary on the passage in *EN* 5.10 where Aristotle says that "the defect [ἁμάρτημα] is not in the law or in the lawmaker but in the nature of the affair" and that, were the lawmaker present when the law actually misses its mark, he would certainly correct the shortcoming and legislate accordingly (1137b17–24).[48] This section of his commentary concludes with the remark: "and so here it is necessary to bring the legally just into line with the naturally just."[49]

The case mentioned in no way eludes the reasonability—the light—of justice. As Aristotle says, "'just' and 'reasonable' are the same thing and both are good but the reasonable is better" (*EN* 5.10.1137b10–11). There are occasions when one must take into consideration the supposed—but no less authentic—"mind of the legislator" or "the intention of the law."[50]

V. Conclusion

The Socrates of the *Crito* conducts his inquiry at the level of moral perception: the level at which *any* moral agent senses when he is about to do something wrong—or not quite right—but the practically wise man can explain why and counsel accordingly. It is, of course, true that in Socrates's inquiry an important and ultimately decisive factor is the voice of the laws. But just as important even there, is what is often missed in readings of the *Crito*: that this Socrates has unswerving confidence that reason can bring us as close as is possible to moral truth. If one is conscientious in applying reason—including especially the reason inherent in law—in debate with others and with oneself, one will have fulfilled one's moral obligation toward the truth and can proceed with a clean conscience.

This is the core meaning—the substance—of Socrates's personal axiom that he knows nothing other than that he knows nothing. His knowing-that-he-knows-not is his knowing that moral situations are such that he must be constantly open to the recognition of additional factors (or "circumstances"). Without minimizing in any way the role of law in moral formation and ethical decision making—and that is the main message of the *Crito*—it must also be affirmed that the practically wise man is one who is aware that the law itself recognizes (at a certain level) the possibility of *defectus*. This is not, however, a defect of reason in moral reality itself. Quite the contrary: the *defectus* has to do with the intelligibility—the inherent reason of—the particular situation that presents itself to the moral sensibility of the practically wise man.

Pontifical Gregorian University (Rome)

Notes

The notes are followed by a reference list, which includes bibliographic details for the works cited.

1. I thank a number of people who made comments on an earlier version of this paper, including Michael Bradley, Randall Smith, Jennifer Frey, Alessandra Tanesini, Kristján Kristjánsson, Luca Tuninetti, Arianna Fermani, and Germain Grisez. Indeed, I would like to dedicate this article to Germain, who died while it was going to press, and whose thought propelled me—sometimes by way of provocation—into the world of philosophical ethics.

2. George Grote, *Plato, and the other Companions of Sokrates*, v.1 302.

3. A. D. Woozley, *Law and Obedience*, 72.

4. Richard Kraut, *Socrates and the State*.

5. *EN* 2.6.1106b6–7; see Kevin L. Flannery, *Action and Character according to Aristotle*, 163–169.

6. In the *Crito*, for instance, he states in the strongest terms that he believes that we ought never voluntarily to act unjustly or to requite wrong with wrong. See 47a13–c4, 48a5–7, 49a4–b6, and 49d5–e2. And in the *Apology*, he states quite flatly says that he knows this; that is, he says he knows that one should not do injustice or disobey a superior, whether man or god: τὸ δὲ ἀδικεῖν καὶ ἀπειθεῖν τῷ βελτίονι καὶ θεῷ καὶ ἀνθρώπῳ, ὅτι κακὸν καὶ αἰσχρόν ἐστιν οἶδα (29b6–7). But he also knows that moral situations are such that he must be constantly open to the recognition of additional factors—and in that sense he knows nothing. One finds this attitude also at *Gorgias* 508e6–509a7 where the character Socrates, acknowledging his own ignorance, expresses a commitment to rational inquiry regarding ethical matters. Writes R. E. Allen: "The man who in the *Apology* knew only that he did not know does not in the *Crito* lay claim to full knowledge of justice and virtue. The *Crito* presents, not demonstration, but dialectic, with the provisional quality which dialectic entails. But when dialectic has been carried through as far as possible and when such degree of clarity has been attained as human limitation permits, one must act—act on the conclusions that appear true" (R. E. Allen, *Socrates and Legal Obligation*).

7. The words "the laws and the commonwealth" translate οἱ νόμοι καὶ τὸ κοινὸν τῆς πόλεως (50a6–9). Burnet points out that "[i]n *Lysias* 16 §18 τὸ κοινὸν τῆς πόλεως is opposed to ἰδιῶται, 'private citizens'" (John Burnet, *Plato*: Euthyphro, Apology of Socrates, *and* Crito, ad 50a8).

8. *Iliad* 9.363: ἤματί κε τριτάτῳ Φθίην ἐρίβωλον ἱκοίμην. In the *Crito*, however, the words are addressed to Socrates and so are in the second person: Ὦ Σώκρατες, ἤματί κεν τριτάτῳ Φθίην ἐρίβωλον ἵκοιο (44b1–3).

9. προτιθέντων ἡμῶν καὶ οὐκ ἀγρίως ἐπιταττόντων ποιεῖν ἃ ἂν κελεύωμεν (52a1–2).

10. ἄλλο τι ἢ τούτῳ τῷ ἔργῳ ᾧ ἐπιχειρεῖς διανοῇ τούς τε νόμους ἡμᾶς ἀπολέσαι καὶ σύμπασαν τὴν πόλιν τὸ σὸν μέρος; ἢ δοκεῖ σοι οἷόν τε ἔτι ἐκείνην τὴν πόλιν εἶναι καὶ μὴ ἀνατετράφθαι, ἐν ᾗ ἂν αἱ γενόμεναι δίκαι μηδὲν ἰσχύωσιν ἀλλὰ ὑπὸ ἰδιωτῶν ἄκυροί τε γίγνωνται καὶ διαφθείρωνται (50a9–b5).

11. See Woozley, *Law and Obedience*, 111–140.

12. Regarding "reasonable law," one notes that Aristotle recognized that some version of the principle of non-contradiction applies in practical reason and that the solutions to moral problems not resolvable by applying general precepts are to be found through the application of reason. See *Metaphysics* 4.4.1008b12–19; also *Nicomachean Ethics* 6.10.1142b31–33, 6.3.1144b17–32, 9.2.1164b27–1165a14. In the *Rhetoric* 1.13.1373b4–6, Aristotle speaks of two kinds of law [νομός]: the "proper" [ἴδιος] and the "common" [κοινός]. Proper law, he says, can be either written or unwritten; "common law," he says, "is according to nature [κοινὸν δὲ τὸν κατὰ φύσιν]." A couple of chapters previously he speaks of the latter as "as many unwritten things [ὅσα ἄγραφα] as are regarded as agreed upon by all" (*Rhet.* 1.10.1368b8–9). Obviously, however, "common law" can be talked about and taught: Aristotle engages in such activity in the *Rhetoric* itself and elsewhere (*Nicomachean Ethics* 5.7.1134b18ff., for instance). If such things are agreed upon, they must be propositional.

13. See *ST* 1-2.91 and, in Augustine, *De libero arbitrio* 1.6.48–49 and *Contra Faustum Manichaeum* 22.27.

14. On Leon, see W. James McCoy, "The Identity of Leon," 187–199.

15. παρανόμως (32b4), παρὰ τοὺς νόμους (32b6).

16. 54d2–4. Burnet makes reference in this connection to Aristotle's *Politics* 8.7.1342a7–11, where Aristotle speaks of certain possessed individuals [κατοκώχιμοί] who achieve catharsis through melodies.

17. In the *Phaedo*, a later dialogue, the character Socrates, as he approaches death, says that he is most concerned to convince himself of the soul's immortality (*Phd.* 91a9–b1). This is his attitude not just regarding the issue of the soul's immortality but regarding all argumentation.

18. See Germain Grisez, *Christian Moral Principles*, 5D. Says Grisez in introducing that section: "Since human goodness is found in the fullness of human being, one begins to understand what it is to be a good person by considering what things fulfill human persons. Things which do so are human goods in the central sense—that is, intelligible goods" (121).

19. "The general determinations of the first principle of practical reasoning are these basic precepts of natural law. They take the form: Such and such a basic human good is to be done and/or pursued, protected, and promoted" (Grisez, *Christian Moral Principles*, 7D, 180).

20. "The practical principle which directs thinking to each basic human good is a self-evident truth" (Grisez, *Christian Moral Principles*, 7D, 180).

21. See also Germain Grisez, "The First Principle of Practical Reason," passim.

22. The laws speak of laws regarding marriage and education (50d1–5, 51e1–52c3). On laws regarding marriage, see Hadley Arkes, "The Family and the Laws," 120–121.

23. ἐπειδὰν δοκιμασθῇ καὶ ἴδη τὰ ἐν τῇ πόλει πράγματα καὶ ἡμᾶς τοὺς νόμους (51d3–4). See also Aeschines, *In Timarchum* 18.5–4: ἐπειδὰν δ' ἐγγραφῇ εἰς τὸ ληξιαρχικὸν γραμματεῖον, καὶ τοὺς νόμους εἰδῇ τοὺς τῆς πόλεως; also Aristotle, *Athenian constitution* 42.

24. ἀρκτέον μὲν γὰρ ἀπὸ τῶν γνωρίμων, ταῦτα δὲ διττῶς· τὰ μὲν γὰρ ἡμῖν τὰ δ'ἁπλῶς (*EN* 1.4.1095b2–3). See Thomas Aquinas, *Sententia libri Ethicorum*, 1.4.120–122 (§52). The *sensibilia* of which Thomas speaks here are moral *sensibilia*: see again Flannery, *Action and Character according to Aristotle*, ix–x, 1–38. I translate the word γνωρίμων (γνώριμος) as "intelligible" for reasons that have to do both with Aristotle and with Thomas's interpretation of Aristotle. (See Herbert Weir Smyth, *Greek Grammar*, 858.9 which notes that adjectives whose nominatives end in -ιμος often denote "able to" or "fit to." The Liddell-Scott-Jones *Greek-English Lexicon* translates the adverbial form of γνώριμος as "intelligibly.") Aristotle's discusses the "to us/simpliciter" distinction in the first chapter of the *Physics*, where he explains that "the intelligible to us and the intelligible simpliciter are not the same" [οὐ γὰρ ταὐτὰ ἡμῖν τε γνώριμα καὶ ἁπλῶς—*Phys.* 1.1.184a18]. In fact, the simpliciter (simply) intelligible may not be *known* at all. This suggests that "known" is not the best translation of γνώριμος. Aristotle also speaks of that which is intelligible simpliciter as intelligible (or more intelligible) "by nature" [τῇ φύσει—*Phys.* 1.1.184a17]. In his commentary on this chapter, Thomas says that the things which are *nobis magis nota* are *intelligibilia in potentia* (Thomas Aquinas, *In octos libros physicorum Aristotelis expositio*, 1.1, §7). He also says that that which is *magis notum naturae* is not more *notum* by nature but rather more *notum* "with respect to itself and with respect to its proper nature": *Non ergo dicit notiora naturae, quasi natura cognoscat ea; sed quia sunt notiora secundum se et secundum propriam naturam.* So Thomas's

own understanding of the word *notum* coincides with Aristotle's understanding of γνώριμος. The translation of *notum* as 'intelligible' is consistent with Luca Tuninetti's decision, in his definitive study of the *per se notum* in the thought of Thomas Aquinas, in order to avoid immediate association with epistemological issues, to translate *per se notum* as *selbstverständlich* ["self-understandable"] (Luca F. Tuninetti, *'Per se notum': Die logische Beschaffenheit des Selbstverständlichen im Denkens des Thomas von Aquin*, 9). (That which is understandable is not yet understood.) I am grateful to Germain Grisez for urging me to clarify my position with respect to these matters.

25. διὸ δεῖ τοῖς ἔθεσιν ἦχθαι καλῶς τὸν περὶ καλῶν καὶ δικαίων καὶ ὅλως τῶν πολιτικῶν ἀκουσόμενον ἱκανῶς (*EN* 1.4.1095b4–6).

26. Thomas Aquinas, *Sententia libri Ethicorum*, 1.4.98–161 (§§51–54).

27. Thomas Aquinas, *Sententia libri Ethicorum*, 1.4.125–129 (§52).

28. *Talis autem, qui scilicet est expertus in rebus humanis, vel per se ipsum habet principia operabilium quasi per se ea considerans, vel de facili suscipit ea ab alio* (Thomas Aquinas, *Sententia libri Ethicorum*, 1.4.150–153 [§54]).

29. "Nothing prohibits there being two effects of a single act, only one of which is intended, the other being beside the intention. Moral acts, however, receive their species according to what is intended, not from that which is beside the intention, since this is per accidens. . . . From the act of someone defending himself, a double effect can follow. One indeed is the preservation of one's own life; the other is the killing [*occisio*] of the assailant. Such an act, therefore, in as much as what is intended is the preservation of one's own life, does not have the character of something illicit, for it is natural for anything to maintain itself in being, as far as that is possible" (*ST* 2-2.64.7c).

30. "But because it is unlawful to take a man's life, except for public authority acting for the common good . . . , it is not lawful for a man to intend killing a man in self-defense, except for such as have public authority, who while intending to kill a man [*intendens hominem occidere*] in self-defense, refer this to the public good, as in the case of the soldier fighting against the foe and of the minister of a judge struggling with robbers—although even these sin if they are moved by private animosity" (*ST* 2-2.64.7c).

31. On these matters, see Kevin L. Flannery, "Thomas Aquinas and the New Natural Law Theory on the Object of the Human Act," 81–94.

32. I follow here the division of chapters used in the Revised Oxford Translation; according to this division, *EN* 5 finishes at Bekker line 1134a16. Aristotle calls universal justice also legal, but, in order to avoid confusion, it is best to avoid that label here. I examine Thomas's interpretation of the first five chapters of *EN* 5 in a paper scheduled to appear in a festschrift for David Solomon edited by Raymond Hain.

33. The word used is κινητὸν (1134b29). Since in this section Aristotle is contrasting the justice of the gods (who are unmoved movers), 'moveable' is perhaps the better translation. They are moveable in the sense that they belong to the human rather than the divine realm.

34. ταὐτὸν ἄρα δίκαιον καὶ ἐπιεικές, καὶ ἀμφοῖν σπουδαίοιν ὄντοιν κρεῖττον τὸ ἐπιεικές. ποιεῖ δὲ τὴν ἀπορίαν ὅτι τὸ ἐπιεικὲς δίκαιον μέν ἐστιν, οὐ τὸ κατὰ νόμον δέ, ἀλλ᾽ ἐπανόρθωμα νομίμου δικαίου (*EN* 5.10.1137b10–13).

35. ὁ γὰρ τῶν τοιούτων προαιρετικὸς καὶ πρακτικός, καὶ ὁ μὴ ἀκριβοδίκαιος ἐπὶ τὸ χεῖρον ἀλλ᾽ ἐλαττωτικός, καίπερ ἔχων τὸν νόμον βοηθόν, ἐπιεικής ἐστι (1137b35–1138a2).

My translation tracks fairly closely William of Moerbeke's Latin translation (a revision of the translation of Robert Grosseteste) apparently used by Thomas: "Talium enim electivus et operativus, et non acrivodikeos ad deterius, sed minorativus, quamvis habens legem adiuvantem, epiikes est."

36. "[E]tsi in communibus sit aliqua necessitas, quanto magis ad propria descenditur, tanto magis invenitur defectus" (*ST* 1-2.94.4). In ethics, principles (or precepts) that do not allow of exceptions—such as 'do not murder,' 'do not commit adultery,' and 'do not lie'—are located in immediate proximity to the common principles such as, "act according to reason"; principles such as 'deposits are to be returned" [*deposita sint reddenda*] are located farther away. Thomas borrows the terms "common" and "proper" from the harder sciences. Certain principles are called 'common' because they are shared with other such sciences (although in each science even the common principles are appropriated to the individual science); a science's own principles are, therefore, its 'proper' principles. Thomas sees the distinction between *principia communia* and *principia propria* in the opening lines of Aristotle's *Physics*: "Ad rationem autem pertinet ex communibus ad propria procedere, ut patet ex I *Physica*" (*ST* 1-2.94.4). See also Thomas's comment on *Phys.* 1.7.189b30–32 (Thomas Aquinas, *In octos libros physicorum Aristotelis expositio*, 1.12.2 [§99]).

37. "In operativis autem non est eadem veritas vel rectitudo practica apud omnes quantum ad propria, sed solum quantum ad communia" (*ST* 1-2.94.4c).

38. Elsewhere Thomas uses the word *deficere* in the sense of disparate, that is, without any sense of (as we understand the word) deficiency. He says, for instance, in the *Quaestiones disputatae de malo*: "omnis effectus per se habet aliqualiter similitudinem suae causae, vel secundum eandem rationem, sicut in agentibus univocis, vel secundum deficientem rationem, sicut in agentibus equivocis" (*De malo* 1.3.161–163). Thomas is alluding here to *Metaph.* 7.9.1034a21–28, commenting upon which he identifies three ways in which an effect might be related to a cause per se. The first involves nothing but univocity; he uses the example of fire generating fire; in this case, "the form generated has prior existence in the generator according to the same mode of being and in similar matter" ["quando forma generati praecedit in generante secundum eumdem modum essendi, et simili materia"—*in Metaph.* §1444]. The second such per se relationship involves univocity and equivocity, as when the idea of a house, in the architect's mind, generates a house—which is different with respect to matter but not form (*in Metaph.* §1445). The third involves nothing of univocity, as when the heat produced in a cure precedes the heat that is part of health (there being no formal correspondence between heat and health, nor is there a material correspondence) (*in Metaph.* §1446). All three are described as per se relationships, although in *De malo* 1.3c Thomas describes at least the third (and perhaps also the second) as *deficiens*. Thomas makes use of the same passage in *Metaph.* 7.9 in *Quaestiones disputatae de veritate* 11.2c.

39. The document was written in French, which, in paragraph 53 (section 2.5) has: "plus on aborde les choses particulières, plus il y a d'indétermination. . . . Dans le domaine de l'action, la vérité ou la rectitude pratique n'est pas la même chez tous dans les applications particulières, mais uniquement dans les principes généraux." The corresponding Latin runs: "etsi in communibus sit aliqua necessitas, quanto magis ad propria descenditur, tanto magis invenitur defectus. . . . In operativis autem non est eadem veritas vel rectitudo practica apud omnes quantum ad propria, sed solum quantum ad communia."

40. "Although there is necessity in the general principles, the more we descend to matters of detail, the more frequently we encounter defects. . . . In matters of action, truth or practical rectitude is not the same for all, as to matters of detail, but only as to the general

principles." The translation and use of *ST* 1-2.94.4 occurs in section 304 of *Amoris laetitia*. The Italian has: "Sebbene nelle cose generali vi sia una certa necessità, quanto più si scende alle cose particolari, tanto più si trova indeterminazione. [. . .] In campo pratico non è uguale per tutti la verità o norma pratica rispetto al particolare, ma soltanto rispetto a ciò che è generale" (not even mentioning, that is, that what are general are principles). The Spanish has: "en los principios generales haya necesidad, cuanto más se afrontan las cosas particulares, tanta más indeterminación hay. [. . .] En el ámbito de la acción, la verdad o la rectitud práctica no son lo mismo en todas las aplicaciones particulares, sino solamente en los principios generales."

41. Later in *ST* 1-2.94.4, Thomas writes: "Et hoc tanto magis invenitur deficere, quanto magis ad particularia descenditur." The word *hoc* refers to the proper principle, "deposita sint reddenda." It is this principle that is said sometimes to fail of application; the moral situation itself, however, is still susceptible to moral analysis.

42. "Quia enim materia humanorum operabilium est indeterminata, inde est quod eorum regula, quae est lex, oportet quod sit indeterminata, quasi non semper eodem modo se habens" (*in EN* 5.16.169–173 [§1087]).

43. In this same chapter of the commentary, he compares the lawgiver to the natural scientist who says that men have five fingers although he knows that, "by an error of nature," they might have more or less than five (*in EN* 5.16.11–115 [§1084]). See also *in EN* 5.12.180–196 (§1028), where, following Aristotle (*EN* 5.7.1134b34–35), he speaks of a principle of nature giving men the stronger right hand, although some people can become [*fieri*] ambidextrous, with the result that their left hand is as strong as their right ("contingit ut in paucioribus aliquos fieri ambidextros qui sinistram manum habent ita valentem ut dexteram"). There is nothing lacking in those who make themselves ambidextrous. However, in the earlier *Sent.* 3.37.4 obi. 2 ("cum contingat aliquos ambidextros esse"), Thomas understands Aristotle to be speaking of those who are ambidextrous rather than become so. In his response, he appears to regard ambidexterity as a *defectus*: "potest in paucioribus deficere . . . ; quod contingit ex hoc quod justum hujusmodi est applicatio quaedam universali et primae mensurae ad materiam difformem et mutabilem." There is a similar remark at *ST* 2-2.57.2 ad 1, where Thomas accounts for exceptions to the law by noting that it can happen that the will of a man is depraved; if human nature was always upright, there would be no such exceptions. But even here in *ST* 2-2, as in *Sent.* 3.37.4 obi. 2 ("difformem et mutabilem"), he is as ready to attribute the disparity to mutability as to deformity ("Natura autem hominis est mutabilis; et ideo id quod naturale est homini potest aliquando deficere").

44. On the proper understanding of "circumstances," see Flannery, *Action and Character according to Aristotle*, chapter 4. Thomas explains in this same section of *ST* 1-2.94.4 that, the more stipulations a legislator might attach to a proper principle, the more likely it is that, in a particular situation, it will not correspond to the concrete moral truth determinable by reason. ("Et hoc tanto magis invenitur deficere, quanto magis ad particularia descenditur, puta si dicatur quod deposita sunt reddenda cum tali cautione, vel tali modo.") I understand him to be saying that, the more particular a legislator gets, the more likely it is that a countervailing morally relevant "circumstance" might present itself. This would not happen, however, in situations involving actions that are evil according to their species (see *ST* 1-2.18.8–9). An act evil in its species cannot become a good act with the addition of a positive factor. For instance, an act of adultery or a lie does not lose its lack of inherent intelligibility if it is performed for a good remote end. This is not to say, however, that in certain situations an act lacking in intrinsic intelligibility might not be of minimal moral gravity. The lie told to Nazis at the door ("there are no Jews here") is unlikely to be other than a venial sin.

45. See *Republic* 1.331c1–d3. Many scholars believe that this first book is an early dialogue to which, in his "middle period," Plato added the subsequent nine books. The book constitutes in itself a complete dialogue in which Socrates is seeking the definition of justice. One proposal would be that justice means telling the truth and returning that which one has received. But, says Socrates, "everyone would say that, if one receives from a friend, a man of sound mind, weapons and if, having gone mad, he demands them back, one ought not to return them and one who returns them would not be just—nor should one be willing to tell the whole truth to someone who is in this condition." In the metaphysical sections of the subsequent books of the *Republic*, it appears that Plato is prepared to say that the answers to such concrete moral questions is beyond the reach of reason since knowledge is only of the Forms. But the theory of the Forms belongs to Plato, not Socrates.

46. "Apud omnes enim hoc rectum est et verum, ut secundum rationem agatur. Ex hoc autem principio sequitur quasi conclusio propria, quod deposita sint reddenda. Et hoc quidem ut in pluribus verum est, sed potest in aliquo casu contingere quod sit damnosum, et per consequens irrationabile, si deposita reddantur; puta si aliquis petat ad impugnandam patriam" (*ST* 1-2.94.4c). For another such example, see *ST* 1-2. 96.6.

47. I go into these matters more thoroughly in Kevin L. Flannery, "Determinacy in Natural Law," 763–773.

48. See *in EN* 5.16.116–151 (§§1085–1086). Thomas also employs here another example concerning a law prohibiting foreigners from scaling the city walls but which does not apply when they are actually defending the city.

49. "et ideo secundum iustum naturale oportet hic dirigere iustum legale" (*in EN* 5.16.150–151 [§1086]).

50. See *Sent.* 3.38.4c (where Thomas speaks of the *intentio legislatoris* and also of not returning a deposited weapon) and *ST* 1-2.96. 6 ad 2. See also 2-2.120.1 ad 1, where Thomas, in connection with reasonableness [*epieikeia*], says that "to follow the words of the law in matters when one ought not is immoral." He goes on then to quote the *Codex Iustinianus* (1.14.5 "Codex Iustinianus," 68a): "There is no doubt that he fights against the law who, seizing upon the words of the law, strives contrary to the intention of the law" ["contra legis nititur voluntatem"]. The same law (which doubtless Thomas knew) goes on to say that a lawgiver will say some things explicitly; "others, it is permitted to gather from the intention of the law as if expressed" ["cetera quasi expressa ex legis liceat voluntate colligere"]. See also *EN* 5.10.1137a31–1138a3. See also Russell Hittinger, "Thomas Aquinas on the Natural Law and the Competence to Judge," 279–280.

Bibliography

Allen, R. E. *Socrates and Legal Obligation.* Minneapolis: University of Minnesota Press, 1980.

Aquinas, Thomas. *In octos libros physicorum Aristotelis expositio*, ed. P. M. Maggiòlo. Turin/Rome: Marietti, 1965.

Aquinas, Thomas. *Sententia libri Ethicorum.* Vol. 47 of *Opera Omnia*. Rome: Commissio Leonina, 1969.

Arkes, Hadley. "The Family and the Laws." In *The Meaning of Marriage: Family, State, Market, and Morals*, ed. Robert P. George and Jean Bethke Elshtain, 116–141. Dallas, TX: Spence Publishing Company, 2006.

Burnet, John. *Plato:* Euthyphro, Apology of Socrates, *and* Crito. Oxford: Clarendon, 1924.

"Codex Iustinianus." Ed. Paulus Krueger. In *Corpus Iuris Civilis*. ed. Paulus Krueger and Theodorus Mommsen, vol. 2. Berlin: Weidmann, 1900.

Flannery, Kevin L. *Action and Character according to Aristotle: The Logic of the Moral Life*. Washington, DC: Catholic University of America Press, 2013. https://doi.org/10.2307/j.ctt4cg8k2

Flannery, Kevin L. "Determinacy in Natural Law." *Nova et Vetera (English)* 9 (2011): 763–773.

Flannery, Kevin L. "Thomas Aquinas and the New Natural Law Theory on the Object of the Human Act." *National Catholic Bioethics Quarterly* 13 (2013): 79–104. https://doi.org/10.5840/ncbq201313172

Grisez, Germain. *Christian Moral Principles*. Vol. 1 of *The Way of the Lord Jesus*. Chicago: Franciscan Herald, 1983.

Grisez, Germain. "The First Principle of Practical Reason: A Commentary on the *Summa Theologiae* 1-2, Question 94, Article 2." *Natural Law Forum* 10 (1965): 168–201. https://doi.org/10.1093/ajj/10.1.168

Grote, George. *Plato, and the other Companions of Sokrates*. London: John Murray, 1875.

Hittinger, Russel. "Thomas Aquinas on the Natural Law and the Competence to Judge." In *St. Thomas Aquinas and the Natural Law Tradition: Contemporary perspectives*, ed. John Goyette, Mark Latkovic, and Richard S. Myers, 261–284. Washington, DC: Catholic University of America Press, 2004.

Kraut, Richard. *Socrates and the State*. Princeton: Princeton University Press, 1984.

McCoy, W. James. "The Identity of Leon." *American Journal of Philology* 96 (1975): 187–199. https://doi.org/10.2307/294382

Smyth, Herbert Weir. *Greek Grammar* (revised by Gordon M. Messing). Cambridge, MA: Harvard University Press, 1956.

Tuninetti, Luca F. *'Per se notum': Die logische Beschaffenheit des Selbstverständlichen im Denkens des Thomas von Aquin*. Studien und Texte zur Geistesgeschichte des Mittelalters. Leiden: E.J. Brill, 1996.

Woozley, A. D. *Law and Obedience: The Arguments of Plato's* Crito. London: Duckworth, 1979.

Life and Work of Adriaan T. Peperzak, 2016 Aquinas Medal Recipient

Jeffrey Bloechl

I t goes without saying that it is an honor for me to stand in this position this evening. It also goes without saying that I stand here with some regret, since Adriaan Peperzak, the well-deserved recipient of the 2016 Aquinas Medal, cannot himself be present. I can assure you that from the moment Adriaan was informed of this award, he has looked upon it with humility and gratitude. In a smaller way, I feel much the same about my own brief role here. Adriaan Peperzak is a longtime friend and has often been a model for how to conduct oneself as a Christian and a philosopher, in one's scholarship, one's teaching, and one's place within the wider academy.

Adriaan Peperzak was born in Indonesia, studied in the Netherlands, Belgium and France, and taught for decades each in the Netherlands and in the United States. He held numerous positions in the Netherlands before settling primarily in Utrecht and Nijmegen from 1971 to 1991. Here in the United States, he became Arthur J. Schmitt Professor of Philosophy at Loyola University of Chicago in 1991, where he remained until retiring one year ago. Were that not enough, he has also been a visiting professor in Mallorca, Nice, Paris, Pisa, and Poitiers, and in the United States at my own Boston College, Duquesne, Penn State, Villanova, and nearby Stanford University. I could add many, many short-term engagements in still other places, and frankly wonder if Adriaan himself has a complete list—it would be very long—ranging across North and South America, through Europe, and into several universities in Asia. Somehow, while all of this claimed his time and attention, he managed to publish over twenty-five books, 300 articles, and several lengthy translations often with annotation and commentary. His work has appeared, by his own hand, in Dutch, English, French, German, Italian, and Spanish.

From the beginning of his career, Adriaan Peperzak has maintained a close and steady interest in both philosophy and theology, and though he has committed occasional works to each of these disciplines as if in isolation from one another, it is a defining characteristic of nearly all of his work—and, I venture to say, his way of life—to refuse to separate them. Or rather, it is his conviction that at real depth, philosophy and theology meet and inform one another without contradiction,

© 2017, *Proceedings of the ACPA*, Vol. 90
doi: 10.5840/acpaproc20169077

though to be sure *not* without challenges and, on occasion, productive reciprocal critique.

Adriaan's early advanced study of philosophy concentrated on German idealism. After a licentiate thesis on Hegel's critique of Fichte, completed in Leuven, he committed his doctoral dissertation to the philosophy of the young Hegel, completed in Paris under the supervision of Paul Ricoeur, and published in 1960. The philosophy of Hegel is one major recurrent interest in his work. During the next forty years, Adriaan published six more books on Hegel, including studies of his moral and political philosophy, his phenomenology, and his conceptions of self-knowledge and freedom, as well as two translations with commentary. Another recurrent interest has been the philosophy of Emmanuel Levinas, which Adriaan discovered through a yearly gathering of the association of former students of Leuven. Perhaps it would have happened anyway: Ricoeur was on close terms with Levinas, Levinas's *Totalité et Infini* appeared with the same publisher as Adriaan's first book on Hegel, in 1961, and the two shared convictions that contemporary thought can and must hold fast to themes like transcendence and the goodness of the good, that ethics and religion are intimately related, and that philosophy has a dimension that deserves to be called "spiritual"—though this is a word that Levinas did not much like, whereas for Adriaan it is essential. As for interpreting and responding to the work of Levinas, Adriaan has committed all or significant parts of at least ten different books to the task, and he has played an important role in the reception of Levinas by the Dutch-language and English-language worlds (and I should add that he has also had a significant impact on Levinas's reception in Italy).

None of this is meant to suggest that Adriaan has been simply a Hegelian, a Levinasian, or a philosopher provoked by their many differences. Perhaps that does describe the field of forces in which he works, but even then I would want to insist on the importance of his regular appeal to a line from Plato through Bonaventure to Levinas, and in more recent years the work of people like Jean-Louis Chretien. This, I think, would have been at least some of what Adriaan intended to offer us in his lecture tonight, which was advertised with the title "A Great Tradition." But evidently, it is a matter not so much of names and texts as an orientation and a perspective. Let me invoke some of it, by reading the final lines of his *Elements of Ethics*:

> To bring thinkers together in mutual service and dedication—or even friendship—the gathering must be 'in-spired.' Does this (in-)spiration, this life-giving breath, come from a spirit? A Spirit that devotes the thinkers to one another on their various paths to the sought? A nonhuman fountain of life that sanctifies them through a passion for the unique Good, which, although totally Different, does not lack anything of all that can be desired because it already has it and gives it by way of foretastes? If philosophy is the attempt to discover and meditate on traces and shadows of that which, in the end, matters, it cannot avoid entering into the realm of religion, even if thinking cannot embrace of deduce it. Hope, accompanied by trust, reaches further—and fortunately they are

stronger—than argumentation. If trust and hope fade away, how would we be able to continue searching despite overwhelming evidence of darkness and injustice? Only the clear obscurity of Grace in the dusk and the dawn of our universe can save the ongoing quest for truth.[1]

This general vision notwithstanding, Adriaan has never ceased to be a careful historian of philosophy, with all of the patience and intensity that that requires. This is a matter of far more than the two or three favorites on record in his curriculum vitae. Adriaan has not written books on Plotinus or Kant, for example, but as his friends and students will surely report, his recourse to them can be formidable. So likewise, John of the Cross, Plato, or Heidegger. An eagerness to keep philosophy fresh and an insistence on communicating its lasting importance for a meaningful life do not become excuses for shortcuts. And this, I submit, is how to approach another sort of work that he has given to us in several books during the past fifteen or so years: *Reason in Faith: On the Relevance of Christian Spirituality for Philosophy*; *The Quest for Meaning: Friends of Wisdom from Plato to Levinas*; *Thinking: from Solitude to Dialogue and Contemplation*; *Trust*; and *Savoir et sagesse*, his 2010 Etienne Gilson lectures given in Paris.

There is still another sort of work to which I would like to call attention. I alluded to it as I began these remarks. Adriaan does not fail to consider his philosophical, and to some extent theological, work from the lens of a concern with Catholic identity at the university and even beyond. Here I will content myself with mention of only one highly indicative title: *Philosophy between Faith and Theology: Addresses to Catholic Intellectuals*, in which one finds texts of lectures given mainly in the United States and Europe over a twenty-five-year period beginning in the mid-1970s. One cannot read them without becoming convinced of our duty as philosophers to think institutionally even while we are possessed by the love of wisdom. And these lectures are replete with advice, exhortation and precautions of all sorts, in many cases long before the American academy began to demand that philosophy become a number of things it has never been and may have good reason to resist.

I do not want to end without emphasizing Adriaan's particular manner of pursuing the things he judges most serious and worthwhile—questions, problems, phenomena—without willingly excluding any single approach to them. I have observed that he is a leading scholar of Hegel and yet also of Levinas, a tremendous historian of philosophy who never ceases to ask for the import of great texts for our effort to live well, and a lover of wisdom who recognizes and attends to his responsibility to the institution in which that love may animate a profession. All of this bespeaks, at least to my ear, a deep and vital confidence in things which this Association, and each of its members, will surely wish to honor: (1) that good thinking begins not simply from unquestioned premises, but an encounter with profound and enduring questions, questions that touch us in our minds and hearts, and again and again; (2) that philosophy neither pretends to answer those questions with definitive solutions nor, however, surrenders to a vision of their impossibility and undecidability, but instead promises us an entire way of life that can find fulfillment and even joy in the peculiar response to enduring questions that takes the form of understanding them, and ourselves, a little better; and (3) that it is precisely this that philosophy has to offer a world that, perhaps increasingly, has too little time for it, and yet stands in need of it as much as ever.

On behalf of Adriaan Peperzak, and his wife Angela, I am pleased to thank the members of the American Catholic Philosophical Association who have awarded him the 2016 Aquinas Medal.

Boston College

2016 Conference of the American Catholic Philosophical Association
San Francisco
November 5, 2016

Note

1. A. Peperzak, *Elements of Ethics* (Palo Alto: Stanford University Press, 2004), 262.

A Great Tradition

Adriaan T. Peperzak

I thank the Association of Catholic Philosophers in America for having honored me by deeming me worthy to receive the Thomas medal of 2016, and I am particularly grateful for the appreciative words that my dear friend Jeffrey Bloechl has spoken at the occasion.

However, it remains a serious question, whether the kind of "philosophy" that I like most of all can be associated with one of the greatest thinkers of our European history: Thomas Aquinas. Although I have with admiration and pleasure studied and taught large parts of Thomas' oeuvre, I never published any book or article on his contributions to theology or philosophy. There are several reasons for this omission, some of which have to do with the insufficiency of my acquaintance with his extensive oeuvre. Many of his rational analyses have convinced and impressed me; but my admiration has not been perspicacious enough to discover and sympathize with the deepest motivations of his engagements. Especially his pious devotion and his mystical attunement remained more hidden for me than the rational and reasonable connections he clarified brilliantly as no other. If I might interpret professor Bloechl's words as saying that, even without focusing on Thomas, all those who, like he, try to participate in a contemporaneous retrieval of the same great Catholic tradition, deserve to be considered friends and followers of the angelic doctor, then I, though aware of my many failures, am glad for the association.

If we, Catholics, who are also philosophers, try today to retrieve again our own Catholic tradition, this can be done in various ways. Not forgetting such great pillars of philosophy as Plato, Aristotle, Plotinus, Augustine, and Dionysius is certainly a condition of our discussions.But if we, even in philosophy, are called to retrieve the laws and lessons of Jesus' kingdom or *basileia*, we cannot neglect to ask what our tasks within that great tradition are and how we today—like Bonaventura and Thomas in the thirteenth century with their possibilities—can fulfill those tasks in the twenty-first century with ours.

Philosophy is not recognized in Christ's realm as the supreme and wholly autarchic authority of all knowledge. Before we, Catholics, apply what we have

© 2017, *Proceedings of the ACPA*, Vol. 90
doi: 10.5840/acpaproc20169078

learned in a steady consultation with modern and postmodern philosophers, who proclaim philosophy's independence, we are well-advised to investigate its relations to other disciplines of primary interest for Catholics and Christians in general. And especially, how does philosophy relate to the competence and authority of faith, theology, devotion, and mystical life?

We could maintain that Jesus, like the prophets who preceded him, does not present an entirely new ethics, but rather insists on the well-known commands of the Jewish Thora: "Do not kill; do not send your wife away; do not steal; do not deliver false testimony; honor your father and your mother; and love your neighbor as you love yourself" (Mt. 19:16–19). We might add to this catalogue that Jesus gave examples and extended the signification of those commands. "Do not kill," for example, encompasses also the avoidance of anger, grudging, and using abusive words (Mt. 5:22–24, 38–41), while loving your neighbor involves visiting the sick and the prisoners and complete hospitality in food, drinks, and clothes (Mt. 5:17–21; 25:34–40). Instead of fighting for your rightful demands, forgive and live in peace (Mt. 18:21–22).

However, beyond such expressions of a generosity intimately connected with one's love of God, Jesus also sketches a deep-seated and fundamental mentality in which the faithful's fidelity takes its root. Confronted by a young and serious observer of the Thora (Mt. 19:16–23), Jesus gives him a glimpse of that underlying mentality, when he answers the interlocutor's question of what, beyond his observance of the commands, he should do to acquire "eternal life" (Mt. 19:16): "If you want to be perfect, sell all your possessions and give the proceeds to the poor. You will have a treasure in heaven. Then come and follow me" (Mt. 19:21). That, however was too much for the young man. The radical fall from being protected within his own wealth (Mt. 19:23) into the destitute situation of Jesus and his companions must have been seen by him as a kind of death instead of the beginning of a new, eternal life. Apparently he did not feel ready to accept such a passage from his wealth to the "eternal life" of the "poor in spirit" (Mt. 5:3), as Jesus understood it.

All the Gospels tell us that Jesus was ready and willing to accept the extreme and definitive poverty of his shameful and unglorious dying. What is the secret that motivated Jesus and his followers to accept such an end of their lives? Which primary inspiration mobilized all those who accepted to die for the joyful promise of entering here and now the *basileia* of heaven (Mt. 5:23)? Which "purity" of "heart" (Mt. 5:8), and what kind of fundamental experience allowed them to embrace persecution, poverty, and contemptible death (Mt. 5:4,10–12)? Is it still possible for us to discover, behind and beyond all learned studies of the Scriptures, such a death-accepting and death-embracing attitude as a most faithful way of *sentire cum Ecclesia*? Is it still or again possible to form one *Catholica* on the basis of a shared attunement that provokes a profound cooperation of piety, theology, and, as an element, philosophy?

When a holy person like Pope Francis does not address theologians or philosophers, but rather everyone who hungers and thirsts for justice and peace in this world of overwhelming malignity and less exposed goodness,he apparently knows how to connect with their heartfelt and still-amazed experience. Like Jesus, he represents the prophetic tradition that is meant for everyone. What is the secret of its language? What, in Jesus' own proclamation of his realm (*basileia*) reached, touched, moved, turned, converted those who belonged to it? And how could a philosopher of our time whose study has been dominated by the proud conviction of its sovereignty speak in a comparably naïve and humble way?

A well-educated philosopher might look for an ancient or contemporaneous message concerning the happiness, the well-being or the *eudaimonia* of his audience, but the word "*eudaimonia*" cannot even be found in the entire New Testament. Instead we are surprised when, at the beginning of his preaching, Jesus offers us a kind of hymn about those whom, as members of his *basileia*, he calls *makarioi*, blissful or even glorious (Mt. 5–7; cf. Lk. 6:20ff.):

> *Makarioi*, glorious, are the poor in the spirit, because the realm of the heavens belongs to them.
>
> Glorious are those who grieve, because they will be consoled.
>
> Glorious are the gentle, because they will inherit the earth.
>
> Glorious are they who hunger and thirst for justice, because they will be fulfilled.
>
> Glorious are the compassionate, because they will receive compassion.
>
> Glorious are those whose hearts are pure, because they will see God.
>
> Glorious are those who make peace, because they will be called children of God.
>
> Glorious are those who are persecuted for the sake of justice, because the kingdom (*basileia*) belongs to them.
>
> Glorious are you when they slander and persecute you and falsely accuse you of all that is evil, because of your relation to me; be glad and exult, because your reward is abundant in heaven; in the same way they also have persecuted the prophets who preceded you."(Mt. 5:3–12)

How can Jesus speak to us, who are confronted with so much poverty and sadness, hunger and thirst for the justice that the earth continues to miss? How can he, for example, speak about the reality of peace, while we, every day through radio or TV, observe the terrible consequences of egoism from all sides: violent disagreements, combative greed, persecution of the well-intentioned, murders, wars, and the misery of the poor, the refugees, the homeless, the exploited, and all other victims of widespread arrogance?

Apparently, despite our almost omnipresent exploitation, Jesus has found persons whose pure hearts and compassion have generated the right kind of profound but not ultimate sadness, an amazing gentleness despite their own and others' poverty, and the ability to always prefer peace over fighting and injustice. Most or perhaps all of us know such people who, despite a world of arrogance in conflicts, persecution, and exclusion, have preserved their patient and holy sadness and their never-exhausted compassion to restore true peace. Amazingly, the desire of justice prevented them from combative explosions of revenge, because they preferred reconciliation over anger and violence. Instead of trying to become the lords of the earth, they prefer to be poor instead of making themselves angrily unjust.

Jesus himself demonstrated that, as the exemplary king of his *basileia*, he was driven by the gentle spirit of poverty (Mt. 5:3) and purity of heart (Mt. 5:8) that should also characterize his followers. They are poor insofar as they have received all that makes them good without boasting about their own proud passion for justice (*dikaiosynē*). All the Gospels illustrate how Jesus himself responded with sadness but patience and gentle compassion even toward those who persecuted him because of his own hungering and thirsting for justice. But also and above all, the Gospels tell us how Jesus' own proclamation of his *basileia* and its manners was rejected in the cruel way of his crucifixion. Jesus' death does not seem glorious, but rather the merciless culmination of a failure. All who belong to his kingdom, however, venerate his cross as the fundamental poverty that made him and his followers not only the "heirs of the earth" (Mt. 5:5), but also citizens of the kingdom of heaven (Mt. 5:10). All who are, in Jesus' way, poor, sad, gentle, compassionate and persecuted, are not only praised as *makarioi*, blissful, blessed, or glorious; they will be seeing Godself, because they already share their lives as children—sons and daughters—of God's own life.

What those words "children of God" and "seeing God" exactly mean, we do not know—it will be revealed when our own singular lives—including the secret of each one's own death—have become a fact. But that those who live the beatitudes are already very close to God's life and associated with his ongoing creation, can hardly be doubted. If God's creation is life-giving and intent on making it succeed from beginning to end, our participation in that creation is a good performance of the given gifts each one has received for nothing.

Theology is one of the activities to which a faithful person can be called, and the philosophy that inevitably plays a role in the unfolding of theology shares its vocation. A theologian who to the end of his life is utterly dedicated to his essential tasks, prepares his death as a sign of having exhausted the possibilities of elucidation that were granted through him or her. Insofar as philosophy is an inevitable component of any up-to-date theology, the same is true for the participating philosopher. However, since philosophers, through their studies, have acquired a more extensive acquaintance with those types of philosophy that avoid all contact with Catholic theology, they might be better equipped to discuss its philosophical components in an encounter with those who deny any relevance of a theological perspective for philosophy. Catholic philosophers have then two main tasks. Besides practicing what they, as Catholic thinkers, teach about the Christian reality of faith and love, they assist the theologians in elucidating what their deepest convictions mean for the organization of the world they share with those who disagree with their convictions. With philosophers who maintain their own autonomy, they discuss how a peacefully shared common world would be possible without committing practical or theoretical infidelities against one's own basic perspectives and experience. That such a discussion, despite great efforts of benevolence on both sides, may lead to painful conflicts and suffering of truly Christian philosophers, is historically not excluded, but suffering and death have their own "glorious" meaning within the realm of Christ's *basileia*.

Arthur J. Schmitt Chair Emeritus
Loyola University Chicago

Mercy Beyond Justice:
The Tragedy of Shylock and Antonio

John O'Callaghan

Abstract: Shakespeare's *Merchant of Venice* provides a dramatic setting for thinking about the relationship of mercy to justice, a topic of great concern to contemporary ethical and political thought. Traditionally classified as among Shakespeare's comedies, the play can also be analyzed as a tragedy in which Shylock is the protagonist. The tragedy is driven by the relatively weak conception of mercy in relationship to justice that informs Portia's famous soliloquy "the quality of mercy . . . ." The mercy she praises is closely related to the stoic conception of mercy that Seneca urges upon Nero, a mercy that is bound within the confines of justice. Examining Aquinas' discussion of misericordia in relation to justice and forgiveness provides a more robust conception of mercy that is closely associated with friendship, particularly the friendship Aquinas argues is owed by all human beings to all human beings. This concept of mercy can rightly be said to be a mercy beyond justice, a mercy that justice strives to attain.

The mercy of God is as beautiful in a time of
tribulation as a rain cloud in a time of drought.[1]

The quality of mercy is not strained;
It droppeth as the gentle rain from heaven
Upon the place beneath. It is twice blest:
It blesseth him that gives and him that takes.
'Tis mightiest in the mightiest, it becomes
The thronèd monarch better than his crown.
His sceptre shows the force of temporal power,
The attribute to awe and majesty,
Wherein doth sit the dread and fear of kings;
But mercy is above this sceptred sway.
It is enthronèd in the hearts of kings,
It is an attribute to God himself,
And earthly power doth then show likest God's
When mercy seasons justice.[2]

© 2017, *Proceedings of the ACPA*, Vol. 90
doi: 10.5840/acpaproc201822372

The court scene in *The Merchant of Venice* provides an exemplary opportunity to think about the relationship of mercy to justice. My particular
interest in it is driven by its use in the contemporary philosophical
discussion of that relationship.[3] I cannot rehearse the details here, other than to say
that mercy does not fare well in the hands of both the utilitarians and deontologists
who dominate the contemporary scene. Alex Tuckness and John M. Parrish have
shown in their recent work *The Decline of Mercy in Public Life*[4] how the phenomenon
of mercy in relation to justice has in the modern period for the most part come under
increasing pressure from, or at best been narrowly circumscribed by various theories
of justice. And yet I think it can also be said, but I only wish to suggest here, that the
notion of forgiveness that philosophers are struggling to develop in such discussions
requires a mercy much more robust than is allowed for in the contemporary debate,
so long as mercy is bound narrowly within the confines of justice.

However much contemporary scholars may wish to cite it, the mercy that
Portia praises and urges upon Shylock does not initially fit well the contemporary
discussion of offense and punishment. At the beginning of the climactic scene in
the Venetian court the concern is the role of political authority not so much in
the imposition of punishment for an offense or crime against the community and
its laws, but, rather, the political authority's interest in enforcing contracts among
individual parties within its jurisdiction; that is what Antonio points out earlier
when Salarino suggests that the duke will "never grant this forfeiture to hold," on
behalf of the Jew. Antonio responds:

> The Duke cannot deny the course of law;
> For the commodity that strangers have
> With us in Venice, if it be denied,
> Will much impeach the justice of the state;
> Since that the trade and profit of the city
> Consisteth of all nations.[5]

Antonio's defense of the law here involves a kind of consequentialist reasoning concerned with the common good of Venice. It will be important to keep in mind for
later that Shylock is described here as a "stranger" in Venice amongst citizens like
Antonio, Salarino, Bassanio, and all the rest, a stranger to them, as if from another
land or city. Justice applies to this stranger for fear that other strangers with whom
Venice wants to do business will not accept its bonds, not giving it credit if they
perceive Venice to be an unjust city.

However, Portia's praise of mercy is not directed at the duke who will enforce
the bond, but, rather at one of the parties to it: Shylock. It is the governing authority of the duke and in his power to execute justice and to grant mercy in relation to
justice. The content of Portia's praise of mercy explicitly relates it to this governing
authority by reference to the king and God himself—it is higher than the crown
that represents his authority and greater than the scepter that represents his power.
But Shylock is neither king nor God; he has no authority or power over Antonio,
which is why he has to approach the duke to have his bond justly enforced.

I do not want to claim, however, that therefore the term 'mercy' should not be applied to what Shylock is being urged to do, forgive or remit the debt; I just want to point out that the sort of governing and judicial mercy that Portia praises seems out of place as addressed to Shylock. In that regard it is no surprise that he does not care for what she says, and responds:

> My deeds upon my head! I crave the law,
> The penalty and forfeit of my bond.[6]

So, if Shylock were to release Antonio from his bond, it would not be the exercise of the mercy that Portia praises, but mercy of some other form in the forgiveness of a debt owed to him.

Still this initial stage of the scene does portray what seems to be the fundamental conflict in contemporary discussions. Either Shylock in virtue of some form of mercy gives up his claim for justice or his demand for justice will exclude such mercy. In addition, the duke is powerless to grant his sovereign mercy in the face of Shylock's demand for justice. Justice reigns supreme in Shylock's heart and the duke's court.

On the other hand, the dramatic reversal by the end of the scene that turns the tables on Shylock ends up fitting the contemporary discussion quite well. Shylock refuses to forgive Antonio's debt and demands strict justice from the duke. However, Portia, in the guise of the young doctor of the law, points out that the strict justice of the bond demands that Shylock shed no blood in the taking of the flesh, for blood, which is not flesh, is not specified in the bond.

This dramatic distinction between flesh and blood, and the strictness with which Portia applies it is perhaps a play on the strictness of *kashrut*, Jewish dietary law.[7] After all, it is the pivot upon which the scene turns, the classical reversal of fortune in a tragedy, an ironic reversal from the law and justice favoring Shylock to them threatening him with the strictness that he has just demanded. The scene itself is reminiscent of the blood libel against Jews that originated in Norwich, England in the twelfth century.[8]

Shakespeare is clearly familiar with Jewish kosher practices, since internal to the play itself Shylock refuses to eat with Bassanio because he would have to eat pork, and Lancelot jokes with Jessica that converting Jews to Christians raises the price of pork, presumably because becoming a Christian means eating pork, which then increases demand.[9] But, according to *kashrut*, when an animal is slaughtered, the blood, which contains the life of the animal, must be completely drained from the flesh before the flesh may be consumed—flesh and blood may not be mixed. The law of *kashrut* on this point is based upon Leviticus 7:26–27 and 17:10–14, which forbid consuming the blood of mammals and birds because it is the blood that contains the life of the animal; on the contrary that blood must be offered as a sacrifice at God's altar to atone for committing bloodshed. To take Antonio's blood is to take his life, and Shylock will be guilty of bloodshed. So Portia explains to Shylock about removing Antonio's flesh:

> This bond doth give thee here no jot of blood.

> The words expressly are 'a pound of flesh'.
> Take then thy bond, take thou thy pound of flesh,
> But in the cutting it, if thou dost shed
> One drop of Christian blood, thy lands and goods
> Are by the laws of Venice confiscate
> Unto the state of Venice.[10]

And:

> Tarry, Jew:
> The law hath yet another hold on you.
> It is enacted in the laws of Venice,
> If it be proved against an alien
> That by direct or indirect attempts
> He seek the life of any citizen,
> The party 'gainst the which he doth contrive
> Shall seize one half his goods, the other half
> Comes to the privy coffer of the state,
> And the offender's life lies in the mercy
> Of the duke only, 'gainst all other voice.
> In which predicament I say thou stand'st;
> For it appears by manifest proceeding,
> That indirectly, and directly too,
> Thou hast contrived against the very life
> Of the defendant, and thou hast incurred
> The danger formerly by me rehearsed.
> Down, therefore, and beg mercy of the duke.[11]

So Portia is here charging Shylock with plotting bloodshed against the life of Antonio, by contracting to take the flesh with its natural bloody effect, unless he shows that he can take the flesh without the blood.

Earlier we saw Shylock identified with a stranger. Here he is identified as an alien in Venice subject to the otherwise unknown Venetian law. So if he takes more than the flesh, and sheds Antonio's blood, then he will be an alien guilty of bloodshed, of having taken Antonio's life. Taking and consuming the life of the animals is at the heart of the prohibition of consuming blood in Leviticus, since the blood consumed cannot be offered at the altar to atone for the blood that is shed. In addition, Leviticus makes it clear that aliens living among the House of Israel are subject to the same law of *kashrut* concerning bloodshed; and of anyone guilty of such bloodshed, including an alien, God "will set [Himself] against that individual and will cut that person off from among the people, since the life of the flesh is in the blood."[12] So this scene looks like a reversal, with Venice in the place of the House of Israel, Shylock the alien living amongst them forbidden to shed blood, and the duke according to his office standing in for the divine as is clear in Portia's soliloquy in praise of mercy.

The point of the dramatic reversal, this change of fortune from good to bad, is that having had justice and the duke on his side in a private arrangement with Antonio but refusing mercy to the Venetian, Shylock has now given evidence against himself of having violated the public laws of Venice, and thus become subject to its punishment, again subject only to the sovereign mercy of the duke—the duke will otherwise "cut [him] off from among the people." Of course, the duke, who can put aside what justice demands in the case of an offense against the city, extends his sovereign mercy by sparing Shylock's life, but still applies the penalty of the forfeiture of his goods half to the state and half to Antonio.

The reversal of fortune continues with Portia turning to the now saved Antonio and asking him, "what mercy can you render [Shylock], Antonio?"[13] It is clear, however, that it is the duke who actually has the power to grant the mercy, not Antonio, since Antonio says "so please my lord the Duke" that Shylock be allowed the half of his goods that would go to the state and that he Antonio be allowed the use of the other half, the whole to be given to Shylock's daughter and son-in-law upon Shylock's death. Where Shylock had demanded strict justice and shown no mercy, the duke at the pleading of Antonio appears to show sovereign mercy again by putting aside justice as determined by the law.

But notice also the apparently arbitrary character of the duke's mercy in sparing Shylock's life—he does it simply "That thou shalt see the difference of our spirit."[14] One of the main modern objections to mercy is its arbitrariness, violating equality and impartiality in the application of law.[15] Earlier Shylock had made his motivation clear—he is pursuing vengeance because of the way in which he, a Jew, had been treated by the Christian Venetians:

> If you prick us, do we not bleed?
> If you tickle us, do we not laugh? If you poison
> us, do we not die? And if you wrong us, shall we not
> revenge? If we are like you in the rest, we will
> resemble you in that. If a Jew wrong a Christian,
> what is his humility? Revenge. If a Christian
> wrong a Jew, what should his sufferance be by
> Christian example? Why, revenge! The villainy you
> teach me I will execute, and it shall go hard but I
> will better the instruction.[16]

So to show that Venice is not vengeful like Shylock, the duke by his mercy foreswears vengeance upon the Jew here in the court.

But if Shylock is right about what he has been taught by Christian example, then the duke's mercy cannot help but look arbitrary. Why has this mercy not been shown to Shylock and his fellow Jews before? Why are they not treated equally and impartially in other legal contexts as the Venetians are amongst themselves? Why is mercy not displayed in the laws of Venice that forbid him to own land and engage in retail trade in merchandise?[17] Why are Christians allowed openly to exact vengeance upon Jews?

As with Seneca's advice to Nero in *De clementia* and *De ira*, it would be better for the duke to attend to establishing a just social order that is then strictly and mercilessly enforced, than to tolerate an unjust social order only to later claim to display his benevolence with Johnny-come-lately and arbitrary mercy remitting punishment that he thinks is due. Rather than determining what justice demands according to a strict law and then lessening it, better to begin by taking into consideration particularities of the case in determining what justice demands.[18] It is this *ex post facto* arbitrariness of mercy that the defenders of justice object to; it looks whimsical, and anything but Godlike. Or perhaps to the contemporary philosophical spirit, it is in fact too godlike in reflecting the mythical whimsicality of the pantheon, and perhaps even Christianity in practice.

Notice in particular the irony of Portia's soliloquy. Portia praises mercy as more becoming to a king than his crown and greater than the temporal power represented by his scepter. It is an attribute of God that a king may embody, indeed an attribute according to which a king may be an image of God in his rule. And yet, one should not miss the fact that the beauty of the passage ends with a metaphor that, if thought through, suggests that justice is much greater. The metaphor is of a meal in which mercy is portrayed as a kind of seasoning. But salt has no substance. Salt makes meat and potatoes taste better, and may even be part of a healthy diet; but apart from the substance of the meal, salt is awful and practically inedible. So the metaphor is an implicit praise of the substance of the meal, justice, as even greater than mercy, which latter may need to be sprinkled upon this justice to make it more palatable. But the substance remains justice. To avoid an open conflict with the substance of justice, mercy must be conceived of as a mere spice—salt and pepper to taste.

So, for all the great artistry that Shakespeare pours into crafting Portia's soliloquy, all its extraordinary beauty and eloquence in praise of mercy, it turns out mercy is extraordinarily impotent. It fails. Not only does the beauty of the words not move Shylock, but also with the greater force of justice on his side mercy must flee, and he will have his bond. In the end the only mercy displayed is the capricious mercy of the duke extended spitefully to Shylock simply to distinguish Venice and the Venetians from him, once again underlining the fact that Shylock is a stranger and alien among and to them.

Mercy Beyond Justice

I want to make an argument about mercy and justice, with the play being the occasion for thinking it through. The first part of the argument is that *The Merchant of Venice* can plausibly be thought of as a tragedy not a comedy. The second part of the argument is that the cause of the tragedy is the absence of genuinely godlike mercy that does not merely "season" justice, but is beyond justice. To understand this second point, I will need to introduce, however briefly, the thought of Aquinas on forgiveness and mercy. In the midst of making this argument, the character of this missing mercy will be detailed. Although I will not have the space to argue the point here, it is perhaps this missing notion of mercy that might have a role to play in contemporary discussions of justice and mercy.

First Part: Comedy or Tragedy

Aquinas tells us to begin arguments by looking to the *usus loquendi*, the common use of words by those who speak them. So looking to the ordinary use of 'merchant' in the play, conventionally *The Merchant of Venice* is classed among Shakespeare's comedies. Antonio is identified several times within the lines of the play as a merchant by Portia and the clerk, and indeed a "royal merchant" by the duke and Gratiano. When Portia enters the court scene, she asks "which is the merchant here and which the Jew?" The Duke then commands, "Antonio and old Shylock, both stand forth," implying of course that Antonio is the merchant.[19] Antonio the merchant comes to a good end in a story that ends as he frolics in Belmont in the midst of his newly married friends. So conventionally he is the protagonist of a comedy and Shylock is then the antagonist who does battle with him. Were Antonio to come to grief, conventionally it would be a tragedy, with Antonio's *hubris* his tragic flaw, shown in his foolishness as a great man and merchant of Venice of having sent out all of his ships simultaneously, trusting them to the winds of fortune, with the result that all of them come to grief by a turn of good fortune to bad with the loss of significant goods; it is that turn of fortune that renders him incapable of repaying the bond. But it all works out in the end—so a comedy.

However, arguably there is a play on words in the title of the play. Lost perhaps to our contemporary English speaking ears in the twenty-first century are the etymological roots and nuances of the term 'mercy' in economic relations. The English term 'mercy' comes through Anglo-Norman from the French *merci*,[20] which now primarily means "thank you." The French in turn derives from the Latin *merces*, *mercedis* meaning pay, recompense, hire, salary, reward, rent, price, or bribe and *merx*, *mercis*, meaning commodity, merchandise, or goods. Other words in English in addition to 'mercy' that we derive from the Latin are market, merchandise, and mercenary.

Consider a classical Roman who might say "*Da mercedem mihi.*" In one's schoolboy Latin, noting the possibility of a transliterated word, one might guess and translate that as "give mercy to me." And yet the real sense of it would be better "give wages to me." If a public official were to say it, the sense would be, "give a bribe to me." If there were bounty hunters, "give to me a reward." Were a beggar to utter "*Da mercem mihi,*" the sense would be "give goods to me." Notice also that both '*merces*' and '*merx*' are unrelated to the Latin noun '*miser*' from which we get such terms as 'misery' and 'miserable,' also the English noun 'miser' itself, but also the now obsolete noun 'miseration' meaning pity or compassion, and finally the current noun 'commiseration.'[21]

While in contemporary English we may think of mercy in highly abstract moralistic terms having to do with an inner intentional act or disposition to forgive another, followed perhaps by an external act of mitigating punishment or penalty, its linguistic roots are found in the much more concrete setting of an economic exchange of some good. A beggar would presumably ask for a mercy (*merx*), that is, some coin or good to assist her in her poverty—it is the coin or good that is concretely the mercy asked for.[22] Someone in debt to another according to an agreement, but given a mercy by his creditor, retains the goods he would otherwise have to hand over to the creditor; the debtor benefits materially by the creditor's mercy. Mercy in this concrete understanding is an economic good exchanged either as alms[23] to a beggar or forgiveness to a debtor.

The etymological concreteness of an exchange of some economic good, commodity, or value, is preserved in the related English noun 'amercement' and verb 'amerce' from English law. An amercement is a discretionary fine of arbitrary value imposed by the one who governs as opposed to a statutory fine the value of which is set by the statute. So the prince in Romeo and Juliet says to Montague:

> I have an interest in your hate's proceeding,
> My blood for your rude brawls doth lie a-bleeding;
> But I'll amerce you with so strong a fine
> That you shall all repent the loss of mine:[24]

By contrast the fine imposed upon Shylock is not an amercement, because even though it is in the mercy of the duke to remit, its limits are set by Venetian statute, and not arbitrarily imposed by the duke.

Now permit me to make an admittedly large but perhaps not too implausible assumption: Shakespeare had a way with words. The play on the words of the title "Merchant of Venice" is that the merchant, Antonio, is a beggar for a mercy from Shylock. This mercy is more a concrete physical and economic benefit to him, Antonio, rather than, or at least in addition to a highly charged and morally fraught intentional act of forgiveness that Portia praises as godlike. If granted the mercy, neither his flesh nor his life will be taken and he will have had the use of 3000 ducats without cost or penalty to him.

For my argument, most important for the play on words in the title is that it may allow us to see Shylock as the protagonist.[25] 'Merchant' is ultimately derived from the Latin verb *mercari*, which is to purchase or buy, and which is of course cognate to *merces* and *merx*. As late as 1903 a meaning for 'merchant' is listed in the English Dialect Dictionary as 'buyer,' 'purchaser,' or 'customer' with the example "have ye found a merchant for your horse," as well as 'shopping' or 'the purchasing of goods' as in "I'm ga'un to mak ma marchand."[26] Indeed it appears in that sense as late as 1965 in the Dictionary of the Scots Language with the example, "It's guid gear that pleases the merchant."[27]

As a Jew in Venice, Shylock is not allowed to own land or property to be bought and sold in the market as merchandise, that is, to engage in retail trade.[28] But he is of course a buyer of merchandise for his own use. Indeed, because of the forfeiture of the bond, Shylock has purchased a pound of Antonio's flesh; as Portia says, "the law allows it, and the court awards it." This purchasing of Antonio's flesh is signaled early in the play but perhaps forgotten by the climax when Shylock, arguing on behalf of his bond says:

> A pound of man's flesh taken from a man
> Is not so estimable, profitable neither,
> As flesh of muttons, beefs, or goats. I say,
> To buy his favour, I extend this friendship.

That particular bit of dialogue is put forward in that scene ironically and dripping with sarcasm, because it is clear there and as the play develops that Shylock certainly does not intend to purchase Antonio's friendship; he is literally purchasing Antonio's pound of flesh with the intended effect to follow. But, lest we forget, we are reminded in the court scene that he is in fact a buyer when in response to the Duke, who says to him, "How shalt thou hope for mercy, rendering none?," Shylock responds:

> What judgment shall I dread, doing no wrong?
> You have among you many a purchased slave,
> Which, like your asses and your dogs and mules,
> You use in abject and in slavish parts,
> Because you bought them: shall I say to you,
> Let them be free, marry them to your heirs?
> Why sweat they under burthens? Let their beds
> Be made as soft as yours and let their palates
> Be season'd with such viands? You will answer
> 'The slaves are ours:' so do I answer you:
> The pound of flesh, which I demand of him,
> Is dearly bought.[29]

This passage underlines the capricious mercy of the duke and Venice by making clear that Venice itself owns the flesh of others to do with as it will, and yet shows no mercy to those whose flesh it owns; why should Shylock do otherwise with the flesh he now owns and be merciful.[30] What is important in both passages is the identification of Antonio's flesh with the flesh of other animals one might purchase in the market; goods, commodities, to be bought. Shylock is not a seller; he is a buyer of merchandise, a *mercans* in Latin; even a merchant in English as late as 1965.

So if we take the merchant, the buyer, to be Shylock, it appears rather that the play is in conventional terms a tragedy, with the protagonist Shylock coming to grief in the end, because of his tragic flaw, his blindness driven by vengeance; he suffers a turn of fortune from good to bad, involving the loss of significant goods—his 3000 ducats, his wife's ring, his daughter married to a Christian, half his estate, and in the end even his faith and Jewish friends, as he is compelled by the court at Antonio's request to convert to Christianity, a compulsion that violates the Decretals as Aquinas points out in his argument against compelling Jews to convert.[31] Antonio is the antagonist. Recall his dismissive words to Shylock when Shylock had spoken of buying his friendship:

I am as like to call thee [dog] again,
To spit on thee again, to spurn thee too.
If thou wilt lend this money, lend it not
As to thy friends; for when did friendship take
A breed for barren metal of his friend?
But lend it rather to thine enemy.[32]

Here Antonio makes explicit his antagonism, and that he is Shylock's "enemy." This play is a tragedy.

Mercy Beyond Justice

So what explains this tragedy? What explains it is the absence of a particular form of mercy in Venice, different from the mercy that Portia praises as godlike as well as the sovereign judicial mercy that is in the power of the duke to grant. To make this argument, I want to borrow from Aquinas three different senses of forgiveness that he discusses, and specifically two different forms of mercy related to these forms of forgiveness.

1) The first sense of forgiveness Aquinas discusses in the second part of the second part of the *Summa* at question 157. It is the forgiveness of punishment that expresses the virtue of *clementia*. *Clementia* is a part of the cardinal virtue of temperance and is concerned with the passion for vengeance. There are two such virtues concerned with this passion: *mansuetudo* (meekness) and *clementia*. *Mansuetudo* regulates the internal passion itself, while *clementia* limits the severity of the vengeful act that proceeds from the passion.

The major source for Aquinas's discussion of *clementia* is Seneca's *De clementia*, which I mentioned above. By and large following Seneca in his own account, Aquinas differs on one point in particular, and that is that the remission or forgiveness of punishment expressed by this virtue may be motivated in part by love for the offender. It may also be motivated in part by an aversion to the infliction of pain. But strictly speaking, its defining object is with Seneca to regulate well the inner passion for vengeance in its external manifestations. So the forgiveness that proceeds from this virtue does not bear upon the good of the offender, but rather upon the good of the one offended. The good done for the offender is, in effect, a side effect. And this is why *clementia* falls under the cardinal virtue of temperance, rather than the cardinal virtue of justice.

While it is evident that Shylock in his desire for the pound of flesh lacks this virtue, it does make an appearance in the play, namely, in Portia's soliloquy. For all practical purposes, even though directed at Shylock, when she praises mercy as befitting kings and godlike, as seasoning justice, she might as well be cribbing from Seneca's various urgings directed at Nero to reign in his vengeful punishments for the sake of his own glory. The greatness of the emperor is most manifest in the fact that while he possesses great power to punish justly but also harshly, motivated by his vengeance against those who have committed offenses, his true greatness rests in reigning in that passion, subjecting it to reason, and mitigating the vengeful act that would otherwise proceed from it.[33]

Considering Seneca and Nero, it is important to recognize that by and large the ancient Greek and Roman discussion of forgiveness related it to offenses against honor or dignity, particularly the honor or dignity of those in power.[34] To be forgiven one had to re-acknowledge that honor or dignity. Nero's vengeance arises from the attack upon his honor as emperor by those who disobey him or those who attack him. Earlier, Julius Caesar's imperial pretensions were thought by many to be manifest in his tendency to grant clemency to the enemies of Rome, as if they dishonored him rather than the republic he was to serve.[35]

Part of the Stoic aversion to forgiveness of this sort is the principle that the wise man, the sage, cannot be harmed, so there is nothing personally to forgive.[36] Forgiveness in effect is an indirect sign of one's own weakness and lack of wisdom. And yet it has a place particularly in the life of those in power, because they do in fact have to govern and punish.[37] So a main goal of Seneca's in *On Clemency* is to distinguish a good ruler's justice and clemency from a tyrant's injustice and cruelty. Now consider that in the court Antonio, addressing the duke, explicitly compares Shylock to a tyrant:

> I do oppose
> My patience to his fury, and am arm'd
> To suffer, with a quietness of spirit,
> The very tyranny and rage of his.[38]

Notice also that Shylock's reason for pursuing vengeance against Antonio is the dishonor with which Antonio regularly treated him:

> Signior Antonio, many a time and oft
> In the Rialto you have rated me
> About my moneys and my usances:
> Still have I borne it with a patient shrug,
> For sufferance is the badge of all our tribe.
> You call me misbeliever, cut-throat dog,
> And spit upon my Jewish gaberdine,
> And all for use of that which is mine own.
> Well then, it now appears you need my help:
> Go to, then; you come to me, and you say
> 'Shylock, we would have moneys:' you say so;
> You, that did void your rheum upon my beard
> And foot me as you spurn a stranger cur
> Over your threshold: moneys is your suit
> What should I say to you? Should I not say
> 'Hath a dog money? is it possible
> A cur can lend three thousand ducats?' Or
> Shall I bend low and in a bondman's key,

With bated breath and whispering humbleness, Say this;
'Fair sir, you spit on me on Wednesday last;
You spurn'd me such a day; another time
You call'd me dog; and for these courtesies
I'll lend you thus much moneys'?[39]

Shylock's bond is his honor. Notice his ironic and biting comment about Bassanio's and Gratiano's cheap fidelity to their marriage bonds, when they wish their wives dead for the sake of Antonio. He cuts them with, "these be Christian husbands."[40] Antonio's failure to pay is yet another dishonoring of Shylock. So, Shylock has been dishonored, and he demands that his honor be acknowledged and restored or that the offender suffer the penalty of the loss of his very flesh. In addition to the similarity to Seneca in Portia's words, the fact that Shylock is pursuing vengeance adds to the evidence that Portia is commending *clementia* to Shylock, who will, nonetheless, have his bond.

The final bit of evidence that it is *clementia* that Portia is urging is shown by the duke's action of pardoning Shylock. Shylock has, in pursuing his vengeance, committed an offense against the laws of Venice, their honor and dignity. But as mentioned above, the duke, who represents in his person the honor and dignity of Venetian law, explicitly says that the motive of his pardon is, "That thou shalt see the difference of our spirits, I pardon thee thy life before thou ask it."[41] Venice as represented by the person and dignity of the Duke does not possess the "spirit" of vengeance. The duke stands in for Nero, and Portia's beautiful words find in him an avid listener, distinguishing himself from a tyrant.

2) The second form of forgiveness expressing mercy one might look at in Aquinas pertains directly to the role of the duke in administering justice. It comes up in Aquinas somewhat oddly when he discusses the injustices of a judge in judging, ST IIaIIae, 67. In that place Aquinas argues that ordinary judges or magistrates do not have the power to remit the punishment or penalty that is due according to the law. Such power of remission belongs solely to the sovereign acting for the sake of the common good. This sovereign forgiveness, this remission of punishment as mercy, is not *clementia*, since it is not concerned with the passion of vengeance and is not directed to the good of the one who remits the punishment as *clementia* is. On the contrary, it is directed to the common good.

But Aquinas places a crucial limit upon this sovereign judicial mercy. The sovereign may only exercise it for the sake of the common good with the consent of the one who has been harmed or offended. The power of the sovereign to punish or forgive such punishment is not absolute or arbitrary, but is conditioned by joint considerations of the common good and the consent of the offended party. So when Antonio points out to Salerino that the duke cannot pardon him at the cost of Venice losing its credit with others, that exchange presupposes that Shylock will not consent. In fact it occurs just after Antonio pleads with Shylock to "hear me speak," to which Shylock responds:

I'll have my bond; I will not hear thee speak:
I'll have my bond; and therefore speak no more.
I'll not be made a soft and dull-eyed fool,
To shake the head, relent, and sigh, and yield
To Christian intercessors. Follow not;
I'll have no speaking: I will have my bond.[42]

This condition upon the duke's sovereign judicial power to forgive is signaled when Bassanio pleads with Portia in the guise of the young doctor of the law:

I beseech you,
Wrest once the law to your authority:
To do a great right, do a little wrong,
And curb this cruel devil of his will.

But Portia responds:

It must not be; there is no power in Venice
Can alter a decree established:
'Twill be recorded for a precedent,
And many an error by the same example
Will rush into the state: it cannot be.[43]

The duke's sovereign judicial mercy is not Shylock's to give, but it is premised upon his consent, lest, as Aquinas argues in question 67, the original harm or injustice done to the one offended be compounded by the state.

Both of these forms of forgiveness or mercy, *clementia* and sovereign judicial mercy, share in common at least two features. First, they are not concerned with the good of the offender—*clementia* is concerned with the good of the one who punishes, while sovereign judicial mercy is concerned with the good of the community primarily, and only secondarily the one who has been offended. Second, they both involve the mitigation of punishment—its relaxation or lessening. But they are not arbitrary or whimsical in the way in which modern and contemporary authors fear the arbitrariness of mercy in relaxing the demands of justice. As virtues they require the exercise of the virtue of prudence, both personal and political. Still neither go beyond justice, but remain within its bonds, seasoning it to taste, as it were.

3) There is however a third sense of forgiveness in Aquinas in which we see a mercy that goes beyond justice. It is the forgiveness found in the discussion of the atonement. Since that is a properly theological topic I want to discuss very little about it here, other than to point out that the account is one of substitutionary satisfaction of punishment due or paid to divine justice.[44] The forgiveness or remission of the eternal punishment justly due a sinner is achieved by Christ's sacrificial act. Crucial to Aquinas's account is that justice is not relaxed as it is in both *clementia* and sovereign judicial mercy. The eternal debt of punishment remains in place but is paid in full by Christ.

Again, I do not want to enter into theological debates about the appropriateness of this theory of the atonement. But, in terms of our ordinary English term 'forgiveness' it is a little awkward since we do not usually think of a debt being *forgiven* when it is actually paid by oneself or another. The Latin verb '*remittere*' is different, however. It can certainly mean to relax or loosen. But it can also mean to give back, send back, restore, indeed to repay. In that sense, it is not at all incoherent to suggest that one person can pay back a debt owed by another person. In our etymological sense of 'mercy' which emphasizes the concreteness of a good exchanged, mercy as remission would be exhibited either by the creditor relaxing or lessening what must be paid back, forgiving or relaxing the debt in that sense, or by someone else paying it on behalf of the debtor. Indeed, this second sense of a mercy, that of someone else paying the debt, makes a brief appearance in concrete terms in the play, when Bassanio, newly enriched by his marital union with Portia in Belmont and at her urging, offers to pay back Shylock double the bond at 6000 ducats, indeed even triple at 9000. Shylock, however, refuses this substitutionary mercy.

For my point, however, what is important in introducing into the discussion this substitutionary mercy in Aquinas is that he associates it with friendship.[45] Christ's act of atonement through substitution, in which the demands of justice are not relaxed but rather satisfied, fulfilled superabundantly, is associated by Aquinas with a divine act of friendship for human beings. It is not an exercise of divine *clementia*, since God cannot have the passion for vengeance that expresses itself in punishment.[46] Nor is it an exercise of sovereign judicial mercy, since it does not relax punishment of an offender for the sake of the common good; on the contrary it is directed to the good of the individual who is suffering or will otherwise suffer punishment. In addition, as opposed to *clementia* and sovereign forgiveness, this mercy does bear primarily upon the good of the offender.

That context of divine friendship fits well with the spousal friendship that motivates Portia to give the money to Bassanio who is to give it in turn on behalf of his friend Antonio. And the doubling of the amount to 6000 ducats is oddly coincidental to Aquinas's discussion of *misericordia*. I would like to switch now to the Latin term, because I think the English term is a bit misleading given the etymological roots of it in economic transactions bound by justice that I discussed above. Recall that I pointed out '*merx*' and '*merces*' are unrelated to '*miser*.' '*Misericordia*' however is clearly related etymologically to '*miser*.'[47] Even though '*misericordia*' is often translated into English as '*mercy*,' as in "*Mater Misericordiae*" as "Mother of Mercy," it has a quite different etymological sense. Aquinas, following Augustine, points out that its etymology is "suffering [or distressed] heart," which is clearly not captured by the quite different etymology of 'mercy' in economic transactions bound by justice. So it is apposite that Portia disguised as the young doctor of the law urges Shylock to mercy, not *misericordia*, immediately upon specifying that the pound of flesh must be taken nearest the heart according to the economy of the bond:

Why, this bond is forfeit;
And lawfully by this the Jew may claim

A pound of flesh, to be by him cut off
Nearest the merchant's heart. Be merciful:
Take thrice thy money; bid me tear the bond.[48]

The coincidence of Bassanio offering double on behalf of Antonio is that in attributing *misericordia* to God Aquinas has to deal with the following objection. *Misericordia* relaxes justice. But God cannot relax his own justice. Therefore, *misericordia* cannot be attributed to God.[49] Notice the presupposed sense of *misericordia* in the objection tracks closely the problem I have been considering at the heart of the contemporary discussion where mercy and justice seem to be opposed. Aquinas does not challenge the presupposition of the objection, but introduces another sense of *misericordia* that does not relax justice, a sense different from the sense of the objection. He writes, "God acting with *misericordia* does not do something *against* (*contra*) his justice, but rather he performs an act *beyond* (*supra*) his justice, just as someone who owes someone else one hundred *denarii* pays him back two hundred." There is the coincidence—paying back double what is owed. Aquinas then concludes, "hence, it is clear that *misericordia* does not take away from justice, but is instead rather its fullness or [superabundance]." And he quotes James, "*misericordia* exalts itself beyond justice."[50]

Aquinas's conclusion is perfectly general as he extends it beyond simply the question of divine *misericordia* to *misericordia* itself. In fact he makes that generality explicit in paraphrasing the passage from Paul in Ephesians 4:32, "therefore, give to one another as Christ has given to you."[51] The passage from Paul is regularly translated into English with 'forgive' taking the place 'give,' and 'forgiven' taking the place of 'given.' However, I have translated it more literally because it is clear from Aquinas's explanation of the Pauline text that he is reading it more broadly as "give," rather than the more narrow "forgive." The notion of "giving" fits better the debtor who pays back more than is owed, and for Aquinas foreshadows the substitutionary account of atonement, whereby Christ gives himself on behalf of and in place of. So, in context, the point of the debt metaphor is that it sets up in the first part of the *Summa* Aquinas's discussion of substitutionary satisfaction later in the third part.

Important for my point here is the identification of this *misericordia* with a divine attribute. Despite Portia's praise of mercy as an attribute to God Himself, the *clementia* she praises cannot in fact be attributed to God, since God cannot suffer the passion for vengeance that drives excessive punishment and needs to be reigned in. Aquinas does not even raise the possibility of attributing *clementia* to God.

Sovereign judicial mercy, in which a punishment is relaxed, can, however, be attributed to God. And yet it is not the *misericordia* displayed in the atonement. Quite the contrary, Aquinas asserts that it is the mercy shown to the damned in Hell (*in damnatione reproborum*). Aquinas argues that God's sovereign judicial mercy is found in the punishment of the damned, for, he writes, "while [their punishment] is not *totally* relaxed, it is alleviated somewhat insofar as they are not punished as much as they deserve."[52]

But the *misericordia* manifested in the atonement does not involve relaxation of justice; the debt to be paid according to justice is fully paid, indeed it is paid superabundantly beyond what justice demands because it expresses the communion of divine friendship for human beings.

This identification of *misericordia* associated with friendship that goes beyond justice is made explicit in the discussion of the infused natural virtue of *misericordia* in question 30 of the second part of the second part. It is infused as an effect of *caritas*. But it is a moral virtue, the acquired correlate of which Aquinas with some stretching of the text struggles to attribute to Aristotle's mere mention of ἔλεος in the second book of the Nichomachean Ethics.[53]

Aquinas himself distinguishes two forms of the human virtue of *misericordia*. One is associated with ἔλεος, described at length by Aristotle in both the *Poetics* and *Rhetoric*, but merely mentioned in passing in the *Nichomachean Ethics*. This passion is experienced when one sees someone like oneself suffer some undeserved evil or harm. Aquinas argues that one is motivated by this passion to assist the one suffering, because one fears that a similar fate may befall oneself because of the likeness to oneself. This *misericordia* is fundamentally self-interested as motivated by one's fear for one's own future.

Under the guise of pity, Martha Nussbaum has analyzed at great length over a number of years the passion of ἔλεος, focusing upon Aristotle's discussion of tragedy in the *Poetics* and also the broad discussion in the *Rhetoric*, and then again later in Rousseau and Adam Smith on the sentiments. The self-interest at the heart of it informs and enriches for her a theory of justice very much like a Rawlsian theory, although it admits of the cognitive importance of the passions, and allows for taking seriously a particular conception of the human good forbidden by Rawls. But she finds no distinct virtue in ἔλεος apart from justice.

One might naturally associate this form of *misericordia* with the biblical injunction to do to others as you would have them do to you.[54] If you would like to be treated a certain way when you suffer, you should treat others the same way in the hope that they and others will return the assistance when you are in need. This fearful self-interested form of *misericordia* requires no friendship, just an observed likeness to the one suffering. So the Duke says, "How shalt thou hope for mercy, rendering none?" and Portia adds to conclude her great soliloquy:

Though justice be thy plea, consider this,
That, in the course of justice, none of us
Should see salvation: we do pray for mercy;
And that same prayer doth teach us all to render
The deeds of mercy.[55]

We are all alike in needing mercy, so extend it here. However, Aquinas identifies a second form of *misericordia* which is associated with friendship for those who suffer, friendship in which we make the suffering of others our own through the union of love and affection by which we identify with them. We do not fear future suffering for ourselves, since their very suffering is our suffering, just as in friendship one makes the *good* of the other one's own. We do not fear for our own future, because we are already suffering with our friends in their present suffering. The association with friendship is confirmed when Aquinas identifies this form of *misericordia* not with Aristotle's ἔλεος, but rather with the latter's discussion of συναλγεῖν, the act by which we grieve with our friends, discussed at some length in the ninth book of the *Nichomachean Ethics* on friendship.

Where Aristotle thinks such an act of grieving with friends is a reason to limit the number of one's friends to a small number, in Aquinas it is extended to all human beings through the natural friendship he thinks we do not choose but are all born into and respond well to or fail to live up to. This *misericordia* is associated with the second great commandment to love your neighbor as yourself, and is the *misericordia* expressed by the alien Good Samaritan when he befriends the stranger suffering in the ditch who had been set upon by thieves, the stranger whom the priest and the Levite move away from.[56]

Notice by the way that the story of the Good Samaritan is told by Christ to a "man of the law" who had asked "who is my neighbor," and who after Christ's story responds to Christ's question "so who was neighbor to the man," with, as the Vulgate has it, "*qui fecit misericordiam*," or "the one who achieved *misericordia*." Recall here that Portia is herself disguised as a "doctor of laws." Most importantly for my claim, it is this *misericordia* that Aquinas identifies explicitly as the greatest of all virtues, greater even than *caritas*, because considered in itself it is most proper to God and thus considered in itself the most godlike virtue.[57] It is the mercy of friendship beyond justice.

One more point from Aquinas. In attributing *misericordia* to God, Aquinas argues that it is to be found in all God's works, including the very act of *creation ex nihilo*.[58] God's *misericordia* is the precondition for the existence and sustenance of a creature in being at all. In the specifically human case, it is God's primeval friendship of *misericordia* that causes us to be created and born to friendship with Him and one another in Him.[59] So the effect of divine *misericordia* does not first appear on the scene after the fall in Christ's incarnation and atoning sacrifice; the Incarnation and Atonement restore and elevate that original *misericordia* of divine friendship expressed in creation.

Now back to the tragedy. All three forms of mercy under the guise of forgiveness show up in the play; *clementia* in the praise of Portia and the arbitrariness of the duke distinguishing "our spirit from yours;" sovereign judicial forgiveness in the power and authority of the duke to relax the penalty of the bond but only with the consent of Shylock, which Shylock does not in fact give. However, it is the third form of mercy, *misericordia*, that is at the heart of the tragedy.

Shylock has neither form of *misericordia* described above. He does not have the form associated with ἔλεος in which one fears for one's own future, which is shown when Portia says in the soliloquy:

Therefore, Jew,

> Though justice be thy plea, consider this,
> That, in the course of justice, none of us
> Should see salvation: we do pray for mercy;
> And that same prayer doth teach us all to render
> The deeds of mercy.[60]

Shylock, however, does not fear that he will one day be in precisely Antonio's predicament, much less by the end of the scene. This passage is a warning and foreshadowing—do unto him, as you would have done unto you, or else it *will be* done unto you as *you will have done* unto him. Shylock rejects that warning with:

> My deeds upon my head! I crave the law,
> The penalty and forfeit of my bond.

But Shylock's lack of the second form of *misericordia*, the truly godlike mercy, is signaled early on in the making of the bond when, with dripping irony and sarcasm, he points out the lack of friendship between him and Antonio just after Antonio identifies them as enemies.

> Why, look you, how you storm!
> I would be friends with you and have your love,
> Forget the shames that you have stain'd me with,
> Supply your present wants and take no doit
> Of usance for my moneys, and you'll not hear me:
> This is kind I offer.

With this passage, Shylock conceals his genuine hatred for Antonio and desire for vengeance, as Antonio responds,

> Content, i' faith: I'll seal to such a bond
> And say there is much kindness in the Jew.[61]

However, it would be a mistake to identify the cause of the tragedy with the lack of godlike *misericordia* in Shylock. That lack in Shylock is rather the effect of the cause of the tragedy. The cause of the tragedy is the lack of godlike *misericordia* in and amongst the Venetians themselves. In their words Shylock is an alien and a stranger; to Antonio specifically he is an enemy. But how does *misericordia* respond to the enemy? To the stranger? To the alien amongst us? Portia comes to the court disguised as a young doctor of laws; a reader of the Gospels cannot help but be reminded of the man of the law whom Christ taught the meaning of neighbor—*misericordia*. Commenting on the second great commandment "love your neighbor as yourself," Aquinas argues that "it does not matter whether he is called 'neighbor' or 'brother' according to 1 John IV or 'friend' according to Leviticus 19, because all of these express the same affinity."[62] And specifically discussing the love of enemies he writes, "someone loving God and neighbor does not exclude his enemies from the generality [of the need to love] one's neighbor."[63]

In Venice, justice applies to the stranger, but not *misericordia*. We know that there is no *misericordia* among the Venetians from Shylock's great soliloquy quoted earlier: "if you prick us do we not bleed?" His eloquence there on behalf of vengeance surpasses Portia's eloquence on behalf of mercy, precisely because it is a heartfelt plea for the acknowledgment of his common humanity with the Venetians, the common humanity that Aquinas argues is the basis for the natural friendship with one another that we do not choose, but by divine *misericordia* are created and born to; but at the same time it is also Shylock's stern verdict upon the Venetians before God, indeed before Christ, convicting the Venetians for their lack of god-like *misericordia*. There is no godlike *misericordia* in the courts of Venetian justice, because prior to those courts of justice there is no *misericordia* in Venice itself, no genuine friendship. That is the tragedy.

In conclusion, "friendship seems to hold states together, and lawgivers to care more for it than for justice; for unanimity seems to be something like friendship, and this they aim at most of all, and expel faction as their worst enemy; and when men are friends they have no need of justice, while when they are just they need friendship as well, and the truest form of justice is thought to be a friendly quality."[64] That friendly quality that Aristotle praises and the Venetians do not know is the quality of mercy, or rather, the quality of *misericordia* that "droppeth as the gentle rain from Heaven upon the place beneath."

University of Notre Dame

Notes

1. *"Misericordia Dei in tempore tribulationis quasi nubes pluviae in tempore siccitatis."* Sirach 35:26.

2. William Shakespeare, *The Merchant of Venice*, ed. M. M. Mahood (Cambridge: Cambridge University Press, 2003), Act IV, Scene 1, p. 155.

3. See for example, Jeffrie G. Murphy and Jean Hampton, *Forgiveness and Mercy* (Cambridge: Cambridge University Press, 1998); J. Adler, "Murphy and Mercy," *Analysis* 50.4 (1990); H. R. T. Roberts, "Mercy," *Philosophy* 46, no. 178 (1971); E. A. Christodoulidis, "The Irrationality of Merciful Legal Judgement: Exclusionary Reasoning and the Question of the Particular," *Law and Philosophy*, 18.3 (1999): 215–241; J. Diller, "Merciful Justice," *Philosophia* 41.3 (2013): 719–735; H. S. Hestevold, "Justice to Mercy," *Philosophy and Phenomenological Research*, 46.2 (1985): 281–291; C. A. H. Johnson, "Entitled to Clemency: Mercy in the Criminal Law," *Law and Philosophy*, 10.1 (1991): 109–118; S. Kershnar, "Mercy, Retributivism, and Harsh Punishment," *International Journal of Applied Philosophy*, 14.2 (2000): 209–224; S. Kershnar, "Respect for Persons and the Harsh Punishment of Criminals," *International Journal of Applied Philosophy*, 18.1 (2004): 103–121; N. Markosian, "Two Puzzles about Mercy," *Philosophical Quarterly*, 63, no. 251 (2013): 269–292; J. G. Murphy, "Forgiveness, Mercy, and the Retributive Emotions" *Criminal Justice Ethics*, 7.2 (1988): 3–15; J. Rothchild, "Dispenser of the Mercy of the Government: Pardons, Justice, and Felony Disenfranchisement," *Journal of Religious Ethics*, 39.1 (2011): 48–70; M. Sigler,

"The Story of Justice: Retribution, Mercy, and the Role of Emotions in the Capital Sentencing Process," *Law and Philosophy*, 19.3 (2000): 339–367.

4. Alex Tuckness and John M. Parrish, *The Decline of Mercy in Public Life*, (Cambridge: Cambridge University Press, 2014).

5. *The Merchant of Venice*, Act III, Scene 3, p. 139.

6. *The Merchant of Venice*, Act IV, Scene 1, p. 155.

7. This point about *kashrut* and the court scene seems to go unnoticed by and large in Shakespeare scholarship. A title search of the World Shakespeare Bibliography with the words 'kashrut' or 'kosher' comes up empty. I have found only three other instances of scholarship that take note of it. David B. Goldstein, "Failures of Eating In *The Merchant of Venice*," *Actes des congrès de la Société française Shakespeare* 29 (2012): 31–46; Joan Fitzpatrick, "Early Modern Dietaries and the Jews: The Merchant of Venice and The Jew of Malta," in *Shakespeare's World/World Shakespeares: The Selected Proceedings of the International Shakespeare Association World Congress Brisbane, 2006*, ed. R. Fotheringham, C. Jansohn, and R. S. White (Newark, NJ: University of Delaware Press), 104; David Conter, "Eagleton, Judge Posner, and Shylock v. Antonio," *McGill Law Journal* 35 (1990): 105–130. However, this story element of the flesh versus the blood in the bond is not due to the genius of Shakespeare's imagination. It, along with the story of Portia and Bassanio, is borrowed from an Italian novella, *Giannetto of Venice and the Lady Belmont*, in *Il Pecorone* by Ser Giovanni of *The Merchant of Venice*, "Introduction," by M. M. Mahood, pp. 2–3. In that Italian story, there is no praise of mercy or request for it; no appearance of the Italian words, '*misericordia*,' '*pieta*,' '*grazia*,' '*clemenza*,' or '*carita*,' any of which could be used in Italian for some form of mercy. There are a number of offers to pay the merchant's debt. And the lady from Belmont, here disguised as a judge, suggests that the Jew will be glad if he "releases" or "frees" the merchant from the debt; the Italian uses '*libera*' in "*Io voglio che tu ti tolga questi Cm fiorini, e libera questo buono uomo, e anco te ne saronno sempre tenuti*." (*Il Pecorone* [Ravenna: Longo Editore, 1974], 112.) Thus, it has a purely contractual and legal or judicial sense in the story, missing the religious and moral connotations that accompany the term 'mercy' and its Italian equivalents. With the Jew refusing, the tables are turned on him on precisely the point about shedding no blood. The "flesh-bond" story itself was a common folk tale. Mahood, "Introduction," 5.

8. See E. M. Rose, *The Murder of William of Norwich: The Origins of the Blood Libel in Medieval Europe* (Oxford: Oxford University Press, 2015).

9. I am indebted to my colleague Michael Novick for reminding me of the scene involving Shylock and his refusal to eat pork with the Christians.

10. *The Merchant of Venice*, Act IV, Scene 1, p. 159.

11. Ibid., pp. 160–161.

12. Leviticus 7:26–27, "Wherever you dwell, you shall not eat any blood, whether of bird or of animal. Every person who eats any blood shall be cut off from the people." Leviticus 17:10–14: "As for anyone, whether of the house of Israel or of the aliens residing among them, who consumes any blood, I will set myself against that individual and will cut that person off from among the people, since the life of the flesh is in the blood, . . . That is why I have told the Israelites: No one among you, not even a resident alien, may consume blood." Notice the parallel with Shylock in the scene—he is a "resident alien" in Venice who will be "cut . . . off from among the people." Both taken from New American Bible, Revised Edition online.

13. Act IV, Scene 1, p. 161.

14. Ibid.

15. *The Decline of Mercy*, pp. 141–246.

16. *The Merchant of Venice*, Act III, Scene 1.

17. *The Merchant of Venice* is dated to the theatrical year 1597–1598. See Mahood, p. 2. According to Benjamin Ravid in "The Legal Status of the Jewish Merchants of Venice, 1541–1638" (*The Journal of Economic History* 35.1 [1975]: 274–279), Tedeschi Jews coming from German lands were first allowed permanent residence in Venice in 1509, and after 1516 confined to the *ghetto nuovo*. They were allowed to operate pawnshops for the poor and trade in second hand goods, under charters renewed every five years. Later in 1541 Levantine Jewish subjects of the Ottoman empire were settled in the *ghetto vecchio* next to the *ghetto nuovo*, for the purposes of promoting Venetian trade with the Turks, but under the restriction that the Jews were "prohibited from engaging in moneylending, the sale of second hand goods, and all activities other than overseas commerce." Their residency was restricted to four months and they were not allowed to bring their families with them. Some of these restrictions, particularly concerning residence, were either formally abandoned in subsequent Venetian legislation or tacitly ignored by the government. After several failed formal petitions, in 1589 Jews obtained the right of permanent residence in Venice.

18. Lucius Annaeus Seneca, *On Clemency*, in *Anger, Mercy, Revenge*, trans. Robert A. Kaster (Chicago: University of Chicago Press, 2010), 172–176.

19. *The Merchant of Venice*, Act IV, scene 1, p. 154.

20. *Oxford English Dictionary* (*OED*) Online.

21. *OED*.

22. Indeed Jewish beggars address those from whom they beg with "*zeki bi*" which means "acquire a merit in heaven through a gift to me." See Gary A. Anderson, *Charity* (New Haven: Yale University Press, 2013), 67.

23. 'Alms' comes through the Latin '*elemosyna*' meaning, among other things, pity, compassion, or an act of mercy, from Hellenistic Greek ἐλεημοσύνη meaning the same, and then ultimately from Ancient Greek ἐλεήμων meaning compassionate or merciful. *OED*.

24. *Romeo and Juliet*, Act III, Scene 1.

25. Even apart from my argument, that claim may not seem so odd if we consider that the play was registered in the Stationer's Register as "The Merchant of Venice, otherwise called The Jew of Venice." See Mahood, p. 22. The latter part of the title calls to mind Christopher Marlowe's earlier *The Jew of Malta*. For the complicated relationship of *The Merchant of Venice* to *The Jew of Malta*, see Mahood, pp. 7–8. And on the treatment of alien Jews in *The Jew of Malta* see James Shapiro, *Shakespeare and the Jews* (New York: Columbia University Press, 2016), 157–158 and 184–187.

26. *English Dialect Dictionary* online edition.

27. *Dictonary of the Scots Language* online edition.

28. Act I, Scene 3.

29. Act IV, Scene 1.

30. *The Merchant of Venice: Introduction*, 37.

31. *Summa Theologiae* IIaIIae.10.8 *respondeo* and *ad* 2.

32. Act I, Scene 3.

33. "One can more easily forgive ordinary people who are implacable in pursuing vengeance: they can suffer real harm; their pain comes from actual wrongs; . . . they appear weak, not clement, when they don't return the favor to people who harm them. But the person who has vengeance at his beck and call can be sure he'll be praised as gentle if he lets an opportunity for revenge go by . . . blows traded by equals do little harm. But for a king, even raising his voice to use intemperate language is at odds with his majesty" *On Clemency*, 151. "Surely we will admit that clemency is all the finer and more magnificent the grander the power in which it excels—a power that cannot rightly be harmful if it is ordered according to nature's law" *On Clemency*, 163–164. "Even a slave can kill a king, and so can a snake, or an arrow. But to preserve life—that can only be done by one who is greater than the man he saves. And so one with the power to give life and to take it away ought to use the gods' great gift in a high-minded way" *On Clemency*, 166.

34. *On Clemency*, 165. See David Konstan, "Assuaging Rage: Remorse, Repentance, and Forgiveness in the Classical World," in *Ancient Forgiveness: Classical, Judaic, and Christian*, ed. Charles L. Griswold and David Konstan (Cambridge: Cambridge University Press, 2011), 17–30.

35. Cato the Younger famously chose suicide rather than accept the dishonor of being granted mercy by Julius Caesar his equal in the Roman republic, the latter known for his clemency directed at his enemies by contrast to the earlier harshness of the dictator Sulla. Barry Strauss, "Caesar and the Dangers of Forgiveness," *The Octavian Report* 1.4. In "Clemency as a Virtue," David Konstan surveys the literature of what he calls the "*communis opinio*" that Caesar's clemency was cynical and self serving, although only to argue that this common opinion is a misunderstanding of the role of clemency in Rome at that time. *Classical Philology* 100.4 (October 2005): 337–346.

36. See Charles Griswold, *Forgiveness* (Cambridge: Cambridge University Press, 2007), chap. 1, pp. 1–37.

37. *On Clemency*, 166–168.

38. Act IV, scene 1.

39. Act I, scene 3.

40. Act IV, scene 1.

41. Act IV, scene 1.

42. Act III, scene 3.

43. Act IV, scene 1.

44. In Anselm, satisfaction had to be made to God's honor as in more ancient accounts of offense and forgiveness involving the powerful—a human being's sin in reference to God consists primarily in disobedience to God, which dishonors Him. See *Why God Became Man*, in *Anselm of Canterbury: The Major Works* (Oxford: Oxford University Press, 1998). Aquinas shifts the ground of satisfaction away from God's honor toward His justice—sin alienates the sinner from the eternal law and original justice, and satisfaction is made to God's justice that otherwise holds the sinner to the debt of punishment. See *ST* IIaIIae.48.4 and IaIIae.82.2–3.

45. See *Summa Contra Gentiles* IV.21.10, 54.6 and *ST* IIIa.48.2 *corp.*

46. *ST* Ia.19.11 *respondeo.*

47. The English term 'miser' is taken directly from the Latin '*miser*,' for the miser is wretched and suffering the vice of inordinate attachment to money; he is miserable in that vice. But see the *misericordia* of the miser in Eliot's *Silas Marner*, who responds in tenderness to the baby by his fire, the baby he had initially mistaken for the gold that had been stolen from him now returned.

48. Act IV, Scene 1.

49. *ST* Ia.21.3 *obj* 2.

50. *ST* 21.3 *ad* 2.

51. The passage in Aquinas is "*donate invicem, sicut et Christus vobis donavit*," while the Vulgate is slightly different as "*donantes invicem sicut et Deus in Christo donavit nobis.*"

52. *ST* Ia.21.4 *ad* 1. This astounding claim of Aquinas's about Hell and the damned invites the question what the common good is that is served by relaxing the punishment of the damned. Aquinas writes nothing of it. So perhaps this mercy shown to the damned is not divine sovereign forgiveness after all, but rather the arbitrary mercy contemporary authors fear, a mercy extended to the damned for God's own inscrutable reasons. Or perhaps it is the closest thing to attributing *clementia* to God that Aquinas can manage, *clementia* without the passion of vengeance, just as Aquinas attributes *misericordia* to God without the passion of suffering.

53. See my "*Misericordia* in Aquinas: A Test Case for Theological and Natural Virtues." *Jaarboek 2013* (Thomas Instituut te Utrecht, 2014).

54. Luke 6:31 and Matthew 7:12.

55. Compare 2 Samuel 2:26, Luke 6:36, Matthew 5:7, Matthew 18:33, James 2:13.

56. Luke 10:25–37.

57. *ST* IIaIIae.30.4 *respondeo.*

58. *ST* Ia.21.4 *ad* 4.

59. See *ST* IaIIae.1–5 for the sustained argument that by nature we are ordained to beatitude and joy, and the disputed question on *Caritas* for the claim that we are "companions in beatitude." "*proximum autem ut socium in participatione beatitudinis.*" Sancti Thomae de Aquino *Quaestiones disputatae de virtutibus quaestio II: De caritate. Corpus Thomisticum* online. See also Josef Pieper, *Happiness and Contemplation* (New York: Pantheon Books, 1958), 93.

60. Act IV, scene 1.

61. Act I, scene 3.

62. *ST* IIaIIae.44.7.

63. *ST* IIaIIae.25.8.

64. *NE* VIII.1 1155a21–28.

Aristotle's Second Thoughts on Justice

Terence Irwin

Abstract: The Aristotelian Corpus contains two extended treatments of justice as a virtue of character: *Magna Moralia* i 33 and *Nicomachean Ethics* Book V (or *Eudemian Ethics* Book IV). Differences between the two treatments include these: (1) *MM* denies, but *EN* V affirms, that natural justice is part of political justice; (2) *MM* denies, but *EN* V affirms, that general (or 'universal') justice is an other-directed virtue that should concern us in the treatment of justice as a virtue; (3) *MM* does not discuss the relation between equity (*epieikeia*) and justice, while *EN* V affirms that equity and justice do not conflict. Are these differences connected? How are they to be explained? Might they help us to answer questions about (a) the relation of *MM* to the other two ethical treatises, and (b) the relation of *EN* V to the *EE* and to the *EN*?

1. The Origin of Our Texts

Aristotle's main treatment of justice as a virtue of character appears in Book V of the *Nicomachean Ethics* (*EN*). Philosophical readers naturally want to understand the argument of this book, and to form some idea of the strengths and weaknesses of the theory that Aristotle sets out there. Such readers may be impatient if they are told that the book contains literary, historical, and textual difficulties that need to be resolved before we can state its philosophical doctrine with any confidence. But in this case I believe that some attention to these difficulties will help us to appreciate the philosophical doctrine more accurately.

I have two difficulties in mind:

1. Book V of *EN* is also Book IV of the *Eudemian Ethics* (*EE*). Most students agree, on the basis of vocabulary and style, that its original home is *EE*.[1] But agreement on this point does not show that Book V, as we have it, belongs to *EE*, and not to *EN*. The linguistic facts leave open three possibilities: (1) It was not Aristotle, but an editor, who put this book in *EN*. Either Aristotle never wrote the corresponding part of *EN*, or it has been lost. (2) Aristotle put this book in *EN*, but without alteration. (3) Aristotle revised the version he had written for *EE*, and inserted it in *EN*, so that, strictly

© 2017, *Proceedings of the ACPA*, Vol. 90
doi: 10.5840/acpaproc20182870

speaking, this book in its present form is part of *EN*, but not of *EE*, and we do not know exactly what the version in the *EE* contained.

2. *EN* V is not the only extended treatment of justice in the Aristotelian Corpus. This virtue is also treated at length in the *Magna Moralia* (*MM*). Students of Aristotle disagree about whether this is a later Peripatetic work that is derived from *EE* and *EN* or an early work of Aristotle.[2] I assume that facts about the vocabulary and syntax of *MM* do not settle the question about authenticity, and that we need to answer questions about its authorship by close attention to its philosophical content, in comparison with *EE* and *EN*.

I will come to the first question, about *EN* and *EE*, later on. I will mostly discuss the second question, about Book V and the *MM*, because I believe a comparison between the two treatises points to some of the themes about justice that Aristotle emphasizes in Book V.

2. Natural v. Political Justice in *MM*

I begin the comparison in the middle of the discussion of justice, with the section on natural justice. This section is historically important; Aquinas uses it to show that Aristotle recognizes the distinction that jurists mark between natural right and legal right (ius: *in EN* §1016). If he is right, the doctrine of natural law has an Aristotelian basis even though Aristotle does not formulate it in exactly these terms. But if we ask what role the passage plays in Aristotle's argument, the answer is less clear. We may even be inclined to treat this as an isolated passage, added for the sake of a complete treatment of the types of justice.

To grasp the significance of the remarks on natural justice, it will be helpful to compare the treatments of it in *MM* and *EN*. The main differences will help us to see the work that it does in *EN*.

In *MM* Aristotle introduces natural justice in order to show why he is not concerned with it in his discussion of general and special justice. After the discussion of the varieties of other-directed justice (as *MM* calls it) or special justice (as *EN* calls it), *MM* introduces the multivocity and homonymy (taken to be equivalent) of justice, with the aim of distinguishing political justice, which is the topic of the present discussion, from other types of justice, which are not under discussion (1194b3–1195a7).

> But since the just is spoken of in many ways, we should determine what sort of just our inquiry is about. There is, then, a sort of just, as they say, for a servant in relation to his master, and for a son in relation to his father. But the just in these cases would seem to be spoken of homonymously with the politically just. For the just that our inquiry is about is the politically just. (1194b3–8)

Aristotle argues that the relations of slave to master, of son to father, and of wife to husband involve only household justice, rather than political justice. Political justice involves the appropriate sort of equality (1194b21–22).

A more surprising example of non-political justice is natural justice. We might think questions about natural justice are irrelevant to political justice if we thought there is no such thing as natural justice. But this is not Aristotle's reason. On the contrary, he argues that the usual objections to natural justice do not prove that there is no such thing. He affirms that there is such a thing as natural justice, and that it is better than legal justice (1195a5–6). But still he denies that natural justice is relevant to political justice.

> Among just things some are by nature and some are by law. But we must not suppose that [the things that are by nature] are things that would never change. For things that are by nature also share in change. I mean, for instance, if we were all to practise always throwing with the left hand, we would become ambidextrous. But it is still by nature the left hand, and the right things are none the less naturally better than the left hand, even if we do everything with the left as we do with the right. Nor because things change does it follow that they are not by nature. Rather if usually and for the greater time the left continues thus to be left and the right right, this is by nature.
>
> Similarly in the case of things that are just by nature it is not true that, if things change because of our use, because of that there is no just by nature. On the contrary, there is [something just by nature]. For what usually remains [just] this is evidently just by nature. For whatever we lay down and recognize, this is also just thereby, and we call it just in accordance with law.
>
> Well, then, what is just in accordance with nature is a better [form of] just than what is just in accordance with law. But what we are looking for is the politically just, and **the politically just is what is just by law, not what is just by nature.** (1194b30–1195a7)

Aristotle acknowledges that natural justice is better than legal justice. He does not say what is better about it, but perhaps he means that it is better to be naturally just than to be politically just. But at any rate his acknowledgment that natural justice is better does not persuade him that it is relevant to his inquiry into justice. His inquiry is about political justice, and political justice depends on law. Natural justice, however, is unaffected by law.

3. Natural Justice in *EN* V

In Book V, however, Aristotle rejects the conclusion that natural justice is irrelevant to political justice.[3] Here he affirms that one part of political justice is natural justice. His discussion of natural justice draws the main distinction between the natural and unchangeable that is drawn in *MM*.

But of the politically just one [part] is natural, and the other part legal—natural the [part] having the same power everywhere, and not by seeming so or not, but legal [the part] that originally makes no difference [whether it is done] one way or another, but makes a difference whenever they have laid down the rule—that a mina is the price of a ransom, for instance, or that a goat rather than two sheep should be sacrificed, and further whatever things they legislate in particular cases—for instance, that sacrifices should be offered to Brasidas—and enactments by decree.

But it seems to some people that all are of this sort, because what is by nature is unchangeable and has the same power, as fire, burns both here and among the Persians, but they see the just things changing. But this is not so, though in a way it is so. Though presumably this is not so at all with the gods, with us there is something that is also by nature, but everything is changeable, but still one thing is by nature and another is not by nature.

But what sort of thing, among those that admit of also being otherwise, is by nature, and what sort is not, but is legal and by convention, if both alike are changeable, is clear. And in the other cases also the same distinction will apply; for by nature the right hand is superior, even though it is possible for everyone to become ambidextrous. (1134b18–35)

The conclusion, however, omits the points in *MM*, that what is naturally just is what is usually just, and that it is not the politically just. Instead Aristotle inserts a new comparison with measures and a new observation about natural justice among different political systems.

But the things that are in accordance with convention and expediency among just things are similar to measures. For not everywhere are measures for wine and for corn of equal size, but in wholesale markets they are bigger, and in retail smaller. And similarly the just things that are not natural but human are not the same everywhere, since neither are the political systems. But still, only one political system is everywhere in accordance with nature the best. (1134b35–1135a5)

MM says nothing about the area in which we might expect to find natural justice, and says nothing about different political systems. In our present passage Aristotle alludes to the different political systems that he discusses more fully in the *Politics*. In Book III Aristotle discusses the nature and goal of the polis, and in Book VII he describes the sort of polis that fulfils this nature and achieves these goals. This best polis embodies natural justice.

Since the best political system requires both the appropriate environment and the appropriate people to be its citizens, it is not a suitable pattern for every actual polis. Though the best system does not vary, constitutions vary in different cities. This is partly, but not wholly, because people have different views about justice and express these different views in different constitutions. A further reason for variation is the fact that different cities have different circumstances and different sorts of people, and no one type of constitution is naturally suitable for every sort of people. This variation is a variation in what is naturally just, because it suits the nature of the different people in different environments.

But though the naturally best constitution is not naturally suitable for everyone with their nature and their circumstances, it is none the less relevant to the constitutions that are naturally best in different circumstances. We find what these constitutions are by reference to the best constitution, and we try to reform actual constitutions so that they embody, as far as possible, the principles that underlie the best constitution, to the extent that these principles are relevant to the actual circumstances. This relation of what is naturally suitable in this or that city to what is naturally suitable in the best city is the basis for Aristotle's advice for the reform and moderation of oligarchic and democratic constitutions. What suits democracies is different from what suits oligarchies; but the different provisions are naturally suitable because they bring a given city closer to fulfilling the conditions that are set out in Books III and VII.

Aristotle's allusion to this aspect of his political theory explains why natural justice is a part of political justice. *MM* is right to say that political justice (i.e., justice in a city) is about legislation and what is required by law, and so it is not the same as natural justice. But the *EN* replies that legislation may be, and indeed should be, influenced by reflexion on natural justice, in the ways that the *Politics* describes. The best political system does not provide a programme for immediate political reforms that will bring it into existence. But it is relevant to questions about political reform. It offers some guidance about the sorts of changes that should be encouraged or resisted in actual cities.

It is clear in the *Politics* that Aristotle takes natural justice seriously both for the analysis and for the criticism of actual cites and their constitutions. It is not so clear that he takes it seriously in his discussion of justice. I remarked at the beginning that the section on natural justice is not obviously connected with the rest of treatment of justice. In the *MM* this is just what we ought to expect, given the separation of natural from political justice. But in *EN* it would be surprising if natural justice were irrelevant; for Aristotle recognizes it as a part of political justice, not a separate form of justice.

Does he, then, recognize its relevance at appropriate places in his argument? To answer this question, I turn to two other questions about justice. Here again it will be useful to consider the differences between the two treatises. If the *MM* asserts that natural justice is irrelevant to political justice, but the *EN* asserts that it is part of political justice, we might reasonably expect this difference to result in further differences elsewhere. I will try to show two things: (1) The two treatises differ on these other questions about justice. (2) The differences can plausibly be explained by the difference over natural justice. The first claim is relatively easy to defend, but the second is less straightforward.

4. Justice as Observance of Law

The first type of justice that Aristotle discusses is called 'general justice,' and is identified with observance of law. We might think he introduces it only to get it out of the way, so that he can concentrate on the subject that he really wants to discuss, which is 'special justice.' This special justice is involved in distribution, restoration, and correction which are treated at length.[4] And so we might take him to indicate that justice is a topic for serious study in so far as it involves distribution, restoration, and correction.

This view that the study of justice is mainly about special justice is confirmed by the *MM*. Aristotle distinguishes the type of justice that is about obedience to law in general from the more specific type that is about equality.

> It remains to speak about justice—what it is, in what things, and about what sorts of things. First, then, if we were to grasp what the just is, the just is in fact of two [sorts] of which one [sort] is in accordance with law. For people say that the things that the law prescribes are just. Now the law commands us to do the brave and the temperate actions, and in general to do all the actions that are spoken of in accordance with the virtues.
>
> (That is why also, they say, justice seems to be some sort of complete virtue. For if the actions that the law commands us to do are just, and the law prescribes the actions that are in accord with all virtue, then the one who abides by the just actions in accord with law will be completely excellent, so that the just person and justice is a kind of complete virtue.) (1193a39–b10)

In support of his description of general justice, he cites the common belief that it is just to follow the law. He adds his own comment that the law commands the actions in accord with all the virtues. This feature of the law explains why people think justice is a sort of complete virtue.

The description of legal justice explains why it is not the main topic of our inquiry into justice. The justice that concerns us is an other-directed virtue, but general justice includes all the virtues, as prescribed by law, and some of these virtues are self-regarding virtues, not directed towards other people.

> One sort of just, then, is in these things and about these things. But it is not this sort of just, nor the justice about these things, that we are looking for. For in accordance with these just things **it is possible to be just when one is by oneself**—for the temperate or brave or continent person is such also when he is by himself. But the just towards another is different from the just according to law that we have spoken of. For in the just things that are towards another it is not possible to be just when one is by oneself. And what we are looking for is this sort of just and the justice about these things. (1193b10–18)

If legal justice is not essentially other-directed, we need not and should not examine legal justice as such, since we would simply reduplicate our examination of the other virtues.

The argument is simple and plausible. If the laws simply recommend the practice of the virtues, and if this is general justice, we learn nothing further by studying general justice beyond what we have learned by studying the other virtues. We are looking for justice as a special virtue that is essentially other-directed, and legal justice is not what we are looking for.

5. Justice, Law, and Legislative Science

Book V, however, disagrees with *MM* on both points. First, it takes general justice to be relevant to our main concerns. Secondly, Aristotle affirms, contrary to *MM*, that general justice is essentially other-directed.

These differences from *MM* result from a disagreement about whether general justice is legal justice. *MM* says Yes, but *EN* says Yes only with qualifications that undermine the argument in *MM*.

> (1) But since the lawless person was unjust, and the lawful person is just, it is clear that all lawful things are in some way just; for the things defined by legislative [science] are lawful, and we say that each of them is just. (2) But the laws speak about all matters aiming either at the common benefit of all, or of the best people, or those in control in accordance with virtue or in accordance with some other manner of this sort. **And so in one way we call just the things that produce and maintain happiness and its parts for a political community.** (3) Now the law prescribes doing both the actions of a brave person—for instance, not to leave the battle-line, or to flee, or to throw away one's weapons—and those of a temperate person—for instance, not to commit adultery, or wanton aggression—and those of a mild person—for instance, not to strike or revile another—and similarly also in accordance with the other virtues and vices commanding the one lot [of actions], and prohibiting the other lot—**the correctly established law correctly, and the carelessly framed law worse.** (1129b11–25)

Aristotle does not straightforwardly identify the provisions of law with the requirements of justice. The account of the just ('we call just the things . . .') refers to the production of happiness and its parts in a political community. Different political systems and legal codes meet this condition to different degrees. Some have the right intention, but fail in execution ('The correctly . . . worse'), while others have a defective intention. The description of justice as prescribed by law is only a step on the way to the correct account. It leads us in the right direction by means of an analysis of the aim of law.

Aristotle recognizes different types of constitutions that determine the character of different legal systems, and that promote the common good to different degrees.

The observation that the laws require action in accordance with all the virtues tells us how they succeed (to different degrees) in promoting the common good. Aristotle therefore assumes that virtues are different ways of promoting the common good. Hence general justice is not simply obedience to law, but obedience to the correct law, the one that actually promotes the common good.

If justice has this role, it is complete virtue in relation to another. Aristotle does not mean that only some virtuous actions promote the common good. He means that complete virtue is justice because it promotes the common good.

None of these claims about justice has a parallel in *MM*, and indeed they disagree with it about legal justice. The aim of correct law shows that the laws aim at the common good, and that therefore just actions are those that produce and maintain the common good. Since the common good is different from my self-confined good, and involves the good of others, the justice that promotes the common good is other-directed. Aristotle has now answered the reason that the *MM* gives for taking general justice to be irrelevant to our inquiry. The *EN* argues, contrary to *MM*, that general justice is necessarily other-directed.

The *EN* has not simply asserted what *MM* denied. Aristotle argues that general justice is not simply observance of law, but observance of the correct law, the one that really promotes the common good. This reference to correct law and the common good is absent from *MM*.[5] The thesis that *EN* defends is not the simple thesis that justice as law-observance is essentially other-regarding, but the more complex thesis that justice, as understood by the correct laws that aim at the common good, is essentially other-regarding.

> This justice, therefore, is complete virtue, but not without qualification, but in relation to another. And because of this justice often seems to be supreme among the virtues, and 'neither the evening star nor the morning star is so marvellous,' and in the proverb we say 'And in justice all virtue is summed up.'
> And it is complete virtue most of all because it is the exercise of complete virtue. And it is complete because the person who has it is able to exercise virtue in relation to another also, but not only on his own; for many in their own concerns are able to exercise virtue, but in things that relate to another they are unable. (1129b26–1130a1)

Contrary to *MM*, Aristotle argues that general justice is not simply complete virtue, but is complete virtue in so far as it is directed to the good of another. Virtue and justice are the same state, but their essence is not the same.

> But in what respect virtue differs from this justice is clear from what we have said. For it is the same, but the being is not the same, but rather, in so far as it is related to another, it is justice, and in so far as it is this sort of state without qualification, it is virtue. (1130a10–13)

Since general justice is complete virtue in a special role of advancing the good of others, the study of other-regarding justice ought to include the study of general as well as special justice.

Aristotle separates correct from incorrect laws in accordance with their degrees of success in achieving the appropriate end of correct law—the common good, which is the aim of legal justice and complete virtue. Different constitutions and laws succeed to different degrees in achieving the common good. The constitution that succeeds completely is the best constitution, which is the one that achieves natural justice. Aristotle relies on his views about natural justice and the best constitution in order to describe the proper scope of general justice. Though he still speaks of legal justice, he does not mean that actual laws all achieve the proper aim of laws, the maintenance of the common good.

Since Aristotle relies on natural justice in order to evaluate actual laws and constitutions, the disagreement about natural justice explains the disagreement between *EN* and *MM* about general justice. This disagreement rests on his claim that natural justice is a part of political justice. Since the *MM* separates natural from political justice, we should not be surprised that it does not rely on any claims about natural justice in its discussion of legal justice. Equally, since the *EN* takes natural justice to be an aspect of political justice, we should not be surprised that it relies on natural justice to support its account of legal justice. The influence of Aristotle's doctrine of natural justice is conspicuous by its absence in one discussion and by its presence in the other.

6. Equity in *MM*

Both *EN* and *MM* discuss equity (*epieikeia*), but in quite different contexts. In the *MM* equity has no role in the treatment of justice. Aristotle mentions it (II 1) in the series of puzzles that form an appendix to his treatment of the virtues.

> After this we ought to make our inquiry into equity, about what it is, and in what things, and about what sorts of things. Equity and the equitable person is the one who takes less of the things that are just according to law. For on the points that the legislator is unable to determine particular points precisely, but speaks universally, the one who gives way on these points, and chooses those things which the lawgiver wished to determine in particular points, but was not able to, this sort of person is equitable. But he does not take less of the things that are just without qualification; for he does not take less of the things that are by nature and in reality just, but only less of the things that are just in accordance with law, which the legislator omitted because of inability. (*MM* 1198b24–33)

Equity is about taking less than your share of what you are justly entitled to according to the law, in particular cases where the legislator was unable to determine the appropriate division of goods. Aristotle remarks that it is not about taking less than your share of what you are entitled to by unqualified justice and natural justice; this is not the concern of law, and equity is about entitlements according to law.

7. Equity and Natural Justice in *EN*

In the *EN* the treatment of 'equity' or (more exactly) 'decency' (*epieikeia*) is part of the book on justice, but it is probably in the wrong place in the manuscripts, since it interrupts a discussion of doing injustice to oneself, in chapters 9 and 11. A better place would be after the account of justice as a mean. The question naturally arises about whether it really is justice that achieves the mean, given the connexion between justice and law, and the apparent fact that sometimes equity rather than justice hits the mean.

> But about decency and the decent, how decency is related to justice and the decent to the just, is the next topic to speak about. For they appear as neither the same thing without qualification nor as different in kind, when we examine them. And sometimes we praise the decent and the decent man, so that even when we praise someone for other things we transfer it instead of 'good,' making it clear that the more decent is better. But sometimes, when we follow the argument, it appears strange if the decent, while being something beyond the just, is praiseworthy; for either the just is not excellent or what is decent is not just, if it is something else, or, if they are both excellent, they are the same. (1137a31–b5)

In Aristotle's view, these different views about justice and equity turn out to be compatible as soon as we understand the type of justice we are talking about in different contexts.

> The puzzle, therefore, about the decent comes about more or less because of these things. But they are all correct in a way, and [contain] nothing contrary to themselves. For the decent, being better than one way of being just, is just, and not as being some different kind is better than the just. The same thing, then, is just and, both being excellent, the decent is superior. (1137b5–11)

To resolve the puzzles about equity, we need to notice that justice is not confined to law. It is sometimes just to exercise discretion in cases where simply following the unqualified law would lead to an unjust outcome.

> But it produces the puzzle because the decent is just, but is not the [just] in accordance with law, but a rectification of a legally just thing. (1137b11–13)

This is not the fault of the legislator, but it is explained by the nature of the case:

And the cause is the fact that all law is universal, but about some things it is not possible to speak correctly universally. And so in the things where it is necessary to speak universally, but it is not possible [to do so] correctly, the law chooses the usual, not being ignorant of the error being made. And it is no less correct; for the error is not in the law, nor in the legislator, but the nature of the object itself—for the matter of things achievable in action is by its nature of this sort. And so, whenever the law speaks universally, but in this case it comes about beyond the universal, in this case it is correct, in so far as the legislator falls short, and has made an error by speaking without qualification, to correct what is deficient, which the legislator would have said himself if he had been present there, and would have legislated, had he known. (1137b13–24)

Aristotle appeals to the intention of the legislator—'what the legislator would have said if he had been there'—to justify not following the written law. This counterfactual claim about the legislator is absent from *MM*. It explains how the error is not in the law or in the legislator.

What is assumed about the legislator? If a rich citizen takes advantage of the law to press a poor citizen to repay a very small sum that the poor citizen cannot afford, and the rich citizen does not need, and if the poor citizen will easily be able to pay the money back within the next month, it would be reasonable and equitable to extend the loan for another month. But perhaps we live under an oligarchic regime in which the legislators approve of enforcing the repayment of loans in all circumstances. In this case an appeal to the intention of the legislator would not support the equitable course of action.

Aristotle's appeal to the counterfactual intention of the legislator gives the answer that favours equity only if he restricts it to certain kinds of counterfactuals. He knows that there are unjust regimes where efforts to follow the intention of the legislator would not support the equitable choice. His claim about what the legislator would say if he were present applies only to the legislator who does what legislative science is supposed to do. Legislative science does not try to make laws that suit the prevailing regime; it tries to find the laws that suit unqualified justice, and therefore promote the common good. The correction of legal justice in the direction of unqualified justice matches the counterfactual judgment of the legislator if and only if the legislator aims at unqualified justice.

This treatment of equity differs from the treatment in *MM* for the reason that also explains the difference between the treatments of general justice in the two treatises. In *EN* Aristotle identifies general justice with legal justice, which he finds not in positive law, but in legislative science, which aims at unqualified justice and the common good. This conception of legislation justifies the treatment of equity as the correction of the law in accordance with the intention of the legislator. The *MM*, however, does not separate general justice from the provisions of positive law.

These disagreements between *MM* and *EN*, about general justice and about equity are explained by the disagreement about the relevance of natural justice to political justice. *MM* denies its relevance, but *EN* affirms it.

8. Natural justice and Aristotle's second thoughts

The point of my argument so far has been to affirm the theoretical significance of the section on natural justice in both treatises, and to point out the implications of this section for other parts of each discussion. While the rest of *EN* V does not discuss natural justice explicitly, I have argued that it implicitly relies on claims about better and worse constitutions that rest on assumptions about natural justice. Reliance on natural justice explains the differences I have pointed out between *EN* and *MM*. If *MM* is an earlier statement of Aristotle's views, Aristotle's appreciation of the importance of natural justice helps to explain a development in his views. In particular, it explains the greater interest that he shows in general justice in *EN*.

How are we to explain Aristotle's emphasis on natural justice? We have seen that he does not change his mind about the reality of natural justice. The *MM* affirms its reality no less clearly than *EN* affirms it, but denies its relevance to political justice, the justice to be found in actual societies. This combination of views is perhaps intelligible if we think of Plato's *Republic* (cited by *MM*, 1194a7). Plato does not present the ideal city as a basis for the reform of actual cities, or as a basis for understanding their political life. The sort of reform that he actually envisages is a radical reform that requires philosophers to rule. We might, indeed, suppose that the task of understanding and reforming actual cities requires a different set of principles and strategies, and that reference to the ideal city is a distraction in these tasks. There is no reason to believe that Aristotle knows of Plato's *Laws* when he is writing the *MM*, but even if he did know Plato's later work on political theory, he might not draw a different conclusion from the one I have suggested about the *Republic*. Though the *Laws* makes less radical proposals about the structure of the best city, its aim is the construction and maintenance of this best city; it does not give advice for those who want to improve actual cities rather than replace them.

Such an attitude to Plato may explain Aristotle's attitude to natural justice in the *MM*. He acknowledges the Platonic enterprise of constructing an ideal city based on principles of natural justice, but he takes his investigation of justice as a virtue to be part of a quite different enterprise. The *MM* is a work of politics, but only in a restricted sense. It is addressed to those who want to achieve something significant in political life, and so it describes the virtues that are needed for the right sort of success (1181a23–b28). For this purpose it may well seem irrelevant to discuss institutions, laws, practices, or virtues, that are based on natural justice; for those institutions and so on belong to the ideal city, not to the one in which we want to achieve something in political life.

This is not the attitude of Aristotle's *Politics*, as we now have it. The *Politics* is different from Plato's two major works in so far as it discusses theoretical principles, ideal cities, the structure of actual cities, and the ways of reforming different types of cities. The same principles underlie both the construction of the ideal and the analysis and reform of the actual. These principles are the principles of natural justice. These two roles for natural justice express the outlook of *EN* V as well as the *Politics*. They do not express the outlook of the *MM*.

We now have a possible explanation of the difference between the *EN* and the *MM*. The *EN* presupposes the existence of the *Politics*, or at least of a plan for the *Politics*, in the order in which we now have it; this plan concludes with an account of the best city (1181b12–23). If, then, Aristotle has formed the outlook of the *Politics*, whether or not he has actually written it, his attitude to natural justice in *EN* V is appropriate. If the *MM* precedes the formation of this outlook, its exclusion of natural justice from political justice is intelligible.

In these remarks about the *Politics* I have passed over a complication that I need to mention, though I cannot stop to explore it. The composition of this work has often been discussed, and one of the reasons for believing that it is not a unified treatise is highly relevant to the questions we have been exploring about justice. Many modern students have argued that the books dealing with Aristotle's political ideal do not really match his empirical treatment of actual states, and that the 'ideal' books should be placed earlier, both in order of composition and in the order of the treatise, than the 'empirical' books. Quite a lot can be said for and against these arguments about composition and arrangement. For present purposes I will simply make three remarks: (1) The end of the *EN* implies that the present order of the books of the *Politics* is Aristotle's order. (2) The use of principles of natural justice to analyse actual constitutions and to construct the best constitution is characteristic both of *EN* V and of the *Politics*, in its present order. (3) If some parts of the *Politics* seem to treat the ideal separately from the actual, we might ask whether this is the result of the attitude that we find in *MM*.

Whatever we decide on these questions, a glance at the *Politics* shows us that the attitude to natural justice that Aristotle takes in *EN* V fits the *Politics* well, whereas the attitude that he takes in the *MM* does not fit it. Here as elsewhere the *MM* shows no knowledge of the political theory that underlies the *Politics*. *EN* V marks a clear contrast. Like the rest of the *EN*, it takes ethics to be part of the systematic study of actual and ideal forms of social and political life, and so to be part of the systematic study that is continued in the *Politics*.

9. The Relation between the *EN* and the *MM*

My comparison of *EN* with *MM* has treated *MM* as an earlier version, and *EN* as the result of reconsideration and revision of the *MM* version. I believe this is the most plausible account of the relation between the two treatises. But it is not the only defensible account. It is difficult to exclude the possibility that *MM* is a later version, and that the direction of revision is the reverse of the one I have suggested.

If *MM* is later and is not by Aristotle, our discussion has cast doubt on some views about its origin. Some readers have suggested that it differs from *EE* and *EN* because the author was summarizing one or both of the other two courses on ethics, and misunderstood what he read. This hypothesis of an unintelligent editor or copyist does not fit the section on justice. For in this section the differences from Book V are not random misunderstandings. If the author is post-Aristotelian, his discussion of justice is designed to express his disagreements with Book V. He presents a distinct philosophical viewpoint, not a misunderstanding of Aristotle's viewpoint.

If, then, the author of *MM* is either early Aristotle or a later critic of Aristotle, can we choose between these two possibilities? If he is a later critic, he ignores Aristotle's arguments for the position that he opposes. He is intelligent enough to alter Aristotle on the points where he disagrees, but apparently not intelligent enough to argue even briefly against Aristotle. If, however, we try the other direction of comparison, we see that Aristotle in Book V always gives some reason for his departure from the position of *MM*. We have seen that on the relation between general and special justice, and on the relation of equity to justice, Aristotle says something to make it clear why he does not agree with the position of *MM*. These facts about the two treatises are easily explained if Aristotle wrote *MM* before he had thought of the different position that he takes in *EN*. They are less easily explained if the author of *MM* was aware of Aristotle's arguments, but rejected them silently.

We ought to be cautious in any efforts to trace the development of Aristotle's position, but not so cautious that we never even consider the possibility of a development. In this case, I believe we can be reasonably confident that his views about justice develop, that two stages of his thought can be seen in *MM* and *EN*, and that his views about natural justice help to explain the development.

10. *EE* or *EN*?

I have not answered the question about whether the book on justice belongs to the *EE* or to the *EN*. Can we decide which it properly belongs to?

A passage in *EN* I shares some of the concerns that we have noticed in the book on justice.

> But our discussion will be adequate if we make things perspicuous in accordance with the subject matter; for we should not seek exactness in the same way in all sorts of arguments, just as [we should not seek it] in [all] manufactured objects [in the same way]. Now fine and just things, which politics examines, have much difference and variation, so as to seem to be by convention only, not by nature. But goods also have some variation of this sort, because harms result from them for many people; for some have been destroyed because of wealth, others because of bravery. It is satisfactory, therefore, if those whose statements are about things of this sort and from premisses of this sort display the truth roughly and in outline, and, given that their statements are about usual things and from premisses of this sort, if their conclusions are also of this sort. (1094b11–22)

This section immediately follows the description of politics in *EN* I 2—hence the remark 'which politics examines.'[6]

Aristotle makes two claims that are connected with points we have already noticed in Book V.

1. Variation is not a good reason for denying that things are fine and just by nature. Hence it is not a good reason for denying that politics is concerned with natural justice.

2. Variation is only to be expected in the matter of ethics. We cannot expect an absolutely precise account.

Each claim prepares us for the argument of Book V.

The first claim is relevant to the contention of Book V that politics is about natural justice, so that natural justice is part of political justice. On this point Book V disagrees with *MM*. Aristotle suggests that if we think some things are good by nature, even though their goodness is subject to change, we also ought to agree that some things are just by nature even though changing circumstances determine whether they are just in one case or another. The variations do not count against the view that politics deals with natural justice. On the contrary, politics is the basis for legislative science, which aims at the common good.

The second claim is partly repeated in the discussion of equity. There Aristotle says that the imprecision and fallibility of generalizations about justice is not surprising, because it simply reflects the lack of fixity that is characteristic of the matter (*hulê*) of actions. This is a familiar theme in *EN*, beginning in the passage we discussed, and present also in I 7, in II, and IX.

The two claims in *EN* I 3 mark a clear connexion with Book V. There is nothing similar in *EE* or *MM*.[7] The *EE* outside the Common Books nowhere comments on the imprecision of ethics, or the way in which this imprecision might seem to undermine any belief in natural justice. But if such a comment had occurred to Aristotle, it would be highly relevant. The fact that justice varies according to circumstances does not show that there is no such thing as natural justice. The fact that even the best general rules may not deal with all particular circumstances does not show that they do not capture natural justice, in so far as it can be captured in generalizations. If, then, Aristotle had formulated and accepted this view about imprecision when he was writing *EE*, he would have had no reason not to mention it. It would have been entirely apposite, since it would have strongly supported his claims about justice.

For this reason the passage on imprecision probably belongs to the revision of *EE* IV that produced *EN* V. If the passage belongs to *EE*, it is the first mention of the imprecision of ethics, and we might get the impression that this doctrine has been invented to deal with questions about equity. But if we read this book as part of *EN*, Aristotle has already prepared us for his remarks about imprecision and equity, and we know that they fit into his wider claims about ethics.

It would be too bold to claim that all the differences I have mentioned between *MM* and the book on justice are really differences between *MM* and *EN*, and that the *EE* version is closer to *MM* on these points. I have remarked that the doctrine of ethical imprecision makes it easier to defend an appeal to natural justice in ethical theory. We might conjecture that the differences between *MM* and the book on justice all result from the greater confidence in natural justice that results from the recognition of ethical imprecision. But it would probably be wiser to conclude simply that we do not know that these differences from *MM* were already present in the *EE* version.

University of Oxford

Notes

1. This paper was the basis for the lecture I gave to the ACPA. In order to keep it within the necessary limits of space, I have omitted many details, including many questions about the relations between the three ethical treatises in the Corpus. The most detailed defence of the Eudemian character of Book V is offered by A. J. P. Kenny, *The Aristotelian Ethics* (Oxford: Oxford University Press, 1978). Kenny also argues (a) that *EE* is later than *EN* and (b) that *MM* is spurious. More recent students have agreed with Kenny (and others) on (b) than have agreed with him on (a).

2. F. Dirlmeier, *Aristoteles: Magna Moralia* (Berlin: Akademie-Verlag, 1964), argues that the substance of *MM* is a third course of lectures by Aristotle. A similar (in this respect) view is defended by J. M. Cooper, "The *Magna Moralia* and Aristotle's Moral Philosophy," *American Journal of Philology* 94 (1973): 327–349. Cooper's argument is criticized by C. J. Rowe, "A Reply to John Cooper on the *Magna Moralia*," *American Journal of Philology* 96 (1975): 160–172. A recent defence of the authenticity of *MM* is offered by Peter Simpson, *Great Ethics of Aristotle* (New Brunswick: Transaction, 2014).

3. F. Dirlmeier, *Aristoteles: Nikomachische Ethik*, 6th edn. (Berlin: Akademie-Verlag, 1974), 324, rejects the contention of J. A. Stewart, *Notes on the Nicomachean Ethics* (Oxford: OUP, 1892), i.493–494, that *MM* disagrees in substance with *EN* on the relation of natural justice to political justice. His attempted reconciliation of the two works is unconvincing.

4. Aristotle's use of two Platonic phrases to describe aspects of special justice may seem to confirm this view. Plato speaks of justice as doing and having one's own (*ta hautou*), and avoiding overreaching (*pleonexia*). Aristotle takes these two features of justice to belong to special justice.

5. Its absence is not surprising. The simple view that one type of justice is law-observance is familiar in the Athenian context, as we can see from the use of '*adikein*' and '*adikos*' in legal contexts. See, e.g., the indictment of Socrates that begins 'Socrates commits injustice' (*Sôkratês adikei*, Plato, *Ap.* 19b4).

6. A discussion of the different descriptions of politics in the three ethical works tends to support some of the arguments I have offered about their relations. I omit that discussion here.

7. Daniel Devereux draws attention to this difference between *EE* (apart from the Common Books) and *EN*, in "Particular and Universal in Aristotle's Conception of Practical Knowledge," *Review of Metaphysics* 39 (1986): 483–504, at 499. He does not mention *MM*.

Religious Liberty and the Limits of Rawlsian Justice

V. Bradley Lewis

Abstract: Religious freedom is included among the basic liberties to which persons are entitled in John Rawls's account of Justice as Fairness. Rawls's revised presentation of this as a political conception of justice in *Political Liberalism* aims to show how it can be (along with the other parts of Justice as Fairness) the focus of an overlapping consensus of reasonable comprehensive doctrines. As an example, Rawls contends that his understanding of religious freedom is consistent with that of the Roman Catholic Church, at least since the Second Vatican Council. I argue that he was mistaken in this in so far as other aspects of his political conception, especially its characterization of citizens as normatively having the power to form their own conceptions of the good, puts it at odds with the teaching of the Council's Declaration on Religious Freedom, *Dignitatis humanae*. This suggests more generally that the limits of consensus in modern pluralist societies are greater than Rawls's theory holds.

It has become something of a commonplace within contemporary political philosophy to lament the influence of John Rawls and/or to suggest that that influence is overstated, that Rawls's views are not nearly as important as they once were. I think this is a mistake, or, at least, a mistaken judgment about the saliency of political ideas. For if Rawls's importance has declined in some manner within academic political philosophy, it has become even more entrenched in common political reasoning, even if not always self-consciously. No other contemporary political philosopher has been cited by name in popular television programs[1] and no other contemporary political philosopher's views have been voiced (if not by name) in speeches given by the President of the United States,[2] or (by name) by candidates for president.[3] Doubtless, an important part of the success of Rawlsianism in this respect is internal to Rawls's own project, for he set out to articulate a conception of social justice implicit not just in the practice of modern liberal democratic societies, but specifically in the institutions and practices of American democracy.[4] Rawls not only presented a political philosophy, but a way of doing political philosophy that involved a continuing back-and-forth conversation between philosophical principles and the ideas that informed political institutions and practices more concretely.

© 2017, *Proceedings of the ACPA*, Vol. 90
doi: 10.5840/acpaproc201822374

pp. 71–84

This is a pervasive aspect in Rawls's work and shows up in at least four important ways. First, one can see it in his notion of "reflective equilibrium," in which
our considered convictions are compared to the principles arrived at through more
rigorous and systematic thought aiming for convergence.[5] Second, it is somewhat
differently indicated in Rawls's most programmatic statement about political philosophy, in which he distinguishes four roles, one of which he calls (after Hegel)
that of "reconciliation." In this guise, political philosophy "may try to calm our
frustration and rage against our society and its history by showing us the way in
which its institutions, when properly understood from a philosophical point of
view, are rational."[6] "When we look at the world rationally," Rawls quotes Hegel as
saying, "the world looks rationally back." Both the notion of reflective equilibrium
and the role of political philosophy as reconciliation are the background to a third
aspect, Rawls's idea of political philosophy as "realistically utopian."[7] The realism is
related to the embeddedness of Rawls's conclusions in actual institutions and values. Finally, the two volumes of Rawls's lectures on moral and political philosophy
illuminate a continuous dialogue between Rawls's own canon of seminal texts and
thinkers from the history of philosophy and his own systematic work. Rawls was
always moving back and forth between the tradition of liberal moral and political
philosophy, on the one hand, and the public values, institutions, and practices of
liberal democracy, on the other.

    This aspect of Rawls goes some way towards explaining his continuing rel-
evance. Rawls's way of doing political philosophy is not the only one; one could
occupy oneself with, as it were, the metaphysics of politics, adopting a largely
speculative mode distantly related to practice. But the main stream of political
philosophy, since Socrates began questioning his fellow citizens in the marketplace
of a democratic city, has been practical, and the context in which political thinkers
did their work is always an important part of understanding them, no matter how
abstract their political thought. This is even more true of the late Rawls than the
early Rawls, although this point has not always been adequately appreciated. The
problems for political theory and practice associated with the pluralistic character
of modern democratic societies have only become more evident since Rawls began
revising his theory of justice in light of them in the 1980s. A theory of justice, no
matter how painstakingly worked out in the abstract, is worth little if it does not
connect with our actual sense of the problems that really generate social and political
dilemmas of justice. Rawls was asking the right questions. Assessing the value of his
answers is more complicated, however. In what follows I consider in some detail one
of Rawls's answers to the dilemmas for political justice caused by modern pluralism,
one of particular salience in recent political conflicts in the United States, that of
religious freedom. Rawls's account is sufficiently in tension with the way at least one
comprehensive doctrine, Roman Catholicism, understands it as to raise questions
about the prospects for his approach to pluralism more generally. On the basis of
this example, I want to suggest that even liberals should scale back their expectations
for the achievement of something like a Rawlsian overlapping consensus, even if
the core idea remains politically attractive. The management of political pluralism

nevertheless remains a daunting challenge both theoretically and practically, and it is a very great merit of Rawls that he looked this extremely difficult problem in the face and worked hard at finding a workable solution to it. Here I, first, look at the general form of Rawls's proposal for a political conception of justice and, second, I critically examine his specific application of it to the question of religious freedom and compare this to some aspects of the Second Vatican Council's 1965 Declaration on Religious Freedom, *Dignitatis humanae*. I refer to this document in particular because Rawls himself points to it as supportive of his own account. In this, however, I argue that he was mistaken, since, although his political conception aims to abstract from the deeper commitments of philosophical and theological doctrines, it fails to do this in a crucial respect involving its characterization of persons. The implications of this failure go beyond the immediate issue of religious freedom.

I

When illustrating the process of reflective equilibrium that I just mentioned, Rawls uses as an example the problem of religious intolerance. Rawls's procedure involves the derivation of principles of justice in the famous "original position," a point of view one can adopt at any time for considering possible normative principles that simulates a system of pure procedural justice. That is, if the original position is set up properly, then any principles selected in it by the parties that inhabit the original position will be just. The parties are not actual people, but representatives who judge on the basis of only commonly available information and have no knowledge of their own particular situations, either their personal characteristics or their conceptions of the good. This is the famous "veil of ignorance." The point is to simulate a deliberative context that controls for the essentially arbitrary characteristics that could influence persons in their choice of principles, it aims to achieve fairness by situating everyone symmetrically. It is, moreover, related to the tradition of liberal political philosophy mentioned earlier in that it clearly bears some relationship to Rousseau's notion of the general will and Kant's categorical imperative as well as to the general idea of the social contract. It is similarly related to our ordinary ideas about justice as a kind of equality.[8]

Reflective equilibrium calls on us to compare the principles that emerge from the original position with our already most confidently held principles, our answers to "questions which we feel sure must be answered in a certain way," our moral deal-breakers.[9] Neither the principles nor the considered convictions are based on appeals to self-evidence.[10] The original position yields two principles of justice: first, what Rawls originally called the equal liberty principle, which holds that citizens should be equally entitled to an adequate scheme of equal basic liberties compatible with the same scheme of liberties for all; and second, social and economic inequalities should be attached to offices and positions open to all under conditions of fair equality of opportunity and to the greatest benefit to the least advantaged members of society (the second part of this is called the "difference principle").[11] These principles are understood to apply to the basic structure of society, which includes the political structure, forms of property, economy, and the family. There is much to be said about this derivation, which has been criticized on a number of grounds, not least because the decisions of the parties to the original position are modeled on a kind of rational choice theory that deploys an excessively thin version of practical reason.[12] But this and other such issues are beside my present interest.

Rawls's turn to political liberalism in the two decades that followed the publication of *A Theory of Justice* was caused by his reflection on the pluralistic character of modern democratic societies, which raised questions about the stability of a society's commitment to the principles of justice defended in his theory. His two principles were presented in *A Theory of Justice* as explicitly liberal principles. Free democratic societies, however, are necessarily home to many different "comprehensive doctrines," that is, philosophical, moral, or religious doctrines that cover all subjects and encompass all values. Rawls held that pluralism under such conditions is ineliminable save through political oppression and thus poses a stiff challenge to political philosophy, at least insofar as it was concerned to defend adequate principles of justice that could inform a society with such deep differences about moral and political values. His answer was that principles of justice needed to be part of a political conception that was not explicitly based on any comprehensive doctrines, but was free-standing.[13] Such a conception could then become the focus of what Rawls called an "overlapping consensus of reasonable comprehensive doctrines." The idea is that since there are many comprehensive doctrines, those doctrines cannot be the source of a public philosophy accepted by all and serving to justify the most important public decisions, especially those that entail coercion. We should justify the most important public decisions by reference to political values that can be endorsed by many different reasonable comprehensive doctrines on their own.[14] Those doctrines might have very different deeper reasons for endorsing these ideas, but all would accept the public presentation of them.

It is very important that these political values are not simply the result of a kind of empirical assessment of public opinion; they do not arise out of a survey of extant comprehensive doctrines.[15] Nor are they simply institutions or practices; they are ideas and they are genuinely moral ideas, but limited to the political sphere so as to be acceptable to adherents of the different doctrines. Rawls works up these ideas out of those that are found already in the public political culture of free democratic societies and much of his argument involves sketching out political conceptions of these ideas that support the other parts of the theory. The original position is accordingly presented here as part of this political conception as distinct from its status as part of the comprehensive doctrine of liberalism in *A Theory of Justice*. Among the most important of the ideas that goes into this account concerns the idea of persons that is crucial to understanding the parties to the Original Position and the kinds of reasons deployed by citizens in actual political discourse. Persons are conceived as having two moral powers: the capacity for a sense of justice, and the capacity for a conception of the good. Moreover, political power flows from citizens of this type and is the power of such citizens as a group.[16] It is important that this psychology is, Rawls claims, both a "moral psychology" and is part of the political conception, and thus not based on empirical psychology, much less any more elaborate philosophical anthropology.[17]

Once the principles of justice are adopted in the Original Position, they are used to construct a constitution, which necessarily includes protections for basic rights. In a third stage, the principles and the constitution serve as the basis for appropriate enabling legislation. Finally, the principles, constitution, and legislation inform the actual choices and decisions made by citizens and political officials in their civic activities. This process is referred to by Rawls as the "four-stage sequence"[18] and is related to the point I made above about the genuinely moral character of political values. A people could live together simply on the basis of rules agreed to for whatever reasons each individual person or group might pragmatically have. Such a community would be neither grounded in moral ideas nor particularly stable. Members could eventually and more deeply bind themselves by means of a constitution and this would provide more stability, but not enough since the constitutional provisions could mean radically different things to different groups. Rawls calls this a constitutional consensus or *modus vivendi* and holds that it fails to deliver the kind of stability that a just society requires. That stability is achieved in the move from a mere constitutional consensus to an overlapping consensus, since, in the latter, the institutions and practices are supported by genuinely shared moral ideas, albeit limited to the political domain.[19] Without this, the various contending comprehensive doctrines would be tempted to simply impose their own doctrines whenever the political correlation of forces allowed it. The achievement of a just and well-ordered free society, therefore, depends on the formation of an overlapping consensus of reasonable comprehensive doctrines around principles of political justice. While Rawls thinks the best such principles are the two principles of his own Justice as Fairness conception, he does think there could be a case made for others. Justice as Fairness is ultimately grounded in his own comprehensive doctrine, liberalism, but it is presented for purposes of political liberalism as a purely political idea that can be endorsed by other comprehensive doctrines and not in such a way that it is or is only intelligible from the perspective of a comprehensive doctrine. It is accepted as a conception within *political* liberalism only.

II

Religious freedom, I argue, presents a serious problem for Rawls's account. The problem is this: while one can concede to Rawls that political liberalism is not necessarily a comprehensive doctrine, it is still a doctrine. The very solution to the problem of stability is that political liberalism's principles of justice can be the focus of an overlapping consensus of reasonable comprehensive doctrines. These comprehensive doctrines provide the deep roots of the principles and must (at least initially, but perhaps more extensively) account for much of the public support for such principles. At several points in his later work Rawls gives examples of the sort of agreement that adherents to comprehensive doctrines can give to principles of political justice and the most significant of these concern specifically Catholic beliefs. One is Rawls's (in)famous discussion of abortion.[20] The other two concern the Church's understanding of religious freedom and the idea of the common good. While these two are clearly related, I can only consider the first here.

It is noteworthy that religious freedom itself is not at first explicitly listed as part of the scheme of basic rights and liberties to which citizens are equally entitled; when Rawls describes the basic liberties he mentions the more general liberty of conscience (and seems greatly to prefer that formulation).[21] Nevertheless, he makes clear in various places that this includes religious practice.[22] This equal liberty precludes not only persecution but also religious establishment.[23] Limitations on religious freedom can only be justified by considerations of public order, which is to say that it can be limited only for the sake of liberty itself. Liberty of conscience is chosen by the parties in the original position because it is essential to the development and exercise of the second of the two moral powers that Rawls describes as the core of the political conception of citizenship. The first of these is a capacity for a sense of justice and the second is the capacity to form a conception of the good. This capacity is integral to the way in which political liberalism is liberal: it describes the most important sense in which persons are free. This freedom is the freedom to adopt conceptions of the good, but also to revise and change them and thus always to be seen as "independent from and not identified with any particular such conception with its scheme of final ends."[24] Religious liberty is thus a specific application of liberty of conscience which itself means this freedom with respect to one's ends.

The background that Rawls gives for his theory of political liberalism emphasizes the origins of liberalism in the religious wars of the sixteenth century and the persecution that Christianity historically perpetrated against both non-Christians and those faithful to rival Christian denominations. He held that such persecution was integral to societies based on comprehensive doctrines since only oppression could prevent the growth of pluralism under conditions of freedom. "In the society of the Middle Ages, more or less united in affirming the Catholic faith, the Inquisition," Rawls writes, "was not an accident."[25] Three years after publishing those words Rawls had occasion to discuss the specifically Catholic attitude towards religious liberty in an article further refining (and to some degree revising) his idea of "public reason," the sort of reasoning appropriate in pluralistic societies when deliberating about the use of coercive power by the state, especially in constitutional essentials and matters of basic justice. In a lengthy footnote appended to a discussion of one objection to the restrictions that public reason imposed on political argument he discussed the history of the Church's changing views by noting that in the Second Vatican Council's Declaration on Religious Freedom, *Dignitatis humanae*, the Catholic Church "committed itself to the principle of religious freedom as found in a constitutional democratic regime."[26] He went on to note that the Church rested its argument for religious freedom on ideas about the dignity of the human person, the limits of government related to religion, and the freedom of the Church relative to the political world. He then quoted with evident approval John Courtney Murray's claim in his commentary on the document that it constituted a repudiation of the Church's older thesis-hypothesis account of religious freedom.[27] The suggestion, then, was that the Church had embraced something like the view of political liberalism or, more precisely, that the Church's view of religious freedom was evidence that Catholicism is a reasonable comprehensive doctrine and therefore could be part of an overlapping consensus supporting the equal liberty principle of Justice as Fairness.

This implication seems, however, to rest on a misreading of *Dignitatis humanae* that points to tensions rather than harmony between the Catholic view of religious freedom and that of political liberalism.[28] The Council did indeed explain religious freedom in terms of human dignity, and both the limits on government and freedom of the Church are important themes. But it also, and most importantly, explicitly characterizes religious freedom as immunity from coercion.[29] It is of equal importance that the Council explained its notion of dignity in terms of personhood: persons are endowed with reason and free will, and, moreover, this reason and free will place on them a responsibility, indeed an obligation, "to seek the truth, especially religious truth" and to "adhere to the truth once they come to know it and to direct their whole lives in accordance with the demands of truth." This obligation cannot be satisfied unless the person is free of coercion in this search.[30] We should note three aspects of the Council's statement: first, the right to religious freedom is characterized as an immunity; second, this immunity grows out of a prior obligation; and, third, the freedom of those who err in their search for the truth about God is derived from the possibility and necessity of freely adhering to the truth. Put another way, the freedom of persons to practice false religions is a kind of collateral effect of the need to freely adhere to true religion.[31] It is finally worth noting that this freedom grows out of the very notion of personhood as comprising reason and the power of free deliberate choice.[32]

Freedom of conscience for Rawls is a principle of justice because it would be identified as such by the representative parties in the original position, and they would identify it as a fundamental right because of their status as representatives of free citizens, free, again, because they can attach and detach themselves from their chosen ends at will. They can form conceptions of the good, adopt them, revise them, and abandon them. They are to be identified with no ends beyond themselves. This picture of freedom is quite different from that endorsed in *Dignitatis humanae*. Rawls does not describe this explicitly as a right, but as either liberty or freedom; nevertheless it does seem to have the character of a right and any constitutional protection of it would need to take the form of a right, but what kind of right? The sort of right of conscience that Rawls describes would seem to be a Hohfeldian liberty-right, that is, a liberty enjoyed by one if no one else has a contravening claim-right.[33] Rawls's account also seems to see rights according to the will or choice theory of rights endorsed generally by Kantians as distinct from the benefit or interest theory of rights usually endorsed by utilitarians.[34]

Dignitatis humanae explicitly describes the right to religious freedom as an immunity, which suggests a Hohfeldian immunity-right, that is, a right that exists in virtue of the non-existence of any contravening power. This is generally the way constitutional scholars interpret the right to free exercise of religion in the First Amendment to the U.S. Constitution ("Congress shall make no law . . .") and many other modern constitutions. But, of course, the Council went further by rooting the right in a prior obligation. Indeed, when considering the rootedness of the right in a duty, one is tempted to describe it as a claim-right belonging to God.[35] However that may be, the Council's account is quite different from Rawls's description of it and it is difficult to see how on those terms it isn't fatally connected to a comprehensive doctrine.[36] But Rawls's account is also connected to doctrine, whether comprehensive or not. It is a doctrine because it understands the freedom of conscience by reference to an allegedly political idea of free citizenship, but that idea seems to go further than political ideas need to go or can go in Rawls's theory. This is because it understands the freedom of citizens in such a way that implies a very serious and substantial doctrine about human affairs: that human beings are their own ends. This isn't simply abstraction from human ends, but holds on two different grounds that human beings are the sources of their ends. One ground is the second moral power by which citizens have the capacity to form conceptions of the good. The other is the related idea of free citizens developed in terms of the freedom to adopt, revise, and abandon one's ends. On such a view the power of choice is crucial and this shapes Rawls's account of religious freedom: one is free to adopt, revise, or repudiate one's religious views and commitments. Moreover, this is not simply an empirical description of human abilities or practices; that would be the sort of empirical psychology that Rawls eschews in his account of the political conception of citizens.[37] His conception is altogether normative. It aims, however, to be normative only as a political conception and so is presented as different from the version presented in *A Theory of Justice*, which was a part of the comprehensive doctrine of liberalism (and as informed by the thought of Kant). But I do not see how it really is different. To conceive of persons in this way is to conceive of them according to the same ideas internal to liberalism as a historical philosophical movement: calling it a political conception and denying that it need have any deeper moral or metaphysical roots does not change the effect that it has on the self-understanding of persons or the character of political discourse with its consequences in the rest of the moral and cultural life of individuals and peoples.[38] This is especially the case if we expect, as Rawls does, that political values will normally override conflicting values.[39] It is, therefore, difficult to see how *Political Liberalism*, on its own terms at any rate, successfully meets a key challenge that it sets for itself. The case of religious freedom is a crucial one in showing up this problem.

It remains true that the view of *Dignitatis humanae* is derived from what Rawls would call a comprehensive doctrine in that the arguments described above are explicitly said to follow from the content of the natural law. But one might reply that it is only the bare idea, and more the practice of, religious freedom that must be accepted; moreover, *Dignitatis humanae*, like Rawls, holds that the right includes an immunity for those who change or abandon their religious beliefs. It does seem to be the case that the vast majority of people in this country and in all the countries of the developed world (at least) agree that there is a right of freedom of belief and practice, and that with respect to constitutions and laws this takes the form of an immunity from coercion. But the reason for this right seems in Rawls's account to be grounded in the political notion of the person which is not only at odds with the idea of personhood in *Dignitatis humanae*, but itself at least implies a far-reaching thesis about human beings, one that seems to go beyond what is strictly necessary for politics. Again, it may well not be a fully "comprehensive" doctrine, but it is a kind of doctrine and conflicts with (among others) the comprehensive doctrine of the Catholic Church.

One route out of the dilemma would be to scale back the demand for an over-lapping consensus. *Dignitatis humanae* does agree with the practice, that is, the most well-known instruments of both the international legal system and most municipal legal systems (in the West, at any rate) that protect fundamental human rights. One could therefore consider this good enough. But that is not Rawls's position: the overlapping consensus must be a consensus around moral views, albeit moral views that are limited to the domain of the political. To accept the institutions and practices simply as matters of constitutional law would be a mere "constitutional consensus," which according to Rawls, would lack the sort of stability that a viable conception of justice needs. If religious freedom were accepted simply as a matter of constitutional law by the adherents of rival comprehensive doctrines, they might well try and change it if and when they become a large majority, and religious persecution could gradually creep back into the political system. Just this sort of thing seems to be suggested by the older "thesis-hypothesis" account of religious freedom that Catholics once held, and the repudiation of which Rawls credited to Murray and the Council, with which we began. Certainly, there is no necessity in this, however, and I do not see why a constitutional consensus could not be quite stable even if there were disagreements about the moral or religious roots of some of the constitution's provisions. Stability is not only an effect of moral ideas, but can grow out of customs and mores that are less specified in terms of moral values. The *determinationes*, to use Aquinas's term, of very general parts of the natural law to specific practices or rules, *determinationes* that are not themselves specified by the natural law, but which derive their force simply from the practical judgment of authorities or even custom, often seem quite stable.[40] I grant that practices or provisions rooted in some moral value will likely be more stable, especially in the short run, but—and this is important—agreement on such values may be asking too much, given the pluralism of contemporary societies.

But one could still, granting the theoretical disagreement between Rawls and the Council about the character of religious freedom, ask why the account Rawls gives is such a sticking point. Surely Rawls would deny that his view entails any deep theoretical principles; rather, it is a merely political conception of citizenship that is appropriate to a democratic society. Citizens cannot be held to some determinate set of religious beliefs or practices by the state, and so they must be conceived as free to adopt, revise, or abandon such commitments. This is simply a way to explain and justify a constitutional practice that is the same as that endorsed by *Dignitatis humanae*, and no Catholic need embrace the kind of voluntarism implied by the political idea. But even to state the objection is, I think, to suggest the problem. The political ideal is still a kind of doctrine and it is a liberal doctrine, indeed, one might say that the way I characterized it earlier, as the thesis that man is his own end, is really the very essence of liberalism as a doctrine, and so despite Rawls's effort to scale back the comprehensive liberalism of *A Theory of Justice* to a merely political liberalism, it remains a liberal doctrine—perhaps less comprehensive, but no less liberal. As such it will be taught and will be held as part of the object of the overlapping consensus that makes a free pluralistic society possible, but it is a teaching very much in conflict with the core of *Dignitatis humanae*, which explicitly accounts for religious liberty in terms of what is necessary for human beings to "come to God, who is their last end."[41] Beyond this, religious freedom is for the sake of private and public religious acts that "transcend of their very nature the earthly and temporal order of things" such that "the civil authority to which is committed the care of the common good in the temporal order . . . must be judged to have exceeded the limits of its power" if it presumes to interfere with religious acts.[42] This is important because it indicates a related point of disagreement between Rawls's political conception of citizens and the Council. For Rawls citizens must conceive of themselves not only as free with respect to their conceptions of the good, but also as themselves the source of political power, "which they impose on themselves."[43] The whole tradition of Christian political thought has held that political power has its origin in God, although how this power is licitly used by human beings has been explained in various ways. Indeed, when the popes of the nineteenth and twentieth centuries opposed democracy, their opposition was to what they took to be the commitment of democratic movements to the proposition that the people were themselves the source of legitimate political authority, and the subsequent embrace of democracy by the Roman Catholic magisterium has not been inconsistent with this, but rather grounded in a different understanding of what claims democracy makes for itself.[44] Religious liberty is thus related to a more general thesis about the limits of politics, of, one might say, the domain of the political. While the limits of the political are understood by Rawls as a consequence of the unavoidable pluralism of reasonable comprehensive doctrines that is characteristic of free democratic societies, those limits are understood by the Council fathers as a consequence of the transcendence of God and thus of those acts by which human persons are directed to God, which lack efficacy unless they are free acts.

This connection between freedom and truth is at the heart of *Dignitatis humanae*'s account of religious freedom and at the heart of the Christian understanding of the nature of religious acts as instantiating a kind of good, one that is uniquely related to other human goods and that, with them, participates in the universal good that is God. It is not a feature of·all religious traditions and so how other such traditions relate to political liberalism and Justice as Fairness would need to be investigated independently.

III

While Christians can accept and, indeed, should insist on political institutions that include religious liberty, including the freedom to adopt, revise, and abandon religious commitments without legal or political consequence, I do not see how they can accept Rawls's political conception of free citizens as an explanation of religious freedom. Assuming that many other citizens would reject the account of religious freedom in *Dignitatis humanae*, the most we could hope for is a constitutional consensus supported by strong traditions of toleration, accommodation, and mutual forbearance, emerging from a shared history and perhaps supported by other political ideas that are shared at least to some degree.[45] Could Rawls's account be amended in such a way as to avoid this problem, perhaps by the formulation of some less obviously liberal conception of citizen-freedom that would still be genuinely moral and a potential component of a more general conception of justice that could be the object of an overlapping consensus? I don't rule that out, but it would be a less liberal version of political liberalism, and whether even this really could attract the support of enough citizens with their own views about religious liberty remains a question.

The character and place of religious liberty in any scheme of political freedom, then, suggests a real limit to Rawls's project and thus to his account of the structure and content of political justice in modern political communities. We may wish to consider the possibility that an overlapping consensus is simply not possible or, alternately, that the sort of overlapping consensus that may be possible must be conceived of in terms different from Rawls's. For example, perhaps we should think of it less as a consensus about liberal *principles* than as some complex of *practices* (historically associated with liberalism, but not exclusively so) and perhaps other sorts of principles, some of which may well be broadly associated with religious traditions. Such a complex of practices and principles would be far messier than what Rawls proposes in *Political Liberalism*, but this may simply reflect the fact that politics is far messier than Rawls's "realistic utopianism" can contend with. Against Rawls's invocation of Hegel, it may be that when we look rationally at the political world, it does not always look rationally back. Certainly this was the view of classical political philosophy, which can be said to have combined utopianism and realism in a different way than Rawls.[46]

If even a constitutional consensus, as distinct from the more demanding overlapping consensus, is too much to achieve (as it may be, at least with respect to certain issues, but not all), it may well mean—even granting the suggestions I made above about customs and other determinations from principles of natural law—that free political institutions are less stable than we would like. This is certainly a concern, but it may simply be an empirical aspect of free societies that they generate a kind of diversity that can threaten their stability. It may imply further that this latent risk of instability could limit just what and how much governments can do consistent with what stability liberal institutions can achieve. That is, it may imply more about the limitedness of limited government. This would be quite important to know. Therefore, even if one considers this aspect of Rawls's enterprise a failure, it is an illuminating failure, one that may reveal to us more problems to investigate, and so, from the perspective of political philosophy, not a failure at all.

The Catholic University of America

Notes

1. *The West Wing*, "Red Haven's on Fire," NBC, 26 February 2003, written by Aaron Sorkin.

2. See "Obama's Rawlsian Vision," *The Economist*, 19 February 2013; and Paul Schumaker, "John Rawls, Barack Obama, and the Pluralist Political Consensus," *American Political Thought* 5 (2016): 628–657.

3. Ted Cruz, "GOP Needs Message of Opportunity Conservatism," *The Washington Post*, 3 January 2013.

4. See Thomas Pogge, *John Rawls: His Life and Theory of Justice* (Oxford: Oxford University Press, 2007), 15.

5. The idea is most fully described in *A Theory of Justice* (originally published, 1971), rev. ed. (Cambridge: Harvard University Press, 1999), 17–19, 42–45.

6. John Rawls, *Justice as Fairness: A Restatement*, ed. Erin Kelly (Cambridge, MA: Harvard University Press, 2001), 3; see also Rawls, *Lectures on the History of Political Philosophy*, ed. Samuel Freeman (Cambridge, MA: Harvard University Press, 2007), 10.

7. See *Justice as Fairness*, 4–5; and Rawls's *The Law of Peoples* (Cambridge, MA: Harvard University Press, 1999), 3–23, 126–128.

8. *Theory*, ch. 3; *Political Liberalism*, Expanded Edition (New York: Columbia University Press, 2005 [1st ed., 1993]), 304–310; *Justice as Fairness*, 14–18, 80–100.

9. *Theory*, 17.

10. Ibid., 19.

11. My statement is based on the last version formulated by Rawls, that given in *Justice as Fairness*, 42–43. See also *Theory*, 52–78, 220, 266–267; and *Political Liberalism*, 5–6, 261, 271, 291, 331–334.

12. See, e.g., John Finnis, "The Authority of Law in the Predicament of Contemporary Social Theory," *Notre Dame Journal of Law, Ethics, and Public Policy* 1 (1984): 128–133.

13. *Political Liberalism*, 11–15, 223; *Justice as Fairness*, xvii, 26–29.

14. It is important that Rawls does not claim that an overlapping consensus can encompass all comprehensive doctrines, but only those that are "reasonable," by which he means doctrines that recognize the limits of what adherents of different comprehensive doctrines can justify to one another and that are willing to offer and abide by fair terms of cooperation with adherents to other doctrines. This includes the recognition of the political conception of persons as free and equal and values like freedom of conscience. Practically speaking, this means an abstention by adherents of a doctrine from any attempt to use especially coercive state power to enforce the views of their doctrines on others. See *Political Liberalism*, 48–66; *Justice as Fairness*, 191–192. Comprehensive doctrines that do not recognize these things are to that extent unreasonable and so cannot be part of an overlapping consensus.

15. *Political Liberalism*, 11n11, 147; *Justice as Fairness*, 37, 61.

16. For the two moral powers see *Political Liberalism*, 18–19, 29–52, 280, 302; and *Justice as Fairness*, 18–24. For political power as that of the people see *Political Liberalism*, 136, 216, 431; and *Justice as Fairness*, 40, 90, 195–197.

17. *Political Liberalism*, 86–88.

18. *Theory*, 171–176; *Political Liberalism*, 397–409; *Justice as Fairness*, 48.

19. *Political Liberalism*, 147–49, 159–168, 208, 249, 389–392; *Justice as Fairness*, 192–195.

20. I discuss this in "Natural Right and the Problem of Public Reason," in *Natural Moral Law in Contemporary Society*, ed. Holger Zaborowski (Washington, DC: The Catholic University of America Press, 2010), 204–207.

21. *Theory*, 53, 180; *Political Liberalism*, 291, 308, 227, 291, 308, 310–315, 335, 341, 424; *Justice as Fairness*, 44, 113, 143.

22. *Theory*, 186; *Political Liberalism*, 221–222, 424.

23. *Theory*, 181, 186.

24. *Political Liberalism*, 30 and texts cited above at n16. While the notion of the two moral powers is part of Rawls's political conception, the idea that the freedom of persons is seen in their freedom to adopt, revise, and change conceptions of the good is already an important part of his original account: see *Theory*, 131–132.

25. *Political Liberalism*, 37.

26. "The Idea of Public Reason Revisited" (originally published in 1997), as reprinted in *Political Liberalism*, 477n75.

27. Murray's comments are in Walter Abbott, S.J., ed., *The Documents of Vatican II* (New York: Geoffrey Chapman, 1966), 673. The Thesis-Hypothesis view of religious freedom held that the ideal arrangement (the thesis) was legal establishment of the Catholic church and public recognition of its unique status, but under factual conditions of great religious pluralism, especially when Catholics constituted a religious minority (the hypothesis), there need be no religious establishment. The preeminent example of the hypothesis was the US constitutional arrangement. For discussion see E. A. Goerner, *Peter and Caesar: Political Authority and the Catholic Church* (New York: Herder and Herder, 1965), 153–172.

28. Leaving aside the related but clearly distinct question of the history and content of the law of religious freedom according to the U.S. Constitution.

29. Second Vatican Council, Declaration on Religious Freedom, *Dignitatis humanae* (7 December 1965), art. 2, in *Vatican Council II: The Sixteen Basic Documents*, ed. Austin Flannery, O.P. (Northport, NY: Costello Publishing, 1996), 552 (DS 4240).

30. Ibid. (Flannery, 553) (DS 4241). Also art. 3 (Flannery, 554).

31. The history of the drafting of the document suggests that the Council fathers, partly as a result of interventions by then-Bishop Karol Wojtyła, wished to particularly emphasize this point as they worked out the final text. See the valuable account in David L. Schindler and Nicholas J. Healy, Jr., *Freedom, Truth, and Human Dignity: The Second Vatican Council's Declaration on Religious Freedom: A New Translation, Redaction History, and Interpretation of "Dignitatis Humanae"* (Grand Rapids, MI: William B. Eerdmans, 2015).

32. For a philosophical account very close to this see Patrick Lee and Robert P. George, "The Nature and Basis of Human Dignity," *Ratio Juris* 21 (2008): 173–193.

33. W. N. Hohfeld, "Fundamental Legal Conceptions as Applied to Judicial Reasoning," *Yale Law Journal* 23 (1913): 16–59.

34. N. E. Simmonds, *Central Issues in Jurisprudence: Justice, Law and Rights*, 2nd ed. (London: Sweet & Maxwell, 2002), 304–312.

35. Certainly, for Aquinas, the virtue of *religio* is a part of justice, a virtue that disposes one to give to God His due: see *Summa theologiae* 2a2ae, 80.1c.

36. It seems likely that Rawls's reading of *Dignitatis humanae* was influenced by Murray's own interpretation (see above n27), which tended to underplay the theological and anthropological elements of the Declaration in favor of a more simply juridical reading that assimilated its account of religious freedom to American practice in particular. See Schindler's discussion in Schindler and Healy, *Freedom, Truth, and Human Dignity*, 43–59. On Murray's grasp of the American situation see Gerard V. Bradley, "Beyond Murray's Articles of Peace and Faith," in *John Courtney Murray and the American Civil Conversation*, ed. Robert P. Hunt and Kenneth L. Grasso (Grand Rapids, MI: William P. Eerdmans, 1992), 181–204.

37. See above, n17.

38. Moreover, it seems to me that Rawls as much as admits this in admitting that the degree to which the specific political conception of justice that is the object of an overlapping consensus will likely modify the content of comprehensive doctrines: see *Political Liberalism*, 12, 24–25n27, 38, 52, 68, 126–127, 134, 140, 145, 147, 160, 169, 246.

39. Ibid., 139, 146, 155, 209.

40. On *determinatio* see Aquinas, *Summa theologiae* 1a2ae, 95.2c; and John Finnis, *Aquinas: Moral, Political, and Legal Theory* (Oxford: Oxford University Press, 1998), 266–274. On customary law see *Summa theologiae* 1a2ae, 97.3c.

41. *Dignitatis humanae*, art. 3 (Flannery, 554).

42. Ibid., art. 3 (Flannery, 554–555).

43. *Political Liberalism*, 136, 216, 431; *Justice as Fairness*, 40, 90.

44. V. B. Lewis, "Democracy and Catholic Social Teaching: Continuity, Development, and Challenge," *Studia Gilsoniana* 3 (2014): 167–190.

45. I agree here with Martin Rhonheimer, "The Political Ethos of Constitutional Democracy and the Place of Natural Law in Public Reason: Rawls's Political Liberalism Revisited," *American Journal of Jurisprudence* 50 (2005): 55–66.

46. To note only a few examples, consider: Plato, *Republic* 545c–547c, 592a–b, *Laws* 627c–628a, 690a–691d, 709a–d, 757e–758a; Aristotle, *Nicomachean Ethics* 1179b18–20, *Politics* 1293b22–1294a30, 1295a25–1296b13; Cicero, *Republic* 2.33.57. It is noteworthy in this regard that Rawls's courses on the history of moral and political philosophy began with Hume and Hobbes respectively.

Beginning and Ending with Hestia: Finding a Home for Justice in Plato's Political Philosophy

Terence Sweeney

Abstract: In my essay, I examine Plato's understanding of justice and injustice within the home and the city. For Plato, the home, as private, must be suppressed to bring about a common *polis*. I critique Plato's conclusions regarding the home and the city, especially his privative definition of justice, which loses the complexity of justice in-between persons, families, and communities. To critique Plato, I rely on his own doubts about his project, especially in his portrayal of the city of sows. The city of sows and the city of guardians both show that we need a politics guided by justice with prudence. The space of justice exists in the needs and obligations that lie between us, our homes, and our cities; it is in this space alone that political prudence can grow in the weaving together of *oikos* with *oikos* in the rich tapestry of the *polis*.

> Mortals have no feast
> without you—they begin by pouring
> honey sweet wine first and last to Hestia.
>
> — *The Homeric Hymns*

In the *Phaedrus*, when Socrates describes how the gods rise-up to contemplate the forms, he includes an odd detail: "Hestia is the only one who remains at the home [*oikos*] of the gods."[1] This essay will be an attempt to recover Hestia, as left behind, in the context of the Plato's politics. The suppression of the Hestian element of human life pervades Plato's political vision. Nevertheless, Plato points to the people and spaces he leaves behind—Hestia, Cephalus and the city of sows—the spaces of the home and the familial. For Plato, the entrance into the political necessitates the suppression and elimination of the private and familial. The city of sows, which is abandoned at the origins of politics, shows the inadequacy of such a politics. This true city haunts Plato's attempts to drive out the *oikos* and the *idiōn* in favor of the *polis* and the *koinon*. The suppression of the private and familial leads to univocal collectivism and to the atomization of political subjects.

© 2017, *Proceedings of the ACPA*, Vol. 90
doi: 10.5840/acpaproc201822777

The pre-political grounds of the *polis*, which make possible intersubjectivity and the dialogue between private and public, is left behind. These abandoned grounds destabilize any possibility of justice as an in-between and so as a rich complexity of the intersubjective giving of what is owed. This complexity is the space of justice united with prudence, a unification flowing from the weaving of relations between persons, homes, and the city. The task then of politics is to negotiate the complicated interrelations between private and common, between *oikos* and *polis*, and between multiplicity and unity. Plato's politics, by reducing persons to their *idiopragein* (private business), eliminates the complex horizontal relations of justice leaving only a vertical relation that produces a univocal polity of 'idiotic' subjects. A human city cannot exist unless we commence with Hestia, dwell in and between the *hestia* of each home, and end our day back by the *hestia* of our *oikos*. The *Republic* paradoxically shows that the space of justice lies in the needs and obligations that lie between us, our homes, our sub-communities, and our polities; it is in this space alone that political prudence can grow in the weaving together of *oikos* with *oikos* in the rich tapestry of the *polis*.[2]

Justice in the True City

Early in the *Republic*, Socrates asks: "If we should watch a city coming into being in speech . . . would we also see its justice coming into being and its injustice?"[3] All his 'cities' will have their own characteristic styles of justice and injustice. The reader must track what makes varying cities just and/or unjust. The first step in this process is to note that the origin of city-life lies in an anthropological claim: "each of us isn't self-sufficient but is in need of much."[4] To fulfill these needs "men gather in settlement as partners and helpers" and "one man gives a share to another . . . in the belief that it's better for himself."[5] Having initially shown bodily needs as originating the city, Socrates asks: "Where in it, then, would justice and injustice be? Along with which of the things we considered did they come into being?"[6] Adeimantus responds, "I can't think, Socrates . . . unless it's *somewhere in some need these men have of one another*."[7] He tentatively locates a justice that lies between individuals and communities. This justice does not neglect bodily justice: the need the shoemaker has for the farmer and the farmer for shoemaker. The rest of the *Republic* tends to neglect or distort these needs. The first city, which foregrounds need, keeps the body in play showing that a central locus of a community lies in these humble bodily needs.

There is a second feature of Adeimantus's hypothesis that justice lies in the need we have for each other. In the *Laws*, there is a similar description of the origins of the city. When the Athenian imagines the origins of city life, he posits a first reason for the coming together of humans. He asks, "Weren't they glad whenever they saw each other?"[8] In the *Laws*, the initial situation before the city is one of isolation, and so when they see each other, they are glad. The need, and its concurring justice that Adeimantus speaks to, is not just our bodily needs (though these are important). Our insufficiency runs deeper. We need each other for companionship and so we are glad when we see each other. We will see this play out in the city of sows, a city which is characterized by human intimacy. Socrates's later cities, and political philosophy in general, neglect this constitutive need for gladness-upon-seeing-each-other.

Socrates wonders if the location of justice might be proper: "Perhaps what you say is fine. . . . It really must be considered and we mustn't back away."[9] He then proceeds to consider this through a beautiful depiction of the first city. It is a city of good measure without excess or want, a city of peace with health, a city related to its past and future, and a city marked by community. It is a city of celebration, gatherings for meals, and "sweet intercourse with one another."[10] This sweet intercourse indicates a free and intimate need that lies between us. Further, the people worship the gods crowning their heads with wreathes and singing of the gods.

Scholars tend to accept Glaucon's subsequent attack on this city as the city of sows. It is *supposedly* insufficiently human in that it only attends to our basic human needs. This degradation of basic human needs is part and parcel of a neglect of the bodily communion, which undergirds any community. Further, the city of sows is *not inhuman at all*. Marina McCoy writes: "It is not immediately obvious what is 'inhuman' about such a city that values craft, music, religion, and community."[11] In the *Laws*, when the Athenian describes a comparable city, he says that such gatherings "were simpler and more *courageous*, and also more *moderate*, and in every way more *just*."[12] They know the correct measure and how to share amongst various 'partners and helpers.' Nor should it be taken as a certainty that philosophy could not arise in this city. Plato wrote in the *Phaedo* that war and desire for wealth "leave us no leisure for philosophy."[13] This community has no place for war or desire for wealth and so has the leisure for philosophy.

Why then does Glaucon reject this city? McCoy rightly argues that "Glaucon rejects this city because it is built upon feminine practice; it is a city that lacks the masculinity of politics, war, and the honors that accompany war."[14] Furthermore, the *Laws*' parallel account of the origin of the city points to another feature of this 'city.' In the *Laws*, the community of simplicity and virtue, which is in every way more just, is the family. Prior to the city in the *Laws*, we have families with their traditions, the elders and young, and their familial gods.[15] Socrates is describing the family, the home, the private. The broader community is the gathering together of families to form a community without negating those families.[16]

It is in this community that we till the garden, build the home, prepare the meal, attend to proper garments, eat dinner together, honor the gods, share drinks, have sweet intercourse, raise our children, live out our lives, grow old, receive from the old, and pass on to the young. This is not yet a city of war, excess, luxury, honor, and legislation. Instead, it is the community dwelling in proximity to nature and to the gods of whom we sing. It is guided by the natural cycles: from youth, to *eros*, to sex, to children, to old age, the handing on of authority and tradition, and then death. This is accompanied by the rituals of home: work, food, clothing, nudity, rest, sex, drinking, all of which is saturated by the divine. Glaucon attacks this city as subhuman because it is too feminine, too familial, and too natural. He rejects this city as insufficient for *aner* not *anthropos*. He does so because he sees something subhuman about the feminine and the familial. He consequently degrades the familial features of women and men, both of whom live in and depend on the *oikos*. This space is not subhuman; it is natural to *anthropos*, male and female. It has the features characteristic of humans and their needs: for the gods, for peace, for food and drink, and for each other. Adeimantus unwittingly shows that the justice of the *oikos* is the need we have for each other. These needs—bodily, intersubjective, and religious—are contrary to autarky and self-honor. They occur between and so lend themselves to sharing.

Recall Hestia who remains home. Plato knows that we must "begin, as is customary, with Hestia."[17] However, the Greeks began *and ended* with Hestia because all prayers and sacrifices begin with her, because we begin and end our days and our lives with Hestia. Ultimately, we begin in the *oikos* as the origins of human intimacy, gladness, community, in the pre-political grounds of the city. The space of Hestia and the city of sows is not without justice for in this space justice is first born. It is born between family members who share what is needed among partners and helpers. It is not a closed-in justice for it dwells in the need families have of each other in that a solitary family cannot survive or reproduce. Further, as Patricia Thompson writes, "the hearthfire where family intimacy is protected and where, once strangers receive a family's hospitality, they are honor-bound to respect their hosts."[18] This honor is justice in which what is needed is shared, in which bodily needs are attended to, in which the violence of Glaucon is inadmissible, and in which the gods and tradition are honored.

This seems like a rosy image of the first city, but Socrates is looking for the justice and injustice in each community. Thompson is right that Plato has a "bias toward the polis at the expense of the oikos" and thus has a politics that is "exclusively *polis*-centric."[19] Plato privileges the common, the polis, the unified, and the male over the private, familial, multiple, and female. However, Plato has a unique ability to keep track in his language of what he leaves behind. Like a good hiker, he frequently looks back on his trail to remember how to get back should he stumble upon an *aporia* that would leave him at a loss. He leaves these traces so that we too can double back if we identify an impasse in Plato's thought. He provides the stirring image of the *oikos* so that we can know what we leave behind when we enter the political. In the *Laws*, Plato makes clear that the community of families must give rise to a *polis* in which legislation comes into being.[20] You cannot stay home. In a text that demolishes the home and the family, it is notable that the beginning of the *polis* lies in the home but does not return to it. We should ask: if we must leave the home, how are we to leave it and can we return to it?

In the *Republic*, the transition to the political is motivated by Glaucon's desire for relishes, couches, and glory and these desires rupture the dialogue. Socrates shifts from a healthy city to an unhealthy one. "We are, as it seems, considering not only how a city, but also a luxurious city, comes into being."[21] Before he abandons the city of sows, he says: "The true city is in my opinion the one we just described—a healthy city, as it were."[22] We have caught a glimpse of the *aletheia polis*, the healthy and true city, in which justice resides in the complex needs we have for each other. Nonetheless, Socrates agrees with Glaucon to pursue not this city but an unhealthy city, the city of luxury, excess, and war. Plato's politics begins with a lost beginning. This is not a second sailing necessitated by an *aporia*; rather, Plato delves forward from a place of inadequacy without fully considering an open way. As McCoy writes, "the first city in speech is left behind, and while Socrates attempts to purify the second, more 'feverish' city of its excesses, no return is made to the 'city of sows.'"[23] Plato pursues a politics in the luxurious city and leaves Hestia—the *oikos* and the *idiōn*—behind for the *polis* and the *koinon*.

Idiopragein and 'Idiot' Subjects

Socrates must now establish the just and the unjust in the unhealthy city by reforming it, which requires the development of a guardian class. Socrates no longer attends to the mundane practices of sharing a home or making shoes. Developing the guardian class is now the only task of the political thinker and this depends on destroying the private and familial. The guardians are characterized by "their possessing nothing private but the body, while the rest is in common" without the "possession of money, children, and relatives."[24] The private pleasure and pains of family, home, and personal occupation will be purged leaving our citizens with "the same thing in common, which is that very thing they will name 'my own'. And having that in common, will they thus more than others have a community of pain and pleasure?"[25] This is not an incidental feature of the city. "The community of pain and pleasure is the greatest good for a city"[26] and requires the elimination of anything private, particularly the family, the greatest source of private pains and pleasures.

To see how this functions, let us consider the sexual lottery. The guardians are told that the lot is random but in truth it is rigged so that the better guardians frequently have sex and so produce acceptable children. Presumably, this means that the top tier of guardians often has sex, whereas the bottom tier never or very rarely does. George Klosko writes that "Plato also recognizes that sexual deprivation will generate hostility even among the guardians, a problem he addresses with the rigged lottery. If Plato had wished to create a system of instructions that could not possibly work, his proposals would have been more obviously outlandish."[27] Klosko's fails to see just how outlandish Plato is being. It is 'outlandish' to think that constantly losing a lottery would somehow cause the sexual desire of spirited (and often naked) guardians to dissipate. Further, the inferior guardians would presumably be aware: that the other guardians are better fighters, that the superior guardians have frequent sex, and that the inferior guardians never or very rarely do. They would have to be oblivious to not notice the pattern, a pattern that would presumably play out over years.

Here the Straussian argument that this is a satire meant to show the limits of politics is at its strongest. However, Plato did believe that this was the ideal city even if only as a necessary paradigm. In the *Laws*, he again argues that the city with everything in common and nothing private is the best city but that it was, tragically, an unlikely accomplishment. Nonetheless, it should be the constant goal and paradigm of the lawmaker. "One should not look elsewhere for the model . . . of a political regime, but should hold onto this and seek with all one's might the regime that comes as close as possible to such a regime."[28] Further, interpreting the *Republic* as being only about the soul is implausible. It is political paradigm in which soul, city, and cosmos are supposed to have parallel structures. This is why the Western tradition, starting with Aristotle, reads it as a political text.[29]

Nonetheless, Plato grapples with a nearly impossible arrangement. Consider an inferior guardian who has been deceived into celibacy. Why wouldn't he figure out that the lottery must be rigged? The reason is simple. *He minds his own business (idiopragein).* The city of the common is both a system of collectivization and atomization. The young guardian does not question the arrangement, because to question would be to meddle, to move out of one's assigned role into a space between, and to become plural.

Socrates explains this atomized collectivity through the assignment of tasks. Each performs the task that "naturally suits him—*one man, one job*—so that each man, practicing his own, which is one, will not become many but one; and thus, you see, *the whole city will naturally grow to be one and not many.*"[30] The guardian would not question the lottery because the lottery is not his business. He is one subject with one task in a city that is one. "Justice is the minding of one's own business and not being a busybody."[31] In the unified collective, an atomized privacy returns in that minding one's business is *idiopragein*. Each citizen is one, has one task, and so the city is one. When the *idiōn* is completely gotten rid of, the private is transformed from sub-communities to privatized subjects. The individual is solitary with a solitary identity subservient to the city as sole determining marker of the individual.

Solitary citizens lack real interactions because they have no sub-communities. Plato purges the complicated assortment of sub-communities, which are the small personal communities that, when woven together, make up the complex texture of a citizen's life, a life woven into a broader weave of a political community. Plato's ideal city, and other visions of statist utopias, stamp out or neutralize sub-communities by forging a united polity of isolated subjects. Consider a hypothetical citizen in an 'unreformed' city. They are a member of a family, of a shoemakers' guild, of a club, and of a neighborhood watch; they have familial gods, a local temple, and a shared duty to civic defense. What would *idiopragein* mean for them? It could only be plurivocal, entailing complicated negotiations of obligations and loyalties with others. Only if everything is made common can one have a unified obligation that structures one's entire identity.

The city of sows or *aletheia polis* was characterized by household practices and by family life. As the related passage in the *Laws* indicates, this original city was a community of familial households. Justice in this city lies in the in-between: "some need these men have of one another."[32] It is a justice of multiplicity. The needs we have for each other include: food, shoes, religion, sexual intimacy, and the gladness of seeing each other. The 'idiotic' subject of the ideal city has lost their multiplicity of tasks and, in a sense, has lost their multiple interconnections of needs. The 'idiot' citizen has one task and one source that provides all its needs, the *polis*. This is how the lottery system works: the guardian minds their own business, and does not meddle by questioning.

Politics and the Familiarity of Justice and Prudence

Here again we can double back to another missing figure. Cephalus left the conversation to offer his familial sacrifices at his familial shrine centered on the hearth. He represented the family and its traditions that have been left behind. His absence haunts the text because the text cannot account for the home, the familial, and the private. Consequently, it cannot do justice to the familial and so cannot hear the definition of justice that Cephalus gave. Hestia has no voice in the dialogue. To hear her, we need to return to what exactly was deficient in Cephalus's familial definition of justice. "It is just to give to each what is owed."[33] This justice lies in-between persons. The obligations of justice link people who are sharers and partners. The various obligations in-between exist because of needs humans have for each other.

This definition of justice is absent from the city of guardians. If subjects have nothing of their own, they would have nothing they could owe or be owed. The 'idiot' citizen has a solitary and vertical obligation to the *polis*. They have no horizontal obligations or needs to/for others because they themselves have nothing except their one task. A neighbor could not ask to borrow a tool because no one *owns* any tools. The 'idiot' citizens have neither horizontal needs nor horizontal intimacy. They have sex with whomever the lot determines; each 'idiot' is replaceable by another. Nicholas Jones writes regarding the *Republic*, "Humans are social beings, but the utopia was to permit no affiliation other than that with the state itself."[34] This affiliation is limited to one's task and to the reception of all human needs from the *polis* alone.

One does not have to be anxious about giving what is owed if everyone just minds their business. The absence of anxiety is the absence of thought. This makes the implausibility of the lottery plausible. The guardian, who has not had sex for years, would not notice that he never wins because noticing would be meddling. The guardian keeps performing their *'idiopragein'* and receives whatever the *polis* gives. The only way to note the pattern of loss would be to pay attention. This paying-attention, as meddling, is political thinking. To find a pattern requires thought, comparison of differences, attention, and ability to unify what is multiple without obscuring the multiplicity. It requires *phronesis* or prudence. Prudence is a virtue of thinking, questioning, and even meddling. The best example of meddling is Socrates, who never minded his own business. In contrast, the guardian does not have prudence because he/she does not need it. Someone else has prudence for him/her. The philosopher king(s) manage the lottery and the complex system of lies. The rest of the citizens—artisans, farmers, and *regular guardians*—neither have nor need prudence.

Consider Cephalus's failure to defend his definition of virtue. It is not the definition but *the enactment and the enactor of the definition that is missing something*. This absence discloses a necessary feature of justice as a virtue in-between. Socrates challenges Cephalus to explain what he would do if he owed his neighbor a sword that he had borrowed. This would be a simple transaction under normal circumstances. In Socrates's scenario, the neighbor has gone mad and will harm himself if you give back the sword. Socrates challenges Cephalus, asking if it would be just to not return what is owed. Cephalus cannot coherently answer. We seem to have arrived at a contradiction, an *aporia*. One is obliged to and obliged not to give back what is owed. Cephalus promptly leaves and Polymarchus abandons the familial definition.

What exactly is missing in the first definition? Prudence is absent from the definition and from Cephalus himself for he receives from the tradition unthinkingly. In the *Laws*, the origins of the city are in the family. This family is ruled by a "monarchy that is the most just of all monarchies."[35] It has moderation, courage, and justice and roughly parallels the city of sows, the *oikos*. This familial community, which is pre-political, is good by "what is called naïve simplicity."[36] The Athenian says that "they believed that what they heard about gods as well as about human beings was true, and lived according to these things."[37] This early community lives "guided by habits" and "ancestral laws"[38] without understanding. Lack of prudence is its central flaw. The Athenian explains that when families come together and found a city, they select from their various traditions, customs, and laws. They must leave behind some of their private familial laws to form the city, which requires prudence to determine what should be retained and what abandoned. In the *Republic*, there is no prudent dialogue about what should be retained from the city of sows; they leave everything without prudence or deliberation.

Cephalus affirms that one should both give what is owed and not give what is owed, but he cannot articulate why. His justice has no prudence. Prudence supplies the art and knowledge to negotiate the complex web of obligations. The problem with the 'crazed neighbor' is that you have *many* obligations between you and your neighbor. Justice without prudence cannot adjudicate this in-between space. Justice without prudence cannot *articulate itself*. It cannot bring into speech the nature of justice or the form of the community. The political task is to enact prudence and this requires bringing-into-speech. To adjudicate our obligations and needs, we need spoken deliberation guided by prudence. With prudence, Cephalus would understand that he has many needs and obligations between himself and his neighbor. These overlap, conflict, and sometimes cancel each other out. There is no pure *episteme* or political science to determine these tasks. We need *phronesis* and dialogue to truly be just because of the plurality of goods, persons, and communities within the polity.

Hannah Arendt writes that "plurality is specifically *the* condition—not only the *condition sine qua non*, but the *condition per quam*—of all political life,"[39] and "men in the plural . . . can experience meaningfulness only because they can talk with and make sense to each other and themselves."[40] This plurality entails humans with a plurality of commitments. An 'idiot' citizen knows his/her role and so need not deliberate. From the need to manage the weaving of communities and persons in the city, justice with prudence and deliberation arises. In other words, there is no politics or polis without the *oikoi*. Plato, and political philosophy since, develop "various attempts to find theoretical foundations and practical ways for an escape from politics all together."[41] When people have been reduced to one task and one source of need-fulfilment, they are not agents because they have no need for prudence or even language. They have neither an independent space to speak from nor an independent space to speak on behalf of, because they no longer need to negotiate the complications of many hearths. The injustice of the city of guardians is that there are no homes or sub-communities and so no politics, no prudence, and consequently, no justice.

While Arendt sees that the household is necessary for politics, she views the household as merely a prerequisite for the more important domain of the political. She remains *polis*-centric and so does not do justice to Hestia. She agrees with the Greeks for whom "without mastering the necessities of life in the household, neither life nor the 'good life' is possible, but politics is never for the sake of life. . . . Household life exists for the sake for the 'good life' in the *polis*."[42] She does not give enough credit to how homes, and sub-communities, are the loci of intimacy, of gladness-upon-seeing-each other. We start our day and end our day, start our lives and end our lives with Hestia. We need the political in the daytime but need intimacy at the origin and end.

In the city of sows, justice lies in the needs we have for one another and in what we owe each other. This creates a complicated weave formed by a variety of communities. This works well when all is clear but the murkiness of Socrates's challenge discloses the inadequacy of unthinking justice. We have all kinds of obligations to our family, friends, organizations, religious practices, neighbors, work, and state. When people, and families come together, justice needs prudence to guide it. Naïve simplicity just receives and practice justices unthinkingly. Prudence is the habit of practicing the justice-in-between with thoughtful attention.

We are not autarkic; we need each other. The home is the place of intimacy, of gladness-upon-seeing-each other. These intimate needs are as important and anthropologically rich as the political. Without either, our lives are diminished. However, this pre-political community needs deliberation, prudence, in order to have a full justice.[43] Recall that when Plato claims we must look for the justice *and injustice* of each city, he is silent about the injustice of both the city of guardians and the city of sows. The injustice of the city of guardians is that it has no need for prudence; justice has been reduced to unthinking *idiopragein* and so is not really justice at all. The injustice of the city of sows is that it has not developed the prudence that complex communities need to navigate the complicated weave of obligations and rights.

Justice does lie in the various needs and obligations we have with each other but, without prudence, this justice ends up unjust. It strains and cracks under the pressure of challenges that will arise when families come together. Cephalus retreats from this challenge, but so does Socrates. The failure to retain the home and a justice-in-between undermines the ideal city of the *Republic*. The representative of the home leaves the conversation and Hestia is left behind. The first city produced in speech is abandoned and a new city is constructed. The intimacy and complexity of the in-between is lost. Plato's *polis* turns out to be homeless and a-political. The guardian city, without the *oikos*, lacks the pre-political ground of a city. In the absence of a well-articulated *oikos*, we are left with an imbalanced city.

Plato's ideal city centered on the common, destroying the familial and private. By ridding itself of these features, it rids itself of a justice-between, leaving citizens with no horizontal needs or obligations, which are the very tendrils that link them into a web of communities. However, the familial city is a just city without an articulated prudence. In coming together into a community of families, the city must articulate prudence to be truly just. This requires that we move beyond the purely familial into the political. If this means that the familial is destroyed, then we cannot have justice, prudence, or politics. The 'ideal' city has no need for prudence because it no longer requires its citizens to negotiate intersubjective needs and obligations. It reproduces itself by mathematical formula, by a technocracy that eliminates the sub-communities, intimacy, and the deliberation needed for the weaving of politics. In the collectivist city, we have 'idiot' citizens who mind their own business and so are oblivious to the system of lies around them. Its justice is a rump justice, one in which an individual fulfills his/her task and does not meddle. Plato's ideal city is unjust and a-political because it destroys the home and isolates the individual. The just city, as it rises to the political, must give the justice that is owed to Hestia if it is to be a city at all.

Shall We, As Is Customary, Conclude with Hestia?

Greek custom had it that one begins and concludes all prayers and sacrifices with Hestia.[44] This is emblematic of how the hearth, the *hestia*, is the origin and end of lives. Plato's commences with Hestia but he does not expand on this beginning nor does he return to Hestia to cultivate the end. However, Plato—with his *aletheia polis*/city of sows (pre-political communities) and his ideal city/city of guardians (the *polis*, which has no families and so is also a-political)—discloses the very task of the political. If the justice that Socrates fails to consider—the justice that lies in our need for each other—is in fact a true sense of justice, if Cephalus's account of justice is only insufficient because it is not coupled with *phronesis*, and if Hestia is rightly held to be beginning and end, then the task of the political looks very different. It becomes the art of balancing obligations and needs, of measuring out the proper spaces of public and private, home-based and common, familial and political. It takes up our bodily and intersubjective needs while also drawing the individual into the political and common space with its complicated weave of relations and its need for prudence, dialogue, and political justice. A true politics dwells in proximity with nature, receives the wisdom of the past, and honors the gods. It cultivates laws and craft, forges forward by retaining and letting go of the past, and allows the play of public reason in the form of philosophy. This means dealing with competing claims to our loyalty and dwelling in the overlapping sub-communities of human intersubjectivity. This is the task of a politics that does not leave Hestia behind. It allows the hearth to remain, dwells with the goddess, and moves out into the community. Such a politics cannot deliver the ideal city, but it may deliver something more desirable, a human city.

Villanova University
Villanova, PA

Notes

1. Plato, *Phaedrus*, trans. Alexander Nehamas and Paul Woodruff, in *Plato: Complete Works*, ed. John M. Cooper (Indianapolis, IN: Hackett Publishing Company, 1997), 247a.

2. I am re-deploying Plato's image of political weaving from the *Statesman*, I can deploy the paradigm differently because of Plato's own work. Mine is a criticism of Plato dependent on the very ideas of Plato.

3. Plato, *The Republic of Plato* (hereafter, *Rep.*), 2nd ed., trans. Allan Bloom (New York: Basic Books, 1991), 369a. Italics mine.

4. *Rep.*, II: 369b.

5. *Rep.*, II: 369c.

6. *Rep.*, II: 371e.

7. *Rep.*, II: 372a. Italics mine.

8. Plato, *The Laws of Plato* (hereafter, *Laws*), trans. Thomas L. Pangle (Chicago, IL: The University of Chicago Press, 1988), 678c.

9. *Rep.*, II 372a.

10. *Rep.*, II: 372b.

11. Marina McCoy, "The City of Sows and Sexual Differentiation in the *Republic*," in *Plato's Animals: Gadflies, Horses, Swans, and Other Philosophical Beasts*, ed. J. Bell and M. Naas (Bloomington: Indiana University Press, 2015), 149.

12. *Laws*, III: 679e.

13. Plato, *Phaedo*, trans. David Gallop (Oxford, UK: Oxford University Press, 1999), 66d.

14. McCoy, "The City of Sows," 150. McCoy explains the word pig is a derogatory "slang term for female genitalia" (151). McCoy contends that philosophy could have arisen in the city of women; maybe it would have been a philosophy with a less masculinist bent.

15. *Laws*, III: 680a–681d.

16. *Laws*, III: 680a–681a.

17. Plato, *Cratylus*, trans. C. D. C. Reeve, in *Plato: Complete Works*, ed. John M. Cooper (Indianapolis, IN: Hackett Publishing Company, 1997), 401b.

18. Patricia J. Thompson, "Dismantling the Master's House: A Hestian/Hermean Deconstruction of Classic Texts." *Hypatia* 9.4 (Fall 1994): 46.

19. Ibid., 45.

20. *Laws*, III: 681c–d.

21. *Rep.*, II: 372a.

22. *Rep.*, II: 372a.

23. McCoy, "The City of Sows," 149.

24. *Rep.*, V: 464d.

25. *Rep.*, V: 464a.

26. *Rep.*, V: 464b.

27. George Klosko, *The Development of Plato's Political Theory* (Oxford, UK: Oxford University Press, 2006), 155.

28. *Laws* V: 739e. See also Laws V: 744a

29. See Aristotle's *Politics*, Book II.

30. *Rep.* IV: 423d. Italics mine.

31. *Rep.* IV: 433a.

32. *Rep.* II: 372a.

33. *Rep.* I: 331e. The definition is given by Cephalus's son Polymarchus as a kind of familial inheritance, which is then abandoned.

34. Nicholas F. Jones, "The Organization of the Kretan City in Plato's 'Laws,'" *The Classical World* 83.6 (July–August 1990): 473.

35. *Laws* III: 680e.

36. *Laws* III: 679c.

37. *Laws* III: 679c.

38. *Laws* III: 680a.

39. Hannah Arendt, *The Human Condition*, 2nd ed. (Chicago, IL: The University of Chicago Press, 1998), 7.

40. Ibid., 4.

41. Ibid., 222.

42. Ibid., 37.

43. For Arendt, the home is the place of labor constrained by "the biological process of the human body" and to "the vital necessities produced and fed into the life process by labor" (7). She does not see the deliberative practices in the household, the possibilities of creativity within labor, and the need for the union of prudence and justice in the home.

44. Plato himself knew of this tradition (*Cratylus*, 401b), which was grounded in the ancient *Homeric Hymns*. These hymns, with no known authors, date from the time of Homer and Hesiod. The hymn to Hestia reads: "Mortals have no feast /without you—they begin by pouring /honey sweet wine first and last to Hestia" (XXIX). *The Homeric Hymns*, trans. Diane J. Rayor (Berkeley: The University of California Press, 2004).

Plato's Debt: Justice and Nature in Early Greek Philosophy

Justin Habash

Abstract: This paper examines the relationship between justice and nature in key figures in early Greek philosophy in order to understand the idea of nature that grounds Plato's account of justice. Tracing the idea of justice through Anaximander, Heraclitus, and Parmenides, I show that each figure uses justice in unique and innovative ways to explain different concepts of nature. Among the Presocratics then, justice is a heuristic for grasping the newly emerging and evolving concept of nature. It is in turn this evolving concept of nature that ushers in the transformation of justice from the conventional Hesiodic notion of "legal settlement" or "paying one's debts" to Plato's philosophical account of justice based on nature. The transformation is marked by the development of several key epistemological criteria and teleological facets in the earliest concepts of nature. As such, Plato's account of justice in the *Republic* is deeply indebted to Presocratic conceptions of justice and nature.

Introduction

Early Greek thinkers wrestled with philosophical notions of justice (*dikē*) long before Plato dreamed up *The Republic*. In that famous dialogue, Plato rejects the notion of justice based upon custom and tradition, instead attempting to ground his account of justice and the just city on an idea of nature (*physis*). Although the Presocratic notions of justice found in Anaximander, Heraclitus, and Parmenides constitute the initial philosophical treatment of this idea, their versions of justice arise only in the pursuit of the explanation of natural phenomena. In doing so, they lay the philosophical foundations of Plato's account of justice not through the development of the idea of justice but through the idea of nature. Yet the development of the "Greek concept of nature" in the Presocratic period has been largely misunderstood. Much of the scholarly debate has centered around how to understand the Presocratic notion of *physis* but has generally rested on the assumption that an inherent consensus exists among the earliest philosophers regarding the features of this new philosophical concept.[1] But how would such a consensus arise in the founding period of philosophy? We know that the concept is

© 2017, *Proceedings of the ACPA*, Vol. 90
doi: 10.5840/acpaproc2017111366

markedly different from the traditional use of the term found in the poetic predecessors or contemporaries of the early Greek philosophers. There *physis* is generally
used to "refer to the outward, visible characteristics of the object or person under
consideration—to its 'appearance.'"[2] The earliest philosophers are, however, in the
process of debating and discovering a far more sophisticated concept of nature
capable of explaining phenomena in both cosmic and human realms. There is,
in short, no such thing as a "Greek concept of nature" in early Greek philosophy,
and it is, curiously, the different uses of the idea of justice which can perhaps best
illustrate this fact.[3] In this paper, I make the case that the theory of nature Plato
uses to ground his theory of justice in the *Republic* is a hybrid of essential features
of *different* concepts of nature found in early Greek philosophy. Exploring the connections and development of the concepts of nature and justice in Anaximander,
Heraclitus, and Parmenides, I show in each case how the philosopher's notion of
justice reveals important features of their particular conception of nature. In the
final section of the paper, I turn to specific passages in the *Republic* to illustrate how
Plato brings together these features into a concept of nature that is philosophically
robust enough to support his theory of justice.

Anaximander

Although the ancients took Thales to be the first philosopher, modern commentators generally agree that Anaximander of Miletus was the first philosopher
in the West.[4] In the case of Anaximander, we at least have some of his own words
preserved for us. While his theory of the boundless (*to apeiron*) has challenged and
fascinated thinkers since antiquity, we find no mention of the term in the preserved
quotation. Instead, the first words in the history of philosophy present a cosmos
built around a notion of justice, as Anaximander says:

> From what things existing objects come to be, into them too does their
> destruction take place, according to what must be: for they give recom-
> pense and pay restitution to each other for their injustice according to
> the ordering of time. (B1)[5]

Strikingly, however, the natural condition of "existing objects" is not justice, but a
fundamental opposition and violation, or rather "serial *injustice*."[6] Natural objects,
most often taken to be fundamental opposites like hot and cold, invariably commit
the cosmic equivalent of trespass, encroaching upon one another.[7] Anaximander
need not observe the natural world for very long to come to such a conclusion. The
changing of the seasons, the regularity of alteration between night and day, the way
wet things turn into dry things; all of these observable phenomena and more would
have pointed Anaximander in this direction. Individual seasons, celestial objects,
environmental temperatures all eternally contend for rule or dominance, driven by
a natural desire for such. These opposites cannot act otherwise, in fact, since such
movement is by necessity or "according to what must be." This "serial injustice" is,
however, only the *beginning* stage of the cosmic process Anaximander offers that

answers cosmogonical and cosmological questions. Justice (*dikē*) as the forced restitution to the injured party is inexorably meted out for such encroachments. Such
an idea of justice as a form of direct payment or balancing of accounts predates
Anaximander, however. In several detailed studies of *dikē* in ancient thought, Michael
Gagarin maintains that the Greek term most often associated with justice means
only law "in the sense of a process for the peaceful settlement of disputes," and has
no broader moral component to it.[8] In *Republic I*, Plato takes up just such a view
from his predecessors just as Polemarchus inherits the argument from his father that
justice is: "to each what is owed."[9] There, Cephalus's definition as adopted by his son
stands for the traditional view of justice as the paying of debts that stretches back
through Anaximander to Homer and Hesiod. Traditionally, the arbitration of such
disputes in Greek society required a judge or wise man (*histōr*).[10] For Anaximander,
it is Time (*chronos*) that plays the role of cosmic enforcer and ultimate arbiter of
justice. As the "cosmic magistrate," it is Time that "assures continued stability of the
world" through a deliberate arrangement (*taksis*).[11] The Greek term *taksis* conjures
images of precision and foresight in forming an order, which will come to be associated with careful and deliberate arrangement of military forces.[12] In Anaximander's
time the term emphasizes the deliberate order of a court of law that observes a fixed
regularity of decrees.[13]

Implicit in such an account of cosmic justice is a fundamental equality of
elemental opposites, which may have been intended as a correction of poor thinking in the material monism espoused by Anaximander's contemporaries.[14] Gregory
Vlastos controversially infers from this implied idea of elemental equality that
Anaximander derived his idea of justice from a "political assumption that justice
was an affair between equals and that its settlement involved an equation of compensation to injury."[15] Michael Gagarin argues, however, that any idea of equality in
Presocratic philosophy "does not come from the influence of legal thinking or legal
institutions" but only that such legal thinking "may have helped focus the attention
of early Greek thinkers on process or procedure."[16] For Anaximander, the cosmic
back-and-forth process is in effect a "self-regulative equilibrium."[17] Anaximander
mobilizes the concept of equilibrium as the fundamental principle of nature perhaps
most famously in his discussion about the earth being equipoised.[18] In resolving a
question that fascinated his fellow Milesians, and perhaps Xenophanes, Anaximander
maintains that what holds the earth in place is not a material support, such as the
earth floating on water or air as the others claim, but the notion of equilibrium or
symmetry. The aim of justice is not to eradicate transgressions, as this would be
impossible. Rather, justice restores a balance that has been transgressed, thus always
aiming at equilibrium as a kind of *telos*. This idea of justice, regardless of its source,
helps Anaximander articulate the idea that nature itself has equilibrium built into
the process of generation *as a natural telos*.

The *telos* of existence may be a kind of equilibrium, but the cosmos is *driven* by
time itself. Identifying *chronos* with Anaximander's source of all things, the boundless
(*apeiron*), Kurt Pritzl argues that *time* serves as the "divine, surrounding, mastering,
force of the whole determining, according to law-like necessity, the fate or ends of

all within the world."[19] Operating as the force which governs the regulative process inherent in all natural things, on this view time is the indefinite, boundless principle that "rules" the unfolding of both the cosmos and all things in it. The result of such an analysis, as Pritzl notes, is that Anaximander's "conception of the universe, as a bounded whole steered and governed by an all-encompassing, teleologically ordered *archē*, is the conception of the universe that persists as philosophy develops and matures."[20] As the first *physiologos* to articulate the idea of nature as a fundamentally purposive *process*, Anaximander sets in motion the philosophy of nature among the early Greeks as an effort not just to say what things are made of or where they have come from, but *how* they come to be what they are. Implicit here, particularly for Plato, is also the question *why*.

Heraclitus

Less than one hundred years later, Heraclitus offers an account of justice that is both rooted in Anaximander's basic cosmic theory and a sufficient departure from it. Adopting Anaximander's "serial injustice" as the basic condition of existence, Heraclitus casts aside any doubt concerning the fundamental existence of opposition in the basic nature of things. Yet such natural opposition or inherent conflict (*eris*) is precisely what Heraclitus labels as justice. "One must realize that war is shared and Conflict is Justice," he tells us, "and that all things come to pass (and are ordained) in accordance with conflict" (B80).[21] Rather than a simple extension of Hesiodic justice to the cosmos, Heraclitus maintains that conflict, not Time, is the teleological, cosmological force that shapes all things.[22] Famous for his ridicule of other early Greek figures including Pythagoras, Xenophanes, and Hecataeus, Heraclitus simultaneously aims his penetrating criticism at Hesiod's view of justice and the Milesian understanding of *archē* as origin and guiding principle when he says: "War is father of all and king of all. He renders some gods, others men; he makes some slaves, others free" (B53). Rather than avoid or ameliorate conflict, Heraclitus reminds us in his critique of tradition that conflict plays *the* vital role in cosmic and biological processes: "Homer was wrong when he said, 'Would that Conflict might vanish from among gods and men!' For there would be no attunement without high and low notes nor any animals without male and female, both of which are opposites" (A22). Justice as strife shapes things *through* conflict and opposition, not by resolving it through some sort of cosmic restitution.

Such an account of justice rests on a conception of nature in Heraclitus which aims not at equilibrium, but rather at an attunement (*harmonia*) of opposites. Not a question of equals, *harmonia* as a kind of fundamental reality is a literal "fitting-together" of conflicting forces in a "unity of opposites."[23] This unity takes many forms: Night and Day are not separate things, as Hesiod claims, but unified as a cyclic continuum (B57). In other cases, opposition is merely a matter of perspective: "Immortals are mortal, mortals immortal, living the others' death, dead in the others' life" (B62). The most paradoxical case is the notion of this unity of opposites as strict identity: "the way up and down is one and the same" (B60). Though diversity and opposition are readily apparent to us in observing the world, the *unapparent* connection or unity underlying such opposition is more fundamental, as Heraclitus points out that "the hidden attunement is better than the obvious one" (B54). Most, however, are unable to recognize the hidden attunement of things precisely because they fail to appreciate the fundamental opposition: "They do not comprehend how a thing agrees at variance with itself; it is an attunement turning back on itself, like that of the bow and the lyre" (B51). This unification of conflicting forces or features is what makes the thing what it is. Without the tension, the conflicting pull in opposite directions, neither the bow nor lyre would exist as such.

Aristotle brings these two ideas in Heraclitus together when he reports that the Ephesian maintains that "the counter-thrust brings together, and from the tones at variance comes perfect attunement, and all things come to pass through conflict" (B8). Heraclitus gives many names to this hidden attunement as a unity of opposites that dictates all things. Most famously, it is the *logos* when understood as a rational pattern found throughout the cosmos according to which "all things come to pass" but which "most fail to comprehend" (B1). Alternatively, this hidden unity is God, as when he says: "The god: day and night, winter and summer, war and peace, satiety and hunger. It alters, as when mingled with perfumes, it gets named according to the pleasure of each one" (B67). Yet perhaps the least obvious, and therefore most powerful, understanding is framing this unapparent *harmonia* by the new presocratic watchword: *physis*. Signaling a link with the unapparent attunement, Heraclitus tells us that "nature loves to hide" (B123). The identity of the thing as an obscure unity of opposites is precisely what Heraclitus has in mind for the "nature" of any individual thing. The ability to "distinguish each according to its nature (*physis*) and tell how it is" (B1) is what gives the sage an unprecedented access to the cosmic *logos*. Likewise, it is in the recognition of the *physis* of Night and Day as a unity where Hesiod, the "teacher of most," ultimately fails (B57 and B106). Thus for Heraclitus, the mark of true wisdom is an understanding of the unity in the *logos*: "The wise is one, knowing the plan by which it steers all things through all" (B41). Such wisdom, however, begins with the recognition of the *physis* of things as a hidden yet powerful attunement of opposites.

Parmenides

Although no one could reasonably complain that Parmenides is underappreciated in early Greek philosophy, his account of justice attracts comparatively little attention from scholars.[24] Blending the old medium of poetry with a new method of inference and argumentation, Parmenides' portrays *Dikē* as a divine being holding "alternating keys," and guarding the "ethereal gates." Able to be persuaded by "gentle words," she is, as Mourelatos contends, one of "four or five aspects or hypostases of one and the same divinity."[25] In short, Justice is only one name for the divine force that holds things in place, in poetic language through "bonds" or "shackles," but in philosophical language through the notion of limits or boundaries (*peiras*). On the one hand, we may concur with Mourelatos that "confinement by constraint is the very paradigm of the traditional Greek concept of justice as keeping one's own place."[26]

Yet Parmenides blends the old imagery of a divine Justice with a new philosophical use of the idea *peras* applied to "what is" as the limit of the nature of being.[27]

Though he uses the new Presocratic "watch-word," *physis*, Parmenides relegates this to that questionable part of the poem, *Doxa*, that seems only to contain false human knowledge. Rather than a complete dismissal of the concept of nature, however, when interpreted alongside the development of the "what is" in the *Truth* portion of the poem, it becomes apparent that such a move shows that Parmenides aims to purge the concept of nature "of the implications of dynamism."[28] It is fitting to talk of the *physis* of things only in the cosmological contexts of human opinion. Yet in the "Truth" section of the poem, Parmenides aims at "establishing formal philosophical criteria for an essence or nature."[29] Declaring that "the same thing is there for thinking and being" (B3), Parmenides forges a link between metaphysical and epistemological criteria.[30] To know something, it must have a certain kind of being: ungenerated and imperishable, a whole, unperturbed, and complete (B8). The limits of any "thing" in order to be *something*, must conform to these criteria. The epistemological and metaphysical criteria are, in effect, two sides of the same coin. As Patricia Curd so eloquently phrases it: "Only a nature or essence that meets his criteria is genuinely knowable: such a thing is the proper object of thought and inquiry . . . such a nature is the only appropriate starting point for successful inquiry into the natural world."[31]

These criteria function as the defining feature of Parmenidean nature—that is, nature understood in terms of the limits (*peras*) of being. In mythic terms, Justice has established the limits of each thing, both in terms of what that thing *is* and, as a result, what can be known about it. Parmenides connects this idea to a "deity who steers all things" (B12). Things are steered by means of the limits of their individual nature, that is, by being held within the bounds of the certain route prescribed by the deity. These correspond to the routes of inquiry, as Parmenides himself suggests, which implies that natures are established by Justice and held within their limits, in order to be known. As opposed to the ancient practice of divination, which Parmenides' supposed teacher Xenophanes argued strongly against, routes or paths of inquiry allow for human empowerment with respect to knowledge.[32] Rather than relying on signs to be interpreted, our understanding of the precise limits of the nature of being that Parmenides points to, and knowledge that these are fixed in place by Justice, means that humans can navigate the path to knowledge successfully themselves. Justice then is the guarantor of the possibility of real knowledge, and not simply mere opinion, through the boundaries of nature.[33]

Plato's Debt

Turning to the question of philosophical debt at the origins of philosophy, it is clear that all of Greek philosophy owes Anaximander a great debt insofar as the Milesian at least marks the transition to the use of nature as an explanatory concept. Establishing the fundamental teleological framework that undergirds the dominant Greek view for centuries to come, Anaximander provides the first account of the cosmos as an ordered system grounded on rational principles. Specifically, it is justice as a cosmic principle, and not a divine being, that regularly steers the world through the mechanism of time. Turning more specifically to Plato, who perhaps follows in Socrates' footsteps here when he redirects the notion of justice toward moral and political questions, we find an account of justice that is deeply rooted in precisely this concept of nature. In the *Republic*, nature *prescribes* what is just, so that it is not arbitrarily chosen based upon something as philosophically flimsy as the "advantage of the stronger." In effect, much of Plato's attack on Homer in the early portion of the dialogue represents an assault not only on the particular content of poems and stories which portray heroes and gods as weepy and deceptive, respectively, but also a not-so-subtle dismantling of tradition and custom as proper guides for human life and political community. Plato's ability to articulate a *philosophical* notion of justice that differs significantly from the conventional notion thus rises and falls on a concept of nature sufficiently solid enough to support consistent answers to the many challenging questions in political life. Broadly speaking then, Plato owes a debt to Anaximander for the inception of the idea that nature is a teleological concept powerful enough to dictate what unfolds in the cosmos, and by extension, to prescribe how men should live in community with one another. His debt to Heraclitus is more specific.

The discovery of political justice in Plato's *Republic* hinges on the determination of roles in the just city according to the idea of nature. Given the importance of the guardian's role, Socrates contends, these soldiers should be free from other kinds of labor and possess "the greatest skill and devotion" (374e).[34] Equally important, however, is that this kind of work "also requires a person whose nature is suited to that way of life" (374e). Comparing the guardian to a dog, Socrates makes the case that these guardians need an "invincible and unbeatable spirit" in addition to keen senses, notable speed, and superior strength. Such natures, however, may be far too savage toward the soldier's own citizens. What is necessary, it seems, is to find a nature that is "both gentle and high-spirited at the same time" (375c). Laying out the problem, Socrates says that "a gentle nature is the opposite of a spirited one" and that since these natures cannot coexist in a single individual, it seems there can be no such thing as a good guardian. Socrates is not stalled long, however, referring back to the analogy of good soldiers with well-trained dogs, as he points out that seemingly paradoxical natures do exist "in which these opposites are indeed combined" (375d). The well-trained dog is "gentle as can be to those he's used to and knows, but the opposite to those he doesn't know" (375e). Thus, Socrates adds a philosophical component to the guardian's nature because it guides the individual in judging well and distinguishing based on knowledge. Plato thus specifies the nature of a "fine and good guardian" for us, as it contains the attributes of philosophy, spirit, speed, and strength (376c).

There is no conception of nature as the unification of opposites before Plato except in Heraclitus; the Ephesian sage is the source for this idea. Socrates here plays the role of a Heraclitean sage who is able to recognize the unity in opposites—the existence of an underlying "fitting-together" (*harmonia*) of opposite traits. The *harmonia* is essential to the just city and it is perhaps another nod to Heraclitean views that music plays such a vital role in education in the *Republic*. Broadly speaking, the mark of the philosopher as a leader is the ability to recognize the logos that nature has laid out for a just society, but more specifically through the crucial ability to, in Heraclitus's words, "distinguish each according to its nature (*physis*) and tell how it is." Recognizing such natures and establishing an accompanying system of task assignment is essential to the establishment of a just society for Plato.

Later in the dialogue, Socrates is pushed somewhat unwillingly by his interlocutors to answer the question of the practicality of the just city. Namely, is such a city as they have been exploring even possible or merely a kind of philosophical pipe dream? Making a bold proclamation, he says:

> Until philosophers rule as kings in cities or those who are now called kings and leading men genuinely and adequately philosophize, that is, until political power and philosophy entirely coincide, while the many natures who at present pursue either one exclusively are forcibly prevented from doing so, cities will have no rest from evils, Glaucon, nor, I think, will the human race. (473c–d)

In a fitting and playful turn on the traditional notion of justice, Glaucon warns Socrates that such a claim will inevitably offend many people. Socrates must be prepared to defend himself by means of argument or else he will "pay the penalty of general derision" (474a). The defense Socrates musters centers on defining philosophers and showing that they alone "are fitted by nature" to engage in philosophy and to rule. The rest are "naturally fitted" to leave philosophy alone and follow their leader. In a very Parmenidean fashion, it is the nature of each individual that prescribes his or her limits. It establishes what we can and cannot be, what we can and cannot do, in effect, nature establishes the route or path we must each follow. This is an expansion of the Parmenidean notion of nature into the political and ethical realms. To live the just life entails an understanding of what one is best suited for, just as the just city depends upon each part fulfilling its nature through specific duties.

Immediately following his claim that philosophers ought to rule, Socrates turns to establishing the nature of the true philosopher. Philosophers are those who are insatiable for learning (475c), but unlike the lovers of sights and sounds, they alone are able to "see and embrace the nature of the beautiful itself" (476b). Dividing the "powers" of inquiry into knowledge and opinion, Socrates claims that knowledge is "by its nature set over what is, to know it as it is" (477b). Ignorance emerges as that which is "set over what is not," while opinion is a kind of intermediate between the two (478d). Through cagey linguistic equivocation with the meaning of "to be" (*einai*), an effort that undoubtedly channels Parmenides, Socrates aims to distinguish not just ways of inquiry, knowledge and opinion, but what these are "set over." In other words, he exploits the link forged by Parmenides between metaphysical criteria and epistemological criteria, between what something is and what we can feasibly know about it. Establishing the foundation for the theory of the forms, Socrates asserts that only philosophers are able to have true knowledge. In other words, philosophers alone are able to understand those "forms" which meet the metaphysical criteria established by Parmenides, and by extension, they alone are fit to lead the just city.

In summary, Plato's debt to the Presocratics is considerable. From Anaximander he inherits the idea that nature, both collective and individual, is fundamentally teleological. Political justice is thus rightly grounded in the prescriptive power of nature. From Heraclitus, he takes the idea that the natures of individual things are, at least in some cases, a unity of opposites. The recognition of such unity, and the ability to properly deploy particular natures to the appropriate tasks, are key traits necessary in the political leadership of a just city. Arguably, this also grounds the idea of a tripartite soul which is simultaneously a unity comprised of competing facets. Finally, from Parmenides he gets the idea that nature defined by limits both dictates what something is and allows it to be known. The connection between epistemological and metaphysical criteria allows Plato to establish a link between what a philosopher knows and how this applies to the practical world of political philosophy. He cannot, in short, answer the question of the practicality of the just city without the connection Parmenides has provided. In the end it seems we must pay Plato's debt for him by agreeing that his theory of justice does not get off the ground without a sufficiently dynamic concept of nature that transcends the Homeric view of *physis* as the "outward characteristic" of the thing. And it is just such a dynamic concept that he finds in the endeavors of his philosophical predecessors.

The Ohio State University
Columbus, Ohio

Notes

1. Gerard Naddaf sketches the four ways that the term *physis* in the "*Historia Peri Physeos*" tradition has been interpreted: 1) *physis* in the sense of primordial matter; 2) *physis* in the sense of process; 3) *physis* in the sense of primordial matter and process; 4) *physis* in the sense of origin, process, and result. See *The Greek Concept of Nature* (Albany, NY: SUNY Press, 2005), 17–20.

2. John Walter Beardslee, *The Use of Physis in Fifth-Century Greek Literature* (Chicago, IL: University of Chicago Press, 1918), 8.

3. Commentators consider the wrong question when they want to know about theories of "natural justice" prior to Plato if they assume a shared understanding of *physis* among Presocratic thinkers. At the very least we may judge those like Paul Woodruff too hasty when they presume the existence of a "prevailing concept of nature" that grounds both human and cosmic theories of justice. See Paul Woodruff "Natural Justice?" in *Presocratic Philosophy: Essays in Honour of Alexander Mourelatos*, ed. Victor Caston and Daniel W. Graham (Ashgate: Aldershot, 2002), 195–204, at 196.

4. For modern interpretations that regard Thales as the founder of philosophy see W. K. C. Guthrie, *A History of Greek Philosophy*, 6 vols. (Cambridge: Cambridge University Press, 1962–1981), vol. 1, 45–72 (hereafter, *HGP*) and Patricia F. O'Grady, *Thales of Miletus: The Beginnings of Western Science and Philosophy* (Aldershot: Ashgate, 2002), 1–8. For proponents

of Anaximander as the father of Western philosophy, see Charles H. Kahn, *Anaximander and the Origins of Greek Cosmology* (New York: Columbia University Press, 1960), 3 and Daniel Graham's *Explaining the Cosmos: The Ionian Tradition of Scientific Philosophy* (Princeton, NJ: Princeton University Press, 2006), 4. Kahn's account is still considered the seminal work on Anaximander. Graham's work aims at an ambitious synthesis of early Presocratic thought under the rubric of the "Ionian tradition" which "defined the world as a natural realm governed by lawlike regularities," *Explaining the Cosmos*, 26. According to Graham, Anaximander is the founder of this Ionic tradition which revolutionizes the state of knowledge in the ancient Greek world.

5. This translation is from Daniel W. Graham, *The Texts of Early Greek Philosophy: The Complete Fragments and Selected Testimonies of the Major Presocratics*, 2 vols. (Cambridge: Cambridge University Press, 2010), vol. 1, 51 (hereafter, TEGP). The fragment is quoted by Simplicius in a commentary on Aristotle's *Physics*, and there is considerable debate about where Simplicius's words end and Anaximander's begin. Graham, as indicated by the bold face, suggests here that Anaximander's own words begin with "according to what must be," though he offers no defense of this in his brief commentary. However, I agree with Kurt Pritzl's summation of a "sufficient consensus" in the literature that the selection quoted above is indeed Anaximander's own words. See Kurt Pritzl "Anaximander's *apeiron* and the Arrangement of Time" in *Early Greek Philosophy: The Presocratics and the Emergence of Reason*, ed. Joe McCoy (Washington D.C.: The Catholic University of America Press, 2013), 18–35, at 19.

6. The phrase is used by Graham, *Explaining the Cosmos*, 36; the emphasis is mine.

7. See *Physics* 187a12–23 and Plutarch, *Miscellanies* (A10): "He says that that part of the everlasting which is generative of hot and cold separated off at the coming to be of the world-order" *TEGP*, 67. Also A9 where Simplicius reports of Anaximander: "His contrarieties are hot, cold, dry, moist, and the rest," *TEGP*, 53.

8. Michael Gagarin, "Dikē in the Works and Days," *Classical Philology* 68.2 (1973): 81–94, at 81. For a subsequent study that extends the investigation beyond Homer and Hesiod, see Michael Gagarin, "Dike in Archaic Greek Thought" *Classical Philology* 69.3 (1974): 186–197. For an account which argues against Gagarin's view that *dike* contains no moral sense, see Matthew W. Dickie, "Dike as a Moral Term in Homer and Hesiod" *Classical Philology* 73.2 (1978): 91–101.

9. *Republic* 331d–332a. Cephalus's requirement that justice entails "speaking the truth" drops out so that the view Polemarchus initially defends is the entirely traditional account of giving to each what is owed. Polemarchus attempts to defend this view by citing a traditional authority: the poet Simonides. See Leo Strauss, *The City and Man* (Chicago: University of Chicago Press, 1964), 68. Strauss compares the traditional view of justice in Ancient Greek society to Thomas Aquinas, *Summa Theologica* II-II, q. 58, a. 1.

10. See *Iliad* 18.501.

11. Graham, *Explaining the Cosmos*, 35.

12. See Herodotus VIII.86, Thucydides IV.72, and Xenophon, *Anabasis* II.i.44 for *taksis* used in military contexts.

13. See Kahn, *Anaximander and the Origins of Greek Cosmology*, 191–196.

14. Aristotle seems to infer that Anaximander's theory of the *apeiron* as an *archē* is a criticism of a flaw in the arguments offered by Thales and Anaximenes that one element

constitutes the source of all things. If a single element is the source or is perpetually dominant, as an *archē* must be, the other elements would have ceased to exist. See *Physics* 204b22–29.

15. Gregory Vlastos, "Equality and Justice in Early Greek Cosmologies," *Classical Philology* 42.3 (1947): 156–178, at 172.

16. Michael Gagarin, "Greek Law and the Presocratics," in *Presocratic Philosophy: Essays in Honour of Alexander Mourelatos*, ed. Victor Caston and Daniel W. Graham (Ashgate: Aldershot, 2002), 19–26, at 22–23.

17. Vlastos, "Equality and Justice in Early Greek Cosmologies," 172.

18. See Aristotle *On the Heavens* 295b10–16 and Hippolytus *Refutation* I.6.3–7. Also Kahn's analysis in *Anaximander and the Origins of Greek Cosmology*, 76–81.

19. Kurt Pritzl, "Anaximander's *apeiron* and the Arrangement of Time," 35.

20. Ibid.

21. Charles H. Kahn, *The Art and Thought of Heraclitus* (Cambridge: Cambridge University Press, 1979), 67 (hereafter *ATH*). All translations of the Heraclitean fragments come from this edition. Kahn rearranges the fragments according to his thematic interpretation, resulting in different enumeration from the standard found in Diels-Kranz. I have maintained the DK fragment number for ease of reference.

22. Gagarin contends that Heraclitus merely extends Hesiod's notion of justice to the cosmos, "Dike in Archaic Greek Thought," 195.

23. The existence of an identifiable "unity of opposites" theory in the Heraclitean fragment has been largely accepted since G. S. Kirk first articulated it in *Heraclitus: The Cosmic Fragments*, 2nd ed (Cambridge: Cambridge University Press, 1962), 166–201. Other accounts of the unity of opposites in Heraclitus include but are not limited to Kahn, *ATH*, 185–204 and Michael C. Stokes, *One and Many in Presocratic Philosophy* (Washington, D.C.: The Center for Hellenic Studies, 1971), 89–100. For a recent account which details the problems with attributing such a theory to Heraclitus, see Roman Dilcher, "How Not to Conceive Heraclitean Harmony," in *Doctrine and Doxography: Studies in Heraclitus and Pythagoras*, ed. David Sider and Dirk Obbink (Berlin: De Gruyter, 2013), 263–280, at 263–265.

24. Gagarin notes only that Parmenides "does include [justice] in his poem as an important divine power" ("Dike in Archaic Greek Thought," 195). Gregory Vlastos dedicates a short section of his paper "Equality and Justice in Early Greek Cosmologies" to Parmenides, 161–164. Of the well-known scholarly monographs on Parmenides' thought, Alexander Mourelatos's work is an outlier in considering the theme of justice in Parmenides' poem worthy of any significant attention. See *The Route of Parmenides* (New Haven: Yale University Press, 1970), 25–29 and 151–154.

25. Mourelatos, *The Route of Parmenides*, 25.

26. Ibid., 119.

27. Ibid., 28.

28. See Mourelatos who argues that Parmenides aims to "purge" *physis* and "speculative predication" of the implications of dynamism, *The Route of Parmenides*, 62.

29. Patricia Curd, "Anaxagoras and Theory of Everything," in *The Oxford Handbook in Presocratic Philosophy*, ed. Patricia Curd and Daniel W. Graham (New York: Oxford University Press, 2008), 230–249, at 231. Curd understands Anaxagoras's thought, as many scholars

do, as a response to Parmenides. Her synopsis of Parmenides' thought in this chapter is a succinct version of the conclusions drawn from her longer study *The Legacy of Parmenides: Eleatic Monism and Later Presocratic Thought* (Las Vegas: Parmenides Publishing, [1998] 2004). The interpretation offered here is heavily indebted to Curd's analysis.

30. Ibid.

31. Ibid.

32. For an account of Xenophanes' repudiation of the customary practice of divination in antiquity, see James Lesher, "Xenophanes' Skepticism," *Phronesis* 23 (1978): 1–21, at 7–13.

33. See Descartes' *Meditations* V for a similar role played by God with respect to the possibility of certain knowledge of the natural world.

34. Translations from Plato's *Republic* come from G. M. A. Grube, rev. C. D. C. Reeve as found in *Plato: Complete Works*, ed. John M. Cooper (Indianapolis: Hackett Publishing, 1997).

Why Friendship Justifies Becoming

Will Britt

Abstract: In his discussions of justice and of friendship in the *Nicomachean Ethics*, Aristotle appeals frequently—without much explanation—to temporal considerations. I take these indications as a key for sorting out the systematic significance of Aristotle's claim that "when people are friends, there is no need for justice" (*NE* VIII.1.1155a26). Anaximander's fragmentary claim that coming-to-be is itself an injustice serves as a touchstone for the analysis; I ask whether and how Aristotle might agree with such a claim. I first isolate some problems, especially those involving time, that underlie Aristotle's various dialectical articulations of justice in *NE* V and show that friendship addresses them more beautifully than does justice. Then I try to establish that the ultimate work of friendship is to alter human temporality, interweaving multiple particular lives into a whole that both imitates and fits into the cosmic whole.

> [For Anaximander,] coming to be [is] a wrong for which
> destruction is the only possible penance. . . . [W]hen he saw
> in the multiplicity of things that have come to be a sum of
> injustices that must be expiated, he grasped with bold fingers
> the tangle of the profoundest problem in ethics.
> —Nietzsche, *Philosophy in the Tragic Age of the Greeks*[1]

1. Introduction

I begin with a quotation from Aristotle that will serve as a touchstone for what follows.

Friendship seems to hold cities together [*sunekhein*], and lawmakers seem to take it more seriously than justice, for like-mindedness seems to be something similar to friendship, and they aim at this most of all and banish faction most of all for being hostile to it. And when people are friends there is no need for justice [*ouden dei dikaiosunēs*], but when they are just there is still need of friendship [*prosdeontai philias*], and among all things that are just, what inclines toward friendship [*to philikon*] seems to be most just of all.[2]

Justice finds its fulfillment in friendship.

At the level of the political community, this seems both evident from experience and well-explained by Aristotle. Friendship holds cities together by preventing revolt, for at least three reasons: a) people are most inclined to be generous to their friends, and to share their property with them (cf. *Politics* 1263a30ff.), so the inequalities that remain despite efforts at reciprocity are less onerous among friends; b) "like-mindedness" means that people are more likely to understand—or even to try to understand—the motivations for decisions made by their friends, while they are more likely to misunderstand (willfully or not) the decisions of their rivals; c) it is much harder to revolt against or wish ill toward a friend, since friendship begins with and necessarily contains goodwill (*eonoia*) toward one another (*NE* 1166b30ff.).

But I take the claim that "when people are friends there is no need for justice" to focus primarily on individual friendships, even if it is the city as a whole that is preserved by such relations. And this is where matters are less clear. Why do we not even *need* justice in friendships? If justice is a virtue of character—or even the whole of character-virtue, insofar as that is directed toward others—surely it would be a *necessary component* of complete friendship, which Aristotle says is the greatest of external goods (1169b10)?

There are some straightforward ways to respond to this question. For one thing, approaching the matter negatively, it certainly does seem like an indication that my virtuous friendship is in bad shape if I have to be concerned with justice *as such* in my actions toward my friend. If I find myself keeping records of wrongs or of favors done, demanding reciprocity, it is usually a sign of some problem; similarly, if I have to start setting laws in any serious sense—e.g., 'we can only get together during the week because we make bad decisions together on weekends'—then the excellence of the friendship is already threatened.

Positively, friendship in general gives me a stronger, more internal motivation for helping another, even if I am also obligated by concerns of justice. For example, I may really want to stay in bed one morning, rather than going in to teach. I am free to cancel class. From the point of view of justice, however, I can recognize that my students are paying a great deal of money to be taught, that they may have already made sacrifices in time and sleep to complete the reading for today, and that I am being paid to teach them philosophy, not to give them days off. All of those considerations will, if I am a just person, usually sway me. But if I am friends with them, I will really desire to see them learn, to have a bit of Plato or Nietzsche click into place *for these particular people*, and this will get me out of bed much more happily than my considerations about its being the just thing to do.

Practical responses along these lines are undoubtedly right, but I am not sure that they are theoretically very satisfying. Can we not say more? What is it about friendship that both completes and suspends justice? In what follows, I will argue in the following manner: justice is fundamentally a way of dealing with the temporality of living together, while friendship is a way of living together that *alters* our very temporality, so friendship removes the need for justice by removing the problems that justice solves. Let us look at each of these claims in turn.

2. Justice is a Response to the Time of Community

If we are to answer more rigorously the question about the relation of justice to friendship, we will have to get in view what it is about the human situation that justice responds to. We can fill out my as-yet empty formulation about 'the temporality of living together' by attending to what is presupposed by each of the various articulations of justice, as Aristotle unfolds them in *Nicomachean Ethics* V.

Aristotle first distinguishes two senses of the word "justice," thereby answering Socrates' repeated question (to Meno, among others) about whether justice is virtue (itself) or *a* virtue.[3] Aristotle claims that there is one sense in which justice is the whole of virtue, insofar as the virtues are other-directed; but there is also a second sense in which justice is a particular virtue, having to do with what one owes to others and with profiting at their expense (1129b30–1130b20). Let us begin with justice as one part of virtue, postponing until the end a discussion of justice as virtue itself.

Aristotle distinguishes two aspects of justice as a particular virtue: its distributive aspect, which involves dividing things *proportionally*, and its corrective aspect, which *equalizes* transactions. He will later interweave these in order to account for what he calls reciprocity, which *equalizes proportionally* and turns out to be something like what we call fairness. Finally, near the end of the discussion, he clarifies and transforms the meaning of justice by summing it up in decency (or 'equity': *epieikeia*), which turns out to be the real habit (*hexis*) of justice. Thus, there are four articulations of justice to be considered.

2.1. Justice as Distributive

Aristotle claims that distributive justice, which operates according to geometrical proportionality, has as its proper domain what is divisible, especially, but not only, money and honors. About such things we are most concerned that they be equitably distributed according to merit—however we recognize merit—so the mean here is the equitable (*to ison*; cf. 1131a10ff.). This concern of ours betrays that it is not only divisibility that is presupposed; scarcity, too, essentially underlies distributive justice. When this aspect of justice is in play, we are always playing a zero-sum game. This is no merely accidental scarcity, as if expanding our horizons to another resource-rich planet could change its zero-sum nature. Rather, scarcity is intrinsic to the distribution, since the scarcity is the discriminant of value. If everyone is honored, I do not feel sufficiently honored; if everyone has enough to eat, I want better things to eat.

Although we are indeed driven by need—for Aristotle, as for Socrates in the *Republic*, necessity is the basis and bond of the city (*Politics* I.2)—Aristotle also follows Socrates' concerns about the luxurious city by claiming in the *Politics* that we are *most* driven by excessive desire: "people commit the greatest injustices on account of excesses [*tas huperbolas*] and not on account of necessities; they do not become tyrants, for instance, so they will not be cold" (*Pol.* II.7.1267a13–15).[4] This makes sense, inasmuch as "the nature of desire [*phusis tēs epithumias*] is infinite [*apeiron*]" (*Pol.* II.7.1267b4), exceeding all limits.

So, my first claim is that competition and comparison with regard to structurally scarce goods are what *distributive justice* presupposes.

2.2. Justice as Corrective

Corrective (or retributive) justice, according to Aristotle, seeks not the proportionally equitable but the directly equal;[5] it operates according to arithmetic proportions. Here the proper domain is that of exchange, of transactions (whether willing or unwilling), so the mean is between loss and gain. The target is "having something equal both before and after" the transaction (1132b20).

Equality with regard to the before and the after—rather than the equitable with regard to the relation of persons and goods—makes explicit the temporal aspect in this articulation of justice. It is a way of maintaining stability through time, but since we live forward, this very stability will always primarily require attending to the future in light of the past, i.e., either restoring an already broken equality or ordering the situation so as to prevent such a rupture. Corrective justice is a response to failure, whether already actual or as yet only possible.

My second claim, then, is that *corrective justice* presupposes history as both the story of and the site of failure.

2.3. Justice as Reciprocal

The insights from distributive and corrective justice come together in reciprocity, which is not reducible to either of the other two articulations. To the *domain* of exchange (i.e., that of corrective justice) Aristotle applies the *measure* from distributive justice, namely, geometric proportionality. Not only is it not the same thing to hit a social equal as to hit someone in authority (1132b28–30)—as we all recognize in practice—but, since it is also clearly not the same thing to build a house as to educate a child, we need some way of relating them to one another if we are to have a community of exchange.

The mean here, which gathers up the previous articulations of justice, is a mean quantity that lies between doing injustice and suffering it (*adikein kai adikeisthai*, 1133a32). In the sphere of exchange, that mean is called 'reciprocity' in English and '*antipeponthos*' in Greek—i.e., 'having suffered or been affected in turn' (from the perfect tense of *paskhō*). The just person, then, takes upon herself neither too much nor too little of the hardship involved in living well (where living well is the self-sufficient aim of the city[6]), *and* she only demands of others a similarly moderate amount.[7]

Aristotle's discussion of reciprocity further gathers up the previous two articulations of justice by making clear two related difficulties that were already involved in the earlier discussions but not yet manifest.

The first problem is that of *communication*, taken in the minimal, game-theoretic sense. That is, how can we really equalize suffering between even two different people? Granted that we are not clones,[8] what can give me any confidence that what I judge to be painful for another is sufficiently related to what I experience as painful?[9]

The two solutions that Aristotle suggests here (1133a26–32), though interesting, cry out for something more by their very insufficiency. First, he says that economic demand (*khreia*)[10] is the measure that holds everything together (*sunekhei*), which is only possible since we need (*deontai*) similar things. But since this demand itself is not exchangeable, his second proposal for the criterion is currency, which, just like a measure (*metron*), makes things commensurable (or symmetrical: *summetra*; cf. 1133b18–20). That means that currency functions as an index of need: 'how badly do you need it?' is taken to be adequately indicated by 'how much are you willing to spend?'

This move may be fine as regards exchange-value, but even Aristotle leaves the door open to recognize that price fluctuations may be artificially induced and thus fail as appropriate indices of need. After proposing currency (*nomisma*) as the solution to the communication problem, he explains that it gets its name from the fact that we can change it or make it worthless—it *is* only by custom (*nomos*; 1133a28–31). Even if we construe this broadly, to mean that we can communicate value by conforming to some pre-established custom (and not only through currency specifically), nonetheless it seems as if the very possibility of fluctuations in value for some things calls into question the characterization of them as valuable. When custom fails or conflicts with other customs, on what can we call to provide a just measure for life together?[11]

The second problem that becomes especially evident in Aristotle's discussion of reciprocity is that of *time*. This problem is already involved in corrective justice: we need some way of linking up who and how I was before you assaulted me with who and how I am now, if we are to decide what to do to make things equal in the future. But in distributive justice, so long as the discussion remains at the level of awarding honor or doling out money, it is unclear whether the temporal meaning is primarily futural (as doling out suggests), past (as a reward suggests), or both.

With reciprocity, however, the problem of proportionality is now explicitly two-fold: a) how to gauge, right now, the relation between my four chickens and your one goat, in light of our differing particular needs; b) how to guarantee the possibility of a future exchange, or the meeting of a future need (1133b8–13). Here the work of currency, as such a guarantor, is to raise the economy above a barter system based on immediate need, thus holding together the city in a long-term sense. In fact, reciprocity corrects for our tendency to act only in light of the extended present by orienting us toward the unknown future.

Hence, I claim thirdly that *reciprocity* presupposes both present communal norms for estimating need and the projection of that need into the future.

2.4. Justice as Decency (epieikeia)

The fourth and last articulation of justice once again gathers up what has gone before. Here it is not a matter of adding an additional component but of focusing our gaze within the phenomena already laid out. To explain decency (*epieikeia*), Aristotle says that it is not different from justice understood simply, only from legal justice, which it corrects. Decency is a kind of subjunctive justice: if we take the lawmaker as the paradigm of justice, then the decent action is what the lawmaker *would have done* in the particular case (whether that means make an exception or follow her own rule), if she were there (1137b20–26).

The distinction between legal justice and justice simply (or decency) points out different ways of applying the previous articulations of justice. To rectify an injury, I can simply apply the eye for an eye rule, or I can go to a judge and ask for a more creative verdict that will correct the situation in light of its particularities, and thereby also "correct" the rule (cf. 1132a20ff.). To be able to deliver such a verdict, that judge requires precisely the habit (*hexis*) of decency—as would I in figuring out what should count as merit in distributive justice (1131a25ff.), and as would the parties agreeing to the price in any given reciprocal exchange (1133a32ff.).

For this reason, I think that when Aristotle concludes at the very end of *NE* V.10 that the habit of decency is "some [kind of] justice and not some other habit [*hetera hexis*]" (1138a3), he means that someone who is "rigidly precise about justice to a fault" (1138a1)—i.e., someone who is *only* legally just—actually does not have the habit of justice at all. This is more than he says (depending on how much we can infer from 'to a fault [*epi to kheiron*]'), but it is borne out by considering the phenomenon. For what would it mean to be rigidly precise about justice? Such a person would not have a settled state of character from which he recognized and did what was just for its own sake. Rather, such a person would either be so internally conflicted that he desperately maintained the letter of the law for fear of doing wrong, or he would be someone who had internalized the law itself as a set of rules but not the principles on which it was constructed, and thus would be at a loss in any situation not explicitly covered by a rule.

So far, I have shown that at least corrective justice and reciprocity, if not also distributive justice, are oriented toward bringing temporal beings more into line with universal constancy. But Aristotle's whole discussion of decency—and thus, I suggest, of justice itself as a particular virtue—now turns out to be premised quite explicitly on the assumption that inevitable exceptions cannot be built into good law. Rephrased into my fourth claim, this means that *decency* presupposes the irreducible particularity of situations in relation to the structural universality of laws (1137b18–20).

3. The Wedding of Time and Particularity

But in what way are such exceptions inevitable? Aristotle claims that "the 'error' [*hamartēma*: missing the mark] is neither in the law nor in the lawmaker, but is in the nature of the particular case [*en tēi phusei tou pragmatos*]: for such is the material of actions [*hulē tōn praktōn*] straight-off [*euthus*]" (1137b17–19). Further, "it is impossible to set down a law about some things, . . . for a rule [*kanōn*] for something indeterminate [*aoristos*] is also indeterminate" (1137b28–30).[12] The impossibility here—i.e., the inevitability of error—lies in the nature of the object, specifically the domain of objects proper to justice: actions and the somewhat indeterminate matters (*pragmata*) with which they deal.

Ethics, according to Aristotle, deals with things that are only "for the most part."[13] They usually happen one way, but not always. Thus, the objects of justice are indeterminate *because of* their relation to change, the measure of which is time. In other words, although we just now saw that the problem to which justice is ultimately a response is the mediation of particularity with universality, the part with the whole, this problem gets *interpreted* according to the value of temporal permanence. Consider Aristotle's claim in the *Physics* that "in itself" time is a cause of destruction but only "incidentally of generation and of being."[14] I can put the point most clearly, following Nietzsche, by appeal to what Anaximander is reported to have said. In a very literal translation: "That from which is the coming-to-be for beings, into the same things they also pass away, according to necessity [*khreōn*]; for they must pay penalty [*dikēn*] and recompense to one another for their injustice [*adikia*], according to the ordering of time."[15]

Here injustice most fundamentally seems to consist in *becoming* as such. Being the kind of thing that has begun to be is understood as already an injustice, a mismatch between what is and that from which it comes. The injustice is either through *arising* from sources (in the sense of leaving them behind, striking out on one's own), or through arising *from sources* (in the sense of necessity, i.e., having some other condition on which one's being is dependent). Time, then, appears as the index of the difference, the common measure between crime and payment that allows their just equalization.[16]

Provisionally, we might think that for Aristotle, too, justice not only *presupposes* temporality but is already a corrective *response* to the kind of necessity to which impermanent beings are subject. In other words, perhaps it is not only that time provides a measure for justice, but that being in a certain relation to time *makes one already guilty* by making one too particular, and thus places one in need of justice in its various articulations.

4. Friendship Fulfills and Surpasses Justice

To check this provisional conclusion, I turn now to friendship, focusing on that kind which is most complete.[17] We will see how virtuous friendship more thoroughly addresses each of the underlying problems to which the four articulations of justice are responses. Recall my four claims from section 2: that distributive justice presupposes competition and comparison with regard to structurally scarce goods; that corrective justice presupposes history as both the story of and the site of failure; that reciprocity presupposes both present communal norms for estimating need and the projection of that need into the future; and that decency presupposes the irreducible particularity of situations in relation to the structural universality of laws.

4.1. Friendship and Distribution

First, friendship includes both competition (to do the most beautiful things [1169a9]) and comparison, both of which we saw to be essential to distributive justice, but here they *remedy* the problem of scarcity rather than simply manage it. Since beautiful action is an end in itself, it cannot be made more or less valuable in different situations, hence it cannot be structurally scarce. Nor can it be accidentally scarce, since there is no external limit placed on doing good. How could there be too much of what is most beautiful? To the extent that friendship consists of shared activity (*energeia*; see *NE* VIII.5 and IX.8)—i.e., action intrinsically complete at every moment—an external limit is impossible.[18]

Furthermore, if friendship (*philein*) is shared activity (giving rise to beautiful actions), the competition to do good is inherently unitive rather than divisive: my success is also yours, and yours is mine. In fact, I can better appreciate my own activity through yours (1170b10ff.), which gives me the pleasure that brings activity to completion (1174b34). For example, a friend "would even give up actions to a friend, and it would be a more beautiful thing to become responsible for the friend's performing them than to perform them himself" (1169a35). Thus, unlike distributive justice, there is no way in which the activity of complete friendship can be a zero-sum game.[19]

4.2. Friendship and Correction

Second, while friendship recognizes both the possibility and the reality of failure, to which corrective justice responds, in friendship failure is dealt with through forgiveness. Thus, while a good person values herself properly and is properly indignant about being wronged, she will be most willing to forgive a friend who apologizes. Likewise, the offender will be most willing to apologize to a friend, who will best understand and point her in the direction of becoming better.[20] It is the very history built into a good friendship, then, that allows people effectively to straighten one another out (1172a12–15). In other words, love corrects the disproportion and thus brings about equality (1159b1ff.).

4.3. Friendship and Reciprocity

Third, whereas reciprocal justice orders itself according to the *geometrical* proportion of distribution, the *arithmetical* proportion of corrective justice is raised to the highest principle in friendship. Aristotle claims that equality in friendship is different than that in (reciprocal) justice, since justice is focused primarily on what people deserve (i.e., the proportionally equitable), while friendship is focused primarily on directly equalizing persons (1158b29ff.).

That equalization addresses the problems visible in reciprocity in several ways. It provides a measure for present need that is more accurate than pricing. It unites the friends' systems of value, so that differences of custom do not threaten their most important commitments. And the stability of a complete friendship, based on loving the other for her own sake, serves as guarantee of future goodwill in times of need.

4.4. Friendship and Decency

Finally, friendship is the ultimate experience of attention to the irreducible particular (the friend) in relation to the whole (the good). I know my friend in some ways even better than I know myself, so my judgment of what is likely to be best for her will be maximally informed by the particular background and circumstances. Friendship here surpasses even decency, for which the paradigm example is taking less in an exchange even when the law is on one's side (1138a2). In friendship, I take less not simply because it is the decent thing to do, but *so that my friend may have more*. Not only do I recuperate in a roundabout way my own loss thereby, but I get even more than what was originally on offer, since my joy is greater when my friend receives good things than when I receive them.

5. Friendship and Temporality

Most importantly for my argument here, however, friendship alters the temporal structure of our lives. Aristotle emphasizes that "nothing is so characteristic of friends as living together" (1157b19; cf. 1158a10–11) and that "whatever being consists in for any sort of people—whatever it is for the sake of which they choose to be alive—this is what they want to be engaged in with their friends" (1172a1–3). This is because we are intrinsically political beings. Aristotle claims that living together here means primarily "shar[ing] in a friend's awareness that he is" (1170b11), which is accomplished through shared activity.

But this being-shared is not only an additive property, as if my activity remained the same but were simply joined by your activity, so that doing the same thing with a stranger or in front of a video camera would be just as good. Instead, my very activity is modified by being joined to yours. Aristotle only hints at *how* this happens, but his suggestions are worth pursuing. He says that "it is not easy by oneself to be active continuously [*sunekhōs*], but it is easier to be so among and in relation to others [*meth' heterōn kai pros allous*]; so the activity . . . will be more continuous, which it needs to be in the case of a blessed person" (1170a6–8). And he adds later that contemplation (the most continuous activity), despite being self-sufficient, is nonetheless improved by being done with friends (1177b1).

What are we to make of this? At one level, we could simply take it as a reference back to the first book of the *Nicomachean Ethics* (I.5, I.8), where Aristotle is concerned that we not take virtue to be the same as happiness, lest we be able to sleep through life and still be accounted happy. In this sense, friends make our activity more continuous by being active when we sleep. That seems true, but it is hardly a very satisfying account, not least because it involves a largely extrinsic relation to friendship. (Surely someone who is not my friend can also carry on similar activities while I sleep.)

Within the context of complete friendships, it seems that shared activities, simply by being shared, stretch out into a kind of everlastingness, as if sharing time privately with good friends brought about a reorganization of our relation to time itself.[21] This is because the friend joins in my being and thus also participates in my self-sufficiency without destroying it. Here the joining together or interweaving (*sunekhein*) of persons (as in the city) turns out to be also a joining together of moments into continuous (*sunekhōs*) activity.

Friendships between good people, who are maximally stable, are also most enduring. Hence, Aristotle locates the maturity of complete friendships first of all "in time" (1156b33). Inasmuch as Aristotle privileges the everlasting,[22] taking our relation to time as an indicator of intrinsic worth, the temporal transformation that friends make possible can be seen to upgrade our very ontological status. Like (and often *as*) contemplation, loving (*philein*) brings us into the realm of the gods, where justice, as governing a realm of actions for extrinsic ends, would be simply out of place.

This allows us to see that my earlier, provisional conclusion requires modification. Rather than taking the particular to be guilty in its difference from the structurally universal law, requiring redress from justice as decency, Aristotle shows the rigidly universalizing character of the law to be an inherently unsuccessful attempt at reaching the whole of virtue, which seeks the cosmic whole. Permanent continuity of being, toward which activity (*energeia*) is inherently oriented, cannot be achieved by cancelling particularity, but only by weaving it together into the kind of unity that structures the whole. Friendship, then, justifies particularity by raising it to the level of the whole (*katholou*), but not in the abstracting sense of the universal. According to Aristotle, this is only possible by altering the temporality of the particular being in question.

Loyola Marymount University

Notes

1. Friedrich Nietzsche, *Philosophy in the Tragic Age of the Greeks*, trans. M. Cowan (Regnery Publishing, 1962), 48.

2. Aristotle, *Nicomachean Ethics* (henceforth: *NE*) VIII.1.1155a23–29, trans. Joe Sachs (Newburyport, MA: Focus, 2002). I use this translation throughout, though I have made occasional modifications in accord with the Greek (*Aristotelis Ethica Nicomachea*, ed. Bywater [Oxford Classical Texts, 1894]). Further citations are parenthetical in the text; unless otherwise noted, all such references are to the *Nicomachean Ethics*.

3. Cf. Plato, *Meno* 73e, 79a–b.

4. Aristotle, *Politics* (henceforth: *Pol.*), trans. Joe Sachs (Newburyport, MA: Focus, 2012).

5. Both 'equitable' and 'equal' translate *to ison*, depending on whether the equalization is to take place according to geometric proportionality (indirect equality = *equity*) or to arithmetic proportionality (a kind of direct *equality*).

6. Cf. *Pol.* I.2.1252b28–30.

7. If we wanted to delineate the extremes that constitute unjust transactions according to Aristotle's usual schematic for the virtues, we could say that "having injustice done to one is less than the mean, and doing the injustice is in excess of it" (1134a14).

8. Aristotle accuses Plato's *Republic* of calling for too much similarity in the citizens (*Pol.* II.2–4), as if Socrates were cheating on this problem in that discussion.

9. This is a far-reaching question, and it was already a problem for corrective justice: if having violence done to me, or even life experience in general, changes me, how am I to begin to figure out what could make up for it? And if the making up involves prescribing a penalty for someone else, the problem only deepens. Those not in the grip of revenge recognize that gouging out *your* eye will not help *me* to see any better.

10. *Khreia* is a combination of need with obligation or debt. We would call it 'demand' in the economic sense.

11. I take it this is part of the problem that Aristotle addresses in *NE* V.7, the infamous chapter distinguishing between natural and conventional justice, and that his appeal to natural justice there carries over to his account of decency in V.10, but I cannot make that argument in sufficient detail here.

12. The switch in terminology between rule and law is to allow him to draw an analogy to the flexible rulers (straight-edges) used in housebuilding on Lesbos.

13. He says near the opening of the *Ethics* that "one ought to be content . . . when speaking about things that are so for the most part, and reasoning from things of that sort, to reach conclusions that are also of that sort" (1094b19–20). To distinguish based on the precision of the object seems right (ethics is not and should not be geometry), but it is another step to let this determine worth, as well. Thus, Aristotle will observe (and evidently approve) that "the [activities] most honored are the ones that are more enduring [*monimōterai*]" (1100b15–17).

14. *Physics* 222b20–21. See also 221a32–33, where he comments on the customary saying that time wastes things away.

15. Diels-Kranz, 12B1, my translation, with help from P. Curd via the *Stanford Encyclopedia of Philosophy* entry on "Presocratic Philosophy" (published March 10, 2007; accessed November 13, 2010).

16. It makes sense, given what was said above about the obligation of necessity (*khreia*) as binding together the city (2.3), which is the very *place* of justice, that temporality should be closely tied to necessity, as it is in the fragment.

17. Of course, there will be points of similarity with the other kinds, namely, friendships of pleasure and of use, since they derive from the complete version (*NE* VIII.3–4).

18. The infinite desire that we encountered (2.1, above) as a problem for justice is thus appropriately directed toward such goods, whereby it avoids being excessive.

19. There is an exception: insofar as time spent with particular friends prevents time with others, since we cannot always bring them together. See *NE* IX.10 for Aristotle's acknowledgment of this problem.

20. St. Paul says that love (*agapē*) keeps no record of wrongs (I Corinthians 13), and it seems to me that this could be extended to Aristotelian *philia*.

21. That alteration is integrally related to the way in which contemplation connects us with that which is unmoved. The unmoved obviously bears a different relation to time, since time for Aristotle is the number of motion.

22. See, *inter alia*, *Metaphysics* IX.7.

The Missing Virtue: Justice in Modern Virtue Ethics

M. T. Lu

Abstract: Several commentators have noted that "justice has not fared well in the revival of virtue ethics"; it "has become damagingly marginalized" and "no longer has a starring role." Given its traditional place among the four cardinal virtues this is a remarkable state of affairs and yet exactly *why* this has occurred has not been adequately explored or explained. In this paper, I argue that the particular moral virtue of justice has been largely disregarded by the contemporary virtue theorists primarily because their conception of justice is so different from Aristotle's. Accordingly, they do not need the virtue of justice to do the kind of explanatory work in their systems that it does in Aristotle's.

In Book V of the *Nicomachean Ethics*, Aristotle famously holds that "it often seems that justice is the greatest of the virtues" and "it especially is complete virtue because it is the putting to use of complete virtue" (1129b28–32).[1] And yet, as Christopher Miles Coope has observed, in modern virtue ethics—the putative modern standard-bearer of an Aristotelian approach to morality—the virtue of justice "has become damagingly marginalized" and "no longer has a starring role."[2] In this paper I want to examine how and why this has come to pass. How has one of the traditional cardinal (natural) virtues come to such an ignominious state in contemporary virtue ethics? Further, what does this signify about the relationship between contemporary virtue ethics and the more traditional virtues approach in Aristotle and the subsequent tradition?

We should be clear that by "modern virtue ethics" we are specifically referring to the approach developed over the last 40 years or so by figures such as Philippa Foot, Rosalind Hursthouse, Michael Slote and others. It presents itself, in Hursthouse's words, as "one of the three major approaches in normative ethics" that "emphasizes the virtues, or moral character, in contrast to the approach which emphasizes duties or rules (deontology) or that which emphasizes the consequences of actions (consequentialism)."[3] While it is generally accepted that this approach to ethics got its start with G. E. M. Anscombe's famous "Modern Moral Philosophy" (1958),[4] its codification as a full-fledged alternative approach "in normative ethics" was a later development, spearheaded in many ways by Rosalind Hursthouse.

© 2017, *Proceedings of the ACPA*, Vol. 90
doi: 10.5840/acpaproc20181368

Our focus here will be on the way in which the particular *moral* virtue of justice has become largely overlooked in contemporary discussions. Coope notes that the stark decline in the discussion of justice can be revealed by the simple expedient of "looking up the references to justice in the index" of "any recent book-length treatment of virtue ethics"; if we do so Coope notes "what we find will be quite piffling."[5] Indeed, Coope is not the first to have noticed this. David K. O'Connor has similarly observed that "justice has not fared well in the revival of virtue ethics" and there has seemed to be "little independent interest in justice as a personal virtue."[6]

While Coope's examples of the many ways in which modern virtue ethics has diminished and downplayed the virtue of justice are highly convincing, I do not think his account fully explains just *why* this has occurred. That is, Coope successfully shows that modern virtue ethics largely disregards justice, but his excellent diagnosis of modern virtue ethics as hostile to the virtue of justice needs to be supplemented by a fuller account of exactly what it is about the traditional virtue of justice that makes it seem so dispensable in the modern virtue theories. I take this as my central task in what follows.

Pleonexia and the Virtue of Justice in Aristotle

Let us begin by returning to Aristotle to see just what role the particular moral virtue of justice plays in his ethics. It is important to note that in Book V of the *Nicomachean Ethics* Aristotle draws an important distinction between two entirely different senses of the word 'justice': (1) what has come to be called *general justice*, which he says is in many ways synonymous with virtue as a whole (though directed towards other people), and (2) *particular justice*, which is the specific moral virtue of justice which he views as parallel with the other moral virtues such as courage, temperance, etc. Our focus here will be primarily on (2), particular justice—i.e, the specific *moral virtue* of justice.

We know from Book II that all the virtues are intermediates between vices of deficiency and excess. Further, they are distinguished by focusing on the characteristic passions that tend to lead to vicious action by those who lack the relevant virtues. So, for instance, the characteristic passion related to the virtue of courage is fear. The coward is someone who has become mastered by and gives into his fear in a shameful way. The corresponding vice of excess is "without a name," but it is essentially a kind of irrational *fearlessness* of things that ought to be feared ("not even an earthquake or a flood as people say of the Celts" [1115b25]). For the moral virtue of moderation (*sophrosune*), on the other hand, the characteristic passion is bodily pleasure, with the vice of excess being expressed in a shameful and intemperate pursuit of pleasure and the vice of deficiency (which is much more uncommon) involving a kind of insensitivity to (proper) pleasure.

We come to the virtue of justice expecting a similar structure. What we get at first seems almost tautological. Aristotle says that "it is clear that doing what is just is a mean between doing injustice and having injustice done to one, for the former is having a greater amount and the latter is having a lesser amount" (1133b33). However, he clarifies that "injustice is an excess and a deficiency, because it is concerned with an excess and a deficiency, an excess for oneself of what is simply beneficial and a deficiency of what is harmful, or in the case of two other people, the whole distribution is made in a similar manner and contrary to proportion, in whichever direction it happens to be" (1134a9). Notice that justice centrally consists in getting something right (hitting the mark as he often likes to say). Specifically, "the just person is said to be inclined to do what is just by choice, and inclined to distribute things, both to himself in comparison with someone else, and to another person in comparison with someone else, not in such a way that more of what is choiceworthy goes to himself and less to his neighbor, nor the opposite way with what is harmful, but so that each gets what is proportionately equal" (1134a2).

As we already noted with courage, moderation, etc., there is a specific passion which differentiates the virtue of justice from the other virtues. For Aristotle, much as the coward is overcome with fear, the unjust man is overcome by *pleonexia*. As Terence Irwin notes in his translation of the *Ethics*, this term "is difficult to translate" but it centrally "involves more than a mere desire to accumulate resources; it also includes a desire to have more than I am entitled to, so as to get the better of someone else."[7]

Aristotle is very clear that *pleonexia* is what specifically distinguishes injustice from the other vices: "we are inquiring about the injustice that is particular. Here is a sign that there is such a thing: with the other vices, the one who engages in them—someone who throws down his shield out of cowardice, or speaks ill of people out of harshness, or does not help people with money out of stinginess—is being unjust but is not taking more than his due of anything, but when someone does take more than his due (*pleonekte*), it is often not a result of any vice of that sort, and certainly not a result of all of them, but it is a result of some vice (since we blame it), namely of injustice" (1130a17).

While it is certainly the case that vicious acts from cowardice, etc., are unjust in the *general* sense, he holds that what specifically marks the vice related to the *particular* virtue of justice is *pleonexia*, much as fear marks courage and pleasure marks moderation. This means that if the vicious act is not performed on account of *pleonexia*, it is not a specific vice against the *particular* virtue of justice (though it remains unjust in the *general* sense). Some important modern commentators have regarded this Aristotelian claim as implausible. For instance, Bernard Williams writes:

> Insofar as Aristotle connects injustice essentially with *pleonexia* he is mistaken. The mistake can, moreover, be fairly easily diagnosed at the systemic level: the vice of injustice has been over-assimilated to the other vices of character, *so that Aristotle seeks a characteristic motive to go with it, whereas it must be basic to this vice, unlike others, that it does not import a special motive, but rather the lack of one.*[8]

The last sentence captures the gravamen of Williams's criticism. He thinks that Aristotle has failed to recognize that what characterizes injustice is fundamentally different than what characterizes the vices against virtues like courage or moderation.

In each of those cases he grants that there is a characteristic passion. However, Williams holds that injustice is not properly characterized by the presence of *pleonexia*, but instead by the *absence* of a proper "motive" of justice.[9]

As David O'Connor points out, this means that "Williams will not count some cases Aristotle considers paradigmatic of injustice as injustice at all, and similarly an Aristotelian will not count some of Williams's cases."[10] For Williams, what is central to injustice is the misdistribution of something (e.g., goods or honors) as an offence against fairness. For Aristotle, on the other hand, certain examples of misdistribution do not count as unjust in the specific sense of involving an offence against the virtue of justice if the reason for that misdistribution is not *pleonexia*, but something else (such as lust).[11] It is again worth noting that Aristotle would identify misdistribution out of lust as unjust in the *general* sense, but not as offending against the *particular* virtue of justice.

It is clear that Williams and Aristotle disagree. It is not so clear that Williams is straightforwardly entitled to his claim that Aristotle "is mistaken" because a lack of motive is what is most essential to the vice of injustice. Williams does not seem to consider that his modern conception of justice is simply different in some important ways from Aristotle's Greek notion. In fact, in making these claims about *pleonexia* Aristotle is simply following a general Greek tradition. To give just one example: in Plato's *Republic*, as C. D. C Reeve points out, *pleonexia* "is, or is the cause of, injustice (359c), since always wanting to out do others leads one to try to get what belongs to them, what isn't one's own. It is contrasted with doing or having one's own, which is, or is the cause of justice (434a, 441e)."[12]

When Williams says "the vice of injustice has been over-assimilated to the other vices of character" I think he is basically accusing Aristotle of artificially playing up *pleonexia* in an attempt to shoehorn justice into his preexisting structure of the virtues instead of recognizing (Williams thinks) that justice is fundamentally different from those other virtues. What the evidence from the *Republic* suggests, however, is that Aristotle is simply attempting to accommodate one of the most important Greek *endoxa* (common opinions) concerning justice. Of course, even if Aristotle is following the traditional Greek view that puts *pleonexia* at the heart of injustice that by itself does not make that Greek conception correct. It does, however, suggest that Williams is being somewhat overhasty in essentially accusing Aristotle of artificially overemphasizing *pleonexia* so as to fit his preexisting system. For our purposes here, it is less important to adjudicate this dispute between Williams and Aristotle than simply to recognize that the dispute reveals something important about how different the Greek notion of justice is from the modern one typified by Williams.[13] This in turn is helpful for thinking about our central question of why modern virtue ethicists give so little attention to the virtue of justice.[14]

What we have found is that Aristotle (and the Greeks more generally) had a different conception of justice than modern thinkers like Williams. While the Greeks placed *pleonexia* at the heart of injustice, moderns like Williams are much more apt to focus instead on unfair distribution. I suspect this difference is largely captured by the contrast J. O. Urmson finds between Aristotle's conception of justice and Hume's:

distributive and rectificatory justice fail to conform to Aristotle's general account of excellence of character, not because the latter is defective, but because they are not excellences of character along with the rest. To be a just distributor or rectifier one needs to have many excellences of character and plenty of wisdom, *but there is not a specific state of character which is displayed in acting as a judge.* This sort of justice is what Hume called an artificial, not a natural, virtue. To conform to it is to conform to certain social rules of distribution and there is no special motive for their observance or breach, Hume's "natural" virtues are, his "artificial" virtues are not, settled states in regard to specific emotions.[15]

On Urmson's account of Hume's distinction, there really is no need for a single virtue of justice at all in Aristotle's sense, because justice is best understood more as an external "conformity" to "rules of distribution" rather than the expression of a psychic state of character. I highly suspect many of the modern commentators possess such a Humean outlook (consciously or not).

This is an important clue as to why the contemporary discussion has moved so far away from the virtue of justice. Contemporary commentators essentially do not need the virtue of justice to do the same kind of explanatory work that Aristotle thought it needed to do with respect to *pleonexia*. In contrast with Aristotle's concern about justice as a virtue, the moderns tend to have a more *formal* conception of justice (focused on rights). It turns out this is neatly illustrated in the work of the *doyenne* of the modern virtue ethicists, Rosalind Hursthouse.

Hursthouse and Justice

In many ways Hursthouse's famous "Virtue Theory and Abortion" (1991)[16] set the terms for much of the modern virtue ethics movement which she later developed and deepened in her book *On Virtue Ethics* (1999).[17] In this book Hursthouse has a relatively short discussion of justice in which she mainly tries to justify the lack of a more substantial treatment of that virtue. While she takes "it as obvious that justice is a personal virtue," she declines to discuss it at length because "other virtues are more hospitable to the detailed elaboration of points." This, however, she does "not regard as a fault" because she is "writing about normative ethics, not political philosophy." Indeed, she says that she regards justice as a "corrupted topic" because "it has become all too common to allow a vague concept of justice and rights to encompass large areas of morality that virtue ethicists believe are better dealt with in terms of other, more concrete, virtues."[18]

This is telling because it suggests that she just does not think that the virtue of justice does much important explanatory work regarding the wrongness of particular acts. So while she does not deny that justice is a virtue, it seems largely superfluous in her system owing to its supposed vagueness and the putative greater specificity and concreteness of the other virtues. We saw above that Aristotle does not regard the specific virtue of justice as any vaguer than courage or temperance, etc. Rather, the analysis of (in)justice in terms of *pleonexia* precisely serves to specify the kind of psychic state (*hexis*) that justice is. On the other hand, if Hursthouse is like Williams in downplaying the moral significance of *pleonexia* it is hardly surprising that the virtue of justice will have less of a role to play in her conception of virtue ethics than the "other, more concrete, virtues."[19]

Regardless of her claim that justice is obviously a personal virtue, Hursthouse's work also suggests that she regards justice as belonging more to political philosophy than to "normative ethics." For instance, in "Virtue Theory and Abortion," she claims that the "rights and wrongs of laws prohibiting or permitting" abortion actually have nothing to do with the "*morality* of abortion" as such (234, emphasis in original).

> putting all questions about the justice or injustice of laws to one side, and supposing only that women have such a *moral right*, nothing follows from this supposition about the morality of abortion, according to virtue theory, once it is noted (*quite generally, not with particular reference to abortion*) that in exercising a moral right I can do something cruel, or callous, or selfish, light-minded, self-righteous, stupid, inconsiderate, disloyal, dishonest—that is, act viciously. . . . So whether women have a *moral right* to terminate their pregnancies is irrelevant within virtue theory, for it is irrelevant to the question "In having an abortion in these circumstances, would the agent be acting virtuously or viciously or neither?" (235, emphasis added)

I want to focus on Hursthouse's striking claim that we can have a *moral* right to do something that would nonetheless be vicious.

This earlier statement (from 1991) is largely in line with the above quoted claim (from 1999) that justice properly belongs to "political philosophy" as opposed to "normative ethics." This suggests a rather different understanding of the role of law and justice than we find in Aristotle. Indeed, in Book V he largely equates justice and following the law. In particular, Aristotle insists that it is a central function of the law to promote virtue.

> the bulk of the things that are lawful are the things that are ordered from complete virtue, since the law orders one to live in accord with each virtue, and forbids one to live in accord with each vice. And the things that tend to produce complete virtue are those of the ordinances of law that are enacted concerning education for the public. (1130b25)

Obviously, this Aristotelian conception of law is alien to contemporary liberal polities such as our own.[20] Presumably, when she makes these remarks Hursthouse has in mind a modern conception of law and political justice focused primarily on individual rights. Aristotle, on the other hand, regards the law, including the coercive power of the state, as fundamentally "educational"—i.e., central to the development of individual virtue. As such, for Aristotle the idea that someone might possess a legal—much less a *moral*—"right" to act viciously is incoherent.[21]

Taken together this illustrates how the conception of justice as a virtue has become diminished as questions of "political" (i.e, formal) justice become largely divorced from morality.[22] This is an expression of a fundamentally modern (liberal) conception of politics which is remote from Aristotle's moral anthropology in which there is a deep continuity between the ethical life and politics. Ultimately, he thinks that human flourishing (*eudaimonia*) is only possible in the context of the well-ordered (i.e, virtue-promoting) *polis*. As such, political justice and the virtue of justice are both complimentary and mutually necessary. The *polis* is both the training ground for virtue in the morally immature (not only children), but also the context within which the morally mature express virtue.[23]

What is curious about this is that elsewhere Hursthouse acknowledges this general point. For instance, in a paper attempting to derive a Hume-inspired account of rights that is nonetheless compatible with her virtue ethics she acknowledges that "[r]ights-based theories avowedly attempt to draw a sharp line between political and moral philosophy, to allow for a pluralism in society of widely differing 'comprehensive' moral views. . . . But a *eudaimonia*-based account draws no such line, seeing the investigation of ethics and political science as continuous."[24] So she is clearly aware of the deep tension between the modern liberal conception of rights and the Aristotelian understanding of how the development of the virtues in individual citizens require the exercise of coercive political power to promote a specific "comprehensive" or special conception of the good. It is a mystery to me then how she can so calmly assure us that there is "no reason to believe that a *eudaimonia*-based account of rights would wind up denying the existence of many of the rights dear to the hearts of contemporary liberals,"[25] insofar as those liberal rights include (as I think most liberal theorists believe) rights to activity that would clearly count as vicious on the Aristotelian account.[26]

My general suspicion is that Hursthouse simply wants to have her cake and eat it too. She remarks frankly that while it "would be anachronistic to look for the liberal concept of rights in Aristotle . . . yet many of us are unwilling to declare shamelessly that we want no truck with liberalism and to follow MacIntyre in espousing traditionalist authoritarianism."[27] What exactly is meant by "traditionalist authoritarianism" she does not explain, but the simple fact of the matter is, as we have already seen, Aristotle's conception of the deep connection between individual virtue and the *spoudaios polis* is incompatible with a robust liberal notion of individual rights. That, of course, does not make Aristotle correct, but it does make Hursthouse's irenicism between the Aristotelian and liberal conceptions of justice seem almost glib.

As a whole, Aristotle's understanding of the virtues, including the virtue of justice, is much more tightly integrated than what we find in modern virtue ethics.[28] Given what we have seen above it should not be surprising that Hursthouse makes no real mention of the particular moral virtue of justice in her Hume-inspired account. Ultimately this is of a piece with how Hursthouse presents modern virtue ethics as a third way of doing "normative ethics" (on a par with, and playing by the same rules as, deontology and consequentialism). Insofar as modern "virtue theory" is meant to be a species of the genus "normative ethics," it fails to be the same kind of integrated ethical/political approach we find in Aristotle.[29]

Conclusions

It goes without saying that there is a great deal more to be said about both Aristotle's understanding of the virtue of justice and the conception of justice in modern virtue ethics. However, I do think we now have enough to give some concrete answers to our original question of how one of four cardinal virtues of the classical tradition has become so diminished in the contemporary virtues discussion.

In short, modern virtue ethics downplays the role of the *virtue* of justice compared to Aristotle (and the classical tradition) because the modern theorists have a significantly different understanding of both the virtues in general and justice in particular. As we saw above, Aristotle shares the general Greek concern with *pleonexia* as the passion that specifies the nature of the virtue of justice. In contrast, modern commentators like Bernard Williams deny the centrality of *pleonexia* to injustice, and thus regard Aristotle's corresponding conception of justice as flawed. The moderns tend to focus instead on justice more as a formal (political) concern about fairness and individual rights, and as a such do not give the *virtue* of justice much of a role to play in their theories.

Similarly, in Hursthouse's discussion of justice we saw that while she was willing to pay lip service to the claim that justice is a personal virtue, she nonetheless regards justice as a hopelessly "vague" and indeed "corrupt" concept. In particular, and most important for our purposes here, it is clear that she does not regard the virtue of justice as having a central *explanatory* function in her conception of virtue ethics. In other words, she does not really need justice to explain the wrongness of particular acts because she thinks "other, more concrete, virtues" are more helpful.[30]

It is worth noting that my conclusion here is a limited one; I have only sought to explain *why* modern virtue ethics diminishes the virtue of justice. I have argued that the main reason is that the modern commentators (even ones like Hursthouse who constantly advert to him) have a fundamentally different conception of justice than Aristotle, and as such they do not actually have much *explanatory* need for the particular moral virtue of justice within their theories. What I have *not* tried to do is argue that Aristotle's view is superior (or vice versa, for that matter). Nonetheless, I hope it is now apparent that there is a fundamental discontinuity between a genuinely Aristotelian ethics and the modern virtue ethics that presents itself as a third way alternative to deontology and consequentialism within the genus "normative ethics."

As it happens, I am convinced that Coope is correct that the contemporary attempt to make virtue ethics into a third way fails to recognize just how radical Anscombe's original indictment of modern moral philosophy really was. In contrast with Anscombe's "disconcerting" claims, he notes that "[m]odern virtue ethics has become something soothing, edifying and familiar. It has grown up in the polluted atmosphere of contemporary expectations (assumptions, presuppositions, confusions, distractions) and naturally has quickly become tarnished by them."[31] Instead, Anscombe originally "wanted to reject 'the moral' in its present-day use, as marking a special category of obligation or permission" which would in turn make Anscombe's view "quite incommensurable" with both consequentialism and deontology. Indeed, properly understood Anscombe "would not be offering a better answer to the question" that these modern approaches pose; rather she "would be rejecting" that question altogether.[32]

In some ways, I suspect the modern virtue ethicists will be largely unmoved by this complaint. After all, they might claim that their goal is not to reanimate Aristotle's ethics as a whole, but to speak to modern ethical questions using insights inspired by Aristotle, without the baggage of his putatively outmoded metaphysics and natural philosophy.[33] I strongly doubt that such a project is ultimately coherent, but that is a much larger question and beyond the scope of our discussion here. In any case, I hope that we have at least gone some way to explaining why the erstwhile "queen of the virtues" has been deposed in the modern virtue ethics.[34]

University of St. Thomas (MN)

Notes

1. All the Aristotle translations in this paper are from Aristotle, *Nicomachean Ethics*, trans. Joe Sachs (Newburyport, MA: Focus Publishing, 2002). I prefer Sachs for his attempt to remain as close to the Greek as possible, even when that means the English is sometimes infelicitous.

2. Christopher Miles Coope, "Modern Virtue Ethics," in *Values and Virtues: Aristotelianism in Contemporary Ethics*, ed. T. Chappell (Oxford; New York: Oxford University Press, 2007), 20.

3. See Rosalind Hursthouse, "Virtue Ethics," in *The Stanford Encyclopedia of Philosophy* (Fall 2013), ed. Edward N. Zalta, http://plato.stanford.edu/archives/fall2013/entries/ethics-virtue/.

4. See also Coope, "Modern Virtue Ethics."

5. Ibid., 41. Coope was writing in 2007 so we might wonder whether the matter has improved significantly in the meanwhile. As it happens Hursthouse's 2012 revision of her entry in the *Stanford Encyclopedia of Philosophy* on "Virtue Ethics" contains precisely four uses of the word 'justice' in an article of over 6000 words.

6. David K. O'Connor, "Aristotelian Justice as a Personal Virtue," *Midwest Studies in Philosophy* 13 (1988): 417.

7. Aristotle, *Nicomachean Ethics*, 2nd ed., trans. Terrence Irwin (Indianapolis, Indiana: Hackett Publishing Company, 1999), 340–341. G. M. A. Grube and C. D. C. Reeve try capture it as a kind of desire to "out do" others. The Liddell-Scott-Jones dictionary entry defines it as "greediness, assumption, arrogance," with a secondary sense of "one's own advantage" and a tertiary sense of "excess."

8. Bernard Williams, "Justice as a Virtue," in *Moral Luck* (Cambridge, UK: Cambridge University Press, 1981), 91, emphasis added.

9. He claims that the "disposition of justice will lead the just person to resist unjust distributions—and to resist them *however they are motivated*" (Williams, "Justice as a Virtue," 90, emphasis in original).

10. O'Connor, "Aristotelian Justice as a Personal Virtue," 420.

11. Aristotle himself supplies the following example: "if one person commits adultery for the sake of making a profit, gaining that in addition, while the other gives money and takes the loss on account of desire, the latter would seem to be dissipated rather than greedy, but the former would seem to be unjust and not dissipated; therefore it is clear that the injustice comes from making the profit" (1130a26). Obviously, the adulterer is unjust in the general sense in both cases, but if he commits the adultery because of sexual desire he is "dissipated" rather than unjust properly speaking. It is worth remembering that Aristotle chooses adultery (along with stealing and murder) as one of the actions that "as soon as they are named are understood as having baseness involved with them" (1107a10) about which there is "never any possibility of getting anything right about them" (1107a15).

12. Plato, *Republic*, 2nd ed., trans. G. M. A. Grube (Indianapolis: Hackett Publishing Company, 1992), 20, n.18. I am not sure if this note is from G. M. A. Grube (the translator of this edition) or C. D. C. Reeve (who edited and revised it); Reeve says "many of the notes" in this edition are new, but he does not seem to mark which are new and which are original. Obviously, what is most important here is the observation about the role of *pleonexia* in the *Republic*, whichever of them produced it. In any case, Thrasymachus first identifies justice with *pleonexia* in Book I (344a) and Socrates attacks Thrasymachus's view with an extended argument (349b–350c). Glaucon, with the famous ring of Gyges' ancestor example, then returns to the claim that anybody with power to express *pleonexia* would do so (359c) which is the lead in to the construction of the City in Speech at the end of which Socrates identifies justice with the opposite of *pleonexia* insofar as "each one of us in whom each part is doing its own work will himself be just and do his own" (441e).

13. I say "typified" because as O'Connor points out Williams and Philippa Foot share the same basic conception of justice, see O'Connor, "Aristotelian Justice as a Personal Virtue," 419–422.

14. Ibid.; David K. O'Connor, "The Aetiology of Justice," in *Essays on the Foundations of Aristotelian Political Science*, ed. Carnes Lord and David K. O'Connor (Oxford: University of California Press, 1988), 136–164; and especially Shane Drefcinski, "Aristotle and the Characteristic Desire of Justice," *Apeiron* 33.2 (2000): 109–123, do defend the Aristotelian position from Williams (and other related) criticisms.

15. James O. Urmson, "Aristotle's Doctrine of the Mean," *American Philosophical Quarterly* 10.3 (1973), 227, emphasis added.

16. Rosalind Hursthouse, "Virtue Theory and Abortion," *Philosophy and Public Affairs* 20.3 (1991): 223–246.

17. Rosalind Hursthouse, *On Virtue Ethics* (Oxford; New York: Oxford University Press, 1999).

18. Ibid., 5–6.

19. Recognizing that the virtues are *hexeis* for Aristotle is actually deeply important for understanding the role of the virtues in his moral psychology in general, and for how the agent is the efficient cause of his actions in particular. Modern virtue ethicists tend to gloss over these issues of causation (though, to be fair, so do their consequentialist and deontological

counterparts in "normative ethics"); Aristotle, on the other hand, does not. I discuss the importance of recognizing that the virtues are *hexeis* in "*Hexis* within Aristotelian Virtue Ethics," *Proceedings of the American Catholic Philosophical Association* 88 (2014): 197–206.

20. To be clear, I use 'liberal' here in the sense of "liberal democracy." The difference in Aristotle's approach to the polis is aptly captured in his casual remark late in Book V that "what [the law] does not condone it forbids" (*NE* 1138a6). Indeed, this remark comes in the context of an example he gives against the legality of suicide, which is particularly apt given the modern decriminalization of suicide, and indeed the contemporary demand for the expansion of euthanasia. It makes a kind of perverse sense that a supposed right to kill oneself should become one of the highest expressions of autonomy in the contemporary context. In the Aristotelian *polis*, however, the common good could be no more served by a "right" to suicide than a "right" to cowardice (and indeed largely for the same sorts of reasons).

21. Of course the entire language of "rights" is itself alien to Aristotle, so it is not entirely clear that Aristotle could even make sense of the notion of an individual right in this sense at all. In fact, the modern obsession with "rights" is another measure of the distance between modern political theory and Aristotle. Alasdair MacIntyre's famous rejection of the idea of individual rights in *After Virtue* is *apropos* here: the "best reason for asserting so bluntly that there are no such rights is indeed of precisely the same type as the best reason which we possess for asserting that there are no witches and the best reason which we possess for asserting that there are no unicorns: every attempt to give good reasons for believing that there are such rights has failed" (Alasdair MacIntyre, *After Virtue*, 3rd ed. [Notre Dame, IN: University of Notre Dame Press, 2007], 69). Of course, the later Christian tradition does include a discussion of rights, though that is more derived from Stoic sources (Fulvio Di. Blasi, "Practical Syllogism, Proairesis, and the Virtues: Toward a Reconciliation of Virtue Ethics and Natural Law Ethics," *Nova et Vetera* 1 [2004]: 21–41). In the end, whether there is some way to reconcile the modern concept of rights with Aristotelian virtue ethics is itself a fascinating question, but one well beyond the scope of our discussion here.

22. The examples could be multiplied *ad nauseam*, but this is of course one of the fundamental principles of modern secular (putative) neutrality and the key notion behind the Rawlsian demand that special conceptions of the good (i.e, morality) cannot justly inform public policy.

23. In the *Politics*, Aristotle says that the "excellent" (*spoudaia*) *polis* is excellent precisely because its citizens are *spoudaios* (morally serious) and the "matter we have to investigate, therefore, is how a man becomes *spoudaios*" (1332a35). This shows again the deep connection of political virtue and individual virtue in Aristotle's understanding; the two cannot be separated. I discuss this in "Getting Serious about Seriousness: Aristotle on the meaning of Spoudaios," *Proceedings of the American Catholic Philosophical Association* 87 (2013): 285–293.

24. Rosalind Hursthouse, "After Hume's Justice," *Proceedings of the Aristotelian Society* 91 (1991): 245.

25. Ibid.

26. This may be most easily seen in the modern liberal preoccupation with rights to engage in activities contrary to the virtue of chastity (e.g., pornography, etc.), but this is a much more general point. As Hursthouse herself admits, the structure of modern liberal theories of justice, unlike Aristotle's, requires the possibility that "a just society can be a wicked one" (ibid., 244).

27. Ibid., 229.

28. Another way in which modern virtue ethics fails to express this deep integration between the virtues is the tepid view of the so-called unity of the virtues in modern accounts. Aristotle essentially argues in Book VI of the *Ethics* that "all virtues will be present together when the one virtue, practical judgment, is present" (*NE* 1145a2). In contrast with this robust unity in Aristotle, Hursthouse is only able to bring herself to accept a "limited" or "weak unity thesis" that simultaneously recognizes the fact that practical wisdom cannot occur in discrete packages, limited in its area of competence to just this virtue or that, and also the fact that it is not an all-or-nothing matter. According to this thesis, anyone who possesses one virtue will have all the other to some degree, albeit, in some cases, a pretty limited one (Hursthouse, *On Virtue Ethics*, 156). I suspect the deep reason for this is that Aristotle takes a much more robust view about the fundamental nature of the virtues as efficient causes in his moral psychology than do modern writers like Hursthouse, who mainly prescind from these sorts of issues in common with their fellow practitioners of "normative ethics."

29. As I have already noted, in Aristotle this integration goes "down" into moral psychology as well as "up" into politics. That is, Aristotle's account of the moral virtues as *hexeis* (active psychic conditions/states) is continuous with his analysis of the nature of the human act as efficiently caused by the human agent through the practical syllogism. For an account of the physical nature of the human act see Kevin L. Flannery, *Action and Character According to Aristotle* (Washington, D.C.: The Catholic University of America Press, 2013); for an account of the agent as efficient cause through the practical syllogism see Di Blasi, "Practical Syllogism, Proairesis, and the Virtues: Toward a Reconciliation of Virtue Ethics and Natural Law Ethics."

30. Coope offers an excellent example of this tendency in Hursthouse. Referring to Hursthouse's discussion of justice in *On Virtue Ethics*, Coope notes: "Lying is not unjust, it is dishonest, says Hursthouse firmly, the italics bristling on the page. And though murder might indeed be unjust, we should not be too impressed by that: 'What is wrong with killing, when it is wrong, may be not so much that it is unjust, violating the right to life, but, frequently, that it is callous and contrary to the virtue of charity'" (Coope, "Modern Virtue Ethics," 44).

31. Coope, "Modern Virtue Ethics," 31.

32. See ibid., 39.

33. Interestingly this is parallel with another group of contemporary commentators—the New Natural Lawyers—who also seek to speak to modern concerns with insights drawn from the tradition, but without taking on the entire metaethical and metaphysical structure that informed that tradition. On whether this is a tenable strategy see the "Critiques of the New Natural Law Theory" issue of *The National Catholic Bioethics Quarterly* 13.1 (2013).

34. *Phronesis* (prudence) is more commonly (and properly, from an Aristotelian point of view) identified as the queen of the virtues, but there is a tradition of giving that title to justice; see, for instance, Cicero (*De Officiis*, 3).

Augustine and Aquinas on Demonic Possession: *Theoria* and *Praxis*[1]

Seamus O'Neill

Abstract: Augustine asserted that demons (and angels) have material bodies, while Aquinas denied demonic corporeality, upholding that demons are separated, incorporeal, intelligible substances. Augustine's conception of demons as composite substances possessing an immaterial soul and an aerial body is insufficient, in Thomas's view, to account for certain empirical phenomena observed in demoniacs. However, Thomas, while providing more detailed accounts of demonic possession according to his development of Aristotelian psychology, does not avail of this demonic incorporeal eminence when analysing demonic attacks: demonic agency is still confined to the material body. Aquinas's account of demonic possession need not, on the face of it, require an immaterial cause. In his renouncement of the strong Christian tradition affirming demonic corporeality, Aquinas either conflates the need for a demonic agent with a requirement for a super corporeal one, or subordinates his demonology and angelology to a deeper, more fundamental Dionysian metaphysical principle of creative diffusion to which these adhere in a secondary way.

I. Introduction

The more I study the demonologies of the ancient and medieval philosophers, the more I feel that they are rather like Eliza Doolittle. They have been extirpated from their worlds, or at best have been sterilized, legitimatized, and made presentable for contemporary academic discussion by many a philosophical Higgins. Philosophers who realize that philosophy began before the twentieth century recognised that St. Augustine, Aristotle, and Boethius have something interesting and important to say within sundry compartmentalized philosophical discussions, but vast amounts of their writings are ignored by philosophers of all stripes. When Lucifer rears his head in a heady medieval discussion on the agent intellect, and when Beelzebub pops round during a meticulous scholastic excursus on natural law, we all look the other way in embarrassment while the devils are curtly tucked away and poked back under the bed. At worst the demons

© 2017, *Proceedings of the ACPA*, Vol. 90
doi: 10.5840/acpaproc201822880

pp. 133–147

are ignored; at best, they are psychologized and demythologized, as a report for the Sacred Congregation for the Doctrine of the Faith from the 1970s lamented, in our day "the name of Satan and of the devil are only mythical or functional personifications, the significance of which is solely to underline in a dramatic fashion the hold which evil and sin have on mankind."[2]

But I wonder: can the views, reasonings, purposes, and worries of the medievals surrounding of any piece of philosophical argument really be understood outside of the context of their worlds? Once one's cosmos contains demons, everything seems to change. When we fail to realize this, we cease to attain to anything but a superficial and piecemeal grasp of these philosophers and theologians. The narrow spotlight might suffice for certain and limited philosophical purposes, but it fails to illuminate the minds and overall systems of these figures.

Herein I hope to show some of the implications of demonology for philosophy (and vice-versa) by focusing on just one small part of one singular aspect of their relation. We will look at some accounts of demonic possession, and how, metaphysically and according to natural philosophy, it might occur. We will narrow in here on the explanations of Saints Augustine and Thomas Aquinas, to show how their different premises regarding the nature of the demonic body affect their explanations and understandings of the phenomenon. Augustine asserted that demons (and angels) have material bodies, while Aquinas, for reasons that I will briefly explain, denied demonic corporeality, upholding that demons are separated, incorporeal, intelligible substances. The latter's view became foundational for current Catholic demonic ontology.

While Augustine and Aquinas are important authorities for each view, how demons lost their bodies in Christian demonology, however, is a story involving more characters and plot turns than can be narrated here. But hopefully, by examining the controversy over the demonic body and its metaphysical implications, I might illustrate how the demonologies of these figures are imbedded within their overall philosophical and theological enterprises and how each affects and is affected by the other. Though Thomas cites demonic possession as a reason to prefer the thesis that demons do not have bodies, ultimately, demonic incorporeality does not radically distinguish the Thomistic from the Augustinian explanations of demonic possession.

II. The Demonic Body

Augustine believed, as did his Hellenic and Christian contemporaries, that demons possess a physical body composed of air.[3] Though Peter Lombard claims that during his time it was disputed whether or not Augustine actually believed this or thought that demons were incorporeal beings, multiple references throughout Augustine's works demonstrate his conviction that demons possess aerial bodies, a conviction that grounds much of Augustine's conceptions of demonic epistemology and agency.[4] Augustine explains how demons exploit the nature of their bodies to traverse quickly great distances, remain invisible, appear to foretell the future, and even to possess human bodies.[5] The initially miraculous nature of demonic agency is reduced to demonic biology—given their airy nature, their abilities follow naturally.

Augustine's works are laden with such examples, indicating how important the demonic body is to his demonological explanations. Furthermore, demonic agency and epistemology are more easily explainable if demons are understood to be somehow physical. The doctrine of the demonic body grounds the demonology of Augustine and others who share the thesis, allowing for naturalistic, common-sense, and down-to-earth explanations for otherwise mysterious and supernatural phenomena.

However, current Catholic dogma maintains that demons and angels are incorporeal intelligences, separated from any kind of material body. The shift in doctrine from material angels and demons to incorporeal ones seems to have come about mainly because of the influence of the Pseudo-Dionysius. Transmitted under the great authority of the Areopagite, the position came to Albert the Great and Aquinas, who also concurred that demons and angels are separated substances. Once the Angelic Doctor weighed in on the matter, no one else, it seems, seriously defended the contrary view.[6]

Aquinas argues that demons are separated intelligences and holds that they are "spiritual substances not united to bodies."[7] It is important to note that much expositional power in the realm of demonological explanation is lost along with the abandonment of the demonic body. Aquinas must have something rather more important to gain by dismissing the explanatory force of the material thesis. In the *Summa Theologiae*, Aquinas identifies the doctrine of demonic materiality with the Platonists. According to Thomas, Augustine did not hold this view, but rather, believed what Thomas believes: demons are immaterial substances. Although Thomas raises Augustine as an authority for the materiality of demons in Question 51 of the *Prima Pars*, he says that Augustine only cites the view, not that he holds it himself.[8]

But while Aquinas writes plenty about the nature of these separated intelligences, he does not elaborate very far on *why* he thinks there must *be* such beings. Primarily, the existence of the Devil and his minions is a theological fact, confirmed by Scripture, and indeed, by the very words of our Lord. In addition to this theological premise, however, one gleans from Thomas's discussions two additional reasons to affirm the existence of incorporeal demons: the first more philosophical, and the second more practical and empirical. The first is the Neoplatonic principle of plenitude, or what Fran O'Rourke has called "creative diffusion," and the second is that the empirical phenomena needing to be explained surrounding sorcery and demonic possession require these particularly discarnate agents.[9] Here, I explore the second reason: Aquinas defends demonic immateriality because he thinks that no material cause is sufficient to produce the portents needing to be explained concerning demonic possession and sorcery. He claims, "in such cases, there are manifestly certain works which cannot in any way be reduced to a corporeal cause."[10] But it is not clear why if one grants the existence of demons that they must also be bodiless. The old view was good enough for the Christians and Platonists until the Pseudo-Dionysius, Aquinas's go-to authority on the immateriality of demons. It was good enough, indeed, for Tertullian, Augustine, and all of the pagan authorities that the Doctor of Grace marshals in support for his own cause. Further, Augustine attempts to account for the very incidents that Aquinas tries to explain, but does so with *embodied* rather than *bodiless* demons. Need demons be immaterial to unravel these mysteries?

III. Augustine on Demonic Possession

While Augustine periodically mentions demonic possession throughout his works, he goes into detail about the phenomenon in the *Literal Commentary on Genesis*—not about the possession of a human being, but rather, the Devil's seizure of the serpent in the Garden of Eden, yet here we gain insight into how Augustine views demonic possession generally. Augustine understands the serpent to be a regular snake, not the Devil in disguise or some chimerical apparition.[11] Of course Augustine also knows that snakes cannot speak because they lack reason, as well as the required physiology. Nevertheless, the serpent converses with Eve. Augustine explains:

> [When we speak of 'cunning tongues,' it is] not a power or capacity of the bodily organ which is called a tongue, but of course of the mind which is making use of it. In the same way the typewriters of journalists can be said to lie; while lying, you see, only falls in the province of living and sentient beings, the typewriter is said to lie because a liar spreads his lies by means of it. Indeed this serpent could be called a liar, because the devil used it like a typewriter to spread his lies.[12]

Here, it seems, the Devil physically manipulates the snake like a kind of ventriloquist dummy. The serpent neither understands what it says, nor comprehends the words it hears.[13] Augustine writes, "it was the devil himself who spoke in the serpent, using it like an organ, and moving its nature to give expression to the verbal sounds and bodily gestures by which the woman would be made to understand what he wished to persuade her to do."[14] The snake is physically manipulated by the Devil, who wields its body in a material manner.

If one believes that demons exist as natural creatures enjoying the properties of the aerial body and long lifespan, Augustine's explanation is entirely naturalistic and materialistic. In the same text, he also writes about snake charmers, and suspects that demons control their pets, making them appear to respond to human commands. In fact, he says that demons have a singular familiarity with serpents going back to Eden, and so it is no wonder that they are so adept at managing them: practice makes perfect! Similarly, the demon's physical control of the demoniac's body is accounted for by an appeal to the corporeal nature of the demonic body. The demon physically moves the human body just as it would any other physical object, and, as with the snake, it can speak through the human body foreign languages unknown to the possessed.

In the discussion, however, Augustine cites another accompanying symptom of demonic possession, identified in both serpentine and human victims: the possessed are unaware of their gestures and discussions while seized by the demon. The snake neither understood Eve's speech, nor, Augustine writes, "is it to be supposed that its soul was turned into one of a rational nature, seeing that not even human beings, who are rational by nature, know what they are saying when a demon is speaking in them in that condition for which an exorcist is required."[15] The possessed's consciousness is 'shut off' during the demonic manipulation: perception, speech, and thought cease to be within the subject's command.

While the demon's ability to ply the demoniac's body is understood by Augustine in physical, mechanistic terms, as the airy body works human flesh, what transpires on the mental plane is rather more mysterious. How can the demon affect thought when thinking is not a material operation? The demonic affect on the soul's consciousness, being immaterial, cannot be analysed in the same manner. Augustine has no definitive answer, though he recognises explicitly the difficulty:

> It is not in the least surprising . . . if those who have a demon sometimes say true things which are not apparent to the senses of bystanders. This must certainly happen by heaven knows what hidden mingling of spirits, so that it is as if there is just one spirit of sufferer and tormentor.[16]

Here, Augustine uses the spatial language of mingling. Elsewhere, he suggests that the demon can circumvent or supervene upon the activity of the human soul. Augustine asks, "And what shall I say of those who suffer from demoniacal possession? Where is their own intelligence hidden and buried while the malignant spirit is using their body and soul according to his own will?"[17]

Even here, however, Augustine seems to think according to spatial and local categories. The demon enters in a material, visceral manner, as the aerial constitution merges with the fleshy human form, seizing in a mechanistic way direct control of the body.[18] However, the devil further spreads by some occult power into the immaterial aspects of the human soul. For example, Augustine writes, "the fine, rarefied nature of their bodies enables them to penetrate the bodies of human beings unperceived, unfelt, and to mix themselves into their thoughts, whether they are asleep or awake, through visions intruded into their imaginations."[19] The demon can "pass unhindered through our bodies" to affect our limbs, and seemingly, even our introspective cogitation.[20] Augustine admits that it is obscure business to determine how the demon can divine our thoughts, and if they enter somehow physically, why we cannot 'see' them in our minds.[21]

Nevertheless, Augustine takes it as an empirical fact that demons can divine human thought, and he is convinced of it. Despite these more arcane speculations concerning how demons read human minds during the invasive seizure of the human being during the extraordinary demonic activity of possession, Augustine's more detailed accounts of how demons generally become aware of our introspective life in their ordinary activity return to the more naturalistic and reductive. Augustine argues that given the keen perception and swift movement that demons possess in virtue of the nature of the aerial body and the long span of their lives, demons have knowledge beyond what the human can attain.[22] Just as people can sometimes divine others' thoughts by paying attention to their facial expressions and tone of voice, so too can demons "read the signs by which 'body language' gives away the mind's intentions, and from this source of information too they forecast many future events, which amazes others who have no previous knowledge of these plans."[23]

Augustine's explanation of these symptoms of demonic possession—control over the body, knowing hidden things, and even the ability to override the human soul's 'access' to its body—are explicitly and generally accounted for by an appeal to the material nature of the demonic body. However, he does often speak in ways that suggest an incorporeal mingling. How demonic and human union on the non-physical plane occurs (if at all) is arcane, and perhaps impenetrable, and in the *Retractions*, Augustine appears to walk back his more physical explanations and leaves open the possibility that there is a more occult power at work in demonic possession.[24] On what this other power might be, Augustine does not speculate further.

IV. Aquinas on Demonic Possession

With the Augustinian context in mind, we now turn to the demonology of St. Thomas. Aquinas represents the solidification of the doctrine of demonic incorporeality. His position is clearly articulated and grounded philosophically and theologically, and he mentions, cites, and takes issue with various contemporary and earlier experts. The Pseudo-Dionysius is Aquinas's main authority for demonic and angelic incorporeality, specifically the text of *Div. Nom.* 4, though cited supporters also include Avicenna, Averroës, and Pseudo-Aristotle, the author of the *Liber de causis*. The revolution in demonic ontology occurs before Thomas, but it is he who works out its ramifications in explicit detail, particularly in the realm of demonic agency and possession.

It is important to remember that for Aquinas, angels and demons, sharing a similar nature, have the same natural abilities: "Therefore, regarding their natural power, devils can do the same things that good angels can, since both have the same nature."[25] Thus, the careful reader can often glean certain details about the one from Thomas's comments about the other. Though there are important differences between the two kinds as a result of the angelic fall and confirmation, often what is said of an angel is true of the demon and vice versa.

Like Augustine, Aquinas also weighs in on the demon's ability to manipulate matter, an apparent pre-requisite for possession to transpire. Augustine's explanation of this fact of demonic agency is, to the extent that he speculates on the phenomenon in his works, materialistic and mechanistic. Aquinas, however, because he denies the demonic body, has some extra work to do. He argues that angels and demons are not in place bodily, but rather, are present where they activate their powers, much like how Descartes explains that the soul is not actually *in* the pineal gland, a common misconception, but in fact, the particular gland is the locus where the soul actualises its influence in space. When we say that Gabriel is in Mary's house, or Raphael strolled along beside Tobias, what we really point to is the location of the activation of angelic power, not their extended presence in space.[26]

In fact, for Aquinas, the want of a material body is not a restriction at all, but rather, its lack provides angels greater dominion over the material world since they are not shackled by corporeal confines.[27] Aquinas writes, "But an angel's power is not limited to any body; hence it can move locally bodies not joined to it," unlike us, who have direct control only over our own bodies.[28] The demons' greater mastery over matter can cause in the demoniac grotesque facial and bodily contortions, levitation, as well as other horrific events: unearthly howls, guttural voices, and flying objects, often associated with the activity of poltergeists, which amaze and terrify. In general, angels and demons can still affect the physical world and move material bodies, even though they are not corporeally in the world.

As Aquinas explains, "whatever can be caused by the local movement of bodies is subject to the natural power of the angels."[29] Thus, the ability of an angel or demon to manoeuvre a human body is rather unproblematic given the demonic nature; it's no different than moving any other material thing. Aquinas requires more steps to explain this aspect of demonic possession than does Augustine, since Thomas has to show how non-corporeal entities can act in place, but he does it, and how immaterial substances affect matter is, in the end, a question needing to be answered by anyone who affirms that the human is a union of a corporeal body and an immaterial soul.

The bigger obstacle is not grasping how the demon physically operates the possessed, about which we will say no more here.[30] Rather, it is fathoming how a demon dominates the demoniac's intellective powers. As Aquinas notes in reference to the *City of God* (19.4), "Augustine says that devils . . . sometimes prevent the use of reason in human beings, as is evident in the case of the possessed."[31] In the *ST*, Thomas asserts that the devil, by his own power, can compel anyone to an *act* of sin (defined as an inordinate act) unless God restrains him, though such an act is not necessarily sinful unless the person wills it. While the devil can coerce a *body* to do whatever he pleases, Aquinas asserts that "man does not resist that which moves him to sin, except by his reason."[32] If reason is not fettered, one can resist internally, and thus remain morally blameless, even if one is powerless to thwart the bodily assault. Aquinas chillingly warns, however, that "the devil is able to impede [the use of reason] altogether, by moving the imagination and the sensitive appetite; as is the case with one who is possessed."[33]

Aquinas's explanation of how the demon can affect and arrest the faculty of reason in an incorporeal soul is explained according to his Aristotelian epistemology and psychology. Although the intellect, or *nous*, does not operate through a bodily organ for Aristotle, nevertheless, the power relies upon sensation, which does require physical implements to provide the material with which the intellect operates.[34] Thus, the demon can affect our thought, though not directly, either by presenting it with real objects in the world through the manipulation of the seeds of things, as Augustine explains and Thomas reiterates, or it can manipulate the material organs of the body themselves on which perception and intellect depend. According to Aquinas, "Evident signs and experiences make it apparent that devils' activities manifest things sensibly perceptible to human beings."[35]

Aquinas maintains that demons, despite their incorporeality, do not enter the mind, since the mind is not properly 'a place' to be entered, but rather, they physically manipulate the external sensibles and internal organs that the mind uses to operate. Even while dreaming, for example, the imaginative power can make us 'see' people walking about the square when our eyes are really shut tight as we snuggle in our beds: we see, hear, smell, taste, and touch all manner of things that are not present materially. The imagination can affect the sensible principle insofar as these images are, though derived from the senses, preserved in the imagination. The imagination, an internal sense, having retained the impressed species from the common sense, produces the expressed species, or phantasm. This can even happen to people who are awake in the case of madness. In a reverse order, the phantasms in the imagination move the apprehensive principle, whereby the sense organs 'sense' and cause the perception of things that are not really there. Demons, therefore, can directly manipulate the 'inner senses' to produce various affects within the possessed's perception.[36] They cause demoniacs to perceive chimeras, not by creating the image in the imagination directly, which they cannot do, but by manipulating the "spirits and humors to produce the desired affect."[37] Fundamentally, anything material is up for grabs, and thereby, anything associated with that matter can be influenced, even if not directly manipulated. Yet, the demon has no direct access to the incorporeal reason and will; there is no 'mingling' of the demonic immaterial, separated substance with the incorporeal, formal principle (the rational soul) of the human being.[38]

While the devil has the power, if left unchecked by God, to physically bend a human being to do whatever it wishes, it cannot make one necessarily sin, since it cannot control the will. The will is sacrosanct and cannot, like the inner senses, be directly affected. One's inner predilection is still hidden to the demon, and while it tampers with the matter of one's body, the Devil cannot scrutinize one's inner life; "the inward disposition of man God alone knows."[39] While the demon certainly longs to exploit our thoughts and desires to its own ends, as we read in C. S. Lewis's *Screwtape Letters*, its evidence of these is external and empirical. Aquinas explains, "It is [his] disposition that makes man more prone to one vice than to another: hence the devil tempts, in order to explore this inward disposition of man, so that he may tempt him to that vice to which he is most prone."[40] Just as the demon cannot directly alter one's reason, neither can it alter the will. However, it has access to and control over the matter on which our reason and desires depend. Thus, Aquinas writes, "Although a demon cannot a change the will, yet, as stated above (*ST* I.111.3), he can change the inferior powers of man in a certain degree: by which powers, though the will cannot be forced, it can nevertheless be inclined."[41] Aquinas has a more detailed explanation than does Augustine of the mental aspects of demonic possession, which takes more explicit advantage of Aristotelian psychology, yet there is no argument addressing why demons must be particularly incorporeal to engage in this nefarious and unnerving activity. The demon's direct manipulation is confined to the material realm, and the explanations of the symptoms of demonic possession are worked out from within this restriction.

V. Conclusion

To sum up, while Aquinas denies the demonic body, going so far as to argue anachronistically that Augustine so too denied it, he nevertheless expands upon the material aspects of demonic agency and epistemology along the lines of Augustine's explanations. Yet, Augustine's conception of demons as composite substances possessing an immaterial soul and an aerial or ethereal body is insufficient, in Thomas's view, to account for certain empirical phenomena observed in the possessed and the works of sorcery.

The Thomistic position is limited, however, insofar as it is not clear why demonic beings need to be immaterial to be able to aid magicians in their sorcery and to possess human bodies, since Thomas, while providing more detailed accounts according to his development of Aristotelian psychology, does not avail of the demonic ontological incorporeal eminence when analysing demonic attacks: demonic agency is still confined to the material body of the human being. Aquinas's account of demonic possession, such as it is, need not, on the face of it, require an immaterial cause;[42] he conflates the need for a demonic agent with a requirement for a super corporeal one, i.e., a separated intelligible substance. Also, Aquinas renounces the strong Christian tradition affirming the existence of demonic bodies.

Maybe it is my personal penchant for Augustine or for less metaphysically expensive explanations, but I still find it difficult to assess the benefit of exiling the demonic body from demonological ontology. Thomas works out elegantly the metaphysics and philosophy of nature of immaterial substances, but I find myself unconvinced as to why this is all necessary to begin with. One gets the feeling that he need not have bothered if he just posited demonic bodies as did his forebears. Granted, I have not witnessed the phenomena that Aquinas thinks require there to be immaterial causes, but demonic immateriality seems to me a solution looking for a problem. Further, much explanatory force of the Augustinian type, suggested at the start of this paper, is lost (or at least complicated) in the process.

Finally, one who denies angelic and demonic existence altogether still must somehow account for the events that Augustine and Aquinas attribute to their agency, and supply other explanations, either supernatural, or naturalistic. Scoffing at demonological passages or dismissing them as amusing oddities, relics of the age, without serious consideration just because these books are old has about as much intellectual integrity as preferring Thursday to Tuesday because today happens to be Wednesday. In our attempts to demythologize, or historically or naturalistically to explain away the demonologies of our philosophical mentors, we moderns might seem more skeptical and rational, but in fact, the opposite is true. As Chesterton pointed out, we believe the staggering drunk when he witnesses a murder on the street, but we mock the sober judge when he spies a spectre in the study. If we valued empirical evidence and expert testimony, the reverse should be the case. Our age scoffs at spooks and devils not because there is no evidence or testimony—the whole history of humanity abounds with it, let alone the pages of our preferred philosophers. Rather, it disbelieves because our modern, secular, dogmatic creeds already preclude their possibility. We have been rocked to sleep by the lullabies of a secular materialism against which Catholicism admonishes. Augustine and Aquinas, however, show themselves to be far more temperate and intellectually modest. I am not saying that theirs are necessarily *the* explanations, but nevertheless, they are entirely sensible. They seek empirical evidence, are willing to admit that there are many natural causes beyond the scope of our current or even possible understanding, and they take into account the testimony of trustworthy witnesses; that is, theirs is a *science* of demonology.[43] Most of us know as little about the activities of the exorcist whom we doubt as we do about the affairs of the surgeon whom we trust. Our derision of the former and confidence in the latter have little to do with empirical corroboration and rational investigation, but rather, such is almost always a matter of dogmas.

The Memorial University of Newfoundland

Notes

The notes are followed by a reference list, which includes bibliographic details for the works cited.

1. I would like to thank the Social Sciences and Humanities Research Council for their generous funding and support of this research.

2. *Christian Faith and Demonology.*

3. See my "The Demonic Body."

4. Augustine also explicitly grounds demonic power, including the incorruptibility of their bodies, in demonic ontology. See, for example, Augustine, *On the Literal Interpretation of Genesis* (= *Gn. litt.*) 3.10,14: "it is in virtue of their airy bodies that they have their power, and the reason they suffer no dissolution in death is that the element dominant in them is one that is more suited to acting than to being acted upon or undergoing." For the text in English, I use Augustine, *On Genesis*, trans. Edmund Hill, O.P.

5. See Augustine, *Demonic Divination* (= *divin. daem.*) 3,7 and *divin. daem.* 4,8 and 5,9. For the text in English, I use Augustine, *On Christian Belief*, trans. Edmund Hill, O.P. On a similar argument concerning the *Life of St. Antony* in comparison with Augustine's position, see Gregory Smith, "How Thin Is a Demon?," 504–507. In *The Trinity* (= *Trin.*) Augustine provides a similar explanation: "When the airy powers do this, they are thought to be divining, but it is only like someone standing on a hilltop and seeing someone coming from a long way off, and telling the people in the plain nearby before he arrives" (*Trin.* 4.22). For the text in English, I use Augustine, *The Trinity*, trans. Edmund Hill, O.P. See also *Gn. litt.* 12. 17,34. On the superiority of demons see also ibid. 11.2.4. See also *Gn. litt.* 12. 17, 35: "We have also heard of someone suffering from an unclean spirit, who while confined to his house used to announce when a priest from twelve miles away was setting out to visit him, and then say where he had got to through all the stages of his journey, and how near he was getting, and when he entered the estate, and the house, and the bedroom, until he stood there in from of him. The patient observed none of this with his eyes, but if he was not observing it in some way or other, he would not be stating it all so accurately. But the man was in the grip of a fever, and used to say all this as if he were delirious. And perhaps he really was delirious, but because of all this he was thought to be suffering from a demon."

6. See Fr. Louis Coulange, *The Life of the Devil.*

7. Thomas Aquinas, *Summa Theologica* (= *ST*) I.115.5. For the text in English, I use Thomas Aquinas, *Summa Theologica*, trans. Fathers of the Dominican Province.

8. See *ST* I.51.1: "Augustine speaks, not as asserting the fact, but merely using the opinion of the Platonists [in particular, the Middle Platonic Apuleius], who maintained that there are some aerial animals, which they termed demons." As Peter Lombard attests, there was some debate as to Augustine's own stand on the demonic body: "It seems to some that Augustine did not say this as his own view, but as reporting an opinion. But some say that he did not say this as his own view but as reporting the opinion of others. They wish to conclude this from Augustine's own words, in which he says: 'The demons *are called* aerial animals,' and does not say *are*; for there were some people who said this. But as to their dwelling in the cloudy atmosphere into which they were cast, they say that Augustine did not say this by way of opinion, but asserting the truth of the matter, as is shown by the linguistic distinction which he makes. They also say that many Catholic writers have agreed on this and have taught unanimously that the angels are incorporeal and do not have bodies united to them" (Peter Lombard, *Sentences* (= *Sent.*) 2.8.1.3). Lombard, however, concludes that "Augustine seems to attest that angels [and demons] are corporeal and have their own spiritual bodies" (*Sent.* 2.8.2.5). For the text in English, I use Peter Lombard, *The Sentences*, trans. Giulio Silano. How much of Apuleius's view maintaining demonic materiality Augustine holds has always been debated, even to the present day.

9. See Fran O'Rourke, *Pseudo-Dionysius and the Metaphysics of Aquinas*, 260ff. Given that Aquinas's account of demonic possession need not require an immaterial cause, as we shall see, the importance of this Dionysian principle to his demonology cannot be overstated. By renouncing demonic corporeality, Aquinas either conflates the need for a demonic agent with a requirement for a super corporeal one, or subordinates his demonology and angelology to a prior, more fundamental Dionysian metaphysical principle of creative diffusion to which his demonology and angelology adhere in a secondary way.

10. Aquinas, *Treatise on Separate Substances* (= *De sub. sep.*) 11. For Aquinas, such events "could not be accomplished by any corporeal cause" (*De sub. sep.* 11). For the text in English, I use Thomas Aquinas, *Treatise on Separate Substances*, trans. F. J. Lescoe.

11. Though this is not to say that for Augustine demons cannot sometimes create illusions and appear to human beings in various forms.

12. *Gn. litt.* 11.

13. See *Gn. litt.* 11. 28, 35: "And so the serpent did not understand the sounds of the words which were being uttered from it to the woman. Nor is it to be supposed that its soul was turned into one of a rational nature, seeing that not even human beings, who are rational by nature, know what they are saying when a demon is speaking in that condition for which an exorcist is required. How much less would that creature have understood the sounds of the words which the devil was producing through it and out of it!" An angel can perform the same feat (e.g., the donkey of Balaam), but the angels do so for good, not to deceive.

14. *Gn. litt.* 11. 27, 34.

15. *Gn. litt.* 11. 28, 35. Augustine provides much more literal interpretations of this event in this later commentary, versus his more figurative interpretations in the earlier *On Genesis: a Refutation of the Manichees* (= *Gn. adv. Man.*). For example: "Or even if there is such a place called Paradise, where Adam and the woman were actually living in the body,

are we to understand the devil also making his approach there in the body? Not at all, but he made it as a spirit, as the apostle says: *According to the prince of the power of the air, the spirit who is not at work in the children of unbelief* (Eph 2:2). So then, he doesn't appear visibly, does he, to those in whom he is at work, or approach them by a kind of bodily movement in material places? No, of course not, but in mysterious ways he suggests whatever he can to their thoughts" (*Gn. adv. Man.* 2. 14, 20). I use the text in Augustine, *On Genesis*, trans. Edmund Hill, O.P. See also *Augustine Through the Ages: An Encyclopedia*, s.v. "Adam and Eve," 6–7, where Katherin Rogers points out that in the later *Gn litt.*, Augustine "explains that in an earlier work, *De Genesi adversus Manicheos*, he had overemphasized a figurative or 'spiritual' interpretation of Genesis (*Gn. litt.* 8.2). In the late works he aims at a literal (though certainly not *prima facie*) interpretation."

16. *Gn. litt.* 12. 28. Sometimes the demon desires to remain hidden: "Discernment is certainly extremely difficult when the evil spirit acts as [*sic*] it were in a quieter manner, and without any harassment of the body says what it can through the human spirit it has taken over, or when it even says things that are true and makes useful announcements, *transforming itself*, as it is written, *like an angel of light* (2 Cor 11:14), with the intention of first winning people's confidence in manifestly good matters and then seducing them to its own needs" (*Gn. litt.* 12. 28).

17. Augustine, *The City of God* (= *civ. Dei*) 19.4. I use the text in Augustine, *The City of God*, trans. Marcus Dodds. See also *Gn. litt.* 12. 19, 41: "But when it is an evil spirit that snatches souls away like this, it makes them into demoniacs or fanatical enthusiasts or false prophets."

18. See also *Beata Vita* (= *b. vita*) 3. (18). In what A. A. R. Bastiaensen calls an "outstanding definition of exorcism," in the *Beata Vita*, Augustine explains that possession brings on a kind of madness in the human (Bastiaensen, 133), in A. A. R. Bastiaensen, "Exorcism: Tackling the Devil by Word of Mouth." In the *Beata Vita*, Augustine is wondering, of the three opinions expressed, whether the one who possesses God and is therefore happy is the soul who is free of unclean spirits. He writes, "according to the rites of the most spotless mysteries, the impure spirit, as far as I can see, is usually spoken of in two different ways. Either it is the evil spirit which invades the soul from the outside, perturbs the senses, and brings on men a certain madness; to remove it, the ones who are over us are said to impose hands or to exorcise, that is, they expel it, adjuring it through a prayer to God. Or else, every impure soul, i.e., one defiled through vices and sins, is called an evil spirit" (*b. vita* 3. [18]). I use the text in Ludwig Schopp, ed., *The Fathers of the Church*. See also *civ. Dei* 10.32 where Augustine writes, Christ "cast out unclean spirits from the bodies and senses of men, and healed deformities and sicknesses."

19. *divin. daem.* 5, 9. Aquinas will try to explain in more detail how this works. On the demon entering physically see also Augustine, *Miscellany of Eighty-Three Questions* (= *div. qu.*) 12, where Augustine quotes Fonteius of Carthage's *On Purifying the Mind in order to See God*: "O wretched mortals, act in such a way that the wicked spirit never pollutes this dwelling, that he does not intrude himself into your senses and defile the holiness of your soul or becloud the light of your mind. This evil being slithers through all the openings that your senses provide: he assumes different shapes, adapts himself to colors, clings to sounds, lies concealed in anger and in false speech, hides in odors, pours himself into flavors, and by his turbulent and filthy activity casts the senses into the gloom of dark emotions. With certain vapours he fills the pathways of the intellect through which the light of reason, the mind's

ray, is accustomed to spread." I use the text in Augustine, *Responses to Miscellaneous Questions*, trans. Boniface Ramsey. See also note 13, p. 35 in Ramsey's translation quoted here.

20. In *Letter* (= *ep.*) 9.3, Augustine writes that demons are "beings which act with the powers of an aerial or ethereal body upon our bodies, and are by the constitution of their natures able to pass unhindered through these bodies, should be capable of much greater quickness in moving whatever they wish, while we, though not perceiving what they do, are nevertheless affected by the results of their activity" (*ep.* 9.3). I use the text in Philip Schaff, ed., *A Select Library of the Nicene and Post-Nicene Fathers of the Christian Church*. On the demon's ability to penetrate and perhaps possess the human body, see also *divin. daem.* 5, 9 (Augustine walks this back in *retr.* 2.56), *Gn. litt.* 11. 27, 34, ibid. 12. 13, 27, and *civ. Dei* 19.4.

21. See *Gn. litt.* 12. 17, 34: "It is difficult to find out and explain how these spiritual likenesses of bodily realities in our spirits become known even to unclean spirits, or what kind of obstacle our souls experience from these earthly bodies, so that we are unable in our turn to see them in our own spirits. There have, all the same, been the most definite and certain indications to establish that what people have been thinking has been made public by demons."

22. In *divin. daem.* Augustine writes, "Endowed with these two faculties, in so far as they are the properties of the aerial body, namely, with keenness of perception and speed of movement, [demons] foretell and declare many things that they have recognized far in advance. At this, because of the sluggishness of earthly perception, men wonder. The demons, too, through the long period into which their life is extended, have gained a far greater experience in events than accrues to men because of the brief span of their lives. Through these faculties which the nature of the aerial body has allotted, demons not only foretell many things that will occur but also perform many miraculous acts. Since man can neither tell nor perform these things, certain individuals think it proper to serve the demons and to render them divine honors" (*divin. daem.* 3.7).

23. *divin. daem.* 5.9.

24. In the *Retractions* (= *retr.*) Augustine writes, "I spoke on a very obscure subject with a more daring asseveration than I should; for it has been discovered, through certain actual experiences, that such thoughts come to the knowledge of demons. But whether certain signs, perceptible to them but hidden from us, are given by the body of men when they are reflecting, or whether they learn these things through another power and that a spiritual one, men can ascertain either with the greatest difficulty or not at all" (*retr.* 2.56 [2.30 if restarting the chapters], p. 181). I use the text in Augustine, *The Retractions*, trans. Sister Mary Inez Bogan.

25. Aquinas, *On Evil* (= *De Malo*) 16.12. I use the text in Thomas Aquinas, *On Evil*, trans. Richard Regan. See also, Therese Scarpelli-Cory, "Attention, Intentionality, and Mind-reading in Aquinas's *De Malo*, q. 16, a. 8," 167.

26. See *ST* I.52–53.

27. Though much is said, and there was great debate in Aquinas's time and after, about how demons and angels take on or subsume a body, or even create one out of air in order to appear to human senses.

28. *ST* I.110.3.

29. *ST* I.111.3.

30. The angel's (or demon's) connection to material bodies is different and more excellent than the human composite's connection to bodies. See *ST* I.110.1.

31. *De Malo* 16.12.

32. *ST* I.II.80.3.

33. *ST* I.II.80.3.

34. See Aristotle, *De Anima* 3.

35. *De Malo* 16.11, p. 506. As Aquinas explains, "Devils affect human beings' power of imagination or external senses insofar as they convey proper objects of the power of imagination or the external senses, not as if they present themselves as means or objects." (*De Malo* 16.11, p. 508).

36. See Anthony Kenny, *Aquinas on Mind*, 39ff.

37. *ST* I.111. 2–3. Demons cannot put into the imagination what is not already there, having been attained from sensation. They cannot directly put images into the imagination. See also *ST* I.111.4: "An angel can do nothing outside the entire order of creatures; but he can outside some particular order of nature, since he is not subject to that order; thus in some special way an angel can work a change in the senses outside the common mode of nature." See also ibid.: "By the interior movement of the spirits and humors an angel can do something towards changing the act of the nutritive power, and also of the appetitive and sensitive power, and of any other power using a corporeal organ."

38. See *ST* I.111.2: "The demon cannot put thoughts in our minds by causing them from within, since the act of the cogitative faculty is subject to the will; nevertheless the devil is called the kindler of thoughts, by the desire of the things thought of, by way of persuasion, or by rousing the passions."

39. *ST* I.114.2.

40. *ST* I.114.2.

41. *ST* I.114.2.

42. See Aquinas's naturalistic explanations in reply to *Objection* 1 in *ST* I.115.5.

43. Augustine writes, "For my own part, I do not wish all the marvels I have cited to be rashly accepted, for I do not myself believe them implicitly, save those which have either come under my own observation, or which any one can readily verify." (*civ. Dei.* 21.7).

Bibliography

Aquinas, Thomas. *On Evil*. trans. Richard Regan. Oxford: Oxford University Press, 2003.

Aquinas, Thomas. *Summa Theologica*. trans. the Fathers of the Dominican Province. Notre Dame, IN: Ave Maria Press, Inc., 1981.

Aquinas, Thomas. *Treatise on Separate Substances*. trans. F. J. Lescoe. West Hartford, CT: St. Joseph's College, 1959.

Augustine. *The City of God*. trans. Marcus Dodds. New York: Random House, Inc., 1950.

Augustine. *On Christian Belief.* trans. Edmund Hill, O.P. New York: New City Press, 2005.

Augustine. *On Genesis.* trans. Edmund Hill, O.P. New York: New City Press, 2002.

Augustine. *Responses to Miscellaneous Questions.* trans. Boniface Ramsey. New York: New City Press, 2008.

Augustine. *The Retractions.* trans. Sister Mary Inez Bogan. Washington, DC: The Catholic University of America Press, 1968.

Augustine. *The Trinity.* trans. Edmund Hill, O.P. New York: New City Press, 1991.

Bastiaensen, A. A. R. "Exorcism: Tackling the Devil by Word of Mouth." In *Demons and the Devil in Ancient and Medieval Christianity*, ed. Nienke Vos and Willemien Otten, 129–142. Leiden: Brill, 2011. https://doi.org/10.1163/ej.9789004196179.i-257.37

Christian Faith and Demonology. In *L'Osservatore Romano*, English Edition, July 10, 1975. Accessed 24 January, 2017. http://www.vatican.va/roman_curia/congregations/cfaith/documents/rc_con_cfaith_doc_19750626_fede-cristiana-demonologia_en.html.

Coulange, Louis. *The Life of the Devil.* trans. Stephen Haden Guest. New York: Alfred A. Knopf, 1930.

Fitzgerald, Allan. *Augustine Through the Ages: An Encyclopedia.* Grand Rapids, MI: William B. Eerdmans Publishing Company, 1999.

Kenny, Anthony. *Aquinas on Mind.* London: Routledge, 1994.

Lombard, Peter. *The Sentences.* trans. Giulio Silano. Toronto: The Pontifical Institute of Medieval Studies, 2008.

O'Neill, Seamus. "The Demonic Body: Demonic Ontology and the Domicile of the Demons in Apuleius and Augustine." In *Philosophical Approaches to Demonology*, ed. Benjamin W. McCraw and Robert Arp (New York and London: Routledge, 2017), 39–58.

O'Rourke, Fran. *Pseudo-Dionysius and the Metaphysics of Aquinas.* Notre Dame, IN, University of Notre Dame Press: 2005.

Scarpelli-Cory, Therese. "Attention, Intentionality, and Mind-reading in Aquinas's *De Malo*, q. 16, a. 8." In *Aquinas's Disputed Questions on Evil: A Critical Guide*, ed. M. V. Dougherty, 164–191.Cambridge: Cambridge University Press, 2015.

Schaff, Philip, ed. *A Select Library of the Nicene and Post-Nicene Fathers of the Christian Church*, First Series. Vol. 1: *The Confessions and Letters of St. Augustin, With a Sketch of his Life and Work.* Grand Rapids, Michigan: Wm. B. Eerdmans Publishing Company, 1956.

Schopp, Ludwig, ed. *The Fathers of the Church: A New Translation, Writings of Saint Augustine*, Vol. 1. New York: Cima Publishing Co., Inc., 1948.

Smith, Gregory. "How Thin Is a Demon?" *Journal of Early Christian Studies* 16.4 (Winter 2008): 479–512. https://doi.org/10.1353/earl.0.0229

Thomas Aquinas and Francisco Suarez on the Problem of Concurrence[1]

Steven Baldner

Abstract: Thomas and Suarez understand God's creation and conservation in a similar way: as God's continually giving being to all creatures. The two philosophers also try to explain the way in which creaturely, secondary causality is guaranteed, but they do so in radically different ways. Suarez's doctrine of concurrence is not a progressive development of Thomas's doctrine of secondary, instrumental causality, with which this Suarezian innovation is incompatible. I try to show how different concurrentism is from Thomas's doctrine of secondary causality and to offer some criticism of the former by the latter.

Theists in the broad scholastic tradition of Catholic orthodoxy try to avoid two opposite extremes when they explain God's causality of the world. At one wrong extreme we have deism, the view that God is indeed the ultimate cause of the universe in some way, but that God is not the cause of on-going events or realities in this world. God may have initially created the universe or caused its motion, but he is not now causing anything and he does not enter into our history by causing miracles, answering prayers, or infusing grace. Such a God is a First Cause, but he is a remote one, too remote to be the God of Christian faith. At the other wrong extreme is the occasionalist God, the God who causes everything not only at the beginning of the universe but also now and always.[2] In fact, this God is causing so much that creatures do not themselves exercise any real causal activity. At the most, according to the occasionalist, creatures only *appear* to be causing. Creatures provide the occasion in their apparent activity but God does the real causal work. One wrong extreme, thus, has God causing absolutely nothing in our on-going world, and the other has God causing absolutely everything and creatures causing nothing.

Thomas Aquinas and Francisco Suarez, of course, will avoid these two extreme positions, seeing clearly the dangers in each. In many ways the two scholastic philosophers work out a common, shared position, Suarez building carefully on the broad scholastic tradition that, as he saw it, was always informed by Thomas Aquinas. In

© 2017, *Proceedings of the ACPA*, Vol. 90
doi: 10.5840/acpaproc2017103064

my opinion, however, the two philosophers differ significantly on *concurrentism*, a doctrine formulated by Suarez but, if I am correct, one that is completely absent from the thought of Thomas. In this paper I want to show just what the difference is between these two philosophers on the problem of concurrentism and to show that concurrentism is really incompatible with Thomas's thought.[3] My topic here is the *philosophical* doctrine of creation, a doctrine that natural, unaided human reason can grasp about God as the first cause. First, I shall summarize some major points of agreement between Thomas and Suarez; I shall next explain Suarez's doctrine of concurrentism; finally, I shall conclude with an analysis of Thomas's understanding of secondary causes.

I. Six Points of Agreement on Creation

Thomas and Suarez agree on the basic meaning of creation out of nothing (*creatio ex nihilo*). First, this phrase indicates God's making of things as an efficient cause with no material cause at all.[4] Thomas points out that "out of nothing" really means "not from something," that is, a denial of any material source out of which the creature could be made. Suarez, too, says that "out of nothing" means "out of no subject." Suarez pushes this point farther, arguing that because composites need efficient causes, so too, even more, does the material component of the composite need a cause.[5] If matter itself is in need of a cause, it cannot, obviously, be caused from matter. It could only be caused from nothing.

Second, Thomas and Suarez agree that creation out of nothing also indicates that the creature is in a sense *nothing* on its own, and this nothingness of the creature by nature indicates that the creature is continually in need of a cause of being.[6] Creation for both thinkers is God's causing of being, and this causing is needed for as long as the creature exists. If God were to cease creating, the creature would cease to exist. Another way to express this idea is to say that creatures *participate* in *esse*; they participate or share in a being that, of themselves, they would not have.

This participation in being indicates a third and fourth point of agreement. Thomas and Suarez, in contradistinction to thinkers like Bonaventure or Albert, do not regard *creatio ex nihilo* as indicating necessarily any sort of temporal beginning.[7] To be created is not necessarily to be created *de novo*; it is to receive being continually from God, but this indicates nothing at all about a temporal beginning. To put this in other terms, both Thomas and Suarez think that it is metaphysically possible to maintain that the world could have existed eternally in the past and that this eternal world would still have been fully created out of nothing for all of its duration.

A fourth point of agreement, closely related to the third, is that for both thinkers there is no real distinction between creation and conservation.[8] To say that God is creating a creature right now is identical in meaning with saying that God is conserving the creature in being. Suarez will allow that there is a conceptual distinction between the two terms, insofar as we may think of creation involving a beginning and we do not think of conservation as involving any beginning, but this is merely a reflection of how we use the terms. The act of creating, for both thinkers, is no different from the act of conserving.

Fifth, Thomas and Suarez understand that God is causing not only the *substances* of creatures to exist, but also the accidents of these substances, including their actions. That is to say, all events and all effects at all times are being caused by God. Thomas says that God is operating more intimately in nature than the natural agents themselves,[9] and Suarez develops his famous doctrine of concurrentism precisely to show in part that God is always causing, and necessarily so, even when the creature is causing.[10] For neither Thomas nor for Suarez is God a remote cause; he is always involved in everything.

Sixth, and last, in spite of the fact that God is continually causing everything in creation at all times, creatures are really and fully causes in their own order. Both philosophers knew versions of medieval occasionalism and gave extensive refutations of this position.[11] For Thomas as an Aristotelian it is axiomatic that natural things have their own principles of agency and that they operate in the world. Suarez, of course, again develops the above mentioned doctrine of concurrentism to guarantee true secondary causality, in addition to God's causality.

We have, then, six points of fundamental agreement on a philosophical understanding of creation. Thomas and Suarez agree that creation involves no material cause; that it is the on-going giving of being to creatures; that creation implies no temporal beginning; that creation and conservation are really the same; that God causes all being, events, and effects in the world; and that creatures are true secondary causes.

II. Suarez's Doctrine of Concurrentism

Suarez devotes all of Disputation 22 to show that God is not only the cause of the substantial being of all creatures but also that God is the *per se* and immediate cause of all of the actions and effects of creatures. This means that God is always the *concurrent* cause of everything that creatures do and cause. For any action that is caused by a creature (that is, a secondary cause) it is equally true to say that God as First Cause is fully and immediately also the cause of this same action. The creature and God are both *per se* and immediate causes of the same action. Why must this be so?

For Suarez there is a fundamental distinction between the being (*esse*) of creatures and their action. When he introduces the idea of creation,[12] Suarez points out that creation concerns the substantial being of things; accidents and actions are a separate consideration. This fact stands behind Suarez's argument for concurrentism. Part of what we understand by God's conserving all creatures in being is that he is immediately causing their substantial being at all times. This fact, however, does not say anything about creatures' actions, and these, too, require a divine cause.

> Just as God can deprive a created entity of its *esse* merely by withholding his action, so too he can deprive a created entity of its natural action merely by withholding his concurrence; therefore, just as from the former power

one may evidently infer an immediate dependence in *esse*, so too from the latter power one may infer an immediate dependence in the action itself.[13]

If God were not concurring with creatures' actions, he would be a remote and not an immediate cause. He would be remote from the creatures' actions, because he would only give the creatures the power to perform their actions. The actions themselves would escape his causality.

> Therefore, while they are acting, they are dependent not only because they are being conserved in *esse* by God, but also because in their very acting they require God's influence *per se* and immediately.[14]

It is as impossible for a creature *to be* without God as it is for the creature *to act* without God. Denying that truth, for Suarez, amounts to affirming the position of Durandus of Saint-Pourçain, and the position of that unfortunate Dominican was always for Suarez a *reductio ad absurdum*. Durandus asserted that God only conserves the creatures in *esse* and that God's causality extends no farther than that.[15]

Suarez reports the position of Thomas Aquinas on this problem, who had said that God is not in every sense the immediate cause of a creature's action.[16] Thomas distinguished between two senses in which one cause might be immediate to its effect. There is, he said, an immediacy of *suppositum*, by which he meant that something is immediately present because it is the agent's own action. I am, in this sense, immediate to my own speaking or writing. There is, also, another sort of immediacy, an immediacy of *power* by which something might immediately cause something else, but the subject (*suppositum*) in which the action is located is the instrument. I might, for example, immediately cause my fountain pen to move, but the flowing of ink is not my immediate action. By my power, the pen moves and hence the ink flows, but the flowing of the ink has to do with the gravity and viscosity of the ink and is not something that I immediately do. This distinction, of course, helps to explain instrumental causality, and Thomas intended it also to account for God's being the immediate cause of creatures' actions while the creatures' actions really belonged to the creatures and not to God.

Suarez, however, stoutly rejects this Thomistic distinction as applied in this context. He reasons that any explanation that treats creatures' actions as God's *instruments* has the implication of making God not an immediate cause, but merely some remote cause. And this is the very thing that he is always trying to reject. The creature's action is never to be understood as a sort of medium between God and the effect.[17] It is furthermore wrong, Suarez argues, to say that God acts *through* the creature or *through* the creature's action.[18] It would likewise be wrong to say that God causes the effect partially and that the creature causes it partially, for here, too, we would be making God remote, at least with respect to the part of the effect that he does not cause.[19] In general, Suarez thinks that this Thomistic distinction fails to do justice to the fact that God is immediately present everywhere in creation; it is thus, for Suarez, never really correct to think of the relation between God's causality and the creature's secondary causality on the analogy of principal cause to instrumental cause.[20]

Suarez devotes a whole section (the third) of his Disputation on concurrence to the problem of whether one should think of God's concurrence as establishing the power of the creature's acting or as being the very action itself. That is, does God concur in creaturely action merely by creating the creature's powers and the conditions that are necessary for the action, or does God actually cause the action itself? Suarez argues that God does both; he causes the necessary conditions of every creature's actions, but he also fully causes each action. In this section, he refutes the view, argued by some Thomists, that God only causes the conditions, powers, or capacities of creaturely action, and not also the action itself.

Those who think that God only causes the conditions of creaturely action, think either that God is not causing the action at all, because he is only causing some pre-event; or they think that God is causing the action as a principal cause causes an instrumental cause to act. The first view is obviously wrong, for Suarez, because it clearly makes God a remote cause only. If God causes my action of speaking only in the sense that he creates in me the capacity for reason and speech, he is not involved in this act of speaking, and hence he is only a remote cause.[21]

The second interpretation is again the instrument analogy, God as principal cause and creature as instrumental, secondary cause. This is a better interpretation, because it implies at least that God is now causing something of the creature's action. This instrumental interpretation, however, is also faulty for two important reasons. First, those who think of God as the principal cause of creaturely instruments use a number of images to express this. They say that God *applies* the instrument to the effect, *stimulates* it to act, or *determines* the instrument to act. Suarez rejects these locutions and the interpretation they support because they remove too much from God's causal influence on the creature. If this instrumental view of God's causality is accepted, the problem for Suarez is that there would be no contradiction between saying that God is the principal cause in this sense and that nevertheless the action did not occur.[22] God's concurrence, according to Suarez, must mean that God directs his action toward some effect outside of himself, that God is the *per se* cause of the action, and that the action comes immediately from God.[23] This means that if God is concurring with a creaturely action, the action is necessarily occurring. If God only applies, stimulates, or determines the creature to act, there is no necessity in the resultant creature's action; it might or might not occur, outside of God's causality.

The second reason that Suarez rejects this instrumental interpretation is a reason from the opposite side: the instrumental analogy also removes too much causality from the creature. Strictly speaking, according to Suarez, God does not *cause* the creature's action or *determine* the creature's action, because to talk in these terms is to remove the full causal action from the creature.[24] Suarez insists that, however much it is true that God concurs in the creature's action, the action is still fully the creature's action, as it is also fully God's action.[25]

These two reasons are combined in Suarez's position that God's concurrence in the creature's action is not some sort of separate action or causality apart from the creature's action: it is identical with the creature's action.

> But, surely, if such a power [God's concurrence] cannot be separated—even by God's absolute power—from the secondary cause's actual action, then this is enough to show that it is not an entity distinct from the action and, consequently, that it is not a *principle* of the action, but is instead the *actual emanation* of the action itself from the First Cause.[26]

This is a remarkable claim. When a creature causes some effect (when, for example, the wind blows the leaves in the fall), there is only one action, the blowing of the leaves, and this action is fully the action of the wind and also fully the action of God. Concurrence, then, is a genuine cooperation between God and the creature, or a genuine case of God helping the creature.[27]

How it can be that one and the same action can have two causes is the subject of the third section in Disputation 22. There Suarez makes the distinction between God's immanent or internal action (God's willing) and God's external action. If we think of God's immanent action, this action is really separate from the creature's action, which is dependent on God's action. If, on the other hand, we think about God's external action, this action cannot be distinguished (except conceptually) from the action of the creature.[28] "Thus, what remains is that God's concurrence with respect to outside things is nothing other than the secondary cause's action itself insofar as it flows *per se* and immediately from the First Cause."[29] Further explanation of this is given in the next section (the fourth). There Suarez says that when God acts by himself to produce an effect, his influence is sufficient to produce the effect all by itself. When, however, God *concurs* in a creature's action, "he applies an activity which is such that it would not suffice by itself in the absence of the secondary cause."[30]

Alfred Freddoso, whose scholarship has greatly aided my understanding of Suarez, provides a useful analogy.[31] If one strong man could move a refrigerator by himself, he might nevertheless choose to move the thing with the aid of someone else. His assistant, a weaker man, might not be able to move it alone. In such a case, the action of moving the refrigerator would be one action, but it would be caused immediately and *per se* by both men. The action would truly belong to both, and one would not be an instrument of the other. The stronger man has elected to make the action dependent upon the weaker man, and thus the action really belongs to both. All analogies, like men, have weaknesses, and this analogy should not be taken to suggest that, in the case of God and creatures, each cause is only a partial cause. The point is to show how concurrence is intended to indicate a sharing of an action that the First Cause does not need to share but chooses to share.

To round out the discussion of Suarez's doctrine of concurrentism, let me make two more points. First, Suarez understands concurrence as a series of different acts by God. God grants "numerically distinct concurrences" for numerically diverse effects, and his concurrences are different in kind for diverse kinds of effects.[32] Concurrence should not be understood to be a sort of general or once-only action; it is numerically distinct for each instance of creaturely action. Second, Suarez has, of course, the vexing problem of how to account for human freedom, as does any theist who insists on God's total and immediate causality on creation. This is a big topic well beyond the scope of this paper, but let me say that Suarez provides an answer to this by explaining that God's concurrence with free agents is different from his concurrence with merely natural agents in that God concurs with the free actions in a sort of conditional way, thereby preserving the freedom of the created will.

III. Thomas on Creation, Conservation, and Secondary Causes

Thomas Aquinas has no explicit doctrine of concurrentism. Suarez, however, seems always to have regarded Thomas as holding a doctrine that at least in principle is consistent with Suarez's own.[33] Thomas is the beginning, for Suarez, of a broad scholastic tradition that leads, excepting a few unfortunate dissenters such as Durandus and some later Thomists, from the thirteenth century to Suarez himself. Thus, although Thomas did not explicitly teach concurrentism, Suarez would say that Thomas's doctrine, correctly understood, includes concurrentism, or something very close to it.

This is the thesis that I wish to contest. From his earliest formulations of a doctrine of creation in his Commentary on the *Sentences* until his most mature writings in the *Summa theologiae*, Thomas describes creaturely, secondary causes in terms that are very different from those of Suarez, and I think that the difference is significant. In his Commentary on the *Sentences*, Thomas sets the profound and consistent theme for his understanding of God's causality in relation to secondary causes.

> Now a creature is able to be the cause of the things that are produced through motion and generation, either because it exerts causality over an entire species, as the sun is the cause of a man and of a lion, or because it exerts causality on only one individual, as man generates man, and fire generates fire. Nevertheless, God is also the cause of these things, operating more intimately in them than do the other causes that involve motion, *because He Himself gives being to things.* The other causes, in contrast, are the causes that, as it were, specify that being. The entire being of any thing cannot come from some creature, since matter is from God alone. Being, however, is more intimate to anything than those things by which being is specified. . . . Hence the operation of the Creator pertains more to what is intimate in a thing than does the operation of any secondary causes.[34] [Emphasis added.]

It is important to note from this passage that Thomas maintains two strictly different orders of causality: God's causality of being (*esse*) on the one hand, and the causality in the natural, material realm through motion, change, and generation.

God causes *everything*, but he does so by giving being; insofar as God gives being (by creating or conserving) he causes always, everywhere, all realities and events in the universe. Being, for Thomas, is given to substances, accidents, motions—to whatever is real. Hence, by the very fact of giving being God is more intimately the cause of creaturely effects than are any secondary causes.

Later, in the *De potentia Dei*, Thomas discusses the same problem at length, and does so in the terms that were so troublesome to Suarez. To begin with, Thomas asserts that God operates *in* the natural or volitional agent;[35] God's act and the creature's act are not the same (*contra* Suarez), but God is operating at a more profound level. Thomas proceeds to give four senses in which one thing can be said to be the cause of the action of another. Three of these characterize God's causing of secondary actions, and one does not. Note that Thomas's assumption throughout is that the action in question *is* the creature's action, and not God's, although in some sense God also causes it.

First, one might talk about how one thing causes another's action insofar as the first cause generates something in the second cause. In Thomas's cosmology, the heavenly bodies were obvious natural examples of this: their influence produced the elements with the basic local motions of heavy and light things. God, however, is also a cause in this sense, but with an important difference. God does not just generate the creature's power but he "continually holds the power in being, because God is the cause of the created power, not only as to the coming-to-be of the power but also as to its being." As a result, God causes the action of the creature by conserving the natural power of the creature in being.[36]

In a second way, a first cause conserves the power of the second cause insofar as it aids or restores what is already in existence, as medicine conserves our health.[37] In this way, God does not cause secondary actions, because this sort of conservation is appropriate only to secondary causes that are conservers of other secondary causes.

In a third way, a first cause causes a secondary action insofar as the first cause *applies* or *moves* the secondary cause to action, as a principal cause applies an instrument to act.[38] This sort of causing of secondary causes is relevant to God's causality, but only in an indirect way. The secondary causes are moved, but they are moved by the celestial bodies, which are in turn moved by God. In this sense God is the cause of the secondary action as the *movens et applicans virtutem ad agendum*, but this moving and applying is effected indirectly through the heavenly bodies.

Fourth, there is another, more profound sense in which God is the principal cause and the creature is the instrumental cause. Insofar as the principal cause is higher, more universal, and more powerful (*efficatior*) it operates in the secondary cause more profoundly. Thomas does not explain this sort of causality, but the language here is suggestive of God, again, as the cause of being (the highest, most universal, and most powerful cause). If this is so, the meaning of instrumental causality in this sense would be something like the way in which creatures are ordered providentially toward ends by God.

In view of these four senses, Thomas concludes by saying that we may regard creatures as instruments of the divine power. If we think of the creatures as agents, they are the immediate subjects ("supposites"—*supposita*) of these actions; the actions immediately belong to the creatures. If, however, we think of the power that makes all of this possible, God's power is more immediately united to the effect than is the creature's. This reflects exactly the doctrine of the *Sentences*: God is the principal cause insofar as he is the cause of being. Thomas concludes by saying that, because God is his own power and because he is within all creatures, not as a part of their essence but as the one holding them in being, it follows that he can operate in all things without excluding the operation of nature or will.[39]

In the *Summa theologiae*, I, q. 105, a. 5, Thomas briefly rehearses the same doctrine, although he uses the schema of the four causes to make his point. In the end, he reverts to the language and ideas of his first text in the *Sentences*, saying that God's operation in creatures removes none of their natural causality, precisely because God operates within creatures at the most intimate level of giving being to them. Creatures operate because of their natural forms, but God creates and holds these natural forms in being.[40]

The position of Thomas Aquinas on the problem of secondary causes comes down to this. Thomas does not have a doctrine of concurrentism, even in an embryonic form, because he does not need such a doctrine. Thomas insists in all of his writings that God is always causing all substances, accidents, and actions in our world because he is always giving all of these realities being—that is, creating or conserving them. God's causality is the causality of being (*esse*), and being is the act of every part of the creaturely reality. But being is caused by God and by God alone. No creature causes being or could do so.[41] Creatures cause *in an entirely different order*. Creatures move things, alter things, increase things, generate things, and so on—none of these genuine actions of creatures is the giving of being that God alone effects. These actions are real, important, and a function of the God-given natures of creatures, and as such they are completely other than and unaffected by God's fundamental act of making all things exist. The fact that creatures and God operate at such different levels is the reason why it is true to say that creatures cause their effects completely, immediately, and essentially as their own, and yet it is also true to say that God is the complete, immediate, and essential cause of these same effects. Thomas does not think that God and creatures are cooperating or collaborating in a shared effort in the same action. Rather, the very same action or effect must be understood in two radically different ways: from the metaphysical standpoint of being or existence, and also from the purely natural standpoint of motions, changes, and generations. To ask about God's causality is to ask about the causing of being or existence; to ask about the creature's causality is to ask about the cause of motions, changes, and generations.

There is thus *not* a consistent tradition on this problem from Thomas to Suarez. At some point, a major rupture in the tradition has occurred, and the rupture has resulted in a radically different explanation. Concurrentism is not an extension of Thomistic creation, conservation, and secondary causality; it is a radical revision of Thomistic doctrine.

What, finally, is the philosophical import of my argument? Assume that I am correct in characterizing Suarez's doctrine of concurrentism as a radical change in Thomistic doctrine. Why does this change matter? Suarez is clearly working out of the scholastic tradition, but, like all philosophers, in the end he creates his own doctrine, and we should just take him on his own terms. I agree with this, except for the fact that, on his own terms Suarez does present himself as part of a consistent tradition. Leaving that aside, however, I do have this final criticism. If Suarez is correct in saying that God and the creature cause exactly the same effect and that the action of producing the effect is fully God's action and also fully the creature's action, we have the serious problem, I think, of explaining why in the end creatures are really needed to cause anything. Remember the analogy of the two men moving the refrigerator. The stronger man could move the appliance all by himself, but he *chooses* to allow the weaker man to help. The weaker man, note, *cannot move the fridge by himself.* The weaker man can only move the fridge because the stronger man refrains from doing all that he can do. Likewise, the creature can only do its action because God, who is doing the same action, allows the creature to do so. But God does not need the creature to do this action, although the creature does need God to do it. If that is the case, why bother with the creature at all? Why not just have God do the action? The creature does not really have a role to play, except on God's generous sufferance. In fact, two centuries of occasionalist philosophers after the time of Suarez, starting with Descartes, drew precisely the unfortunate inference that I have just suggested.

St. Francis Xavier University
Nova Scotia, Canada

Notes

1. The texts for Suarez are all taken from the *Disputationes metaphysicae* (Paris: 1866; Reprint, Hildesheim: Georg Olms, 1965). Translations from Suarez are taken from *On Creation, Conservation, and Concurrence: Metaphysical Disputations 20, 21, and 22*, trans. Alfred J. Freddoso (South Bend, IN: St. Augustine's Press, 2002). Translations from Thomas Aquinas's Commentary on the *Sentences* are taken from *Aquinas on Creation: Writings on the "Sentences" of Peter Lombard 2.1.1*, trans. Steven Baldner and William Carroll (Toronto: Pontifical Institute of Mediaeval Studies, 1997).

2. For an excellent account of occasionalism in the mediaeval and early modern period, see Alfred J. Freddoso, "Medieval Aristotelianism and the Case Against Secondary Causes in Nature," in *Divine and Human Action: Essays in the Metaphysics of Theism*, ed. Thomas V. Morris (Ithaca, NY: Cornell University Press, 1988), 74–118.

3. This paper is a response to the excellent case made for concurrentism in Alfred J. Freddoso, "God's Causal Concurrence with Secondary Causes: Why Conservation is not Enough," *Philosophical Perspectives* 5 (1991): 553–585.

4. "Sciendum est autem quod ad rationem creationis pertinent duo. Primum est ut nihil praesupponit in re quae creari dicitur. . . . et ideo creatio ex nihilo dicitur esse, quia

nihil est quod creationi praeexistat, quasi non creatum." Thomas Aquinas, *Sent.* 2.1.1.2. "Significat ergo creatio effectionem alicuius rei ex nihilo. . . . Illa autem particula, *ex nihilo*, ut distinguat hanc actionem ab aliis, excludit omnem concursum causae materialis." Suarez, *DM* 20.1.1; see also *DM* 20.5.11.

5. *DM* 20.1.15–17.

6. Thomas, *Sent.* 2.1.1.2; Suarez, *DM* 21.1.6–15.

7. Thomas, *Sent.* 2.1.1.5; Suarez, *DM* 20.5.11–12. For the doctrines of Bonaventure and Albert, see Steven Baldner, "St. Bonaventure and the Temporal Beginning of the World," *The New Scholasticism* 63 (1989): 206–228; Steven Baldner, "Albertus Magnus on Creation: Why Philosophy is Inadequate," *The American Catholic Philosophical Quarterly* 88 (2014): 63–79.

8. Thomas, *De potentia*, 5.1.ad2; Suarez, *DM* 21.2.7. For an argument based on Thomas and Suarez that creation must imply conservation, see Louis A Mancha, Jr., "Defending God's Strong Conservation," *Proceedings of the American Catholic Philosophical Association*, ed. Michael Baur (Charlottesville, VA: Philosophy Documentation Center, 2003), 144–157.

9. Thomas, *Sent.* 2.1.1.2.

10. Suarez's doctrine of concurrentism will be explained in the second section of this paper.

11. Thomas, *Sent.* 2.1.1.4; Suarez, *DM* 18.1.5–11.

12. Suarez takes his meaning of creation out of nothing from the theologians; it indicates God's causing of substances. "Unde inferunt Theologi, quidquid creatur, debere esse subsistens, aut fieri per modum subsistentis, quia oportet ut fiat extra subjectum seu sine dependentia a subjecto." Suarez, *DM* 20.1.1.

13. Suarez, *DM* 22.1.11 (Freddoso, 156).

14. Suarez, *DM* 22.1.10 (Freddoso, 156).

15. Suarez, *DM* 21.1.2–7. For a good account of Suarez's response to Durandus, see Alfred J. Freddoso, "God's General Concurrence with Secondary Causes: Pitfalls and Prospects," *American Catholic Philosophical Quarterly* 68 (1994): 131–156.

16. Suarez, *DM* 22.1.16. Thomas, *De pot.* 3.7.

17. Suarez, *DM* 22.1.19.

18. Suarez, *DM* 22.1.21.

19. Suarez, *DM* 22.1.22.

20. Suarez, *DM* 22.1.18.

21. Suarez, *DM* 22.2.2–5.

22. Suarez, *DM* 22.2.17.

23. "Dico ergo primo: divinus concursus, quatenus est aliquid ad extra, per se essentialiter est aliquid per modum actionis, vel saltem per modum cujusdam fieri immediate manantis a Deo." Suarez, *DM* 22.2.15.

24. Suarez, *DM* 22.2.25, 31–40.

25. When Suarez gives his general discussion of efficient causality, he gives three marks of what it means to be an instrumental, as distinct from a principal, cause. In the broadest sense, an instrumental cause is any cause that is dependent on another cause in order to be a

cause. In a narrower sense, any part of a substance (such as a hand or the intellect) might be considered an instrument insofar as it is that through which an operation is performed. *DM* 17.1.16. In the most proper sense, however, an instrumental cause is one whose causal power is raised to accomplish an effect that is beyond the power of the instrument on its own. *DM* 17.1.17. A carpenter's saw, for example, cannot of its own power make a bench; its being an instrumental cause in the making of a bench is the raising of the saw's causal powers by the carpenter to produce an effect far beyond the power of the saw alone. This proper sense of instrumental causality shows why Suarez is opposed to calling creatures instrumental causes: the effect of the concurrence of God and creature is not an effect that goes beyond the power of the creature. It is, rather, exactly the same effect that is produced by God and the creature. I am writing these words, and God is also writing these same words. For God to concur with my writing is not for God to produce something greater than what I can produce; it is for Him to produce, along with me, the same effect that I am also producing.

26. Suarez, *DM* 22.2.17 (Freddoso, 180).

27. Suarez, *DM* 22.2.48.

28. Suarez, *DM* 22.3.8.

29. Suarez, *DM* 22.3.5 (Freddoso, 212).

30. Suarez, *DM* 22.4.9 (Freddoso, 221).

31. Freddoso, 221n9.

32. Suarez, *DM* 22.4.8.

33. Throughout his 22nd Disputation, Suarez argues that Thomas is teaching the same position or that, at least, Thomas's position is compatible with Suarez's. In *DM* 22.1.6, Suarez claims that the consensus of all Scholastics is that God acts *per se* and immediately in every action of a creature. In *DM* 22.1.16, Suarez notes an apparent difference between himself and Thomas, that Suarez regards God as immediate to the creature's action both in power and as a *suppositum* and that Thomas regards God as immediate only in power; Suarez, however, responds at length to show that Thomas's position is compatible with his own, *DM* 22.1.17–22. In *DM* 22.2.7–12, Suarez argues that Thomas does not hold the view that God causes creatures' actions "in the manner of a principle"; rather, Thomas, like Suarez, really holds that God concurs with creatures' actions insofar as God causes the creatures' actions. In *DM* 22.2.20, Suarez reports that Thomas says that God concurs in creatures' actions by *moving* them. In *DM* 22.3.2, Suarez claims that, for Thomas, God's action and the creature's action are *one*.

34. Thomas, *Sent.* 2.1.1.4 (Baldner and Carroll, 85).

35. "Non ergo sic est intelligendum quod Deus in omni re naturali operetur, quasi res naturalis nihil operetur; sed quia in ipsa natura vel voluntate operante Deus operatur." Thomas, *De pot.* 3.7.

36. "et hoc modo Deus agit omnes actiones naturae, . . . et conservat virtutem naturalem in esse." Thomas, *De pot.* 3.7.

37. "Nam etiam alio modo conservans virtutem dicitur facere actionem, sicut dicitur quod medicinae conservantes visum faciunt videre." Thomas, *De pot.* 3.7.

38. "Tertio modo dicitur una res esse causa actionis alterius in quantum movet eam ad agendum; in quo non intelligitur collatio aut conservatio virtutis activae, sed applicatio virtutis ad actionem." Thomas, *De pot.* 3.7.

39. "Et cum coniunxerimus his, quod Deus sit sua virtus, et quod sit intra rem quamlibet non sicut pars essentiae, sed sicut tenens rem in esse, sequetur quod ipse in quolibet operante immediate operetur, non exclusa operatione voluntatis et naturae." Aquinas, *De pot.* 3.7.

40. "Unde non solum [Deus] est causa actionum inquantum dat formam quae est principium actionis, sicut generans dicitur esse causa motus gravium et levium; sed etiam sicut conservans formas et virtutes rerum. . . . Et quia forma rei est intra rem, et tanto magis quanto consideratur ut prior et universalior; et ipse Deus est proprie causa ipsius esse universalis in rebus omnibus, quod inter omnia est magis intimum rebus; sequitur quod Deus in omnibus intime operetur." Aquinas, *Summa theologiae* 1.105.5.

41. Early on in his career, Thomas did think that it might be possible, though in fact false, to say that creatures could be instrumental causes in creation or in the giving of being (*Sent.* 2.1.1.3). Later, however, and for most of his career, he rejected this position. It is impossible for any being that receives its being to be the cause, even instrumentally, of being. See *Summa theologiae* 1.45.5.

Is Marriage a Basic Good?

Charles D. Robertson

Abstract: According to the New Natural Law theory, marriage is a basic good. This means that marital society is an end in itself, and that marital intercourse instantiates that end by making the married couple to be "one-flesh." This one-flesh union finds its intrinsic fulfillment in the procreation of children, but should not be seen as a mere means to the begetting and rearing of offspring. This view of marriage represents a departure from the traditional understanding of marriage as having its ultimate *raison d'être* in the begetting and rearing of offspring, and has significant implications for judgments concerning the liceity of embryo adoption/rescue. This paper offers a critical appraisal of the thesis that marriage is a basic good.

For the past several years, Catholic ethicists have been debating whether embryo adoption or rescue is a licit means to preserve the lives of the many cryopreserved and abandoned embryos leftover from IVF treatments. Those opposed to all forms of heterologous embryo transfer object to embryo rescue by arguing that the desire to become pregnant can justly be fulfilled only by means of marital intercourse. In their view, our use of the organs of the reproductive system are governed by the order of the generative faculty to the good of offspring, and so may be licitly used only by directing their activities to marital intercourse. It is a matter of justice between the spouses that they order the use of their generative potential to their spouse and to their spouse alone.[1] Consequently, if a married woman were to undergo embryo transfer, she would be guilty of an injustice to her husband, who has exclusive rights over her generative potential. Likewise, for an unmarried woman to intend embryo transfer would violate the order of general justice that governs the use of our reproductive faculty, reserving that use for marriage. A fairly typical response to this line of argument is that although *procreation* must be the fruit of the marriage act, procreation properly terminates at the fertilization of the ovum or at conception, and so a woman who is impregnated with an already conceived child does not seek procreation apart from her spouse. To help illustrate the point, an analogy between embryo transfer and wet nursing is offered; just as a woman can provide nourishment to a child who is not her own by means of her

© 2017, *Proceedings of the ACPA*, Vol. 90
doi: 10.5840/acpaproc20182871

breasts, so also a woman can provide nourishment to a child who is not her own by means of her womb. Since the former is not morally evil, neither is the latter.

Typically, this line of argumentation in favor of embryo adoption or rescue is employed by those who follow or are sympathetic to the so-called New Natural Law (NNL) theory. According to this theory, it is possible to separate impregnation from the marriage act, not only in the order of nature, but also in the order of morals. This separation is made possible by the way in which marriage is conceived as a basic good, and how marital intercourse instantiates that basic good. It is my conviction that the NNL approach to marriage is problematic, and so the analogy between wet nursing and embryo adoption is improper. I recognize that many NNL theorists have been valiant and articulate defenders of natural marriage in recent years, and that much of what they have to say, even about the relationship between marriage and procreation, is extremely valuable. I do not wish to impugn their good intentions in any way. It is my worry, however that as described by the NNL theory, the relationship between marriage, sex, and procreation is ultimately incoherent. In what follows, then, I will present, as fairly as possible, the NNL view of what marriage is as a basic good and how that good is instantiated in the marriage act and fulfilled in procreation. Then I will indicate ways in which this theory is problematic and offer a corrective according to the teaching of St. Thomas.

First in the order of business is to determine what is meant by saying that marriage is a basic good. According to the NNL theory, basic goods are willed for their own sake as humanly fulfilling, and not on account of some benefit it may bring. By calling marriage a basic good, then, NNL theorists mean that it is not an instrumental good, i.e., that it does not exist for the sake of ends extrinsic to the marriage covenant itself. As explained by Christopher Tollefsen, the good of marriage essentially involves a complete sharing of lives which "would be incomplete if that union were temporary, or open to similar sharing with others,"[2] which entails its permanence and exclusivity. Also included in the good of marriage is the capacity of the married couple to become literally "one flesh" in marital intercourse, which is the physical expression of their love. This ability to form a one flesh union renders them able to "perform a biological act that neither one is capable of performing separately, the act of generation."[3] Since the one flesh union of marital intercourse and its ordination to the good of life are part of the good of marriage, to offend against the good of the one flesh union is to offend against the good of marriage. Thus, it is wrong to engage in the one flesh union apart from marriage. Further, since the good of marriage does not include in itself the effects of that one flesh union, to achieve pregnancy apart from any act of sexual intercourse, does not of itself offend against the good of marriage. In other words, the marital communion is an act of complete self-donation, which is intrinsically fulfilled by the begetting and educating of offspring which itself is fulfilling of the couple both as individuals and as a couple.

Put another way, marriage is a special kind of friendship, whose specific difference arises from the procreative nature of marital communion. As George, Girgis and Anderson define it:

Marriage is the union of a man and a woman who make a permanent and exclusive commitment to each other of the type that is naturally (inherently) fulfilled by bearing and rearing children together. The spouses seal (consummate) and renew their union by conjugal acts—acts that constitute the behavioral part of the process of reproduction, thus uniting them as a reproductive unit. Marriage is valuable in itself, but its inherent orientation to the bearing and rearing of children contributes to its distinctive structure, including norms of monogamy and fidelity. This link to the welfare of children also helps explain why marriage is important to the common good and why the state should recognize and regulate it.[4]

On this formulation, the procreative nature of marital communion seems to provide for a specific difference in light of which permanence and exclusivity are seen as properties of that communion. Whether it is looked at in the former way, in which permanence and exclusivity are seen as necessitated by the "total" nature of the union, or the latter way, in which permanence and exclusivity are seen as necessitated by marriage's order to bearing and rearing children, marital communion itself is a basic good that has an intrinsic relation to the begetting and education of offspring. Sexual intercourse is a sign and seal of this union since by that activity alone do a man and a woman form an organismic unity. Grisez explains it this way:

> Biologically, every animal, whether male or female, is a complete individual with respect to most functions: growth, nutrition, sensation, emotion, local movement, and so on. But with respect to reproduction, each animal is incomplete, for a male or a female individual is only a potential part of the mated pair, which is the complete organism that is capable of reproducing sexually. This is true also of men and women: as mates who engage in sexual intercourse suited to initiate new life, they complete each other and become an organic unit. In doing so, it is literally true that "they become one flesh" (Gn 2.24).[5]

Since the organic one flesh union of marital intercourse is a defining feature of marriage as a basic good, and the one flesh union is that by means of which couples generate new life, to generate new life apart from the one flesh union of marital intercourse fails to instantiate that basic good. In other words, for procreation to be an act that is intrinsically fulfilling of the married couple as such, it must come about as a result of marital intercourse. This is not to say that the end of marital intercourse is procreation, for that would make marriage an instrumental good,[6] but rather that procreation intrinsically perfects and instantiates the basic good of marital communion.

The central feature of this account is that marriage is essentially a comprehensive union of persons. The comprehensive nature of the union demands a bodily component. The only way in which this component can be fulfilled is by means of an act in which the man and the woman become literally one organism. They become literally one organism by performing an act that has a single function or end, namely, the begetting of new life. A major difficulty with this argument, as presented, is the insistence that the man and woman become one organism in a literal and not a metaphorical sense. This thesis seems, on the basis of the Aristotelian-Thomistic notion of substance, to be patently false. An organism, according to the thought of St. Thomas, is "literally" one due to its having a substantial form as the internal principle of its motion and rest. The fact that the activity of generation requires two individual organisms to perform a single action together does not render them a single organism. Edward Feser tries to show the absurdity of this position by saying,

> This is like saying that people engaged in conversation or competitive games make up one organism, since qua individuals they cannot carry out these essentially social activities. (Or are playing solitaire and delivering a soliloquy on all fours with self-abuse? And does the deliberate cessation of copulation constitute the suicide of the "one organism" that the pair make up? Is it therefore a mortal sin to stop copulating once you have started?)[7]

All questions concerning the liceity of the *amplexus reservatus* aside, then, we must ask the question: are the new natural law theorists basing their notion of marriage on an absurd thesis? Perhaps not. They certainly do not seem to be claiming that a man and a woman become a single substance in the act of coitus, even though they use the term "organism," which denotes a substance, to refer to the one-flesh union of intercourse. But why the insistence on this strange terminology?

The answer seems to have something to do with the way in which they conceive of the relationship between marriage, as a formal bond uniting the man and the woman in a marital society, the principal act of marriage, namely, intercourse, as an instantiation of that bond, and procreation as the natural consequence of that act. They want to deny that *marriage*, the formal bond of communion, is ordered to the end of procreation as to an extrinsic good, for that would make marriage an instrumental good rather than a basic good. Consequently, according to Grisez, the bond itself is the common good of the couple: "In sum, marriage is a basic human good, and the married couple's common good is, not any extrinsic end to which marriage is instrumental, but the communion of married life itself."[8] They also want to deny that the *marriage act* is ordered to the end of procreation as to an extrinsic good, for that would make the marriage act itself an instrumental good rather than an instantiation of the marital communion. George and Lee put it this way:

> It is true in general, for any two (or more) people, that actions which they perform make them one only if there is a real, common good of their actions (unity of action). . . . In the case of the sexual act of a married couple, their act of physically or organically becoming one (organic unity) is the common good, the shared pursuit of which (unity of action) also brings about or enhances their interpersonal unity (unity of persons). But if the participants in a sexual act do not become physically or organically one, then, whatever goods they may be seeking as ulterior ends, their immediate goal is mere pleasure or illusory experience."[9]

On this account, the end of the act of sexual intercourse is not procreation, but the one-flesh union. This forces them into the position of claiming that sexual intercourse effects a real, organic union: the spouses become "literally" one organism. If this were not the case, and the spouses become only "metaphorically" one organism, the real end of the act of intercourse in virtue of which the spouses could be seen as a single quasi-organism would be the generation of offspring. Further, since the one-flesh union of intercourse, now found to be ordered to procreation as to an extrinsic end, is that which distinguishes marriage from other forms of friendship as a *total* communion of persons, marriage itself would thus be seen to be ordered to procreation as to an extrinsic end, and thus incapable of being a basic good. Consequently, to avoid this conclusion, the NNL theorist is forced to insist that the spouses become literally one organism in the marriage act.

This result follows from the view that the common good of the spouses is marital communion itself. Grisez explains what this means: "The *communion of married life* refers to the couple's *being* married, that is, their being united as complementary, bodily persons, so really and so completely that they are two in one flesh."[10] This conception of marital communion as the non-instrumental common good of marriage, however, is also incoherent, for it makes the society of married life its own end. The NNL theorists have taken what has been traditionally understood as the form of marriage, namely, the bond of union, and made it the end of marriage. It is easy to see why the form of a society cannot itself be the end of that society; the bond of union exists for the sake of common operation, and so it is the object of operation that is the "that for sake of which" the bond exists. On the traditional account, that for the sake of which marriage as a society exists is offspring, and the begetting and rearing of offspring is the primary common operation of the spouses. In other words, the child, and not the total communion of the spouses, is the common good of marriage.[11] This traditional view is distasteful to the NNL theorist, for it seems to make the spouses subordinate to an extrinsic end; it puts marriage, and those who belong to it, at the service of the good of the species.

They must, however, have an account of how parenthood is related to marriage in order to defend the Church's teaching on contraception and to ground their judgments about the necessity of marriage for the transmission of life; thus they insist that marriage is ordered to parenthood as its intrinsic fulfillment:

> Parenthood is not the end of marriage to which conjugal communion is instrumental; conjugal communion is intrinsically good. But conjugal communion is designed to be, and normally is, an intrinsically good part of a larger, intrinsically good whole: the family. Thus, parenthood is the intrinsic fulfillment of the intimate union of persons and actions. Because parenthood fulfills marriage, it shapes the spouses' interpersonal communion; and the way children come to be sets requirements for marriage as a whole, among them that it be an open-ended community.[12]

Grisez and the NNL theorists would have it that parenthood is not "that for the sake of which" marriage exists, but that marriage is somehow ordered to parenthood as that which fulfills it. But that which is perfective, completive, or fulfilling of a thing has the notion of being an end and a good of that thing. Consequently, the NNL theory wants to have it both ways: parenthood is not the end of marriage, but it is the end of marriage. This contradictory position is disguised by an ambiguous distinction: parenthood is the end of marriage as "a realization of its potency," but not as an "extrinsic end to which one-flesh unity is instrumental."[13] Unfortunately, it is very difficult to divine what it means to say that marriage is ordered to begetting and rearing offspring as its "intrinsic fulfillment" but not as to an "extrinsic end." The affirmation that marriage is ordered to procreation as potency to act is meant to explain why parenthood is fulfilling of couples while the denial that it is the "extrinsic" end of marriage is meant to explain why marriage is not ordered to procreation as a means is ordered to an end. Since a means receives its goodness from its order to the end, its goodness is derived. But marriage is supposed to have underived goodness on the NNL view; that is, it is a basic good. Hence, offspring are supposed to be perfective of the married couple not because marriage is ordered to offspring as a means is ordered to an end, but rather as potency is related to act. However, this is a distinction without a difference, for act is the end of potency, and that for the sake of which potency exists.[14] So marriage has its specific perfection and goodness as the kind of society that it is due to its potential to actualize the good of parenthood, which is to say that it is the means by which the spouses are perfected in becoming parents.

This problem with the NNL theorists' view of marriage as a basic good is connected to the way in which they view basic goods in general, as desired "for their own sake," and thus fit to be a kind of measure with respect to which we can judge our chosen acts. These acts will be good, if they are directed toward the attainment and integration of the goods, or evil, if they offend against these goods. According to Grisez,

> There are different senses in which a good can be said to be "sought for itself." The human goods which fulfill persons should not be considered mere outcomes one wants and seeks—as the goals one will enjoy if action is successful. Such outcomes have the character of accomplishments rather than of self-fulfillment—that is, they remain extrinsic to the person. Basic human goods must instead be considered aspects of what one might call human "full-being." They are sought for themselves in the sense that they are judged to be humanly fulfilling. They provide reasons for intelligently wanting something and choosing to act for it as a goal.[15]

Although he does not tell us what the different senses are in which a good can be said to be "sought for itself," Grisez identifies for us the sense in which basic goods are sought for themselves; namely, because they are judged to be humanly fulfilling.[16] Contrasted to these basic goods, which are intrinsic to persons, are those goods that are not sought for their own sake. These goods are extrinsic to the person, which Grisez defines variously as things that "can be valuable by being useful to persons," or as "mere outcomes one wants or seeks." Since they are not sought for their own sake, they have the character of "means." Basic goods, goods that are intrinsic to persons and fulfilling of them, are thus "ends." Common goods, in the restricted sense that excludes common utilities, are also to be understood as basic goods intrinsically perfective of the members of some community.[17] Consequently, it is necessary to deny that any of the traditional ends of marriage are extrinsic to it, for that would make the whole of married life a means and not sought for its own sake.

In contrast, St. Thomas has no problem saying that "extrinsic" goods are more properly ends than "intrinsic" ones, and that the former are more properly desired "for their own sake" than the latter. Concerning the distinction between goods as intrinsic and extrinsic, St. Thomas says:

> For the good, according as it is the end of some thing, is twofold. For there is an end that is extrinsic to that which is ordered to the end, as when we say that place is the end of that which is moved to a place. There is also an interior end, as form is the end of generation and alteration, and the form already received is a kind of good intrinsic to that of which it is the form.

He then immediately applies this distinction to a whole of order: "But the form of some whole, which is one by a certain ordering of parts, is its order: whence it follows that it (i.e. the order) is its good."[18] The good of a whole of order is its common good, and this common good, then, is twofold: the common good intrinsic to the whole consisting in the order of its parts, and the common good extrinsic to the whole, that is, the end to which the whole is ordered.[19] The communion of married life, then, as the form of marriage can rightly be called the intrinsic common good of the spouses, but must also be understood as being ordered to some extrinsic common good.[20] And it is the extrinsic good that is more fundamental in any order, whether it be the order of the individual to his end, or the order of a whole to its end:

> it ought to be noted that the whole universe is constituted out of all creatures as a whole (is constituted) out of parts. But if we wish to assign the end of some whole and its parts, we find in the first place that the singular parts exist for the sake of their acts, as the eye for seeing. But secondly, (we find) that the less noble part is for the sake of the more noble, as sense is for the sake of understanding and the lungs for the heart. But thirdly, all the parts are for the sake of the perfection of the whole as matter is for the sake of form, for the parts are the quasi-matter of the whole. Finally, however, the whole man is for the sake of some extrinsic end, namely, that he may enjoy God. So also, therefore, in the parts of the universe, each and every creature exists for the sake of its proper act and perfection. But secondly, the less noble creatures are for the sake of the more noble as the creatures that are below man exist for

the sake of man. But after that, individual creatures are for the sake of the perfection of the whole universe. But after that, the whole universe, with every one of its parts, is ordered to God as to its end, insofar as, for the glory of God, the divine goodness is represented in them by a kind of imitation, although rational creatures have, in a special way apart from this, God as their end, whom they are able to attain by their operation, by knowing and loving. And thus it is clear that the divine goodness is the end of all bodily things.[21]

Now, the ultimate end of man, according to St. Thomas, is an extrinsic end, namely, God. According to the NNL theorists, as we saw above, goods extrinsic to persons have the character of being "means" to some further end. On St. Thomas's account, this characterization of goods extrinsic to persons will be true of all such goods apart from the ultimate end, which alone can be "sought for its own sake." Moreover, goods that are intrinsic to the person or a community will also be "means" when related to the ultimate end or even to their corresponding extrinsic end. Considered in themselves, they are a kind of actuality, and thus have the character of goods that can, in some sense, be "sought for their own sake":

> when the will is said to delight in something for its own sake (*propter se*), this can be understood in two ways. In one way, according as the word "for the sake of" (*propter*) refers to a final cause, and in this way someone delights only in the ultimate end for its own sake. In another way, according as it (*i.e., propter*) designates a formal cause, and thus someone can delight in everything that is delightful according to its form for its own sake.[22]

For St. Thomas, then, the communion of married life should be considered the intrinsic common good of the spouses that can be willed "for its own sake" as a certain pleasing form. Moreover, any good intrinsic to persons, insofar as it is a form perfective of persons, can likewise be sought "for its own sake." These intrinsic goods, however, have their goodness, in the final analysis, from their order to their proper extrinsic goods, and so the extrinsic good is the cause of the being and goodness of the intrinsic good. In other words, the extrinsic good is prior in the order of being and causality to the intrinsic good and so serves to explain why the intrinsic good exists. If the so-called "basic goods," then, are intrinsic goods, they can be neither ultimate ends nor the ultimate measure against which we measure the morality of our acts. Further, in beginning ethical considerations by seeking to identify basic goods, NNL theorists end up with theses that are counterintuitive or even absurd, such as the thesis that spouses become *literally* one in the marriage act, when considered from the standpoint of the philosophy of nature.

In the final analysis, it seems that the NNL theory, in its positing of basic goods grasped immediately by practical reason, has served to undermine its own reason for existence. It was supposed that by proceeding from goods understood as indemonstrable first principles grasped by practical reason, natural law ethics would be freed from the charge of having committed the naturalistic fallacy, namely, of deriving statements concerning what we ought to do from statements concerning what is the case. By claiming the epistemological primacy of the basic goods over the discovery of natures, this approach has served to invert the older scholastic order between the speculative study of nature and the practical study of human acts, such that, as John Finnis says, "an adequately full knowledge of human nature is derived from our practical and underived (*per se notum*) knowledge of the human goods of which Aquinas speaks in I-II, q. 94, a. 2."[23] Whereas on the older account, marriage, and marital morality, exists in order to serve the good of the species, on the NNL account, marriage must be seen as something simply to be desired without reference to its extrinsic end. In the former, a speculatively observed order between sex and the begetting of offspring leads to a moral conclusion, namely, that sex should be used only within marriage. In the latter, the existence and goodness of marriage and the marriage act is intuitively grasped, and governs how we are to think about the nature of human generation. Unfortunately, this inversion results in the contradictions observed above, and so the cure seems to be worse than the disease.

University of St. Thomas
Houston, TX

Notes

1. See, for instance, Tadeusz Pacholczyk, "Some Moral Contraindications to Embryo Adoption," in *Human Embryo Adoption: Biotechnology, Marriage and the Right to Life*, ed. Thomas V. Berg and Edward James Furton (Philadelphia: The National Catholic Bioethics Center, 2006), 42; Nicholas Tonti-Filippini, "The Embryo Rescue Debate," in *Human Embryo Adoption: Biotechnology, Marriage and the Right to Life*, ed. Thomas V. Berg and Edward James Furton (Philadelphia: The National Catholic Bioethics Center, 2006), 77.

2. Christopher Tollefsen, "Could Human Embryo Adoption be Intrinsically Immoral?" in *The Ethics of Embryo Adoption and the Catholic Tradition: Moral Arguments, Economic Reality, and Social Analysis*, ed. Sarah-Vaughan Brakman and Darlene Fozard Weaver (New York: Springer, 2007), 91.

3. Ibid.

4. Ryan T. Anderson, Robert George, and Sherif Girgis, "What is Marriage," *Harvard Journal of Law and Public Policy* 34.1 (2010): 246.

5. Germain Grisez, *The Way of the Lord Jesus: Living the Christian Life*, Vol. 2 (Chicago: Franciscan Herald Press, 1993), 570 (henceforth *TWOTLJ*, vol. 2).

6. See, for instance, Robert George and Gerard V. Bradley, "Marriage and the Liberal Imagination," *Georgetown Law Journal* 84.2 (1995): 304: "*The intrinsic intelligible point of the sexual intercourse of spouses, however, is, in our view, marriage itself, not procreation considered as an end to which their sexual union is the means.*" (original italics) These authors hold that to view the marriage act as a means to the end of procreation will vitiate the act such that it

is not truly "marital." One can hope for children as the result of the marriage act, but only as an intrinsic perfection of the union.

7. Edward Feser, "In Defense of the Perverted Faculty Argument," in *Neo-Scholastic Essays* (South Bend, IN: St. Augustine's Press, 2015), 411.

8. Grisez, *TWOTLJ*, vol. 2, 568.

9. Robert George and Patrick Lee, "What Sex Can Be: Alienation, Illusion, Or One-Flesh Union," *American Journal of Jurisprudence* 42 (1997): 147.

10. Grisez, *TWOTLJ*, vol. 2, 568.

11. See St. Thomas Aquinas, *In VIII Ethicorum*, lect.12: "And he says that children seem to be the cause of the stable and firm conjunction. And it is on this account that the sterile, namely, those who lack offspring, are quickly separated from each other. For among the ancients the separation of matrimony came about by reason of sterility. And the reason for this is that children are the common good of both, namely, of the husband and the wife, whose joining is for the sake of offspring." ["Et dicit, quod causa stabilis et firmae coniunctionis videntur esse filii. Et inde est quod steriles, qui scilicet carent prole, citius ab invicem separantur. Fiebat enim apud antiquos separatio matrimonii sterilitatis causa. Et huius ratio est quia filii sunt commune bonum amborum, scilicet viri et uxoris, quorum coniunctio est propter prolem."]; See also Michael Waldstein, "Children as the Common Good of Marriage," *Nova Et Vetera (English Edition)* 7.3 (July 2009): 697.

12. Grisez, *TWOTLJ*, vol. 2, 569.

13. Ibid.

14. See St. Thomas Aquinas, *In IX Metaph.*, lect. 8.

15. Germain G. Grisez, *Christian Moral Principles*, Vol. 1 (Chicago: Franciscan Herald, 1983), 122 (henceforth *TWOTLJ*, vol. 1).

16. However, given that the judgment that these goods are humanly fulfilling is what makes them to be "sought for themselves" makes human fulfillment, then, seem to have more the notion of an end than even the basic goods, which are sought on account of that end. Grisez, Finnis, and Boyle, however, deny that this is the case. See John Finnis, Germain G. Grisez, and Joseph M. Boyle, "'Direct' and 'Indirect': A Reply to Critics of our Action Theory," *The Thomist* 65 (2001): 131–133. For a detailed argument that "integral human fulfillment" implicitly serves as the ultimate end of man in the thought of the new natural law theorists, see Stephen Louis Brock, "Practical Truth and its First Principles in the Theory of Grisez, Boyle, and Finnis," *National Catholic Bioethics Quarterly* 15.2 (2015): 321–325.

17 See Grisez, *TWOTLJ*, vol. 2, 340.

18 St. Thomas Aquinas, *In XII Metaph.*, lect. 12: "Bonum enim, secundum quod est finis alicuius, est duplex. Est enim finis extrinsecus ab eo quod est ad finem, sicut si dicimus locum esse finem eius quod movetur ad locum. Est etiam finis intra, sicut forma finis generationis et alterationis, et forma iam adepta, est quoddam bonum intrinsecum eius, cuius est forma. Forma autem alicuius totius, quod est unum per ordinationem quandam partium, est ordo ipsius: unde relinquitur quod sit bonum eius."

19 See also St. Thomas Aquinas, *In I Ethic.*, lect. 1: "But there is found a twofold order in things. Namely, one of the parts of some whole or of some multitude with respect to each other, as the parts of a house are ordered one to another; the other is the order of things to their end. And the latter order is more fundamental than the former." ["Invenitur

autem duplex ordo in rebus. Unus quidem partium alicuius totius seu alicuius multitudinis adinvicem, sicut partes domus ad invicem ordinantur; alius autem est ordo rerum in finem. Et hic ordo est principalior, quam primus."]

20 In contrast, Grisez and co. collapse the extrinsic common good of marriage into the intrinsic common good of marriage and then simply deny that there is an extrinsic common good of marriage.

21 St. Thomas Aquinas, *STh*, Ia, qu. 65, art. 2c: "considerandum est quod ex omnibus creaturis constituitur totum universum sicut totum ex partibus. Si autem alicuius totius et partium eius velimus finem assignare, inveniemus primo quidem, quod singulae partes sunt propter suos actus; sicut oculus ad videndum. Secundo vero, quod pars ignobilior est propter nobiliorem; sicut sensus propter intellectum, et pulmo propter cor. Tertio vero, omnes partes sunt propter perfectionem totius, sicut et materia propter formam, partes enim sunt quasi materia totius. Ulterius autem, totus homo est propter aliquem finem extrinsecum, puta ut fruatur Deo. Sic igitur et in partibus universi, unaquaeque creatura est propter suum proprium actum et perfectionem. Secundo autem, creaturae ignobiliores sunt propter nobiliores sicut creaturae quae sunt infra hominem, sunt propter hominem. Ulterius autem, singulae creaturae sunt propter perfectionem totius universi. Ulterius autem, totum universum, cum singulis suis partibus, ordinatur in Deum sicut in finem, inquantum in eis per quandam imitationem divina bonitas repraesentatur ad gloriam Dei, quamvis creaturae rationales speciali quodam modo supra hoc habeant finem Deum, quem attingere possunt sua operatione, cognoscendo et amando. Et sic patet quod divina bonitas est finis omnium corporalium."

22 St. Thomas Aquinas, *STh*, Ia-IIae, qu.70, art. 1, ad 2: "cum dicitur voluntas in aliquo propter se delectari, potest intelligi dupliciter. Uno modo, secundum quod ly propter dicit causam finalem, et sic propter se non delectatur aliquis nisi in ultimo fine. Alio modo, secundum quod designat causam formalem, et sic propter se aliquis potest delectari in omni eo quod delectabile est secundum suam formam." See also qu. 2, art. 6, ad 1: "it is according to the same notion that the good is sought and that delight, which is nothing other than the rest of the appetite in the good, is sought. . . . Whence just as the good is sought for its own sake (*propter seipsum*), so also is delight sought for its own sake (*propter se*), if the term "for the sake of" (*ly propter*) indicates a final cause. But if it indicates a formal cause or even a moving cause, thus delight is desirable for the sake of something else, that is, for the sake of the good which is the object of delight and consequently it (the good) is its principle and gives to it its form, for it is from this that delight has that it should be sought, viz. that it (delight) is rest in the desired good." [*eiusdem rationis est quod appetatur bonum, et quod appetatur delectatio, quae nihil est aliud quam quietatio appetitus in bono, sicut ex eadem virtute naturae est quod grave feratur deorsum, et quod ibi quiescat. Unde sicut bonum propter seipsum appetitur, ita et delectatio propter se, et non propter aliud appetitur, si ly propter dicat causam finalem. Si vero dicat causam formalem, vel potius motivam, sic delectatio est appetibilis propter aliud, idest propter bonum, quod est delectationis obiectum, et per consequens est principium eius, et dat ei formam, ex hoc enim delectatio habet quod appetatur, quia est quies in bono desiderato.*]"

23 John Finnis, "Natural Inclinations and Natural Rights: Deriving 'Ought' from 'is' According to Aquinas," in *Lex Et Libertas: Freedom and Law According to St. Thomas Aquinas*, ed. Leo Elders and Klaus Hedwig, Vol. 30 (Rome: Studi Thomistici, 1987), 46.

A Prolegomena to Gender Justice

Alexander Schimpf

Abstract: The paper seeks to identify some of the first principles necessary for an adequate account of gender justice. In the first section of the paper, a recent account of gender justice is analyzed in order to determine its ultimate principles. These principles include a distinction between sex and gender, absolute equality and individual freedom of choice as valuable, the just as the chosen, and gender as a restriction upon freedom. In the second section of the paper, these principles are critiqued, and alternate first principles are proposed. It is argued that an adequate account of gender justice should view sex and gender as a unity, justice as rendering what is due to the other, and gender as a teleological structure. The paper concludes with a brief consideration of what these revised first principles might mean for the question of a gendered division of societal roles.

Introduction

Robert Spaemann has confessed that his philosophical work typically begins with an irritation.[1] The account of gender justice I will begin to sketch in this article has similar origins, though I would prefer to speak of a "provocation" rather than an irritation. In a 2012 article in the *Journal of Ethics and Social Philosophy*, Anca Gheaus proposes a unifying "principle" of gender justice: gender justice is only achieved when "gender-neutral" lifestyles are the least costly option for persons.[2] Lifestyles and behaviors that conform to common gender norms—so-called "gendered lifestyles"—must be actively discouraged by societies and individuals.[3] Such lifestyles must have penalties associated with them, "at least during the transitional phase" toward more just societal forms.[4] Because gender norms "illegitimately interfere with our freedom of choosing what kind of persons we are," Gheaus also argues that gender norms must be abolished in the upbringing of children.[5] There can be no "gender shaping" of children, however spontaneous.[6] It seems that for Gheaus, societal justice can only be achieved if gender is rendered more or less irrelevant.

My paper will disagree in great measure with the account of gender justice offered by Gheaus. However, my disagreement will not focus upon the particular

© 2017, *Proceedings of the ACPA*, Vol. 90
doi: 10.5840/acpaproc201822373

contours of her argument. My objection is far more fundamental: I will argue that the account or "principle" of gender justice she proposes is by no means primitive. It is itself based on more ultimate philosophical principles, and these principles, though widely held, are inadequate to the reality of the human person. The Scholastic adage applies here: *Parvus error in initio, magnus erit in fine.*[7] One cannot construct a satisfactory account of gender justice upon such theoretical foundations.

Thinking well and clearly about gender justice is made possible by a particular set of anthropological and ethical first principles. Through a method of critique, my paper will attempt to identify some of them. I will begin, in my first section, by discussing the ultimate principles upon which Gheaus's account of gender justice is based. These first principles include the goodness of equality and freedom of choice, the distinction between sex and gender, the injustice of burdens being imposed without consent, and gender as a restriction upon human freedom. These are the theoretical principles upon which she bases her more practical "principle" of privileging gender-neutral lifestyles.

In my second section, I will offer a critique of the principles supporting Gheaus's account. In the course of doing so, I will propose some alternate principles, ones better suited to ground gender justice. Three of these will be of particular importance. One principle will be that sex and gender should be thought of as a unified, natural reality. A second principle will be that a burden can sometimes be just even in the absence of consent; justice is rendering to the other what is "due." A third principle will be that gender is an orientation toward particular sets of human virtues; gender is teleological.

The First Principles of a "Gender-Neutral Lifestyle"

I have claimed that my disagreement with Gheaus is ultimately one of first principles. What, then, are some of these principles upon which her account is based? Gheaus herself identifies two as having a fundamental importance: the values of equality and individual freedom of choice.[8] For ease of analysis, we might rephrase these values as statements or principles: (1) equality is good; (2) individual freedom of choice is good. These principles are judgments of value, not statements about the being of the human person. For example, Gheaus's fundamental principle of equality is not that the genders are in fact equal in dignity or power, but more simply, that it is good or valuable when the genders are treated equally. Similarly, Gheaus's principle concerning free choice is not a denial of determinism. It is just a principle about the desirability of free choice within human affairs. We should also note that since these are the foundational principles or "values" in her account of gender justice, Gheaus does not attempt to prove their truth or goodness. However, she does present them as reasonable values to adopt, inasmuch as they are said to be important to "all liberal conceptions of justice."[9]

Each of these values is to be understood in a particular manner. Gheaus specifies that she is working with a "robust" sense of equality. As she explains, equality does not mean that men and women should have different but somehow equal burdens or privileges. She seems to consider that sense of equality to be more of a danger than a good, for it has been used in the past to support a strict gendered division of societal roles.[10] The sort of equality that Gheaus considers a good or value is more univocal: men and women must be burdened or privileged in the same ways.[11] Gheaus also wants the value of freedom to be understood in a robust way: namely, she holds that freedom of choice is a human good no matter what choices are actually made. Human choice has a general, "nonspecific" value, in addition to whatever value it receives from the things chosen.[12]

Gheaus also acknowledges that a distinction between gender and sex is important to her argumentation, and she claims that a denial of this distinction is "one of the most formidable obstacles to gender justice."[13] According to Gheaus, sex refers to the biological features that differentiate the male and female members of the human race. By contrast, gender indicates the "social meanings associated with sex."[14] Gender is therefore socially constructed, not naturally occurring. Gheaus does admit that gender and sex often happen to correspond in human existence. As she says, they "map onto each other—albeit imperfectly."[15] However, she offers no explanation of why the correspondence occurs.

The goodness of equality, the goodness of freedom of choice, and the distinction between sex and gender are all important principles that support and shape the account of gender justice offered by Gheaus. She is reflexively aware of these three principles, and she takes care to draw the reader's attention to them. However, these are not the only principles that shape Gheaus's account of gender justice. There are also a couple of implicit philosophical principles upon which her argumentation depends.

First, there seems to be a general assumption that a burden or responsibility can only be just if it is in some way freely chosen. As she says, "In a just society nobody has to systematically take on more burdens than others—unless they freely choose to and are offered proper compensation."[16] Gheaus's analysis of a traditional division of labor within a family is instructive in this regard. According to Gheaus, if the husband works outside the home, while the wife stays home and cares for the children, our intuitive moral appraisal of the situation will depend upon the degree of choice involved. If the couple has voluntarily chosen to divide the work in such a way, then we are likely to think that "all is fine." However, if "they end up with this arrangement due to the pressure of gender norms" instead of freely choosing the division, then we will feel some injustice has occurred.[17] For Gheaus, then, the paradigmatic case of injustice involves the imposition of burdens without consent. This is why gender norms are so problematic: such norms are generally forces independent of our willing. They give us responsibilities we would rather not have.

A second important assumption is that gender and gender norms primarily act as restrictions upon individual freedom of action.[18] The fundamental action of gender norms is to hinder one from doing or achieving certain things. Gheaus gives examples of gender norms prohibiting men from expressing fear, or from investing a great amount of time and energy in the cultivation of close, fulfilling human relationships. She also offers examples of gender norms aimed at discouraging women from engaging in abstract thought, or from pursuing careers outside of the home.[19]

In fact, Gheaus's account of gender and gender norms is so pervasively negative that one begins to wonder why such things came to exist at all. Why would so many human beings throughout history have chosen to formulate, or at least follow, rules that pushed them away from some of the essential elements of human happiness and hindered their freedom to make choices? Gheaus is mostly silent on the question. However, in one spot in her article she does suggest that gender norms have some sort of survival value: "'feminine' as well as 'masculine' functional spheres are necessary for individual survival and social reproduction."[20] Gender and gender norms have functioned as a way of ensuring that the basic goods of individual and societal survival are achieved.

Critiquing the Principles of Gender Justice

Both the explicit and implicit principles upon which Gheaus bases her account of gender justice are thought by many to be true and in need of no defense. However, I do not think such widespread endorsement is warranted, especially when these principles are meant to ground an account of gender justice. While some of these principles are fairly innocuous and non-controversial, some are quite contentious and in need of substantial revision.

Among the more contentious of these first principles would be what Gheaus calls the "classical" distinction between sex and gender. The term "classical" is somewhat jarring in this context. As Prudence Allen has shown, the roots of the sex/gender distinction might be found in certain philosophical schools such as Neoplatonism and Cartesianism, but the distinction as it is currently understood (sex as natural, gender as constructed) only came into wide currency in the twentieth century.[21] And even in the late twentieth and early twenty-first centuries, the sex/gender distinction has by no means met with universal approval. Gheaus mentions that the distinction is opposed by some neurobiologists and evolutionary psychologists. One might be tempted to discount such opposition, since members of those disciplines could be seen as having a vested interest in interpreting social phenomena in terms of material, bodily realities. However, the sex/gender distinction is opposed by thinkers in many other fields: it is also opposed by some philosophers, medical doctors, theologians, writers, clinical psychologists, diplomats, and others. The distinction has also been criticized by high-ranking members of the Catholic clergy.[22] Objections to the sex/gender distinction are by no means confined to particular academic fields, or to the academy at all.

The fact that a strict distinction between sex and gender is not accepted by many contemporary thinkers, or most humans throughout history, is by no means a definitive argument against it. Humans make plenty of intellectual errors. Yet the sizeable, longstanding, and distinguished opposition to the distinction does mean that a heavy burden of proof must be placed on any philosophical account of justice built upon it.[23] We would need compelling reasons to accept a theory of gender justice whose theoretical foundations are uncertain.

While not formally admitting the existence of this burden of proof, Gheaus seems at least tacitly aware of the problem. She attempts to render the sex/gender distinction less contentious by citing some research in support of it, and more importantly, by arguing that truth or falsehood of the distinction ultimately has no effect upon her conclusions concerning gender justice. Were we to suppose that gender is natural like sex, it would still not mean that we should treat men and women differently. As she says, it "would not entail that it is just to block individuals' access to very important goods."[24] Rather, the naturalness of gender would simply mean that a just society could not hope to be a maximally efficient society. Gheaus claims that this is not a problem specific to her account of gender justice, but a larger and more general problem about whether societies should aim at efficiency or justice.[25]

However, the problem of inefficiency cannot be so lightly dismissed in terms of the particulars of Gheaus's own account. If, as Gheaus suggests, gender and gender norms are ordered to individual and societal survival, then the inefficiency in question would be inefficiency in maintaining life. Such inefficiency is an entirely different category than an inefficient dry cleaner or an inefficient method of grading papers. Life has the status of a fundamental good; it is a good one must have to achieve other goods such as a successful career and fulfilling relationships. No, if gender is ordered to survival, then the account offered by Gheaus places gender justice and life in a fundamental opposition. Such an account of gender justice would then bear little relation to the "classical" sense of justice as a *virtue*, a perfection of living human beings.

A theory of gender justice could avoid many of these problems, and especially the problem of carrying a heavy burden of proof, by re-adopting the principle that has guided most human thought on these matters: sexual difference arises by nature, and even culturally-influenced expressions of masculinity and femininity (i.e., gender) find their ultimate basis in this natural reality of sex. Gender is not infinitely malleable, but is limited and guided by our bodily constitution as male or female. Put differently, there is no *real* distinction between sex and gender. A conceptual distinction is indeed possible, but sex and gender are ultimately just different aspects of the bifurcation in the human mode of existing. Viewed on the bodily level, humans have a male or female reproductive role and bodily configuration.[26] Viewed on a more spiritual or intellectual level, one might wish to speak of masculinity or femininity, an identifiable set of behaviors, qualities, or social roles. However, while one can conceptually distinguish between these various aspects of being male or female, the human person is a unity of body and mind—and so sex and gender are ultimately united.[27] Thinking well about gender justice requires, in other words, a hylomorphic understanding of the human person.

A second contentious principle in Gheaus's account is that a burden can only be just if it is freely chosen. The principle is used to support the claim that any burden imposed on a person by one's gender is fundamentally unjust. We might call this a "contractual" sense of justice, the just as the agreed upon or the chosen. It is an important sense of justice to recognize, for our free choices do primarily determine what is just in some contexts. But a problem occurs in the *reduction* of justice to this contractual form; justice is a wider, more complex phenomenon, and free choice is not always the most important factor. It might be possible for some burdens to be justly imposed on us by nature or human society, regardless of our lack of consent or choice.

In Book V, ch. 3 of the *Nicomachean Ethics*, Aristotle points out that merit is the key element to consider in distributions of commonly-held goods or property. Although Aristotle speaks primarily of the goods that might come to one from having a share in the constitution, we know that political communities also impose burdens upon their citizens. Such burdens might be just, even if not freely chosen, so long as they are not arbitrarily assigned—that is, as long as the distribution is guided by the consideration of merit (or the lack thereof). One traditional idiom to express this thought is *Noblesse oblige*, "nobility obliges." Few of us would think it fundamentally unjust if a nation in a war for its survival conscripted its best warriors for the struggle. The martial excellence of these warriors imposes certain burdens upon them, even if that excellence owes much to their physical size and other non-chosen characteristics.

In a far less dramatic but still analogous way, the natural "excellences" of being male or female might justly impose certain privileges or certain burdens, even though one does not freely chose one's gender. It seems, then, that an adequate account of gender justice needs to base itself on a more flexible—and much more classical— principle of what justice is: not simply justice as giving the other what has been agreed upon, but instead giving the other his or her *due*. In the context of criminal justice, the "due" would indeed seem to be dignified, equal treatment. As Gheaus rightly notes, it is a clear case of gender injustice when one is victimized because of gender.[28] However, in situations of distribution, strictly equal treatment might fail to recognize and render what is one's due. For example, is it actually unjust that maternity leave is more commonly offered than paternity leave? Or to make the example a bit more difficult, would it be a true situation of gender injustice if both paternity and maternity leaves were legally mandated, yet maternity leave was specified to be of a longer duration? It is true that both father and mother contribute to the existence of the child, but there are several considerations one might offer in support of the idea that more is somehow "due" to the mother, at least during the time immediately following childbirth.[29]

Some of Gheaus's other fundamental principles such as the goodness of equality and the goodness of individual free choice do not seem as contentious. Yet even these principles are open to some mild critiques and revisions. One could certainly grant that human freedom retains some degree of value irrespective of its objects, but an emphasis on this sort of freedom seems most compatible with a view of the human person as lacking any ultimate ends, a non-teleological view of the person. If the human person is instead oriented to the achievement of certain perfections, then far greater value would attach to the appropriate use of freedom than to freedom as such. It is fitting for rational beings to enjoy freedom of choice within the limits imposed by nature; but it is even more fitting for that freedom to be used well, in a way perfective of one's nature. A better principle for gender justice would emphasize the "specific" value of freedom—freedom to pursue the perfections to which one is naturally ordered.[30]

In a similar way one might agree with Gheaus that a univocal, absolute form of equality has some value. We might find such an intuition even in Aristotle—a thinker not typically associated with the notion of male and female equality—in his account of rectificatory or "criminal" justice in Bk. V, ch. 4 of the *Nicomachean Ethics*. Aristotle claims that merit should play no role in criminal justice. Instead, judges should strive to impose a more absolute, arithmetical equality between the offender and the victims. To put Aristotle's thought back into our contemporary context, there would be something fundamentally unjust about a society, a religion, or a culture in which victims were presumed to bear some guilt simply because of their gender. Inasmuch as men and women are equally human, we find it fitting that they should enjoy equal personal dignity.

The problem is that Gheaus does not mean for her account of gender justice to be confined to the sphere of criminal justice, and outside of that sphere, univocal equality is not as obviously valuable. As Harry Frankfurt argues in relation to economic matters, equality "is not a morally compelling ideal."[31] It is not valuable in and of itself. Equality is a mere relation, a comparison of two things. What matters, economically speaking, is that people have enough goods to lead dignified lives, even if others have more of certain goods, or perhaps different goods altogether.[32] We might pursue a similar line of critique in relation to gender justice, especially with regard to the more distributive aspects of the issue. Is absolute, univocal gender equality what matters? Does human flourishing depend on male and female privileges and burdens being the same in every way, or is something else more important? Would univocal gender equality allow us to have "enough" of the good?

If gender is primarily a socially-created restriction upon our actions, something that holds us back from the good, then such absolute equality might indeed appear necessary. Absolute equality would help to ensure that people have enough access to the components of good human lives, components such as close relationships and non-domestic work. However, a problem occurs because gender is more than simply a restriction upon freedom; in fact, gender is an orientation to certain higher-order goods. Gheaus is correct that gender assists in achieving individual and societal survival, but it also seeks to achieve far more. Gender is a predilection to develop particular human perfections or virtues. On this alternative model, gender could be thought of in a positive way as a sort of biological, psychological, and social "jig" that guides us toward the good.[33] As with any jig, such guidance involves restriction. However, the restriction involved is far less significant than the teleological ordering (and the goods that ordering brings).

Pope St. John Paul II, for example, seems to have thought of gender in this teleological way when he wrote of the "genius" of women. As he says, the genius of women is not the exclusive possession of a few exceptional women throughout history: the genius is also seen in "ordinary women."[34] It is a certain set of natural predispositions to develop personal qualities such as empathy, sensitivity to the value of the person, intuition, self-gift, etc. Acting upon these natural dispositions allows women to achieve human flourishing, to "fulfil their deepest vocation."[35]

To speak of gender in this teleological way is not to suggest that there are a great number of virtues, if any, that only men or only women can achieve. Virtues are *human* excellences, not specifically male or female excellences. The point is instead that gender facilitates the acquisition of certain rare goods or virtues, thus making it more likely that those virtues are achieved (and achieved in a higher degree) by one sex or the other. Rather than simply a negative reality, a restriction of freedom locking people away from goods, gender should be understood as bringing about a net gain in the human good. Because of gender, we are able to obtain personal goods that would otherwise be practically inaccessible. Gender is a natural orientation toward the inner freedom that is virtue.

If gender functions in this more robustly teleological way, then a gender-neutral lifestyle would actually have the opposite of its intended effect: namely, both individuals and the wider community would miss out on certain rare human goods. A unisex or gender-neutral lifestyle might indeed succeed in removing some of the external impediments to human goods by allowing greater legal and cultural access to non-domestic work and fulfilling relationships. However, such external impediments are not the only challenges to achieving a good human life. The internal impediments to flourishing, our lack of various virtues, are also formidable obstacles. For example, having close relationships is not likely to be personally fulfilling if one lacks the empathy and intuition that help to sustain such relationships. In like manner, engaging in non-domestic work does not make for a good human life if one is highly inadequate at one's job, or if one fails to find any deeper meaning in one's tasks.

Of the two sorts of impediments, it is the internal impediments to flourishing that are the more difficult to overcome. A country might pass a law granting men lengthy paternity leaves to facilitate the development of close, fulfilling relationships with their children. But the paternity leaves will do no good if the men devote the time to dissolution. The example helps to show that we need the virtues even more than we need access to all possible human goods. We need the virtues to "unlock" these various goods. But the cultivation of virtue typically requires time, attention, and repeated, good actions. Gender gives us a much-needed natural and societal "nudge" toward investing the time and energy needed to acquire those personal perfections.

It is from virtuous agents that one becomes aware of the possibilities of virtue and right action, and so the different goods achieved by men and women under the influence of gender norms can be shared. For example, a wife might cultivate empathy to such an exquisite degree that even her somewhat humanly "dense" husband could suddenly become aware of that moral excellence by watching her. He could even begin to take some halting steps towards the virtue under her tutelage. By contrast, a gender-neutral lifestyle directs one to nothing; it gives no "head-start" towards certain virtues, nor direction, and we should expect only a leveling mediocrity as a result. A gender-neutral or "unisex" lifestyle might allow us to live, but not to live well. In the name of equality, the genderless life would stunt the full possibilities of human development.

Conclusion

In the first section of this paper, I discussed the theoretical foundations of a "gender-neutral" vision of gender justice. Though my analysis focused upon the particular account of gender justice offered by Anca Gheaus, the first principles informing her account are by no means uncommon. I suspect one might find similar principles undergirding many contemporary philosophical discussions of issues relating to gender. If we wish to achieve greater clarity with regard to gender justice, it is thus desirable that these often-tacit first principles be brought to light.

In the second section of this paper, I offered a critique of these principles, and I proposed several revisions of them. I suggested that we deny, or at least rethink, the sex/gender distinction. We should think of gender as based in biological sex, making gender, like sex, a natural reality. I also suggested that gender justice requires a more classical conception of justice: namely, giving the other his or her due, whether that "due" comes through nature or convention. Finally, I have suggested that we adopt a teleological outlook on the reality of gender. Rather than thinking of gender simply as an instrument of societal control, we should understand gender as a natural orientation towards certain virtues, an orientation reinforced through societal gender norms. In other words, gender is good news. The goal should not be to master gender and destroy it, but to be mastered by it, letting it guide us to the good.

This paper has been a prolegomena to gender justice. I have not attempted to give a full account of this form of justice. I have merely sought to identify the starting points for building an adequate account. Nevertheless, I anticipate that some might object even to these elemental principles of gender justice I have proposed. Some will suspect that the adoption of these principles would be likely to lead to a "retrograde step" in gender relations, for it is often assumed that thinking of gender as natural and necessary forces us to embrace a strictly gendered division of societal roles. Women would be restricted to the private sphere of the home, while men would be limited to the more public spheres of government and non-domestic work.

However, I do not think the principles I have proposed would necessarily conclude to such a division of societal roles. If societal roles, or even particular jobs, were completely reflective of particular virtues, and the virtues themselves were strictly divided between men and women, then such a division might make sense. For example, if being a stay-at-home parent merely required only the stoic ability to repress one's emotional expressions, and if only men were capable of such emotional control, then one might have a good argument that only men should be homemakers. But it does not seem to me that either societal roles or gender should be understood in those ways. As I have argued, gender predisposes one to develop certain virtues, but this does not mean that the virtues cannot be developed by the members of the other gender. John Paul II may speak of empathy as part of the feminine genius, but we all know men can be empathetic as well—it is just a more difficult virtue for males to recognize and achieve. Moreover, societal roles typically draw upon many different human qualities, and those qualities in various degrees, so it would not be advantageous to restrict roles or jobs to one sex or the other. Having different sets of virtues causes men and women to "inflect" their societal roles differently, and this diversity in performance is a valuable thing. Difference and diversity are not antithetical to gender justice.

St. Gregory's University

Notes

1. "Am Beginn eines Textes steht für mich fast immer irgendeine Irritation." Robert Spaemann, *Über Gott und die Welt: Eine Autobiographie in Gesprächen* (Stuttgart: Klett-Cotta, 2012), 168.

2. Anca Gheaus, "Gender Justice," *Journal of Ethics and Social Philosophy* 6.1 (January 2012): 1. Gheaus specifies that her term "costs" should be taken in a broad sense that would include material, psychological, and social penalties.

3. Examples of gendered lifestyles and behaviors mentioned by Gheaus include women engaging in domestic work and men typically avoiding direct expressions of sadness or fear.

4. Gheaus, "Gender Justice," 20. However, Gheaus is also careful to indicate that gendered lifestyles should only be made "slightly more costly," not "prohibitively costly." Making gendered lifestyles prohibitively costly would unduly interfere with freedom of choice, a fundamental value in her account. See ibid., 21. Nevertheless, we should take note of the dialectical reversal in her position: the freedom of a gender-neutral world must be achieved by restricting freedom.

5. Gheaus, "Gender Justice," 22.

6. Gheaus does not clearly specify what "gender-shaping" means. I presume she is referring to societal practices such as forbidding boys from wearing dresses, or advising girls that it is "unladylike" to swear.

7. "A small error in the beginning will grow large in the end." St. Thomas Aquinas quotes the axiom at the start of *De ente et essentia*.

8. "The principle of gender justice that I propose here relies on the two values reflected, in different proportions, by all liberal conceptions of justice: equality and individual freedom." Gheaus, "Gender Justice," 12. For a similar statement, see also ibid., 1: "This principle is grounded in the values at the core of liberal egalitarian justice: equality of access and the good of individual choice."

9. Gheaus, "Gender Justice," 12.

10. "The second solution to gender justice, that is, making women and men equally well off by giving more recognition and economic support to "feminine lifestyles," was criticized for entrenching the gendered division of labor and therefore curtailing women's access to "masculine" lifestyles." Gheaus, "Gender Justice," 2.

11. "It is unfair, and therefore unjust, for some people to be worse off than others on account of their sex . . . even if everybody's (lack of) freedom in this respect is equal." Gheaus, "Gender Justice," 12.

12. "Freedom has (also) nonspecific value, deriving from the way it determines agency rather than from the value of things we actually choose." Gheaus, "Gender Justice," 14.

13. Ibid., 16.

14. Ibid., 3.

15. Ibid.

16. Ibid., 5. It is difficult to determine how important the qualifier "systematically" is to her argumentation. Does Gheaus mean to suggest that there is nothing unjust in occasional, non-systematic burdens imposed by one's gender?

17. Ibid., 6.

18. If one views gender as socially constructed (as does Gheaus), then there is not much of a difference between gender and gender norms. The gender norms create gender. Perhaps one could distinguish between gender norms as the rules, and gender as the content of the rules.

19. For examples of male gender norms, see Gheaus, "Gender Justice," 9, 11. For examples of female gender norms, see ibid. 9, 18.

20. Ibid., 2.

21. Prudence Allen, "Gender Reality vs. Gender Ideology," in *Thomas Aquinas: Teacher of Humanity*, ed. John Hittinger and Daniel Wagner (Newcastle upon Tyne, UK: Cambridge Scholars Publishing, 2015), 310–315.

22. See especially the General Audience of April 15, 2015, in which Pope Francis speculates that gender theory is "an expression of frustration and resignation, which seeks to cancel out sexual difference because it no longer knows how to confront it." Pope Francis, *General Audience*, April 15, 2015, https://w2.vatican.va/content/francesco/en/audiences/2015/documents/papa-francesco_20150415_udienza-generale.html.

23. We should recall that an argument from authority is only fallacious to the extent that the authority invoked is not a true expert or is in some other way improper. Appeals to proper authorities are reasonable forms of argument.

24. Gheaus, "Gender Justice," 17.

25. Ibid., 18.

26. We should note, however, that bodily configuration as male or female is not limited to differences in the reproductive organs or other minor cosmetic features. There are also differences in the structure of the brain, of the eyes and ears, and of the cellular mechanisms regulating the perception of pain. While these sexual differences may be fairly minor considered individually, they have a profound cumulative effect on the human experience. For an opinionated but competent overview, see Leonard Sax, *Why Gender Matters: What Parents and Teachers Need to Know about the Emerging Science of Sex Differences* (New York: Doubleday, 2005).

27. There is an attractive "ontological economy" in thinking of sex and gender as united. Only one reality is posited instead of two, eliminating the problem of explaining how sex and gender come to correspond in human life, or how the "construct" of gender can have governing power in the absence of a natural basis.

28. See Gheaus, "Gender Justice," 4: "If those directly responsible for the above injustices are partly motivated by hatred or prejudice against women, the victims of violence and discrimination do not just happen to be women—rather, they become victims of injustice because they are women. Hence, these examples are clear illustrations of gender injustice."

29. For example, one might argue that the great difficulty involved in labor and birth merits a longer recovery period. Or, one might argue that during the so-called "4th trimester," the time immediately following birth, the goods the mother can offer to the child (nutrition, familiarity, etc.) are of paramount importance.

30. The much-debated (but rarely instituted) idea of payments to mothers seems premised upon the value of this sort of freedom. Knowing that they will receive financial support (and social esteem) liberates women to pursue the perfection of motherhood, the perfection to which all other female perfections are ordered.

31. Harry Frankfurt, *On Inequality* (Princeton: Princeton University Press, 2015), 5.

32. Ibid., 7.

33. The philosophical significance of jigs has recently been explored in Matthew Crawford, *The World Beyond Your Head: On Becoming an Individual in an Age of Distraction* (New York: Farrar, Straus and Giroux, 2015). See especially 31 ff.

34. "Necessary emphasis should be placed on the '*genius of women*', not only by considering great and famous women of the past or present, but also those *ordinary* women who reveal the gift of their womanhood by placing themselves at the service of others in their everyday lives." Pope John Paul II, *Letter to Women*, Vatican web site, June 29, 1995, https://w2.vatican.va/content/john-paul-ii/en/letters/1995/documents/hf_jp-ii_let_29061995_women.html, sec. 12.

35. John Paul II, *Letter to Women*, 12.

Aquinas: Justice as a Cardinal Virtue

R. E. Houser

Abstract: This paper has two goals: 1) to understand justice as a cardinal virtue, according to Aquinas; and 2) to use his conception of justice as a cardinal virtue to understand how one engages in acts of "general" justice. The argument proceeds in four stages: 1) how Aquinas understands the virtues by looking to their "objects"; 2) the two distinct "modes" of the four cardinal virtues, as "general" and "specific" virtues; 3) the triangle of three kinds of justice, seen in terms of their "objects"; 4) Aquinas's doctrine of justice as a "general" virtue (*ST* 2-2.58.5–6) shows that we can perform operations of "general" justice in two ways, as do the ruler and his minsters, and as ordinary folk do. Surprisingly, it is the latter mode of acting for "general" justice that is primary, not the former.

E specially in Europe and North America, but increasingly around the globe, human life is now characterized by stark and seemingly irrec- oncilable oppositions, especially in our common life together, the area traditionally called "political." From Louis XIV through Karl Marx and a vast array of socialisms, now including American, to various forms of contemporary Islamism, supporters of a maximal state have advocated sacrificing pursuit of personal goods in favor of the good for the community, traditionally called the common good. At the opposite extreme are advocates of a minimal state, whose current American form is called "libertarianism." And since the Second World War these two extremes have morphed, in Hegelian fashion, into the "social service state," which uses the resources and power of the political community at the service of individuals to realize their personal goods, with one caveat, that those goods must be approved by the "experts" who staff the ever-growing bureaucracy of that state.

Many students of contemporary society have looked for a "third way" to shoot between the horns of this dilemma. And here I propose to use the history of moral and political philosophy to contribute to that quest, in particular, the conception of justice of the medieval friar Thomas d'Aquino.[1] Unlike Aristotle, for whom the *polis* formed the horizon of his political thought, Aquinas was familiar with larger communities, the Roman Empire, the Islamic caliphate, and the Catholic Church. So he could broaden and deepen the understanding of the triangle of three senses of justice he inherited from "the Philosopher"—"legal" or "general" justice, "distributive" justice, and "commutative" justice. Here I shall end by looking to how the latter two, called "particular justice" because they aim at justice for an individual, necessarily contribute to "general" justice, whose end is the common good. Let us begin, however, by looking at how Aquinas understands the virtues by looking to their "objects." Then we will turn to how he distinguishes two distinct "modes" of the cardinal virtues, as "general" and "specific" virtues. Then we can focus on the relation of specific to general justice, which can give us a start in dealing with our current dilemmas.

1. Understanding the Virtues through Their "Objects" (*Objecta*)

Socrates rightly can be said to have begun moral philosophy with two efforts: initiating the search for universal definitions of moral excellences, like piety and friendship, and likening them to "crafts," such as his own skill at stone masonry.[2]

Plato recognized that knowing such crafts requires knowing the inner workings of the soul, to which we have no direct access. So he turned outside, to the polis, in order to explain virtue, and to things in the physical world and beyond, to the world of "forms," to explain knowledge.

In order to explain the attributes which, say, two individual triangles or equal things share, there must exist beyond them a higher world of unchanging and necessary "forms" or "exemplars" in which they share: the "triangle itself," the "equal itself," and the "form of the good." And these same forms are the ultimate source of universal and necessary knowledge, such as the subtraction axiom.

To understand virtue, Plato also looked outside the individual human, but here to the polis, where he saw three classes—craftsmen, warriors, and guardians—and therefore three correlative powers in the soul—desire (*epithumia, concupiscibilis*), emotion (*thumos, irascibilis*), and reason (*logistikon, ratio*). Each power is the seat of a virtue—temperance, courage, and wisdom respectively; and there also must be a virtue for the whole polis and whole soul—justice.[3] Thus were born the four "cardinal" virtues—though this term would not be coined until Ambrose. Finally, virtue, whether in the polis or in a man's soul, requires all four virtues working together.

Aristotle recognized Plato's standards were impossibly high. In morality, he said that virtuous action demands only co-ordination between the practical virtue of prudence and *one* of the twelve moral virtues he recognized. There is no courage, for example, without prudence, and no prudence without virtue; but warriors can be courageous without being temperate, as Homer had shown with Achilles.[4] So Aristotle brought Plato's heavenly forms down to earth, as has been said, in three areas important for our issue: ontology, cognition, and the virtues.

In ontology, Aristotle re-situated Plato's forms within the individual changing things in our world, so form became an *intrinsic* "principle" within an individual "composite substance." Form accounts for a thing's "actuality" as a certain "kind" (*eidos, species*) of "being." But because forms exist within individual things, Aristotle added a second, correlative intrinsic principle: "matter," which is "potentiality" for the "kind" the thing it currently is, and also for other kinds it can "become," in both its fundamental category (i.e, "substance," such as a "human"), and its accidental categories, (i.e., "equal" or "triangular"). Aristotle's new ontology thus provided a firm basis for cognition, both sensory and intellectual, and for moral virtue—but only a basis, one that required our own activity to realize both knowledge and virtue.

In explaining cognition, Aristotle followed Plato in turning to the thing cognized; not to separate forms but to the thing sensed (*aistheton*) or known (*gnôston*), later called in Latin the "object" (*objectum*) of cognition, which is the thing, not as it is in itself, but *as presented* to the knower.[5] Aristotle explained sensation through the example of sight. There are three different modes of an object of sense, "two of which," he said, "we call sensible essentially (*kath hauto*; *per se*)," such as "color, the *proper* object of sight," since only sight senses color, and five "common" objects of sense, which more than one sense power can take in: "motion, rest, number, shape, and magnitude." Aristotle's example of the third kind of sense object was a man such as "the son of Diares," which is an object of sight "accidentally" (*kata symbebekos*, *per accidens*), because being a man or a son is a feature of the thing we see, one that *accompanies* his color or shape and is known intellectually, not through sensation alone. In this way we see the color and the shape and the man, but in different senses of the word "see."[6]

The example of sight was Aquinas's favorite, but he reduced Aristotle's three kinds of sense objects to two: "the visible," the object of sight, "is two-fold, namely, the essential (*per se*), such as color, and the accidental (*per accidens*), such as a human."[7] He also explained why color is the *per se* object of sight in language Aristotle never had used: "Now that is designated properly the object of some power or habit, *under that aspect* (*ratione*) whereby all things are referred to that power or habit, for example, a human and a stone are referred to sight, in so far as they are colored. Consequently, colored thing (*coloratum*) is the proper object of sight."[8]

Understanding a power or habit in this way opened up more than one "aspect" (*ratio*) of the "object," and Thomas then made use of the fundamental ontological distinction between form and matter, conceived as act and potency, to analyze color and sight, and thereby the "objects" of cognition and moral action, in a way Aristotle never had:

> In the *object* we consider something as *formal* and something as *material*. Now what is formal in the object is that based on which the object is referred to a power or habit, while what is material is that on which this is founded. So if we speak of the *object* of the power of *sight*, its *formal object* is *color* or something of this sort, since to the extent that something is colored, to that extent it is visible; but what is *material* in the object is the *body* in which color inheres.
>
> From this it is clear that a power or a habit is referred to the formal aspect of its object essentially (*ad formalem rationem objecti per se*), but it is referred to that which is material in the object accidentally (*materiale in objecto per accidens*). Now things which are accidental do not produce

variation in a thing, but only things which are essential (*per se*). Therefore, *material diversity in the object does not diversify power or habit, but only formal diversity*. For there is but one power of sight by which we *see stones and humans and the heavens*, since this diversity of objects is material, and not based on the formal aspect of what is visible.[9]

Since form and matter are not things in themselves, but principles of a being, its "formal aspect" (i.e., color along with shape and size) causes us to *see* it, while its "matter" (i.e., *this* body) causes us to see this one individual stone or human. By contrast, the "formal aspect" of an object of *intellectual* cognition is not its color but its ontological *form* or essence and its "matter" is the *type* of body it has, for example, the intellectual soul and organic body in a human, or intellectual knowledge of an accidental form and the type of substance that is its "subject." Neither the "formal aspect" nor the "matter" can be omitted from a full understanding of the "object" of cognition, whether intellectual or sensory. Aquinas's account of the objects of knowledge then led to his explanation of the virtues in terms of their "objects," where we will see him use this same distinction between the "formal aspect" and the "matter" of the object to distinguish two senses of the cardinal virtues, namely general and specific. The "object" of a virtue (or vice) toward which human actions are directed will likewise have two features, one analogous to the "formal aspect" of an object of cognition, and the other analogous to its matter. The "formal aspect" will determine the moral type or "species" of the action that causes it to be virtuous (or vicious), while its "matter" will be the area of moral life such a virtue or vice involves.

2. The Four Cardinal Virtues: "Specific" and "General"

Aquinas recognized two opposing conceptions of the cardinal virtues, that between the Platonic-Patristic conception of the cardinal virtues and that of the Aristotelians, both of which he knew from his sources. And he embraced both by making a distinction:

> Some speak about the *four cardinal virtues in two ways*:
> Certain thinkers [Augustine and Gregory] use these four terms to signify *general modes* of the virtues (*generales modos virtutum*). They call all *rational direction* (*cognitio dirigens*) prudence; they call all *correctness producing equity* (*rectitudo adaequans*) among human acts justice; all *moderation* (*moderatio*) restraining human appetites from worldly goods they call temperance; all *firmness* of mind (*firmitas animi*) steadying a human in the good and against the assaults of all sorts of evils they call courage.... *Without all the conditions mentioned above dovetailing together*, one of these conditions by itself is *insufficient* to produce the true nature of virtue. According to this way of thinking, therefore, the four things mentioned are called four virtues, *not* because they are different specific habits understood in relation to different objects, but because they are different formal aspects of virtue (*secundum diversas rationes formales*).

Other thinkers, however, like Aristotle in his *Nicomachean Ethics*, speak about the four virtues under consideration in so far as they are specific virtues limited to their proper matter (*speciales virtutes determinatae ad proprias materias*). Now the quotation from Gregory is true when interpreted this way, as well: Through a kind of overflow, these four virtues concern those areas where the four general conditions of virtue we have mentioned are pre-eminently important.[10]

Aquinas here distinguishes "general" from "specific" senses of a given cardinal virtue by looking at its "object": both the "formal aspect" which describes the general nature of that virtue, and its "matter" which captures its specific area of its operation.

Aquinas makes three points about the "general" virtues. First, his descriptions of them are purposely abstract because they do not include the whole "object" of each virtue, but only its "formal aspect," which functions like a genus. General prudence is "rational direction" guiding the moral agent; general justice engenders "correct" external operations concerning others, based on the "notion of what is right and obligatory" (*ratio recti et debiti*); general temperance is "moderation" of desires that might take us away from our end; and general courage makes us "firm" in overcoming obstacles on the way to that end. Second, *all four* of these "general" conditions must be present *together* in each and every good concrete action; actions cannot achieve any good without all these features working together. Finally, this description explains why it is the "general" cardinal virtues that form the structuring principle of the *Secunda secundae*, since a "specific" cardinal virtue, and all its many subdivisions (its potential parts) have the same "formal aspect," but *different* "matter."

The focus of Aquinas's treatment of the "general" cardinal virtues is on actions that are *morally* good; but such virtues can be stretched to include actions which are morally bad, but teleologically good. Such is the case of a "good robber."

A human is called a *good* robber, and in this way we may speak of a *prudent* robber, by a similarity, because he devises fitting ways of committing robbery. This is the prudence of which the Apostle says: "The prudence of the flesh is death," namely, because it places its ultimate end in the pleasures of the flesh.[11]

Such a man is good in the sense that he has successfully achieved an end, but his prudence is "false" because his end is morally bad. Aquinas, then, recognizes the presence of the "general" cardinal virtues, even when they help bad people do morally bad things.

The "specific" cardinal virtues are not just different from the "general," but are "better,"[12] because they are more fully in accord with the true nature of moral virtue, and this for three reasons. First, such virtues are more real subjectively, since they exist as "habits" in various parts of the soul. So they have a kind of permanence the "general" virtues need not have, one which makes us better at living a good practical and moral life. Second, these virtues incline us only to *morally good actions*, not to bad ones; habits that make us more efficient at morally bad actions, of course, are vices.

Third and the most important, a "specific" cardinal virtue is confined to a limited "matter." This limitation is important because it comports with real world experience where humans can be courageous but intemperate, or magnificent but liars.

What is the "matter" for each of the "specific" cardinal virtues? Br. Thomas narrows down *prudence* to a "specific virtue" by using his action theory. Its "matter" includes deliberation and judgment, but its most distinctive feature is to "plan before acting" (*praemeditari de agendis*) and initiate actions by "commanding" a morally good operation (*bene praeceptiva, imperium*). The "formal aspect" of justice concerns external operations directed toward another and includes the moral notions of the "right and the obligatory"; the "matter" of specific *justice* adds the notion strict "equality" because it concerns "obligatory *actions between equals*," illustrated by the two species of "particular" justice—commutative and distributive justice—whose beneficiaries are particular humans, as distinct from the whole community. To the "formal aspect" of moderating desires, the "matter" of specific *temperance* confines those desires to the area of "the pleasures of touch," Aristotle's polite way of referring to eating, drinking, and sex. And to the "formal aspect" of "firmness," the "matter" of specific *courage* is limited to the "fear of death."[13]

As presented in his broad treatments of the cardinal virtues,[14] then, the "general" cardinal virtues are limited to the "formal aspects" of their objects, without reference to any "matter" or delimited area of application, while the objects of the "specific" cardinal virtues add the premier "matter" each virtue covers. And the subjective and potential parts of each of the cardinal virtues will apply their "formal aspects" to yet other matters. At least, this is the way things turn out for prudence, temperance, and courage.[15]

But justice, as presented in his more thorough treatment in *ST* 2-2, will turn out to be different. To be sure, "general" or, using Aristotle's term, "legal" justice includes the "formal aspect" of its object, namely, external operations, directed "toward another," involving the "notion of right and obligatory." But there is more. Unlike the other three "general" cardinal virtues, "general" justice will also include its own "matter," the common good of the community, in contrast with "particular" justice, which includes within its "object" a different "matter," namely the good of particular persons.

3. The Nature of Justice (*ST* 2-2.57–58)

Aquinas begins his more thorough treatment of justice with its etymological twin *jus*, which sometimes means the subjective "*art* by which we know what is just," or the "place where the *law* (*jus*) is rendered," or the "*judgment* (*ius*) rendered" by a judge, "even when his decision is wrong." But all these are derivative meanings; *jus* is "primarily used to signify a just thing itself (*ipsam rem iustam*)," that is, an external act that is just. This is why "what is correct (*jus*) is the *object* of justice" and why Aquinas's explanation of the nature of justice focuses on that "object."[16]

His explanation of justice itself (2-2.58.1) begins with a standard legal definition, from the *Corpus iuris civilis*: "justice is the perpetual and constant will to render to each and everyone what is correct for him (*ius suum unicuique*). This definition is "fitting if understood correctly," by measuring its "proper matter and object" against a standard provided by the cardinal virtues. "For an act concerning any matter to be virtuous, it is required to be *voluntary*, and that it be *stable* and *firm*." Now voluntary acts necessarily involve "rational direction" and willed "operation," the "general" cardinal virtues of prudence and justice; "firm" is Aquinas's own description of "general" courage; and stability is a feature of "general" temperance. So the standard legal definition shows justice to be a "general" cardinal virtue understood through the "formal aspect" of its "object," and this remains Aquinas's focus in Q. 58.

At 2-2.58.2, Aquinas rejects the Platonic notion of an interior justice within the soul, dismissing it as "metaphorical justice," as had Aristotle. It's not that psychic harmony is unimportant, far from it. But it simply is not justice, which "requires a diversity of subjects and therefore is only of one human toward another (*ad alium*)." This is the "formal aspect" of justice we saw earlier. In order to show that justice is a virtue, Aquinas notes in Art. 3 that "virtue renders a human act and a man himself good," by using "the rule of reason" whereby "justice regulates human operations." Here Aquinas invokes both "operation," a feature of "general justice," as well as the "rational direction" that is "general" prudence. And in Art. 4, he explains that the "subject" power of justice, "the proximate principle of action, is an appetitive power," the will, not the intellect, an argument he had earlier used to establish justice as a "general" cardinal virtue.[17]

Thus far, Aquinas's treatment of justice has followed smoothly along the lines seen earlier,[18] but this is about to change. He now introduces the triangle of the three senses of justice, as determined by their objects, beginning with "general justice" (2-2.58.5–6) and proceeding to "particular" justice (Art. 7–8). But he does not consider "distributive" and "commutative" justice, which are the two types of "specific justice," until he takes up the "parts" of justice (2-2.61).

Aristotle had said that "particular" justice is directed toward the good of an individual human, "distributive" when the community bestows that good on an individual, while "commutative" justice consists in "rectifying the transactions between one man and another."[19] And Aquinas follows suit. But with the third kind of justice, where an individual citizen contributes to the "common advantage" of his polis, they differ. Aristotle had called this kind "legal justice," because the individual obeys the laws of the polis. Aristotle had used this term because he had recognized that laws (*nomoi*) enjoin other virtues, as well justice. "The law bids us do the acts of a brave man, for example, not deserting his post or fleeing battle or throwing away our arms, and those of a temperate man, for example, not committing adultery to gratify lust."[20] So Aristotle had concluded that "this kind of justice is *complete* virtue, not absolutely, but in relation to another." But if legal justice covers the whole range of the virtues, what is the difference between virtue itself and legal justice? Aristotle had left but a single, cryptic answer: "they are the same, but their substance (*ousia*) [*essentia*, in Latin] is not the same; what, in relation to one's neighbor, is justice, is, considered without qualification, virtue."[21]

It is precisely on this point that Aquinas begins to interpret Aristotle in such a way that Aristotelianism turns into Thomism. The distinctions among these three kinds of justice are determined by their "objects." At 2-2.58.5 the issue is this: "Is justice a general virtue (*utrum justitia sit virtus generalis*)? It is, and to explain why Aquinas begins with the "formal aspect" of the object of justice: "Justice, as has been said, orders a human in comparison with another (*alium*)," and then he identifies two kinds of "other": "in one way toward another considered as an individual; and in the other way toward another considered in common, namely, in so far as the one who serves some community serves all the humans who are contained within that community." When the "other" is a particular human, the justice concerned is "particular," and Aquinas will divide it, like Aristotle, into "distributive" and "commutative" justice.

But Aquinas does not explain "legal" justice as Aristotle had done. Rather, Aquinas's argument sticks strictly within the ambit of final causality. Every individual is part of a whole, a community.

> Now every good of a part is ordered to the good of the whole. For this reason, therefore, the good of every virtue, whether it orders a human in relation to himself [such as courage and temperance] or orders him toward some other individual persons [commutative justice], leads us back (*referibile*) to the common good, toward which justice ordains us.[22]

Here Aquinas has taken Aristotle's materials and reshaped his argument.

To know that justice is a "general virtue" because it works for the common good, however, does not explain Aristotle's comment that legal justice and virtue "are the same, but their essence is not the same." So Aquinas directly raises this question, in Art. 6: "Is justice, so far as it is general, the same *in its essence* as all virtue?" Aquinas's answer is that legal justice is "*specific* in its *essence*," because it has "the common good as its *proper object*," but it is "general in its *power*." This clarification is built on a distinction Aristotle never made, one Aquinas takes from another of his favorite authors, Avicenna.[23] Aquinas explains:

> Something is called *general* in two ways. In one way, general *through predication*, as *animal* is general in comparison with human and horse and other such things. Now in this way, what is general must be the *same* essentially as that toward which it is general, because a genus pertains to the essence of its species and falls within its definition. But in another way, something is called general *in power*, as a universal cause is general in relation to all its effects, such as the sun in relation to all bodies which are illuminated or changed by its power. Now in this way, what is general does *not* have to be the same in essence as those things toward which it is general, because the essence of cause and effect are not the same.[24]

In which way is "general" justice general? It is not general through predication, since then the distinction between "general" and "particular" justice would be lost;

but through causality. This makes "general" justice a "specific" virtue *in its essence*, because its *object*, the common good, is *distinct* from the personal good, "but general in its *power*," a power that enjoins individuals in the community to act for personal goods which actually contribute indirectly (*mediate*) to the common good, as well as doing some things that contribute directly (*immediate*) to the common good.

Aquinas offers another particularly apt example to explain the power of "general" justice. "Just as *charity*, which looks to the *divine good* as its proper object, is a *specific virtue* in its essence, so also legal justice is a specific virtue in its essence, in so far as it looks to the *common good* as its proper object." Both charity and "general" justice are "specific" virtues "in their essences," because both have specific kinds of goods as their respective objects: God as the highest good that is loved for charity, and the common good of an earthly community for general justice. Neither charity nor general justice can be virtues "general by predication." Faith and hope are different from charity, just as temperance and courage are different from justice. Rather, charity and general justice are "general through power," their power over subordinate virtues and the individuals who act in accord with them, "which is to move through command all the other virtues." Since in Aquinas's action theory, "command" is a will act exercising efficient causality over the body, one might think that "general" justice exercises efficient causality over "particular" justice. And it is true that the law that governs the community can constrain its members to act in certain ways. But this is not what Aquinas means. He says that "legal justice is said to be a general virtue, in so far as it ordains the acts of the other virtues *to its own end*," that is, to the *common* good, a different end from the end of distributive and commutative justice. Aquinas's argument proceeds in the line of final causality, not efficient causality. General justice is *not* the same as all virtue, even though Aristotle had seemed to say so; the function of general justice is to move pursuit of personal goods onto the plane of communal goods through offering the members of a community a higher good to which their personal goods can and should fit and contribute.

Now there are two ways of acting in accord with "general" justice. In the first and more obvious way, "legal" justice "is *in* the ruler (*in principe*) principally and in the manner of a master craftsman, but it is also in his subordinates (*subditis*) secondarily and as his ministers."[25] Those who perform acts of "general" justice in this way are most obviously those who work directly and professedly (*immediate*) for the common good, as full-time members of the regime—from the prince and his vassals down to town mayors and tax collectors and night-watchmen. But we should also include those whose normal employment is elsewhere, but on occasion act directly (*immediate*) for the common good of the community, such as yeomen when they are jurors or soldiers for a time, or simple peasants who pay taxes or tithes.

Immediately after noting the first way of acting in accord with "general" justice, Aquinas adds a second way: "Nonetheless, *every virtue*, in so far as it is ordered to the common good by the aforesaid virtue ["general" justice], which is specific in its essence but general in its power, *can be called legal justice*."[26] When a particular person exercises moral virtue, say, temperance, or when he exercises commutative justice toward his neighbor, say in paying a fair price for shoes, in such cases he does two things. First, he contributes to someone's personal good, his own when being temperate, and his neighbor's when buying shoes. Second, he also contributes to the "common good" of the whole community, albeit indirectly. Such actions contribute to the common good, even though one is not working intentionally for that end. The normal and natural and, for most people, the best mode of acting for the common good in "general" justice is in this indirect (*mediate*) way; and it is enough to establish the conclusion that "general" justice has, as its "matter," the "other" which is the community and its common good.[27]

Aquinas caps his argument at 2-2.58.7, which is devoted to whether "there is some particular justice, in addition to general justice." There is, but by no means is particular justice isolated from general justice. To the contrary, the difference between them is not *whether* each contributes to the common good, but *how* they contribute to the common good.

General or "legal justice is not in its essence [that is, in its object] every virtue, but in addition to legal justice, which orders a human *immediately* to the common good, there must be other virtues which *immediately* order that human to particular goods. Now these virtues can be either ordered to oneself or ordered to another single person. Therefore, just as in addition to legal justice there must be some particular virtues that order a human in himself, that is, temperance and courage, so also in addition to legal justice there must be a certain particular justice that orders that human concerning those things that are in relation to another singular person.[28]

Aquinas's immediate concern here is to show that general or legal justice being directed to the community absolutely requires particular justice directed toward other individual members of that community. But in order to draw this conclusion, Aquinas also brings in the two cardinal virtues directed toward the good for ourselves, courage and temperance. Why this seeming side trip? The reason comes from the theme Aquinas had struck from the beginning of his treatment of the cardinal virtues, the requirement that the general cardinal virtues must work together and cannot be separated from one another, in contrast with the specific cardinal virtues, which only have to be paired with prudence. In order to function, in order to achieve the common good of the community, its "object," general justice must include prudence, courage, and temperance. If so, then general justice must be built on the exercise of courage and temperance, directly or immediately for the sake of ourselves, and, in addition, it requires particular justice for the sake of other individual humans.

In sum, individuals can perform acts of general justice, in three ways. First, they can do so as the ruler and his ministers do, who work in positions of command directly for the common good. Second, they can work as individual members of the community, directly (*immediate*) for the common good, under the command of the ruler. Third, individual members of the community can work indirectly (*mediate*) for the common good, by exercising virtue in their own regard or for the sake of their neighbors.

It is this *last* way of working for the common good that moved Aquinas well beyond Aristotle; and it can move us beyond our current dilemmas. But for this to happen, we must learn a hard lesson, one that Aquinas, and before him Plato, can teach us. There can be no public morality without personal morality, because, in Thomistic parlance, achieving the common good depends absolutely upon the personal virtues of the community's members. Their contribution is a necessary, though not a sufficient condition for the achievement of "general justice." This is but one of the many consequences of the fact that "man is a political animal."

* * *

We end, then, with one of Aquinas's most important conclusions about justice, one that is historically accurate about his thought and practically important for our time, and for all time. Not only is our pursuit of individual and commutative goods not inconsistent with acting for the common good, but acting morally toward self and toward neighbor is, for the majority of humans, the primary but indirect (*mediate*) way in which they exercise "general" or "legal" justice and thereby build up the common good. So "legal justice sufficiently orders a human in those actions which are toward another; as concerns the common good, *immediately*, and as concerns the good of one single person, *mediately*."[29] And the same is true in reverse. The personal virtues of courage and justice *immediately* produce the personal good for an individual person—ourselves—just as commutative justice produces the personal good immediately for other individual humans; but even more importantly, they produce the common good for the whole community, though mediately.

Aquinas's conception of how the majority in a community contributes to the common good offers us hope, but also a challenge to current political polarities. Exclusively "top-down" rule by powerful elites—whether the secular socialists of the West or Islamists of the East—cannot produce justice and a healthy common life, because they can never substitute for the free exercise of moral character in the general population that is absolutely required to feed into the common good "indirectly." Distributive justice then becomes corrupted when the elites try to use their misconceptions of it as a replacement for commutative justice, whether in totalitarian regimes or in the "social service state." But when "libertarianism" is substituted for commutative justice, the result is equally damaging to the common good. In this case, over-concern for my personal good eclipses the commutative justice we owe other individuals and, most importantly, the indirect contribution to the "common good" that is the benefit contributed to the whole community by its members acting in their personal capacities.

In sum, we should learn from Aquinas that pursuit of the decadent personal pleasures of the West undermines the common good, and that state developed institutions for distributive justice, when created and run by those who no longer understand personal morality and commutative justice, and especially their contribution to general justice, are bound to fail. Though he never read their works, Br. Thomas of Aquino well understood that the route to justice lies in the mean that runs between the absolute "freedom and equality" promised by "libertarians" from Plato's extreme democrat to Sartre and Rawls, as well as the totalitarianism running from Tiberius Caesar and the Caliph Umar to Marx and his epigones, from Lenin to the Ayatollah Khomeinei.[30]

Center for Thomistic Studies
University of St. Thomas, Houston

Notes

1.. Significant recent work on the cardinal virtues and justice in Aquinas: Jean Porter, *Natural and Divine Law: Reclaiming the Tradition for Christian Ethics* (Ottawa: Eerdmans, 1999); Stephen J. Pope, ed., *The Ethics of Aquinas* (Washington, DC: Georgetown University Press, 2002), studies of the cardinal virtues by James Keenan (Prudence), Jean Porter (Justice), Martin Rhonheimer (Injustice), R. E. Houser (Courage), Diana Fritz Cates (Temperance), 259–339; R. E. Houser, *The Cardinal Virtues: Aquinas, Albert, and Philip the Chancellor* (Toronto: Pontifical Institute of Mediaeval Studies, 2004); Jean Porter, *Nature as Reason: A Thomistic Theory of the Natural Law* (Grand Rapids, MI: Eerdmans, 2005); István Bejczy, "The Cardinal Virtues in Medieval Commentaries on the 'Nicomachean Ethics', 1250–1350," in *Virtue Ethics in the Middle Ages: Commentaries on Aristotle's Nicomachean Ethics, 1200–1500,* ed. István Bejczy (Leiden: Brill, 2008), 199–221; Michael Sherwin, OP, "Infused Virtue and the Effects of Acquired Vice: A Test Case for the Thomistic Theory of Infused Cardinal Virtues," *The Thomist* 73.1 (2009): 29–52; Peter Koritansky, *Thomas Aquinas and the Philosophy of Punishment* (Washington, DC: CUA Press, 2011); Michael Pakaluk, "Structure and Method in Aquinas's Appropriation of Aristotelian Ethical Theory," in *Aquinas and the Nicomachean Ethics*, ed. Tobias Hoffman, Jörn Müller, and Matthias Perkams (Cambridge: Cambridge University Press, 2013); Jeffrey Hause, "Aquinas on Aristotelian Justice: Defender, Destroyer, Subverter, or Surveyor?" in Hoffman, Müller, Matthias Perkams, *Aquinas and the Nicomachean Ethics*; Matthias Perkhams, "Aquinas's Interpretation of the Aristotelian Virtue of Justice and his Doctrine of Natural Law," in Hoffman, Müller, Matthias Perkams, *Aquinas and the Nicomachean Ethics*; Fernando Martin de Blassi, "¿Por qué motivo las cuatro virtudes se llaman cardinales? Pedro Lombardo, Alberto Magno y Tomás de Aquino," *Estudios Filosoficos* 63.184 (2014): 547–563; Steven J. Jensen, *Knowing the Natural Law: From Precepts and Inclinations to Deriving Oughts* (Washington, DC: CUA Press, 2015); Jean Porter, *Justice as a Virtue: A Thomistic Perspective* (Grand Rapids, MI: Eerdmans, 2016).

2. Plato, *Euthyphro, Laches.*

3. Plato, *Republic* IV (369a–444a), VI (504d–511e).

4. Aristotle, *Nicomachen Ethics*, VI.12–13 (1143b16–1145a13). See Houser, *The Cardinal Virtues*, 16–31.

5. Lawrence Dewan, OP, "*Objectum*: Notes on the Invention of a Word," *Archives d'histoire doctrinale et littéraire du moyen âge* 48 (1981): 37–96.

6. Aristotle, *On the Soul*, 2.6 (418a7–26). Aquinas, *In de anima*, Bk. 2, lec. 13.

7. Aquinas, *Super Sent.*, lib. 4 d. 49 q. 1 a. 3 qc. 1 ad 1m.

8. Aquinas, *ST* 1.1.7.

9. Aquinas, *De caritate*, Art. 4c. At *Super 1 Sent.*, d. 45, q. 1, art. 2 ad 1m, Aquinas adds the influence of light to his explanation: "color is visible in potency, but is not made

visible in act except through the action of light." Since light is the extrinsic cause of colors becoming visible, Aquinas uses this feature of the example when explaining the theological virtues. The two examples are consistent with each other, because form and matter are understood as act in relation to potency, so the two examples capture distinct features of sight: color makes things visible, while light makes colors, and things, actually to be seen. See Joseph Pilsner, *The Specification of Human Actions in St. Thomas Aquinas* (Oxford: Oxford University Press, 2006), 92–102.

10. Aquinas, *De virtutibus cardinalibus*, 1 ad 1m.

11. Aquinas, *ST* 2-2.47.13c.

12. Aquinas, *ST* 1-2.61.4c.

13. Aquinas, *De virtutibus cardinalibus*,1c and ad 1m; *ST* 1-2.61.2–4.

14. *ST* 1-2.61, *De virtutibus cardinalibus*, 1 and 2.

15. For temperance: *ST* 2-2.141.7; for courage: 2-2.123.2 and 11; for prudence: 2-2.48. un.c. Consider temperance. As a "general" cardinal virtue it is "moderation" in whatever area of life; its "integral" parts are "honest" attraction to the good and "shame" in the face of the bad; "specific" temperance is limited to the "pleasures of touch," whose "subjective" parts, its subdivisions or sub-species, are "abstinence" about food, "sobriety about drink, "chastity" and "purity" about sex; while its "potential" parts, about other "matters," include continence, clemency, modesty, good order, proper adornment, simplicity, humility, austerity, and restraint.

16. *ST* 2-2, 57.1 ad 1m.

17. *ST* 1-2.61.2c, *De virtutibus cardinalibus*, 1c.

18. Aquinas, *De virtutibus cardinalibus*, 1-2; *ST* 1-2.61.2–4.

19. Aristotle, *NE* 5.2 (1130b29–1131a2).

20. Aristotle, *NE* 5.1 (1129b14–22).

21. Aristotle, *NE* 5.1. (1129b24–25, 1130a12–13).

22. Aquinas, *ST* 2-2.58.6.

23. Avicenna, *On the Principles of Natural Science*, 2, Sec. 8–11, tr. J. McGinnis (Provo, UT: Brigham Young University Press, 2009), 8–10.

24. *ST* 2-2.58.6.

25. *ST* 2-2.58.6.

26. *ST* 2-2.58.6.

27. *ST* 2-2.58.7 ad 1m.

28. *ST* 2-2.58.7c.

29. *ST* 2-2.58.7 ad 1m.

30. Let me thank Christopher Tollefsen for his insightful comments on this paper at the San Francisco ACPA meeting, 2016. Informed by his suggestions, I have reworked the first section on understanding the virtues through their objects and the conclusion about contemporary life. Of course, much more must be said about the latter. But let's be clear, "if a Hobbesian or Humean account of reasons for action is true," then it is equally true that Aquinas should be dumped on the ash-heap of history. But they are not true, and the reason for presenting his views about the cardinal virtue of justice is to offer our contemporaries

better options than Hobbes or Hume. Dr. Tollefsen does this through his superb direct interventions into contemporary debates; I try to do so through offering the doctrine of Aquinas himself, in a way that I hope is intelligible to our contemporaries. These roles are complementary, and both necessary.

St. Thomas Aquinas on Original Justice and the Justice of Christ: A Case Study in Christological Soteriology and Catholic Moral Theology

Brandon L. Wanless

Abstract: This paper discusses the theme of "personal justice" in the *Summa theologiae*, a concept inherited from the *Nicomachean Ethics* wherein Aristotle says that a man is just toward himself only *metaphorically*, insofar as the parts of man are appropriately ordered with the higher ruling the lower and the body subjugated to the soul. This paper demonstrates how Aquinas extensively utilizes this concept of metaphorical justice across the tripartite division of the *Summa* in his accounts of original justice in the *prima pars*, the humanity of Christ in the *tertia pars*, and justification of the sinner in the *secunda pars*. As a response to critiques that Thomistic moral theology is not properly centered in the person of Christ, I will show that, for Aquinas, Christ's personal justice both fulfills the right ordering of humanity lost through sin and restores that integrity to mankind in the grace of justification—the root of the Christian's entire moral life.

I. Introduction: The Incarnation and Moral Theology

In Oxford University Press's interdisciplinary symposium on the Incarnation, Linda Zagzebski provides the chapter which relates the Christology of the Incarnation to moral theology, specifically virtue ethics.[1] She is quick to note that although "Christian ethics purports to centre on the life of Christ," it rarely ever does.[2] Instead, moral theologians find themselves adopting at their core either a theory centered upon natural law or some form of a divine command theory, neither of which possess anything distinctively Christian in her view. "Christian thinkers no doubt agree that Jesus Christ was paradigmatically good, but when this belief is incorporated into a theory, it too often amounts to nothing more than secular ethics plus an example."[3] Zagzebski's proposal is to establish an ethical theory with the Incarnation as central and the imitation of Christ as "the basic normative idea." The example of Christ, for Zagzebski, is presupposed to the systematic and theoretical evaluations, and guides all speculative inquiry as the touchstone of Christian morality.

© 2017, *Proceedings of the ACPA*, Vol. 90
doi: 10.5840/acpaproc2017111365

If Jesus did it or would do it, then so too should all Christians. He alone is worthy of perfect imitation and this imitation is at the heart of the Christian moral life.

St. Thomas Aquinas also saw it crucially important to recognize the central role of Christ in Christian moral theology. Most readers of his *Summa theologiae*, however, seem to miss this point due to Aquinas's method of arrangement. The "moral section" of the *Summa* is presented in the massive two-part *secunda pars*, with relatively little reference at all to Christ himself, let alone the Incarnation, until the *tertia pars*, wherein moral theology seemingly has no formal treatment as it is the "Christological/sacramental section" of the work. At *prima facie*, Aquinas seems to follow a rather rigid method of theological compartmentalization that artificially separates the dynamic unity of *sacra doctrina*. This observation, however, is quite flawed. I will argue in what follows that Aquinas sees a deep continuity in his treatments across the sections of the *Summa* wherein the treatment of Jesus Christ serves as the recapitulation and culmination of Aquinas's systematic and moral theology.[4] Working with a close reading of passages from the *Summa theologiae* (plus a few closely related texts), I propose to demonstrate that the theme of personal justice guides Aquinas's investigation of both his Christian soteriology and thus also his moral theology. Jesus Christ reestablishes in his human nature the order of justice lost by Adam in order to restore that same order of justice in the members of his Church by faith and the sacraments. I will proceed along the lines of three main sections: first, Aquinas's treatment of original justice in the *prima pars* and original sin in the *prima secundae*; second, his treatment of Christ's personal justice in the *tertia pars*; and third, a return to the *secunda pars* to examine his account of the justification of the sinner.

II. Thomas Aquinas on Original Justice

Original Justice in the State of Original Innocence

Aquinas maintains that, throughout the course of salvation history (i.e., the whole history of mankind from creation to eternal beatitude), "man has three states," namely, "innocence, sin, and glory," and that in the state of innocence, Adam possessed a gift that we refer to as "original justice."[5] This justification of the first man is called a state of *justice* not as a possession of the cardinal virtue which governs his acts with others, but "as it implies a certain rectitude of order in the interior dispositions of a man, in so far as what is highest in man is subject to God, and the inferior powers of the soul are subject to the superior."[6] Aquinas, following Aristotle, calls this justice "metaphorical" in as much as man is just toward himself, that is, the parts of man are properly ordered with the higher governing the lower.[7]

The relation of the parts of man in original justice are nowhere as comprehensively and succinctly detailed by Aquinas as in the account in his *Compendium theologiae*:

> Man was originally constituted by God in such a condition that his body was completely subject to his soul. Further, among the faculties of the

soul, the lower powers were subject to reason without any rebelliousness; and man's reason itself was subject to God. In consequence of the perfect subjection of the body to the soul, no passion could arise in the body that would in any way conflict with the soul's dominion over the body. Therefore neither death nor illness had any place in man. And from the subjection of the lower powers to reason there resulted in man complete peace of mind, for the human reason was troubled by no inordinate passions. Finally, owing to the submission of man's will to God, man referred all things to God as to his last end, and in this his justice and innocence consisted.[8]

This metaphorical justice of man in original innocence implies a relation of the higher parts of man to the lower consisting of the ruler to the ruled, as Aquinas says commenting on Aristotle's *Nicomachean Ethics*: "The reason is master of the irascible and concupiscible parts and governs them . . . as one who commands and one who obeys."[9] This self-mastery is at the same time a self-possession inasmuch as "possession denotes undisturbed ownership,"[10] denoting a radical body/soul unity in the human person.[11]

This perfect subjection and ordering within man's make-up was "not from nature," according to Aquinas, for thus "it would have remained after sin,"[12] but instead was the result of a supernatural state given by grace to Adam at the moment of creation.[13] "This grace would not have been natural . . . but would have been conferred on man immediately on his receiving a rational soul."[14] Further, this gift of original justice—with the reason perfectly subject to God—is principally rooted in the rational appetite of the will. "Now the whole order of original justice consists in man's will being subject to God: which subjection, first and chiefly, was in the will, whose function it is to move all the other parts to the end."[15] It is interesting to note that for Aquinas, though man in the state of "integral nature" did not need grace in order to love God above all things,[16] the grace of original justice allowed for a perfect subjection of his will beyond nature, that is, according to charity.[17]

Because the will ordered the rest of man to his true end, "the first subjection" of man's mind and will to God "was the cause" of the rest of his integrity: "while reason was subject to God, the lower powers remained subject to reason."[18] Therefore, "in that state the passions of the soul existed only as consequent upon the judgment of reason."[19] In other words, the soul was never impeded by the body, and the body and passions would only act following the movement of the will, as regulated by reason. From this perfect order and unity of man in original innocence, Aquinas says that a perfect harmony and "complete peace of mind" resulted,[20] as well as a preternatural beatitude pertaining to that state of natural integrity.[21]

Original Sin as Privation of Original Justice

Adam, in sinning, removed his will from this state of perfect subjection to God. Aquinas thus holds that, just as "to sin is nothing else than to fail in the good which belongs to any being according to its nature,"[22] so, too, original sin essentially is "the privation of original justice." As a privation, original sin removed that "obstacle" to "inordinate movements" of the lower appetites and the body which was original justice.[23] Therefore, original sin is also positively a quasi-habit insofar as it is "an inordinate disposition of the parts of the soul."[24] Aquinas refers to the privation of the order of justice itself as the formal element of original sin and the inordinate disposition as the material element. Formally, original sin is rooted in the will that is no longer subordinated to God. Materially, original sin consists in the inordinateness of man's powers as they turn to mutable goods, a disposition called concupiscence.[25] "Natural good is corrupted, inasmuch as man's nature is disordered by man's will not being subject to God's; and this order being overthrown, the consequence is that the whole nature of sinful man remains disordered."[26] Original sin thus is the state of corrupted nature which has been passed on from the first man as the principle of human nature. The need for a savior, then, lies in the reality of original sin and the need to reestablish human nature in accordance with original justice. As Sean A. Otto has correctly noted: all throughout this treatise, "Thomas's understanding of original sin points to a more important doctrine, that of the Incarnation."[27]

III. The Grace of Justice in Christ

The Perfection of Christ's Humanity

Aquinas's description of the three historical states of man—innocence, sin, and glory—is found in the *tertia pars*, of all places, in order to show how Jesus Christ, the Incarnate Word, in his humanity, corresponded in different ways to each of those states. "From the state of glory [Christ] assumed comprehension and from the state of innocence, freedom from sin—so also from the state of sin did he assume the necessity of being under the penalties of this life."[28] Later in his treatment of Christ's human and divine wills, Aquinas returns to this correspondence of Christ to the state of innocence, extending the scope of Christ's perfection from a freedom from sin to even a freedom from conflict within the very constitution of his humanity. "In us the desires of the spirit are impeded or retarded by the desires of the flesh: this did not occur in Christ. Hence in Christ there was no contrariety of flesh and spirit, as in us."[29] In the same article, Aquinas makes clear that the unity of order in Christ's humanity was not such that his body and lower passions simply desired everything that the rational will settled upon as good and necessary. "For it pleased Christ, in his divine will, and in his will of reason, that his natural will and will of sensuality should be moved according to the order of their nature."[30] In other words, although the divine will and Christ's deliberative human will were in agreement about his bodily suffering for the sake of man's salvation, it was not necessary for the lower parts of his humanity to be in perfect agreement, but instead were permitted to shrink from the suffering according to their natural disposition. All the while, however, this constituted no contrariety in the humanity of Christ himself. This "freedom from sin" and "lack of contrariety" in Christ corresponding to original innocence implies more than a negation of evil, however, but a positive perfection on the part of Christ's humanity, as is clear when turning to other material from the *tertia pars*.

In speaking of Christ's subjection to God the Father, Aquinas offers an exposition of the three ways in which men are subject to God, with a special allusion to the primitive state of man.

> Now human nature from its beginning has a threefold subjection to God. The first regards the degree of goodness, inasmuch as the divine nature is the very essence of goodness . . . while a created nature has a participation of the divine goodness. . . . Secondly, human nature is subject to God, as regards God's power, inasmuch as human nature, even as every creature, is subject to the operation of the divine ordinance. Thirdly, *human nature is especially subject to God through its proper act, inasmuch as by its own will it obeys His command.* This triple subjection to God Christ professes of Himself.[31]

This third form of submission to God, namely as man is subject to God by obedience, is according to man's proper act, that of the rational will. Clearly Aquinas has the personal justice corresponding to original justice in mind here. Christ is perfectly subject in his human will to the totality of the divine command, most especially in his obedience by which he willingly went to death out of divine charity.[32] Seemingly for Aquinas, this is the type of subjection to the Father that makes all the difference.

Moreover, to denote how Christ in his humanity is subject to *himself* in his divine nature, Aquinas once again explicitly refers to the principle of metaphorical justice inherited from Aristotle. "A certain notion of mastership and subservience may be preserved inasmuch as the same one is master of himself in different respects,"[33] namely according to the diversity of parts. These "parts" in the composite Christ are his humanity and his divinity. This subjection of Christ to himself is located precisely in the coordination of his two wills, human and divine. As Thomas Joseph White says, "The human will of Christ desired, willed, and acted in such a way so as to cooperate with and be in submission to the divine will."[34] Just as the graced state of original justice was rooted in Adam's will above all, so too in Christ, his human will was perfected such that his humanity was perfectly subjected to his divinity, all while constituting one composite subject—the Person of the Word. This perfection of the human will of Christ, just like that of Adam, is by way of sanctifying grace and the infusion of charity.

Aquinas also notes how the lower parts of Christ's humanity were subject to his reason and will, remarkably similar to the state of innocence. "But in the man Jesus Christ there was no motion of the sensitive part which was not ordered by reason. Even the natural and bodily operations pertained in some respects to his will, inasmuch as it was his will that his flesh should do and suffer what belonged to it."[35] Now, although Adam's body was not passible before sin, Christ did assume a passible body and other defects in keeping with the "penalties of this life" incumbent upon the state of sin,[36] in order to effect the work of salvation. So, while Christ did assume bodily defects, his human body was also "endowed with a most perfect constitution," because it was formed miraculously by the Holy Spirit, thereby making his external senses "most acute." Likewise, Christ's soul, in his suffering, "apprehended most vehemently . . . the causes of sadness" in its inferior powers according to their perfection.[37] Moreover, Aquinas posits that if Adam in innocence were passible, his bodily suffering would not have been as acute as that of Christ himself, despite the latter's assumed defects.[38]

Christ Fulfills the Ratio *of Justice Demanded of Mankind*

The soteriology implicit in the composition of Christ in assuming a passible body is further rooted precisely in the relation of his human and divine will. White says further: "If the action of God in Jesus is not truly the action of the Father, and if Christ is not able to act in concert with this action as man, then his 'soteriological' pattern of living on behalf of human beings in fact has no intrinsically salvific value."[39] Clearly, for Aquinas, the perfect subjection of Christ's human will to the divine in supernatural charity was ordered to the end of satisfaction. Thomas Hibbs stresses this point: "The main reason for the Incarnation is the need to satisfy for sin. The satisfying power of Christ's sacrifice results from his 'extraordinary charity' (*propter eximium caritatem*), which unites the human will in perfect obedience to the will of God."[40] In other words, according to the demands of satisfaction, the perfect order of justice in Christ made possible the means of satisfaction. "By his passion, Christ made satisfaction for the sin of the human race; and so man was set free by Christ's justice."[41]

Christ, in the ordering of justice according to the grace of charity in his human will, is himself the New Adam, the new incarnation of primitive justice formed by a perfect love of God and ordering of all things to God. Mark Armitage highlights this reversal of the prideful disobedience of Adam by the humble obedience of Jesus Christ. Armitage notes the central importance of the justice lived according to obediential charity in Christ as the manifestation of the perfect ordering of the man Jesus in the divine sapiential plan of salvation. Christ's justice is established by and for the sake of charity, which state of being enables him to merit in charity for his fellow mankind.

> This divine and sapiential *ordinatio* helps bring about the proper *ordinatio* of the human being both internally (*rectitudo ordinis*) and externally (*ordinatio* towards the goal of eternal life), and merit can be seen as consisting in obedience to the divine commandments inasmuch as the latter denotes both that *rectitudo ordinis* which derives from humility and that co-operation with the divine *ordinatio* which orders the will both internally and externally. . . . The obedience in virtue of which Christ is ruled entirely by his Father's will—that is, the perfect subjection of his will to that of the Father—constitutes Christ as truly just and well-ordered, and is the means by which he merits both for himself and for others.[42]

The establishment of Jesus Christ in the perfect order of justice and charity reestablishes the relationship between man and God lost by the prideful disobedience of

Adam. In Adam's fall, the gift of justice was lost and its recovery impossible to him. In divine wisdom, however, Jesus Christ, the Incarnate Word, would be brought forward as a man from a virgin, who was sinless by the gift of God to be the second Adam who would fulfill that original intention for mankind in his own person, but also in order to bestow it upon mankind.

The Instrumentality of Christ's Humanity

Thus it can be most accurately said that, for Aquinas, God put to use the personal human justice of Christ as the instrument of his sapiential economic plan for man's salvation. "Christ's passion was subject to his will. But his will was ruled by divine wisdom which 'ordereth all things' conveniently and 'sweetly.'"[43] Because an instrument is always put to use in accordance with its own nature, the humanity of Christ was put to use, so to speak, by the Godhead according to its own particular human perfection.

> In Christ, the human nature has its proper form and power whereby it acts; and so has the divine. . . . Nevertheless, the divine nature makes use of the operation of the human nature, as of the operation of its instrument; and in the same way the human nature shares in the operation of the divine nature, as an instrument shares in the operation of the principal agent.[44]

So, how did this instrumentality operate in Christ's humanity? Since it was in accord with the perfection of his human nature, it was by way of the perfect state of justice. That means that in the perfect subordination of his human will to the divine, God worked to achieve salvation, and this subordination of the will was precisely on account of Christ's supernatural charity. Thus, Aquinas can say that, in fact, "God the Father did deliver up Christ to the passion . . . inasmuch as, by the infusion of charity, he inspired him with the will to suffer for us"[45] and that Jesus Christ "as man gave himself up by a will inspired of the Father."[46] The instrumentality was supernatural, of course, because it was beyond the ability of human nature, but that does not mean it was unnatural. In fact, it is precisely the opposite; Christ's humanity as an instrument was put to use according to the supernatural perfection of that humanity and its most proper operation, the love of God.

IV. Christ's Justice as the Source of Our Justice

The Necessity of the Incarnation

The primary motivation for God the Word to become man was to make satisfaction for the sins of the whole human race, to atone for sin by his own suffering and death. Aquinas also points out, however, that this was by no means the singular motive, nor was it isolated from the many other motives whereby God arrived on the scene of human history as a human himself.[47] True, man left to his own devices could never make satisfaction for his sins to God, which had a quasi-infinite character, because of the now defective state of nature. Neither could he retrieve his previous state. "Human nature undone by reason of the act of sin, remains no longer perfect, but corrupted; nor can it be restored, by itself, to its connatural good, much less to the supernatural good of justice."[48] As we have seen above, Christ—who is both God and man—merited satisfaction for the sins of men by his superabundant charity and the suffering of his cross. Aquinas is careful to say, however, that this new relationship of men to God achieved in Christ's satisfaction is not simply a negation of punishment, but that it also bestows positive benefits which require some kind of participation in order for men to receive them. "Christ's passion wrought our salvation, properly speaking, by removing evils; but the resurrection did so as the beginning and exemplar of all good things."[49] In a careful analysis of the whole paschal mystery, Aquinas points out that just as Christ's bodily death was not isolated from his bodily resurrection and ascension into glory, even so is the forgiveness of sins not isolated from the bestowal of the life of grace which leads to glory in his followers.

Christ as Exemplar and Fountainhead

Aquinas, like Zagzebski, holds that Jesus Christ is exemplar of the Christian moral life. But for Aquinas, exemplar seems to have a fuller meaning than it does for Zagzebski. Aquinas holds that Jesus is the true model of the activity of Christians, an example to be followed in virtues such as charity,[50] obedience,[51] humility,[52] prayer,[53] etc.,[54] though it should be noted that Christ cannot be the model of all the virtues, since he had not faith[55] nor hope[56] as he was already a true comprehensor of beatitude. More than an example of virtue, however, Christ is also the very source of these virtues. This is true especially of the justice by which he is perfectly ordered in his humanity. The personal justice of Jesus Christ is the source for the justice by which each Christian is justified before God. The sanctifying grace of justification, for Aquinas, is the same grace by which Christ was personally just and also the same grace of harmony by which Adam and Eve were constituted in original innocence.

Because he was constituted by God as the principle of human nature, if he had not sinned, Adam would have passed on not a defected nature through procreation, but a perfected human nature in the same order of justice as his own. But, as principle and source of humanity, he passed on the kind of humanity which he himself had, namely that of disorder, weakened and prone to sin. Adam was the son of God in time, but Christ, the eternal Son of God, became the new Adam in the incarnation, restoring the order of justice in his own humanity. So Christ is also a principle of humanity. "The sin of Adam, who was appointed by God to be the principle of the whole nature, is transmitted to others by carnal propagation. So, too, the merit of Christ, who has been appointed by God to be the head of all men in regard to grace, extends to all His members."[57] Christ is the principle of redeemed and justified humanity. He does not bestow restored nature through carnal propagation, but through spiritual propagation, which begins in the reason and will of a man and gradually perfects him entirely as he works with the gift throughout his life. As the Jesuit theologian P. De Letter wrote:

Accordingly, if the restoration of original justice in our human race was to happen not by way of pure mercy or pardon on the part of God but by way of immanent reparation, then the re-insertion in the specific nature of its lost preternatural accident could be done only by one of the human species who had a hold on the specific nature and was not held by it. . . . Only God made man could be the second fountainhead of grace in mankind.[58]

It is in this way that Aquinas speaks of Christ as the Head of the Church and the source of all graces given to her members.

Aquinas acknowledges that Jesus Christ is the Head of the Church precisely in regards to the graces of his human soul. In considering the hierarchy of order, "[Christ's] grace is the highest and the first"; according to perfection, Christ had "the fullness of all graces"; finally, his power is such that "he has the power of bestowing grace on all the members of the Church."[59] Because Christ is first in the order of grace, he also has grace in its fullness of perfection, which further enables him to be the cause of grace for everyone else who receives it, according to the instrumental coordination of his two natures. "To give grace or the Holy Ghost belongs to Christ as he is God, authoritatively; but instrumentally it belongs also to him as man, inasmuch as his manhood is the instrument of his Godhead. And hence by the power of the Godhead his [human] actions were beneficial, i.e. by causing grace in us, both meritoriously and efficiently."[60] Further, the grace of Christ's headship is no different from the individual grace of his justice, except according to a distinction of reason. "Hence the personal grace, *whereby the soul of Christ is justified*, is essentially the same as his grace, as he is Head of the Church, and *justifies others*."[61] The very grace by which Christ is ordered in perfect charity and justice is that which each Christian receives and in which he or she participates in their Christian moral life. So, for Aquinas, for Jesus Christ to be the exemplar of justifying grace is by way of example, but first and foremost by way of causality.[62]

The Grace of Justification

The grace "whereby man himself is united to God"[63] and which "makes man pleasing to God"[64] Aquinas calls *gratia gratum faciens*. It is this gift of grace that "heals and justifies the soul,"[65] and thus produces the state of justification, that is, the "rectitude of order in the interior disposition of a man, insofar as what is highest in man is subject to God, and the inferior powers of the soul are subject to the superior."[66] This graced state of justice is, as seen above, essentially identical with the order of justice in the humanity of Christ, and thus, with the grace of original justice. The grace of justification is identified with the grace of Christ and that in Adam, not insofar as the sinner justified now has the perfect ordering of his body and soul, higher and lower parts, but insofar as his reason is subordinated to God by faith and charity. As has been seen in original justice and the personal justice of Christ, the key to the grace is that it is rooted in the will of the possessor.

A movement of free-will is required for the justification of the ungodly, inasmuch as man's mind is moved by God. Now God moves man's soul by turning it to himself. Hence for the justification of the ungodly a movement of the mind is required, by which it is turned to God. Now the first turning to God is by faith. Hence a movement of faith is required for the justification of the ungodly.[67]

In the act of faith, man's reason assents to divine revelation as moved by the will under the guidance of grace. Mark Armitage says: "By justification, God effectively 're-orders' what has become disordered, bringing about a restoration of this *iustitia* or *rectitudo ordinis*."[68] The reordering of man with grace happens first in his mind and will in their direct subjection to God, which further orders all other things according to the end of charity, that is, beatific and eternal union with him. And just as this first subjection was the cause of the lower subjections in Adam and Christ, it is the case also for the justified sinner. This subjection is instantaneous in one respect according to the infused virtues, but is not instantaneous in that this infusion requires the gradual working out of virtue according to the principle of grace. Charles Raith observes that the "life of grace" for Aquinas "begins with initial justification, which transforms a sinner into a just person, and proceeds to final glory, where the process of justification is completed—*all understood as an ever-increasing participation in Christ's justice though the Spirit.*"[69]

The Application of Christ's Justice to His Members

Aquinas repeatedly mentions the need for the efficacy of Christ's work of salvation to be actually *applied* to recipients by some form of spiritual contact. "As the sin of Adam reaches others only by carnal generation, so, too, the merit of Christ reaches others only by spiritual regeneration."[70] The spiritual regeneration into Christ happens in a variety of ways, all of which require the submission of man's mind and will to God. For the apostles, this occurred in their tangible, historical encounters with Jesus in his earthly life.[71] For us, however, "Christ's passion works its effect in them to whom it is applied, through faith and charity and the sacraments of faith."[72] Aquinas uses a variety of terms to refer to this reality of application through spiritual contact, including incorporation, participation, integration, likening, and conformity. "In order to secure the effects of Christ's passion, we must be likened unto him."[73] To share in the grace of Christ's justice means that man becomes part of Christ as a member of his Mystical Body, which happens by being conformed in the likeness of Christ by grace. "Christ's satisfaction works its effect in us inasmuch as we are incorporated with him, as the members with their head. Now the members must be conformed to their head."[74] By the act of faith, man submits his intellect and will to God and receives the grace of justification. The sacraments, too, efficaciously bestow the necessary grace of justification (especially baptism and penance) and the individual graces for increasingly greater conformity with Christ throughout the Christian life (especially in the Eucharist). In this way, Mark Armitage can say: "It is axiomatic for Aquinas that that justification which results in a proper *ordinatio* of the lower part of the soul to the higher and of the higher part to God is the effect of grace, and this grace is in turn the grace of Christ, derived from his passion and accessed by faith and through the sacraments, in virtue of which the justified participate in Christ's *iustitia* and *obedientia*."[75]

V. Conclusion: Christ as Fountainhead of the Grace of the Moral Life

Zagzebski is correct in her intuition that the heart of the Christian moral life is about becoming like Jesus Christ, the man who is God. The point of contention, for me, is how this conformity is accomplished. For Aquinas, it is a matter of causality and incorporation. It is true that Christ is the highest example of Christian virtue and therefore the center of the moral life as model and pioneer, but moreover, Christ is also the fountainhead of the very life of grace which is the principle of Christian morality. For Aquinas, Jesus Christ *is* at the heart of moral theology because he is the source of the graces it requires, first of all the grace of justification, the very supernatural organism itself whereby Christians live their lives in Christ. In the *Summa theologiae*, then, the *tertia pars* should not be read as set apart from what goes before it.[76] Aquinas treated original justice, original sin, the nature of man, man's moral life, and grace and justification before Christology for the simple reason that all these topics point to the treatment of Jesus Christ himself.[77] Whatever is the subject of the prior *partes* is recapitulated in the treatise on Christ and his life. Just as moral theology should not be read in isolation from the *prima pars*, even less should it be read apart from the *tertia pars*. Our moral lives as Christians are not simply multiple imitations of Christ the example, doing what Jesus did, but rather a fuller integration within the very grace of Christ himself whereby his life of grace becomes our life of grace, reaching its fulfillment in the harmony and charity of the beatific vision. Just as Adam is the beginning of the divine economy and Christ is the end, so too does the Christian begin his moral life in sin and come to the grace of Christ in order to finally share in Christ's glory in body and soul at the end.[78]

Ave Maria University

Notes

1. Linda Zagzebski, "The Incarnation and Virtue Ethics," in *Incarnation: An Interdisciplinary Symposium on the Incarnation of the Son of God*, ed. Stephen T. Davis et al. (New York: Oxford University, 2004), 313–331.

2. Ibid., 313.

3. Ibid.

4. Others have made similar arguments in defense of the integral location of the *tertia pars* in Aquinas's *Summa*. See, for example, John F. Boyle, "Is the *tertia pars* of the *Summa theologiae* misplaced?" *Proceedings of the PMR Conference* 18 (1993–1994): 103–109; Thomas

P. Harmon, "The Sacramental Consummation of the Moral Life According to St. Thomas Aquinas," *New Blackfriars* 91.1034 (July 2010): 465–480; Dominic Legge, *The Trinitarian Christology of St Thomas Aquinas* (New York: Oxford University, 2017).

5. St. Thomas Aquinas, *Summa theologiae*, trans. Fathers of the English Dominican Province (Notre Dame, IN: Christian Classics, 1981), *tertia pars*, q. 13, a. 3, *ad 2*. Hereafter, *ST* III 13.3 *ad* 2.

6. *ST* I-II 113.1. For its distinction from the cardinal virtue, see *ST* II-II 58.2. Aquinas is clear elsewhere, however, that this metaphorical justice does not merely concern the parts of man in isolation but indeed regards what is owed to another, namely what is owed to God. Cf. *Commentary on Saint Paul's Epistle to the Galatians*, trans. F. R. Larcher (Albany, NY: Magi Books, 1966), c. III, lect. 3: "Therefore the highest form of justice is to render to God what is God's. . . . Now, whatever is in man is from God, namely, intellect and will and the body itself, albeit according to a certain order; because the lower is ordained to the higher, and external things to internal, namely, to the good of the soul. Furthermore, the highest thing in man is his mind. Therefore the first element of justice in a man is that a man's mind be subjected to God, and this is done by faith. . . . Therefore in all things it must be said that God is the first principle of justice and that whosoever gives to God, namely, the greatest thing that lies in him by submitting the mind to him, such a one is fully just."

7. Aristotle, *Ethica Nicomachea*, trans. W. D. Ross, in *The Basic Works of Aristotle*, ed. Richard McKeon (New York: Modern Library, 2001), Book V, Ch. 11 (1138b, 10–13): "Metaphorically and in virtue of a certain resemblance there is a justice, not indeed between a man and himself, but between certain parts of him; yet not every kind of justice but that of master and servant. . . . For these are the ratios in which the part of the soul that has a rational principle stands to the irrational part. . . . There is therefore thought to be a mutual justice between them as between ruler and ruled." Cf. St. Thomas Aquinas, *Commentary on Aristotle's* Nicomachean Ethics, trans. C. I. Litzinger (Notre Dame, IN: Dumb Ox, 1993), Book V, Lecture XVII, 1106–1107. For a very brief treatment of Aquinas's recognition of the limitations regarding Aristotle's theory regarding divine justice, see Allan H. Gilbert, *Dante's Conception of Justice* (New York: AMS, 1965), 64–66.

8. St. Thomas Aquinas, *Aquinas's Shorter Summa*, trans. Cyril Vollert (Manchester, NH: Sophia Institute, 2002), I.186. Hereafter, *Comp. theo.* I.186.

9. Aquinas, *Commentary on Nicomachean Ethics* V, XVII, 1106–1107. Cf. *ST* I 96.2: "Over the sensitive powers, as the irascible and concupiscible, which obey reason in some degree, the soul has mastership by commanding. . . . But of the natural powers and the body itself man is master not by commanding, but by using them."

10. *ST* II-II 136.2 *ad* 2.

11. Man's mastery over his body and the lower powers of his soul is not according to a Cartesian dichotomy of soul as "I" and body as not-"I", but as both body and soul fully belonging to the reality of man. Cf. *ST* I 75.4: "It is clear that man is not a soul only, but something composed of soul and body"; *ST* I 89.1: "Such union [of body and soul] belongs to [the soul's] very nature."

12. *ST* I 95.1.

13. For a survey of theologians on the precise relation between grace and original justice, see Cyril Vollert, "Saint Thomas on Sanctifying Grace and Original Justice: A Comparative Study of a Recent Controversy," *Theological Studies* 2.3 (1941): 369–387. Cf. Cyril Vollert,

"The Two Senses of Original Justice in Medieval Theology," *Theological Studies* 5.1 (1943): 3–23. For a thorough treatment from a later theologian, see William A. Van Roo, *Grace and Original Justice According to St. Thomas*, Analecta Gregoriana vol. 75 (Rome: Gregorian University, 1955). For a recent treatment of Aquinas's thought on the grace of original justice, see especially Jean-Pierre Torrell, "Nature and Grace in Thomas Aquinas," in *Surnaturel: A Controversy at the Heart of Twentieth-century Thomistic Thought*, ed. Serge-Thomas Bonino, trans. Robert Williams and Matthew Levering (Ave Maria, FL: Sapientia, 2009), 155–188.

14. *ST* I 100.1 *ad* 2. Cf. 95.1 *ad* 5; I-II 113.1: The first man's justification takes effect not by a "transmutation from the state of injustice," like the justification of the sinner, but by "simple generation": "Now this justice may be in man . . . by simple generation, which is from privation to form; and thus justification may belong even to such as are not in sin, when they receive this justice from God, as Adam is said to have received original justice."

15. *ST* I-II 82.3. St. Thomas continues: "Accordingly the privation of original justice, whereby the will was made subject to God, is the formal element in original sin; while every other disorder of the soul's powers, is a kind of material element in respect of original sin."

16. Cf. *ST* I-II 109.3.

17. Cf. *ST* I 95.3: "Charity . . . did exist in the primitive state absolutely, both in habit and in act." See also I-II 109.3 *ad* 1: "Charity loves God above all things in a higher way than nature does. For nature loves God above all things inasmuch as He is the beginning and the end of natural good; whereas charity loves Him, as He is the object of beatitude, and inasmuch as man has a spiritual fellowship with God."

18. *ST* I 95.1. Cf. *Comp. theo.* I.186. Here we discover again that great doctrine of Thomism that grace builds on nature: the higher does not negate the lower, but rather serves to elevate and perfect it.

19. *ST* I 95.2.

20. *Comp. theo.* I.186. Cf. *ST* I-II 82.1–2: *"harmonia originalis iustitiae."*

21. Cf. *ST* I 94.1 *ad* 1, quoting St. Augustine, *De Genesi ad litteram* XI, 18: "Man was happy in paradise, but not with that perfect happiness to which he was destined . . . [but] so far as he was gifted with natural integrity and perfection."

22. *ST* I-II 109.2 *ad* 2.

23. *ST* I-II 82.1 *ad* 1. Cf. St. Thomas Aquinas, *De malo*, q. 4.

24. *ST* I-II 82.1 *ad* 3.

25. *ST* I-II 82.3.

26. *ST* I-II 109.7.

27. Sean A. Otto, *"Felix Culpa*: The Doctrine of Original Sin as Doctrine of Hope in Aquinas's *Summa Contra Gentiles*," in *The Heythrop Journal* (2009): 781–792, at 787.

28. *ST* III 13.3 *ad* 2.

29. *ST* III 18.6 *ad* 2.

30. *ST* III 18.6.

31. *ST* III 20.1 (emphasis mine). See also *Comp. theo.* I.213: "Perfect attachment of the will to God is brought about by love and by grace, whereby man is justified. . . . For man is made just by union with God through love. Perfect knowledge of God is effected by the

light of wisdom, which is the knowledge of divine truth. Therefore, the incarnate Word of God had to be perfect in grace and in wisdom of truth."

32. Cf. *ST* III 20.1: "And this is the subjection [through his human will] to the Father, of obedience unto death."

33. *ST* III 20.2 *ad* 2. Cf. 20.2 *ad* 3. In the *respondeo*, Aquinas is careful to clarify that Christ is only subject to himself according to the diversity of natures, and not at all according to a diversity of *supposita*, the error of Nestorius.

34. Thomas Joseph White, "Dyotheletism and the Instrumental Human Consciousness of Jesus," *Pro Ecclesia* 17.4 (2008): 396–422, at 407n29.

35. *ST* III 19.2.

36. *ST* III 13.3 *ad* 2.

37. *ST* III 46.6.

38. *ST* III 46.6 *ad* 3: "And, though actually suffering, it would have felt less pain than Christ's body."

39. White, "Dyotheletism," 412. White goes on to argue later that this concerted execution of the divine will according to the instrumentality of Christ's humanity required that Christ had full beatific knowledge of *who* he is and the divine plan for his whole life.

40. Thomas Hibbs, *Dialectic and Narrative in Aquinas: An Interpretation of the Summa Contra Gentiles* (Notre Dame, IN: University of Notre Dame, 1995), 156.

41. *ST* III 46.1 *ad* 3.

42. Mark Armitage, "Obedient unto Death, Even Death on a Cross: Christ's Obedience in the Soteriology of St. Thomas Aquinas," *Nova et Vetera*, English ed. 8.3 (2010): 505–526, at 507–508. Cf. J. Mark Armitage, "A Certain Rectitude of Order: Jesus and Justification According to Aquinas," *The Thomist* 72 (2008): 45–66.

43. *ST* III 46.9, quoting Wisdom 8:1.

44. *ST* III 19.1.

45. *ST* III 47.3. Cf. *ad* 2.

46. *ST* III 47.3 *ad* 2.

47. Cf. *ST* III 1.2.

48. *ST* I-II 109.7 *ad* 3.

49. *ST* III 53.1 *ad* 3.

50. *ST* III 49.2.

51. *ST* III 46.3.

52. *ST* III 1.2; 46.3.

53. *ST* III 21.1 *ad* 1.

54. *ST* III 7.2. Reginald Garrigou-Lagrange also has a beautiful meditation on the three-fold harmony of original justice lost by sin and now healed through the three evangelical counsels. See his *The Three Ages of the Interior Life*, vol. 1, trans. M. Timothea Doyle (Rockford, IL: TAN, 1989), 206–213.

55. *ST* III 7.3.

56. *ST* III 7.4.

57. *ST* III 19.4 *ad* 1.

58. P. De Letter, "The Reparation of Our Fallen Nature," *The Thomist* 23 (1966): 565.

59. *ST* III 8.1. One can detect here the Platonic principle put to use by Aquinas in the fourth demonstration for God's existence, namely, that whatever is first in an order both has the fullness of that perfection and also is the cause for the perfection in all the participants in the order. Cf. *ST* I 2.3.

60. *ST* III 8.1 *ad* 1.

61. *ST* III 8.5 (emphasis mine). Cf. St. Thomas Aquinas, *Commentary on Saint Paul's Epistle to the Ephesians*, trans. Matthew L. Lamb (Albany, NY: Magi Books, 1966), c. I, lect. 8: "Everything which is virtually in Christ is, as it were, filled out in some way in the members of the Church. For all spiritual understanding, gifts, and whatever can be present in the Church—all of which Christ possesses superabundantly—flow from him into the members of the Church, and they are perfected in them. . . . Christ makes [a] member of the Church . . . just with his perfect justice."

62. For Aquinas, exemplar causality incorporates efficient, formal, and final causality. Grace is acquired by the merit of Christ (efficiently), grace is of the same substance in Christ (formally), and grace points to Christ as the goal of the recipient (finally). Cf. *Commentary on Ephesians*, c. I, lect. 7: "As the life of Christ is the model and form of our justice, so Christ's glory and exultation is the model and form and exemplar of our glory and exaltation."

63. *ST* I-II 111.1.

64. *ST* I-II 111.1 *ad* 3.

65. *ST* I-II 111.2.

66. *ST* I-II 113.1. For a treatment of justification vis-à-vis deification in Aquinas, see Daniel A. Keating, "Justification, Sanctification and Divinization in Thomas Aquinas," in *Aquinas on Doctrine: A Critical Introduction*, ed. Thomas Weinandy, Daniel Keating, and John Yocum (London: T&T Clark, 2004), 139–158. See also Aquinas's parallel treatment in his earlier disputed question on truth at *De veritate*, q. 28.

67. *ST* I-II 113.4.

68. Armitage, "Obedient unto Death," 508.

69. Charles Raith II, *Aquinas and Calvin on Romans: God's Justification and Our Participation* (New York: Oxford University, 2014), 88 (emphasis mine). Shortly thereafter, Raith also says, "Through the right use of grace, believers obtain the goods that advance them in justification, that is, in the ongoing cultivation of justness in the soul that culminates in eternal life."

70. *ST* III 19.4 *ad* 3.

71. Cf. *ST* III 64.3. This is not to say that the apostles did not have faith in Christ nor that they did not actually receive sacraments, like at the Last Supper, but that their contact with Christ was direct, while ours is mediated.

72. *ST* III 49.3 *ad* 1.

73. *ST* III 49.3 *ad* 2.

74. *ST* III 49.3 *ad* 3.

75. Armitage, "Obedient unto Death," 513.

76. Cf. John F. Boyle, *Master Thomas Aquinas and the Fullness of Life* (South Bend, IN: St. Augustine's Press, 2014), 14: "Although Thomists mine the *Summa theologiae* as if it were an encyclopedia, the fact is that it is a *summa*, which means that Thomas is out to give order to his discipline and to do so precisely along the lines of causality as found in the careful study of things—in this case, first and foremost revealed things."

77. Thomas Hibbs makes this point regarding the structure of the *Summa Contra Gentiles*, which is more evident than in the *Summa theologiae*: "The location of the consideration of original sin is instructive. There is a twofold subordination of the intelligibility of the topic: it is subordinate to revelation and—within revelation—to the topic of the Incarnation. . . . The subordination of original sin to the passion, death, and resurrection of Christ makes clear the Christocentric character of the fourth book, indeed of the whole text." *Dialectic and Narrative in Aquinas*, 155.

78. Many thanks to the program committee of ACPA's 2016 meeting, as well as to Patrick Gardner for his most welcome remarks in response to my presentation.

Public, Private, and Extra-Judicial Killing

Craig Iffland

Abstract: Over the past decade, U.S. officials have taken steps to institutionalize the practice of targeted killing of persons outside an identifiable war zone. In the past, such a policy would have been described as extra-judicial killings. Advocates of this policy claim that the practice is permissible because the executive reviews and authorizes every targeted strike. I examine the tenability of this claim in light of Aquinas's understanding of the natural principles of justice and their implication for our definition of murder and the duties of a sovereign judge to those subject to his judgment. I conclude that Aquinas's understanding of murder is expansive enough to include the use of lethal force by public authorities when it proceeds from an act of judgment that disregards a presumption of innocence for the accused and her right to a fair trial.

Introduction

According to a 2012 piece on drone strikes published in the *New York Times* by Jo Becker and Scott Shane, President Obama believes "that his own judgment should be brought to bear on [drone strikes]." According to former chief of staff Bill Daley, President Obama "accepts as a fact that a certain amount of screw-ups are going to happen, and . . . that calls for a more judicious process" in which the President personally approves of every name added to the list. As a "student of the writings on war by Augustine and Thomas Aquinas," President Obama believes his personal involvement is necessary because he should "take moral responsibility for such actions."

It should be noted that the President *is* tracking the tradition of Augustine and Aquinas. For that tradition of thought, one necessary (but not sufficient) condition of the justice of an act of lethal force is its authorization by a public person, one designated with the responsibility to preserve justice and advance the common good. Only public authorities have the "right" to make use of lethal force and no use of lethal force is "just" if it is not commanded by a public authority. Of course, the "right" of public authorities to wield lethal force, and to do so in accord with the

© 2017, *Proceedings of the ACPA*, Vol. 90
doi: 10.5840/acpaproc201822775

pp. 217–226

demands of justice, is subject to a variety of constraints. No one, not even a public authority, has a "right" to murder.

While not everyone shares the same view of the kinds of actions that can be described as murder, many understand murder to be any deliberate killing of the innocent. A lesser number may hold that most cases of private killing will also count as murder, genuine cases of self-defense excepted. I want to suggest a more expansive definition. Murder is an unjust killing and not every unjust killing has an innocent person as its victim or a private person as its perpetrator. In fact, not every killing of a non-innocent person by a public authority is just. Public authorities can be guilty of murder even if the intended target is not innocent, a suspected "terrorist."

For Aquinas, the "right" of public authorities to command the use of lethal force is inextricably tied to their capacity *ex officio* to render authoritative judgments. Still, it would be wrong to assume that any judgment made by a public official—just so far as *he* or *she* made it—possesses the obliging force of law, a determination of what is "due." This seems to be the operative assumption of President Obama's policy vis-à-vis the use of lethal force against suspected terrorists. The interpretative error here is that public officials, while responsible for the conservation of justice, do *not* determine the *ratio* of justice, which for Aquinas contains a broad ideal of equality of persons grounded in their being made in the image of God.[1] Aquinas's commitment to this ideal is manifested in his conception of the duties a judge *owes* to those he judges. In line with his contemporaries, this conception reflects his recognition of the rights of the accused to a fair trial in accord with established legal and evidentiary norms.[2] In order to be just and possess the obliging force of law, a sovereign's act of judgment must conform to these norms. In this way, Aquinas ensures that the act of judgment proceeds from a public conception of justice rather than the arbitrary will of the judge.

In what follows, I defend the claims made above by examining the general constraints on the use of lethal force offered by Aquinas and their connection with his defense of the immutability of the fifth commandment of the Decalogue (Section I). Thereafter, I turn to discuss the normative requirements of the act of judgment and their implications for the extra-judicial use of lethal force by public officials (Section II). I conclude with a discussion of the implications of each for President Obama's policy of targeted killing.[3]

I.

Aquinas claims that all the commandments of the Decalogue are immutable and non-dispensable just to the extent that these precepts give expression to the intention of the divine lawgiver, which is directed to the common good and the order of justice and virtue by which it is attained (*Summa Theologiae* [*ST*] I-II 100.8).[4] There can be no dispensations from the fifth commandment with respect to this intention, that is, no dispensation from its order to the end of the law, which is the achievement of the common good and the order of justice and virtue necessary for that achievement. Thus, Aquinas claims that "the killing of a man is prohibited in the Decalogue insofar as it has the character of something undue, for this is the sense in which the precept embodies the very nature of justice" (*ST* I-II 100.8 *ad* 3). So, the commandment categorically forbids unjust killing and human law "cannot permit that a man should be killed both lawfully and in an undue way" (ibid.). This implies that our knowledge of the character of an unjust killing must consist in some knowledge beyond the fact that a public authority commanded the killing. At the same time, since the commandment categorically forbids only unjust killing, it is not contrary to the fifth commandment for human law to command the killing of an evildoer granted that the killing of evildoers has the character of something due (ibid.). This analysis has implications for our understanding of murder and the "right" of public authorities to use lethal force.

To begin with the former, it is evident that Aquinas does not treat the fifth commandment of the Decalogue as a moral statement presupposing facts about the victim or the perpetrator. That is, "do not kill" is not shorthand for "do not kill innocent persons" or "do not kill if you are a private person." It is shorthand for "do not kill contrary to the order of justice." Unlike the former statements, this claim does not give us a description of murder in terms of who can or cannot be killed or who can or cannot kill. The point is more basic. Whenever we make a judgment that an action is right or wrong, we are working against the backdrop of some understanding of what justice demands. It is in light of that understanding that we describe acts of killing as right or wrong. It cannot be reduced to a simple identification of certain facts about the victim or perpetrator because it is only in light of our understanding of the *ratio* of justice that the status of the victim or perpetrator becomes morally salient. So, while it is no doubt true that, for the most part, the killing of innocents is wrong, it is important to remember that this is a judgment about what is required by justice rather than a simple matter of equivalence, i.e., "murder = killing of innocents."[5] The chief problem with the claim that "do not kill" is simply equivalent to "killing of the innocent" is that it leaves out the role that judgment plays in our determinations of what should and should not be done. By connecting the immutable and non-dispensable character of the prohibition of homicide (i.e., murder) to the very *ratio* of justice, Aquinas provides us with a more expansive view of the scope of the prohibition, its conceptual dependence on our understanding of the *ratio* of justice, and the role that judgment plays in determining what counts as running afoul of the precept in light of that understanding.

In addition, Aquinas's view of the fifth commandment should help us to see why it is somewhat misleading to speak of the exclusive "right" of public authorities to wield lethal force. That "right" is measured by a judgment about what justice requires—whether the lethal force in question is due to the one at which it is aimed. So while Aquinas claims that only public authorities can wield lethal force, we should not interpret this as a claim that they have an absolute "right" in this regard (*ST* II-II 64.3). Rather, his view is that public authorities can *potentially* wield lethal force in accord with the *ratio* of justice while private persons cannot. This is because only public authorities are charged with making coercive judgments about what should be taken from their subjects for the common good (*ST* I-II 90.3 *ad* 2). As in our analysis above, this calls to mind the role that judgment plays in the determination that a certain lethal action falls under the prohibition against killing contained in the Decalogue. The chief difference here is that the judgment of a public authority, unlike private judgments, binds those subject to that authority. Still, we can ask what counts as a good or bad judgment about what justice requires and our answer would give us some guidelines for discriminating between just and unjust uses of lethal force by public authorities. It is to this question that I now turn.

II.

While anyone can exercise judgment, it pertains chiefly to the sovereign, or his or her ministers, since only they can make authoritative judgments of what pertains to the common good (*ST* II-II q. 60.1 and *ad* 3, 4).[6] Judgment is a determination of the *ius*, which is the object of justice (*ST* II-II 57.1). And it is *this* determination—of what is due in accord with the order of justice—that is necessary for a use of lethal force to be just. The measure of our determination of the *ius* is the extent to which it gives expression to some basic notion of equity or equality among persons subject to said determination (ibid.). Such determinations will fail as expressions of *ius* and so fail to be just judgments about what is due insofar as they manifest or entrench some form of inequity or inequality. In what ways can this occur?

Aquinas identifies three ways in which a judgment can fail to be an act of justice (*ST* II-II 60.2). A bad judgment is (a) manifestly unjust, in the sense of being unfair, (b) beyond the authority of the one making the judgment ("judgment by usurpation"), or (c) when it lacks certainty, i.e., "rash" judgment or judgment by "suspicion" (ibid.). Each kind of defective judgment manifests an unfair relation between the judge and the one being judged. The basis for the injustice of the relation is the claim, advanced by Aquinas, that individual human beings, considered according to their nature, should be loved rather than hated and presumptively immune from harmful actions. This view seems operative in his claims that:

(1) We ought to love sinners in virtue of their nature, but they are to be hated with respect to their fault [*culpa*] (*ST* II-II 25.6).

(2) No sinful human being, considered apart from her relation to the common good of the community of which she is a part (i.e., according to her nature), should be killed "because we ought to love the nature which God has made, which is destroyed by slaying him" (*ST* II-II 64.6).

(3) "It is better to err frequently through thinking well of a wicked man, than to err less frequently through having an evil opinion of a good man, because in the latter case an injury is inflicted, but not in the former" (*ST* II-II 60.4 *ad* 1).

So, one may say that bad judgment presumes that we should harm and hate the one being judged whereas good judgment presumes that we should love the person being judged and not harm him or her without sufficient reason. Thus, Aquinas claims that "rash" judgment or judgment by "suspicion" arises from the fact that the judge thinks "evil of another without sufficient cause," which is to "despise him unduly [*indebite*] and therefore does him an injury [*iniuriatur*]" (*ST* II-II 60.3 *ad* 2). Why? Because unlike our judgments of the goodness or badness of non-intelligent things, the judgments of a human being's goodness or badness can be the grounds for the infliction of various social and bodily harms to the person (*ST* II-II 60.4 *ad* 2). In view of the possibility of our judgment inflicting *harm* on the one being judged, and the presumption of non-maleficence to other human beings, we should assume his or her goodness unless there is sufficient evidence to the contrary (ibid.). Although Aquinas does not say so explicitly, this position seems to express the notion that we should presume the innocence of the one we are judging. For if condemnatory judgment in itself inflicts a kind of harm on individuals, it should not be lodged against a person that has not harmed anyone (i.e., an innocent), since justice requires that we only return what is received and no harm is inflicted by an innocent person (*ST* II-II 61.4). In presuming the goodness of the one being judged, we are presuming they are not a principle of harm, i.e., an innocent, which is another way of expressing Aquinas's view that individuals should be considered objects of love and presumptively immune from harmful actions.

Aquinas goes on to stress that all judgments must be made in accord with the written law since the written law contains both "natural" and "positive" right, although only giving "force" (i.e., the character of obligation) to the latter (*ST* II-II 60.5). This claim stands on the assumption that the written law does not establish anything contrary to natural right, which would nullify its obligatory character as a *determination of natural right* (ibid., *ad* 1). But insofar as both natural and positive right are contained in the written law, it belongs only to public authorities, i.e., those who make and interpret the written law, to give binding determinations of what justice requires (*ST* II-II 60.6). The reason for this is that those who make the written law are in the best position to understand its general aims in light of which one could rightly determine its application to diverse circumstances (ibid.).

From the preceding, we can make the following claims about what is necessarily presupposed by any authoritative determination of *ius* by a public authority. First, determinations presuppose a certain *ratio* of justice (e.g., equality of persons) rather than being determinative of that *ratio*. Accordingly, the authority of public judgment depends, not only on its being pronounced by someone with public authority, but more fundamentally on its being a determination (rather than a usurpation) of natural right, whose force derives from the "nature of the thing" in question rather than the authority of the one making the judgment (*ST* II-II 60.5). Second, there are limits to what can conceivably count as just determinations of *ius*. Public authorities must presume the goodness and innocence of the persons subject to their judgment unless this presumption is defeated by sufficient evidence of fault. Third, a just judgment cannot simply be an *ad hoc* expression of public authority, but rather one that proceeds from a promulgated law in accord with the scope of the authority granted to the one making the judgment. Finally, a sovereign exceeds her authority whenever her judgment deviates from the requirements of natural justice. What is the significance of these claims for our understanding of the limits imposed on the use of lethal force by public authorities?

A sovereign command to kill is no different than a determination of what is "due." It requires an act of general or legal justice, i.e., the judgment of a public authority, directed to the common good of his or her subjects (*ST* II-II 58.6). I would argue that Aquinas presupposes this view when he claims that human beings can be killed in a due manner when considered in their relation to the common good and that only public authorities may kill those at fault, i.e., evildoers (*ST* II-II q. 64.2–3, 6). Public authorities have the power to make authoritative judgments about what is necessary for the common good, but not any judgment about what is necessary for the common good will do (*ST* I-II 90.3). The use of lethal force must not only proceed from a consideration of what is necessary for the preservation of the common good, but also must be the *terminus* of a true act of general or legal justice, i.e., a *just* judgment about what is necessary for the common good. The upshot of this claim is that it applies to public and private persons alike. Let me explain.

Aquinas does not deny that private persons can make judgments about what is necessary for the common good (*ST* II-II 58.5–6, 12 *ad* 1); rather, he claims that they do so in a different mode than that of the sovereign. Legal justice exists in the sovereign as a "master-virtue, commanding and prescribing what is just" whereas it exists in her subjects as an "executive or administrative virtue" (*ST* II-II 60.1 *ad* 4). Consequently, judgments of private and public persons differ in that only the latter has the character of an obligation, i.e., an authoritative command. Only the judgment of a sovereign can impose an obligation, i.e., establish a relation of debt between individual subjects or an individual and the community of which she is a part. Since these determinations may be contrary to the will of those subject to them, they may involve inflicting some form of harm on another, albeit a harm in accord with the order of justice and the common good. For this reason, Aquinas asserts that a private individual can "do anything for the common good, provided it harm nobody, but if it be harmful to another, it cannot be done, except by virtue of the judgment of the person to whom it pertains to decide what is to be taken from the parts for the welfare of the whole" (*ST* II-II 64.3 *ad* 3). The private individual cannot harm another person because of her inability to make a certain kind of judgment, i.e., an authoritative determination of *ius* in view of the common good of all. Yet, as we saw above, the conditions of an authoritative determination of *ius* go beyond mere considerations of civic status. It would be wrong to impose some private judgment on another because in doing so one usurps the judgment of a higher authority—whether this be the judgment of the sovereign or a judgment contained in the written law. So too, the determination of *ius* by a public authority may not usurp the judgment of a higher political authority, but it may fail on other grounds—e.g., lack of sufficient evidence or lacking basis in the written law.

What I'm suggesting is that evaluating the justice of a particular person's judgment to use lethal force does not depend solely on our identification of them as a public official, or even ostensibly carrying out the duties of her office. The judgment of a public official, even when obviously informed by some concern for the common welfare of her subjects, and even when commanded by appeal to the authority vested in her office, can fail as a true determination of *ius*, a just command. When is this the case?

Although the general outline of an answer to this question has been presented above in terms of the principles governing just and unjust judgment, it is worth supplementing that presentation with some considerations Aquinas offers in his discussion of the kinds of injustice that occur in the context of judicial proceedings (*ST* II-II 67–71). This is because, for Aquinas, the primary applicability of the question 'when does a public official use lethal force in an unjust manner?' will be cases in which a judge passes an unjust sentence on some accused criminal. Although much of what he claims in this regard presumes a courtroom setting, the general principles contained therein, much like the general principles governing just and unjust judgment, are relevant to our evaluation of the use of lethal force by public authorities.

To begin with, the use of lethal force must be within the scope of legal authority had by the public official in question, and the object of that force must be someone who is subject to the coercive judgment of that official (*ST* II-II 67.1). This principle would invalidate, from the outset, any targeted killing of persons that is not a *legal* subject of the official in question. For where the individual is not *legally* subject to the official in question, the principles governing their relations with one another cannot be anything other than the principles that govern the infliction of harm between private persons, which is to say that the public official *qua* private person has no legitimate coercive power over the person targeted with lethal force. He may be a public authority, but he kills *as* a private person because he has no legal authority over his intended target. In addition, such a killing would constitute a *usurpation* of the coercive power (judgment) had by those public authorities to whom that person *is* legally subject.

What if those public authorities *consented* to the killing, as some reportedly have, and what if this consent were a *sine qua non* of the killing?[7] In this case, the primary agent of the killing would be the public authority to whom the person killed was legally subject rather than the public authority whose subjects carried out the killing (*ST* II-II 64.3 *ad* 1). Here President Obama would function as an "accuser" of a particular person and the public authority to whom that person is subject would function as a "judge," ascertaining the soundness of the accusation. The problem with this scenario, however, is that while Aquinas conceives of the judge as "an interpreter of justice" with a duty to adjudicate the claims of *two* disputants (an accuser and the accused), the practice of targeting killing presupposes the absence of such adjudication (*ST* II-II 67.3). It is difficult to see how one could, on Aquinas's view, render a judgment *at all*, much less a just judgment, when the accused is absent or where no trial has taken place.[8] And this gets us to the heart of the issue: on what grounds might Aquinas object to extra-judicial killing?

With the exception of cases of manifest, public guilt of the accused,[9] Aquinas holds that judgment of an individual's fault, and infliction of harm on the basis of that judgment, cannot be made in an *ad hoc* manner, lacking sufficient evidential grounds of that individual's fault. Such fault must be established through some *process* in which the evidence in favor of an individual's fault is subjected to critical scrutiny.

Indeed, Aquinas's commitment to a general presumption of innocence for all persons seems to require such a process. The facilitator of this process is the judge whose duty *qua* public authority is to pass *public* judgment, a judgment based on public laws and the evidence presented in court by the accuser, accused, and witnesses (*ST* II-II 67.2). That judgment will be unjust if it is not based on what was made known to all parties involved in the trial, but rather on the private knowledge of the judge (ibid., *ad* 4). So, a public authority cannot inflict punishment on account of a purported fault without an authoritative determination of the accused's fault, which must be based on the evidence presented against the accused at trial and in accord with the "order of public justice" (*ST* II-II 67.3 *ad* 2). This strongly suggests that Aquinas would categorically exclude the infliction of lethal harm by public authorities on individuals legally subject to them without a trial process. Absent such a process, it is difficult to see how the "right" of a public authority to use lethal force would be based on anything other than the *status* of the person occupying a public office and that person's *private, extra-legal* judgment that the person targeted with lethal force deserves to die.

Still, might someone say that there is a difference between the private judgment of a public official and the private judgment of an ordinary citizen? The appeal here is to the moral salience of a person's public status. But this won't do. A person's *status* is established vis-à-vis a certain relation to another that is consequent on some kind of action—one becomes a father by begetting a child, one becomes owner of *this* land by acquiring its title. For this reason, one is a superior to another in certain respects relevant to the nature of the authority had by the superior. Thus, fathers have some claim to obedience on their sons in relation to matters of household governance, but no claim to obedience in matters related to marriage, raising children, or religion (*ST* II-II 104.5). In the case of the public official intending to kill one of his subjects, his sphere of authority derives from the power of judgment associated with his office. Consequently, the "right" of the official to kill a subject is a function of his power to pass *judgment* on that subject (*ST* II-II 64.5 *ad* 2). In other words, the obedience *due* from a subject to the public official in matters of life and death is that the subject must submit to the *judgment* of the public official. Put differently, the public official has no authority over his subjects, and no authority to kill them or anyone else, except in virtue of his power to pass judgment on them. Outside the sphere of public judgment and all its attendant procedural norms, however, the public official stands to his subjects as a mere private person and has no right to kill.

Conclusion

If my above analysis is correct, Aquinas's understanding of the fifth commandment carries with it a range of categorical prohibitions on the use of lethal force by both *public* and *private* persons as well as the use of lethal force against innocent persons *and* evildoers. A critical feature of his account is the view that all human beings possess a presumptive immunity from harm. This places a justificatory burden on the use of lethal force by public authorities. Overriding this immunity requires sufficient evidence of wrongdoing, which is to be established through a trial process that issues in a public judgment of innocence or guilt. This suggests two conclusions regarding the moral permissibility of President Obama's policy of targeted killing. First, any determination by him that a citizen of another nation deserves death will be unjust from the outset. This is because he lacks legal authority over the person in question. Neither being the subject or superior of another in any relevant respect, they stand to one another as complete equals. To permit either to kill the other would be a direct violation of the equality of persons demanded by their common nature. Second, any determination by the President (or a consenting sovereign) that one of his legal subjects is deserving of death will be unjust *if* the presumption of that person's innocence is not overcome by sufficient evidence of fault. A public authority cannot defeat this presumption without appeal to public knowledge made manifest through a trial process that involves both accused and accuser. Finally, a public authority has a "right" to kill his subjects only by virtue of his power to pass judgment on their fault, which may or may not warrant execution. Outside the context of public judgment at trial, a public authority has no authority to command that an individual subject be killed.

University of Notre Dame

Notes

1. On this point, see Jean Porter, *Natural and Divine Law: Reclaiming the Tradition for Christian Ethics* (Grand Rapids, MI: Wm. B. Eerdmans Publishing, 1999), 259–267.

2. For a fuller discussion of this history, see Kenneth Pennington, *The Prince and the Law, 1200–1600: Sovereignty and Rights in the Western Legal Tradition* (Berkeley: University of California Press, 1993), 119–164.

3. In this essay, I do not offer any explicit, critical treatment of the various claims made by the Obama administration in defense of their drone policy. Nevertheless, one particular claim merits mention. The claim is that public authorities can employ lethal force against individuals—without explicit judicial authorization—in order to defend its citizens from the present, certain, and imminent threat these pose, particularly when capture of the individual is not feasible. I believe Aquinas would agree with this claim, at least within the domestic context. He would *not*, I think, agree to the Obama administration's interpretation of a key component of this claim, provided in a leaked Department of Justice white paper on the lawfulness of drone strikes—mainly, that "an imminent threat of violent attack against the United States does not require the United States to have clear evidence that a specific attack on U.S. persons and interests will take place in the immediate future." For an excellent critique of the Obama administration's claims in this regard see Kenneth Himes, *Drones and the Ethics of Targeted Killing* (Lanham, MD: Rowan and Littlefield), 85–168. For a detailed analysis and critique of the legal issues at stake, and the administration's invocation of the Law of Armed Conflict to justify its use of drones outside identifiable war zones, see Mary Ellen O'Connell, "International Law and Drone Attacks beyond Armed Conflict Zones," in *Drones and the Future of Armed Conflict: Ethical, Legal, and Strategic Implications*, ed. David

Cortright, Rachel Fairhurst, and Kristen Wall (Chicago: University of Chicago Press, 2015), 63–73.

4. For Aquinas's discussion of law and the Decalogue, I have relied on the translations provided by Alfred Freddoso, trans., *Treatise on Law* (South Bend, IN: St. Augustine's Press, 2009). For all other texts, I have relied on the translation provided by The Fathers of the English Dominican Province, *Summa Theologica* (New York: Benzinger Brothers, 1947).

5. The qualification is necessary because while Aquinas holds that killing the innocent is contrary to the "ordinary mode of virtue," he argues it is not intrinsically contrary to justice—when, for example, it is done out of obedience to God (*ST* II-II 104.4 *ad* 4).

6. I will not here try to explain the complex connections between the order of justice and the common good. Suffice it to say that there is a conceptual connection between them in the sense that the flourishing (i.e., common good) of any human community consists in their maintenance of a common civic life, which is the subject matter of justice (*ST* I-II 100.2 and II-II 58.6).

7. As Christopher Woods explains, consent of the host nations nonetheless seems to be mostly an "interpretative affair," a matter of presumed rather than explicit consent. See Christopher Woods, *Sudden Justice: America's Secret Drone Wars* (Oxford: Oxford University Press, 2015), 231–236.

8. At least, his discussion of the obligations of the accused to speak truthfully in response to the inquiries of the judge certainly presupposes the presence of the accused at trial (*ST* II-II 69.1).

9. In line with other medieval canonists, Aquinas defended judicial condemnation without trial when the guilt of the party in a particular case was manifest, i.e., known to both judge and the general public. Still, he insisted that both must have *independent* knowledge of the guilt of the party in question (*ST* II-II 67.2 *ad* 3). In this respect, Aquinas would give no particular credence to the claims of public authorities vis-à-vis the guilt of their designated "public" enemies when those claims are invoked in an effort to deny such persons a trial. For more on the history of this position among medieval canonists, see Pennington, *Prince and the Law*, 146–148.

Why Did Aquinas Hold That
Killing Is Sometimes Just, But Never Lying?

John Skalko

Abstract: Aquinas held that lying is always a sin, an evil action (*ST* II-II, Q110, A3). In later terminology it falls under what would be called an intrinsically evil action. Under no circumstances can it be a good action. Following Augustine, Aquinas held that even if others must die, one must still never tell a lie (*ST* II-II, Q110, A3, ad 4, *DM* Q15, A1, ad 5). Yet when it comes to self-defense and capital punishment Aquinas's reasoning seems at odds with itself. One may kill a man in self-defense (*ST* II-II, Q64, A7). Similarly, just as a diseased limb may be cut off for the sake of the good of the whole, so too may an evildoer who is dangerous to the community be killed for the sake of the good of the whole community (*ST* II-II, Q64, A2). Herein lies the tension: why does Aquinas hold that it is licit to kill in self-defense or in capital punishment on account of the common good, but that one may never tell a lie on account of the common good? I argue that Aquinas does indeed have a consistent account. Killing and lying are not analogous, despite the prima facie temptation to lump them together.

Over twenty different times Aquinas insists that every lie is a sin.[1] Throughout his entire philosophical career Aquinas held that under no circumstances could lying ever become a good action.[2] One may not tell a lie even to save one's own life or the life of another.[3] For the purposes of this paper Aquinas's position that all lies are wrong shall be called the absolutist position on lying.

Many today reject Aquinas's absolutist position on the grounds of an analogy with violence. If violence is generally evil, but allowable in exceptional cases, cannot the same be said about lying? Peter Kreeft,[4] Sissela Bok,[5] Sidgwick,[6] David Decosimo,[7] and Alasdair MacIntyre[8] all reject the absolutist position on lying based upon an analogy with violence. They hold that in difficult situations one ought to tell a lie. Sigdwick states his position as follows: "if we may even kill in defence of ourselves and others, it seems strange if we may not lie, if lying will defend us better against a palpable invasion of our rights."[9] Sidgwick's position is a representative sample of

© 2017, *Proceedings of the ACPA*, Vol. 90
doi: 10.5840/acpaproc20184282

the views of this first group of authors: uttering a falsehood is still a lie even if in defense of a life, but it ceases to be wrong in such difficult situations.

This first group of authors, namely Kreeft, Bok, Sidgwick, Decosimo, and MacIntyre, differ slightly in their position from that of a second group of authors. Whereas the first group holds that lying is sometimes permissible, this second group holds that in difficult situations lying ceases to be an act of lying. Abbé F. Dubois,[10] Ruland,[11] Vermeersch,[12] Julius Dorszynski,[13] and Janet Smith[14] fall under this second group of authors. Dubois succinctly sums up their position:

> The saying of a falsity with the intention to deceive is the material element of a lie, analogous to the material act of killing, indifferent like it, that is to say good or evil according to the circumstances and determining the moral conditions of the act, that is, like in the act of killing, the violation of a right, of the right to life in the first case, of the right to the truth in the second.[15]

Effectively, in situations where human lives are at stake, what normally counts as a lie ceases to be so. Despite their differences, what both groups of authors hold in common is that they reject Aquinas's absolutist position based upon an analogy with violence.

In that respect, they have a point. Aquinas allows for killing in self-defense,[16] killing in capital punishment,[17] and killing in a just war.[18] If Aquinas holds that killing is generally evil, but allows for broad exceptions to it in certain contexts, cannot the same be said about lying? The purpose of this paper is to show that the analogy between killing and lying fails to hold up under scrutiny. Aquinas's justifications for killing in certain contexts cannot be used to justify lying. In order to argue for that point, I will proceed as follows: first, I will explicate Aquinas's account of killing, second I will elucidate Aquinas's account of lying, and finally I will conclude by showing that killing and lying are not analogous. Though killing is not always wrong, lying is and remains an intrinsic evil.

Killing in Aquinas

I will begin with an explication of Aquinas's account of killing. Aquinas allows for the killing of plants and animals because they are ordered towards our good. Plants are ordered towards the good of animals, and both plants and animals are ordered towards the good of man. Since it is not illicit to use things for what they are for, it is not illicit to kill plants or animals for man's good.[19] Thus, it is good for man to kill plants or animals for food or for his own use. Life itself is not so absolute a good that it can never rightly be taken away.

Capital Punishment

Killing, however, can occur not only with regard to plants and animals but also with regard to human beings. This killing can be done upon two types of human beings: those who are guilty and those who are innocent. Grievous evildoers may be licitly killed provided certain conditions are met, but the innocent may never be intentionally killed.

In *Summa Theologiae* (*ST*) II-II, Q64, A2, co. Aquinas argues that "if any man is dangerous to the community and corruptive of it on account of some sin, then it is praiseworthy and profitable to kill him in order that the common good be preserved."[20] Aquinas reasons for his conclusion as follows:

> It is licit to kill brute animals inasmuch as they are naturally ordered to the use of man, as the imperfect are ordered to the perfect. Now every part is naturally ordered to the whole as the imperfect to the perfect. Therefore, every part naturally is for the sake of the whole. On account of this, we see that if the cutting off of a member is expedient to the health of the whole human body, as when it is rotten and corruptive of the others, it is praiseworthy and profitable to be cut off. Now any singular person is compared to the community as a part to a whole. Therefore, if any man is dangerous to the community and corruptive of it on account of some sin, then it is praiseworthy and profitable to kill him in order that the common good be preserved.[21]

Now, in the very next article, *ST* II-II, Q64, A3, Aquinas adds the qualifier that only those in public authority may kill in the case of capital punishment.[22] Aquinas's rationale why only those in public authority may execute another person is that only those who have been entrusted with the care of the whole may sacrifice a part for the sake of the good of the whole. The care of the common good has not been entrusted to private individuals as such. It has been entrusted, rather, to those in public authority. Thus, only those in public authority may kill a grievous malefactor for the sake of the common good.

In *ST* II-II, Q64, A4, Aquinas then argues that clerics may not kill another human being. In the reply to the third objection, Aquinas argues that if the cleric happens to hold public office he cannot himself carry out the capital punishment but may delegate others to do so in virtue of his authority.

Just War

Aquinas's justifications for killing in self-defense and killing in a just war are dependent upon his justifications for killing in the case of capital punishment. In *ST* II-II, Q40, A1, co., Aquinas argues that a war may be just provided that three conditions are met: proper authority, just cause, and rightful intention. Proper authority means that not anyone can declare or wage war; only those in public authority have the right to wage war. Because the care of the common good is entrusted to those in public authority, it belongs to those in public authority to gather together the private individuals as needed in wartime. Further, "just as [those in public authority] licitly defend it [the republic] by means of the sword against internal disturbances, as they punish malefactors . . . so too by means of the sword in war it pertains to them to safeguard the republic from exterior enemies."[23] One must note that Aquinas is very adamant here about the fact that only public authority has the proper authority to wage war. The private individual *qua* private individual cannot wage a war that is just. Aquinas's rationale as to why only those in public authority can rightly wage war ultimately must be traced back to the rationale he used in *ST* II-II, Q64, A3, about why only those in public authority can execute criminals for capital offenses: the public authority alone has been entrusted with the care of the common good. Ergo, only the public authority may put a part in harm's way for the good of the whole.

Aquinas's second criterion for a just war is that "it requires a just cause, namely, that those whom one is fighting against deserve to be fought against on account of some fault (*culpam*)."[24] Aquinas's reasoning here echoes back to his reasoning in *ST* II-II, Q64, A2 about the case of capital punishment. Capital punishment may only be done if the person is *periculosus* and *corruptivus* of the community. This implies that the person is guilty of some *culpa*. So though the terminology is different in *ST* II-II, Q40, A1, and *ST* II-II, Q64, A2, the rationale is the same: in order for killing to be legitimate the person to be killed must be guilty of some grievous fault. In a just war, the enemy is guilty and so are all of his soldiers. In capital punishment the criminal is guilty. Aquinas's allowance for killing in war is heavily dependent upon his account as to why killing in capital punishment is allowable.

The third criterion for a just war is that it must be waged with a rightful intention. It must be done for the sake of some good and not out of mere bloodlust or cruelty. The need for a right intention permeates Aquinas's teaching on punishment[25] and his ethics in general. Any action may be rendered evil on account of an evil end intended.[26] Thus, for Aquinas the intention must be good in any type of killing.

Self-Defense

I will now proceed from Aquinas's account of just war to his account of self-defense. Like Aquinas's account of just war, Aquinas's account of self-defense in large part is parasitic upon his account of capital punishment. In *ST* II-II, Q64, A7, Aquinas argues that it is licit to kill another in self-defense, but only those in public authority may intend to kill their attacker. The private individual may perform an action from which the death of the aggressor sometimes follows,[27] but he may never intend to kill his attacker.[28] As support for his contention that only those in public authority may intend to kill another for the sake of the common good, Aquinas explicitly cites the earlier article, Q64, A3, where he had previously argued that in capital punishment only the public authority may intend to kill.[29] Only public authority may intend to kill an attacker in self-defense because only public authority has been entrusted with the care of the whole such that only they may kill a part for the sake of the good of the whole.

ST II-II, Q64, A7, has been the subject of much disputed interpretation.[30] The New Natural Lawyers hold that Aquinas would allow for the private individual to stab the assailant in the heart so long as he does not intend death.[31] Steven Jensen, on the other hand, holds that not only is it illicit for the private individual to stab the assailant in the heart, but that it is also illicit for him to intentionally harm the attacker in anyway.[32] For Jensen, the type of killing that Aquinas allows for by the private individual in Q64, A7, is only that which is purely accidental. The person was a not a very accurate shot, or just a poor swordsman. All he may do is deflect the blows or scare off the attacker or swing his sword so as to knock the blade out of his attacker's hand.

Though Jensen's account is the better interpretation of Aquinas, I merely wish to point out here that on either interpretation of Q64, A7, Aquinas's argument that the private individual may kill in self-defense cannot be used to support lying in self-defense. Lying includes intention in its very definition. An unintentional lie is a contradiction in terms. So even if it were possible for the private individual to stab the assailant in the heart without the intent to kill, in no way could one argue that the private individual may tell a lie to a public enemy without intending to lie.

In sum, Aquinas's entire account of justifiable killing is fundamentally dependent upon his understanding of public authority and the common good. Aquinas's justification of intentional killing in self-defense, intentional killing in a just war, and intentional killing in capital punishment, all hinge upon the fact that only those in public authority have been entrusted with the care of the common good as such.

This care of the common good by public authority is significant for answering the objection to Aquinas's account of lying from the analogy with violence. The only way Aquinas's rationale for killing could be used to justify lying is if the lies were done by one in public authority for the sake of the common good and upon an enemy or a guilty party. Can this justification for killing by public authority be used to show that Aquinas's account of the intrinsic wrongness of lying is incoherent? Before we answer that question we must first investigate Aquinas's account of the intrinsic wrongness of lying.

Aquinas on Lying

Throughout his philosophical career Aquinas time and time again insists that every lie is a sin. He holds this line from his early treatment of the subject in his *Commentary on the Sentences*, Book III, D38, Q1, A3, to *Quodlibet* VIII, Q6, A4, to his *Commentary on the Nicomachean Ethics*, Book IV.7, Lecture 15, n. 837, to *ST* II-II, Q110, A3 and Q111, A1. In all four cases, Aquinas's argument is fundamentally the same. Lying is wrong because it violates the purpose of asserting. I will quote merely from his more mature account of the subject in *ST* II-II, Q110, A3, co. in order to give an overview of Aquinas's argument against lying:

I reply it must be said that what is evil in itself from its genus in no way can be good and licit, since for something to be good it is required that all things rightly concur. Indeed good is from a complete cause, evil from a single defect, as Dionysius says in Chapter IV of the *Divine Names*. Now a lie is evil from its genus. Indeed it is an action bearing upon undue matter, since words are naturally signs of understanding, it is unnatural and undue that one signify by word that which he has not in mind. Hence the Philosopher says in *Nicomachean Ethics* IV that "lying is in

itself deformed and ought to be avoided, truth is good and praiseworthy."
Hence every lie is a sin, as Augustine asserts in the book *Against Lying*.[33]

It appears that from this text the crux of Aquinas's argument is that in lying one is using words contrary to their purpose.[34] Upon closer analysis, however, Aquinas's account is a bit more nuanced. His case against lying is not about the teleology of words or language as such. For Aquinas, lying is contrary to the truth.[35] So a necessary component of a lie is that it contain some falsehood, namely what Aquinas calls "formal falsity." Formal falsity is that one wills to say what one believes to be false. In a lie one intentionally utters what one believes to be false as if it were true. Ergo, if what one says is believed to be true, then what one utters is not a lie.[36]

Words, by themselves, however, do not involve truth or falsity. Aquinas recognizes this in his commentary on Aristotle's *De Interpretatione*.[37] Sentences, also, do not necessarily involve truth or falsity.[38] In questions, requests, petitionary prayers,[39] commands, and hypothetical examples, one is generally not asserting something as true. Questions, for example, in themselves are neither true nor false. This is why it is not possible for one to lie in asking a question. Now, Aquinas was well aware of these distinctions.[40] So when he treats of the immorality of lying in Q110, A3, he is not speaking about words or language as such, but rather about assertions. In A3 he is presupposing that the reader remembers what he had said earlier in A1 that *manifestatio sive enuntiatio* is the type of speech act involved in telling a lie. Further evidence of the importance of assertions for Aquinas's account can be found in Q110, A3, ad 1,[41] Q111, A1, ad 1,[42] *Commentary on the Sentences*, Book III, D38, Q1, A5, ad 1,[43] and in *ST* II-II, Q69, A2, co.[44] Not all types of speech acts involve truth or falsity. Assertions are different from other speech acts. Assertions by their very nature are ordered towards truth as their proximate end. An assertion, by definition, is to present something as if it were true to another.[45] As Christopher Tollefsen puts it, in an assertion one is communicating to another that one believes *that P* is true.[46]

The nature and importance of assertions sheds much light on Aquinas's argument against lying. For in telling a lie one is making an assertion.[47] But the whole purpose of assertions is to convey the truth to another. In lying one is making an assertion, while at the same time deliberately frustrating the natural end of assertions. The disorder is in engaging in an action that has its own natural end, while simultaneously frustrating that end from happening. In this respect, lying is much like contraception. In contraceptive intercourse one is engaging in sex, while at the same time deliberately frustrating its natural end of procreation. To make an assertion while frustrating the conveyance of truth to another is disordered per se. It is due to this fundamental disorder in the act itself that Aquinas calls lying "an inordinacy through the abuse of word" in *Quodlibet* VIII,[48] "acting inordinately" in his *Commentary on the Nicomachean Ethics*,[49] and "unnatural and undue" in the Summa.[50] What is disordered in itself is evil, and evil ought never to be done. Thus, lying ought never to be done.[51]

Is There an Analogy Between Killing and Lying?

This leads to the final section of the paper: Aquinas held that all lying is wrong, but permitted some types of killing. As Janet Smith indicates, was Aquinas not inconsistent here in holding that you could kill the Nazi but not lie to him?[52] Here I argue directly that Aquinas is not inconsistent.

To begin with, killing in itself is a natural species of action,[53] while lying is a moral species. Natural species are morally neutral,[54] while moral species are not. Killing cannot receive its moral species until it is known what the *materia circa quam* of the action is. It makes a world of difference whether the killing is of a plant, an animal, an innocent human being, or a guilty one. Killing in an act of just war and due capital punishment is good, but killing the innocent is evil. Only certain species of killing are morally evil, but killing in itself as a natural species is not. Lying, on the other hand, is not a natural species. It is evil in its genus on independent grounds even before broken down into its species.[55] Ergo, killing and lying are not analogous.

Perhaps the analogy could be recast then as an analogy between capital punishment and lying: If capital punishment is allowable for Aquinas, then so too should lying be in similar cases, such as by a public official, upon a guilty party, for the sake of the common good, etc.

In reply to this objection, it must be said that if one wished to apply Aquinas's account of capital punishment to lying, then only those in public authority may lie for the sake of the common good. Lying by a private individual would be strictly prohibited. So if a Nazi came to your door, then you as a private citizen would still under no circumstances be permitted to tell a lie. Double-effect reasoning that it is allowable for the private individual to kill in self-defense would not apply here.[56] It is possible for the private individual to perform an action that foreseeably may cause death without intending the death that follows. With lying, however, it is not possible to perform an act of lying without intending the lie. Lying by definition includes intention within it. This is why animals cannot strictly speaking tell lies, nor can the insane. This is also why a slip of the tongue, or a drunken man who blurts out something accidentally, is not lying even if what is spoken is what the agent knows to be untrue.

There is a second problem with applying Aquinas's rationale about capital punishment to the case of lying. In capital punishment one is killing or permanently destroying a corrupt part for the good of the whole. In the case of a lie though it is unclear what part of what whole one would be permanently destroying. Lying involves words or assertions. Words or assertions cannot be killed or permanently destroyed, unless of course the whole human race ceased to exist.[57] Further, the larger whole that words or assertions are a part of is language. So if Aquinas's reasoning about capital punishment were applied to the case of lying, this would mean that public authorities could destroy assertions for the sake of language. This, however, hardly makes sense. The reason is the parts and the wholes in the case of assertions and capital punishment are simply not analogous.

A third problem with the analogy between killing and lying is this: lying is disordered in the very nature of its action, whereas killing is not. In lying one is engaging in an action that is naturally ordered to an end, while deliberately frustrating that end from happening. One is engaging in an assertion that is naturally ordered to truth, while deliberately acting against that truth. In killing, even unjustified types of killing, there is no such fundamental frustration of teleology. Murder is wrong, but it does not involve the frustration of the natural *telos* of an action in which one is engaging. Justified capital punishment involves killing the guilty for the common good, but there is no frustration of natural teleology here. Killing, in its various species, is not disordered as a frustration of natural teleology, but lying is.[58] As Edward Feser says, "[lying] is in this respect like contraception, or deliberately vomiting up a meal so one can gorge oneself indefinitely. [The] argument is thus a species of what is known as a 'perverted faculty' argument. Murder and stealing do not involve the perversion of a faculty; they are immoral for other, more complex reasons."[59]

Finally capital punishment aside, killing has no intention involved in it.[60] Killing is still killing even if done unintentionally or accidentally. Killing is still killing even if done by an animal or a bolt of lightning. Killing is not even necessarily a human act. Lying, by contrast, involves intention and by definition is a human act.[61] Lying and killing are not analogous.

Conclusion

I will conclude here with one last argument. The argument for lying based upon an analogy with violence proves too much. If lying may be done for the sake of the common good when lives are in danger, then cannot the same rationale apply to other actions as well? If lying must be justified in order to save innocent lives for the sake of the common good, then why is not adultery, murder, or even sodomy justified in similar situations?[62] Imagine a blackmail situation: a gang breaks into a bank and recognizes you as their old lost enemy. They insist that they will murder everyone else in the bank and leave the gun in your cold dead hands unless you kill one of the innocent bank tellers. If you can lie for the sake of the common good, then why can you not murder? This Augustinian challenge has yet to be answered by advocates of the noble lie.

Aquinas can hold *both* that it is morally good to kill another in capital punishment or just war *and* that lying is always wrong. There is no explicit or implicit contradiction between those two claims, nor can any contradiction be derived. In certain cases, you may kill, but you may never tell a lie. Aquinas's ethics is not inconsistent, but right.

The University of St. Thomas
Houston, TX

Notes

1. Cf. *Summa Theologiae* (*ST*) II-II, Q110, A3, especially obj. 4 and ad 4. Aquinas says "omne mendacium est peccatum" in eight places: *Super Sent. III*, D38, Q1, pr.; A3, s.c.

1; s.c. 2; A3, s.c. 3; A3, co.; Q1, A4, s.c. 2; *ST* II-II, Q70, A4, co.; II-II, Q110, A3, co. He says "omne mendacium peccatum est" in two places: *Super Sent. III*, D38, Q1, A3, s.c. 2; *ST* II-II, Q124, A5, ad 2. In other places he says things like "mendacium omne sit peccatum" (*Super Sent. III*, D38, Q1, pr.), "omne mendacium sit peccatum" (*Super Sent. IV*, D21, Q2, A3, s.c. 1; *ST* II-II, Q111, A1, co.), "mendacium semper est peccatum" (*Quodlibet VIII*, Q6, A4, co.), and "mendacium nullum sine peccato est" (*Super de Trinitate II*, Q3, A1, co.). In *De Malo* Q15, A1, obj. 5 and ad 5 Thomas opposes the view that one may commit adultery in order to kill a tyrant. In condemning the objector's point, Thomas says, "Ad quintum dicendum quod ille Commentator in hoc non est sustinendus: pro nulla enim utilitate debet aliquis adulterium committere sicut nec mendacium dicere debet aliquis propter utilitatem aliquam, ut Augustinus dicit in libro Contra mendacium" (Sancti Thomae de Aquino, *Quaestiones Disputatae de Malo*, in *Opera Omnia Iussu Leonis XIII P. M. Edita*, vol. XXIII [Roma: Commissio Leonina, 1982], 271).

If Aquinas ever indeed held that a lie was justified in some cases, he had plenty of opportunities to say so, but he never did. In multiple contexts where the objection is raised that lying is not a sin or that not every lie is a sin (*Super Sent. III*, D38, Q1, A3, obj. 1, obj. 2, obj. 3, obj. 4, obj. 6, obj. 7; *ST* II-II, Q110, A3, obj. 1 obj. 2, obj. 3, obj. 6; *Quodlibet VIII*, Q6, A4, obj. 2), Aquinas never backs down on his statement that every lie is a sin. If Aquinas really had held that the officious lie is not a lie in some cases, then he would have said so. On the contrary, Aquinas agrees with Augustine that the officious lie is a sin in all cases: "Et sciendum Augustinum, *Nullum mendacium officiosum est sine peccato*: quia si mentiris ut liberes aliquem hoc non est bonum: quia Apostolus dicit Rom. III, 8: *Non sunt facienda mala ut veniant bona*" (Doctoris Angelici Divi Thomae Aquinatis Sacri Ordinis F. F. Praedicatorum, *In Psalmos Davidis 5*, n. 3, in *Opera Omnia* [Parisiis, Ludovicum Vivès, 1876], 249). Aquinas also says in *Super Sent. III*, D38, Q1, A4, s.c. 3 that "Ergo mendacium officiosum est peccatum veniale," and in response to obj. 4 about officious lies in *ST* II-II, Q110, A3, he allows for no exceptions: "Et ideo non est licitum mendacium dicere ad hoc quod aliquis alium a quocumque periculo liberet" (Sancti Thomae Aquinatis, *Summa Theologiae, Secunda Secundae* [Matriti: Biblioteca de Autores Cristianos, 1952]). See also *ST* II-II, Q69, A1–2. According to Aquinas lying is always wrong and ought to never be done in any circumstances.

2. Ibid.

3. *ST* II-II, Q110, A3, ad 4; *De Malo* Q15, A1, ad 5.

4. "Thomas Aquinas said that even torture is sometimes justified; in emergency situations like that; if torture, then *a fortiori* lying," Peter Kreeft, "Why Live Action Did Right and Why We All Should Know That," CatholicVote.org, http://www.catholiceducation.org/en/religion-and-philosophy/apologetics/why-live-action-did-right-and-why-we-all-should-know-that.html (accessed November 06, 2014).

5. Though she does not directly attack Aquinas's position in this regard, Sissela Bok rejects the absolute position on lying and argues for this rejection by means of an analogy with violence. This argument is repeatedly used throughout her book. See Sissela Bok, *Lying* (New York: Pantheon Books, 1978), 41, 45–46, 109, 115, 126, 130, 144, 213.

6. In the appendix Bok also quotes a lengthy passage from Sidgwick who also argues from an analogy with violence (273): "Just as each man is thought to have a natural right to personal security generally, but not if he is himself attempting to injure others in life and property: so if we may even kill in defence of ourselves and others, it seems strange if we may not lie, if lying will defend us better against a palpable invasion of our rights. . . . And again, just as the orderly and systematic slaughter which we call war is thought perfectly

right under certain circumstances, though painful and revolting: so in the word-contests of the law-courts, the lawyer is commonly held to be justified in untruthfulness within strict rules and limits."

7. David Decosimo, "Just Lies: Finding Augustine's Ethics of Public Lying in His Treatments of Lying and Killing," *Journal of Religious Ethics* 38.4 (2010): 661–697.

8. Alasdair MacIntyre, "Truthfulness, Lies, and Moral Philosophers," in *The Tanner Lectures on Human Values*, vol. 17, ed. Grethe B. Peterson (Salt Lake City: University of Utah Press, 1994), 351–352, 356. MacIntyre does not explicitly cite Aquinas in his rejection of the absolutist position that all lies are wrong. Nevertheless, his reasoning logically entails a rejection of Aquinas: "In this type of case [of a Dutch housewife hiding Jews from a Nazi official] the normally illegitimate power exercised by the successful liar becomes legitimate" (356).

9. Sissela Bok, *Lying*, 273.

10. Abbé F. Dubois, "Une Théorie Du Mensonge Replique (1)," ed. M. L'Abbé Duflot, *La Science Catholique* 12 (December 1897–December 1898): 168: "It must be added: *the violation of a right*, which constitutes the *formal* element of a lie and morally *specifies* it. Thus, the saying of a falsity with the intention to deceive is the material element of a lie, analogous to the material act of killing, indifferent like it, that is to say good or evil according to the circumstances and determining the moral conditions of the act, that is, like in the act of killing, the violation of a right, of the right to life in the first case, of the right to the truth in the second" (translation from the French is my own).

11. Cited in Julius A. Dorszynski, *Catholic Teaching About the Morality of Falsehood*, PhD diss., The Catholic University of America, 1948 (Washington, DC: The Catholic University of America Press, 1948), 59.

12. As quoted in Dorszynski, *Catholic Teaching About the Morality of Falsehood*, 60: "Indeed, just as an unjust aggression of another brings it about that an action, which otherwise would be homicide is not homicide as an action, but the defense of self, so also the unjust aggression can be the cause why words, which, if offered outside of aggression would become lies, now also they might be a defense of a secret and are chosen and intended only as such. Nor is it required that the aggressor be aware of his unjust aggression. For one is able to repel by force also one who is materially unjust."

13. Dorszynski, *Catholic Teaching About the Morality of Falsehood*, 88: "We realize that deceptive speech *ordinarily* harms mutual trust in society; but we maintain that there are times when it may be used without injury to mutual trust. One of the times it does not endanger that trust is when it is employed to protect a lawful secret from unjust aggression. We believe that in a conflict of the rights of the speaker and hearer we could aptly apply the usual rules involved in cases of unjust aggression of life and property."

14. Janet E. Smith, "Fig Leaves and Falsehoods, Pace Thomas Aquinas, Sometimes We Need to Deceive," *First Things*, June 2011, http://www.firstthings.com/article/2011/06/fig-leaves-and-falsehoods (accessed October 7, 2014): "Aquinas' rigorism about uttering falsehoods is certainly cogent, but hard to reconcile with some of his other positions. Aquinas (and the Church) approve of killing someone for the sake of protecting innocent life as well as commandeering or destroying the property of another to protect other goods. Thus the question: Why shouldn't Aquinas (and the Church) permit false signification uttered in order to protect innocent life and other important goods?" See also Janet E. Smith, "Why Tollefsen and Pruss Are Wrong about Lying," *First Things*, December 15, 2011, http://www.

firstthings.com/web-exclusives/2011/12/why-tollefsen-and-pruss-are-wrong-about-lying. Accessed October 7, 2014.

15. Dubois, "Une Théorie Du Mensonge Replique (1)," 168.

16. *ST* II-II, Q64, A7.

17. *ST* II-II, Q64, A2; SCG III, 146, n. 4–5.

18. *ST* II-II, Q40, A1.

19. *ST* II-II, Q64, A1.

20. Et ideo si aliquis homo sit periculosus communitati et corruptivus ipsius propter aliquod peccatum, laudabiliter et salubriter occiditur, ut bonum commune conservetur (Sancti Thomae Aquinatis, *Summa Theologiae, Secunda Secundae* [Matriti: Biblioteca de Autores Cristianos, 1952]). All further Latin citations from the *ST* II-II are from this edition, hereby referred to as the BAC. The translation is my own. All further citations from the *ST* II-II are my own unless otherwise indicated.

21. *ST* II-II, Q64, A2, co.: Respondeo dicendum quod, sicut dictum est (a.1), licitum est occidere animalia bruta inquantum ordinantur naturaliter ad hominum usum, sicut imperfectum ordinatur ad perfectum. Omnis autem pars ordinatur ad totum ut imperfectum ad perfectum. Et ideo omnis pars naturaliter est propter totum. Et propter hoc videmus quod si saluti totius corporis humani expediat praecisio alicuius membri, puta cum est putridum et corruptivum aliorum, laudabiliter et salubriter absciditur. Quaelibet autem persona singularis comparatur ad totam communitatem sicut pars ad totum. Et ideo si aliquis homo sit periculosus communitati et corruptivus ipsius propter aliquod peccatum, laudabiliter et salubriter occiditur, ut bonum commune conservetur: *modicum* enim *fermentum totam massam corrumpit*, ut dicitur I ad Cor. 5, 6.

22. *ST* II-II, Q64, A3, co.

23. *ST* II-II, Q40, A1, co.: Et sicut licite defendunt eam materiali gladio contra interiores quidem perturbatores, dum malefactores puniunt . . . ita etiam gladio bellico ad eos pertinet rempublicam tueri ab exterioribus hostibus.

24. *ST* II-II, Q40, A1, co.: Secundo, requiritur causa iusta: ut scilicet illi qui impugnantur propter aliquam culpam impugnationem mereantur. The translation is my own.

25. *ST* II-II, Q108, A1; *ST* II-II, Q64, A6; *ST* I, Q19, A9; *ST* I-II, Q19, A10, ad 2; *ST* I-II, Q87, A3, ad 3. For an excellent analysis of this point see Lawrence Dewan, "Thomas Aquinas, Gerard Bradley, and the Death Penalty: Some Observations," *Gregorianum* 82.1 (2001): 161–164. "*No one* (whether a public official or a private person) is *ever* allowed to 'intend the death of this person', in the way that involves pleasure in that person's suffering, or hate of that person as possessed of human nature" (ibid., 162).

26. *ST* I-II, Q18, A4, co. and ad 3.

27. *ST* II-II, Q64, A7, ad 4: Ad quartum dicendum quod actus fornicationis vel adulterii non ordinatur ad conservationem propriae vitae ex necessitate, sicut actus ex quo *quandoque* sequitur homicidium (emphasis added). This implies that Aquinas would allow for the swinging of one's sword so as to deflect the opponent's blows or so as to strike the opponent's sword out of his hand. From such an action *sometimes* the death of the aggressor follows if accidentally the aggressor steps into the way of the sword and suffers a fatal blow. Decapitating the attacker, however, is not an action from which the death of the attacker merely *sometimes* follows. It follows rather in all cases.

28. *ST* II-II, Q64, A7, co.: Illicitum est quod homo intendat occidere hominem ut seipsum defendat, nisi ei qui habet publicam auctoritatem.

29. Ibid.: Sed quia occidere hominem non licet nisi publica auctoritate propter bonum commune, ut ex supradictis (a.3) patet.

30. I am only mentioning two prominent interpretations here, but there are others. Cf. Steven A. Long, "A Brief Disquisition Regarding the Nature of the Object of the Moral Act according to St. Thomas Aquinas," *The Thomist* 67 (2003): 71. It is there that Long quotes from Francisco de Vitoria as holding the same position. For two other interpretations see Joannis a S. Thoma, *Cursus Theologicus in Summam Theologicam D. Thomae, Tomus Septimus In Secundam Secundae, Q64, Disputatio XI De Homicidio, A4, XV*, ed. Ludovicus Vives, (Parisiis, 1886), 495; Gregory M. Reichberg, "Aquinas on Defensive Killing: A Case of Double Effect?," *The Thomist* 69.3 (2005): 341–370.

31. John Finnis, *Aquinas: Moral, Legal, and Political Theory* (Oxford: Oxford University Press, 1998), 287.

32. Steven J. Jensen, "The Trouble with Secunda Secundae 64, 7: Self-Defense," *Modern Schoolman: A Quarterly Journal of Philosophy* 83.2 (2006): 152–153. Jensen cites *ST* II-II, Q65, A1, Q64, A3, ad 3, and Q41, A1 in support of his position.

33. Respondeo dicendum quod illud quod est secundum se malum ex genere, nullo modo potest esse bonum et licitum: quia ad hoc quod aliquid sit bonum, requiritur quod omnia recte concurrant; *bonum* enim *est ex integra causa, malum autem est ex singularibus defectibus*, ut Dionysius dicit, 4 cap. *De div. nom.* Mendacium autem est malum ex genere. Est enim actus cadens super indebitam materiam: cum enim voces sint signa naturaliter intellectuum, innaturale est et indebitum quod aliquis voce significet id quod non habet in mente. Unde Philosophus dicit, in IV *Ethic.*, quod *mendacium est per se pravum et fugiendum: verum autem et bonum et laudabile.* Unde omne mendacium est peccatum: sicut etiam Augustinus asserit, in libro *Contra mendacium.*

34. This, at first glance, appears to be a very weak argument against lying. We can use plenty of other things licitly against their purpose. Standing on one's hands is certainly not immoral (SCG III, 122), even though the purpose of the hands is for grasping. Using a pencil to poke a hole in the ground is not immoral, even though the purpose of a pencil is for writing. If we can violate the purposes of things in all these instances, then what is so special about words? The answer is that the purpose of the hands is simply movement, local motion. There is no violation of their purpose in handstands. Pencils are artifacts, human creations, and as such their nature is under the authority of man. Man created pencils and gave them their nature. Thus, man may change their nature if he so wishes by using them not as writing utensils but as tools for digging. None of this, however, applies in the case of lying, because man does not have authority over the nature of assertions as such.

35. *ST* II-II, Q110, A1.

36. Aquinas in numerous cases allows for equivocation or various types of mental reservation (Q110, A3, ad 3 and ad 6). For example, when Abraham told Pharaoh that Sarah was his sister, he did not lie, for she was his sister in a sense, though not in the sense of the term as understood by Pharaoh (cf. Q110, A3, ad 3).

37. Aquinas, *Commentary on Aristotle's De Interpretatione* Book 1, Lesson 3; cf. Aristotle, *De Interpretatione* Chapters 1 and 4.

38. Aquinas, *Commentary on Aristotle's De Interpretatione* Book 1, Lesson 7; cf. Aristotle, *De Interpretatione* Chapter 4.

39. Aristotle, *On Interpretation*, trans. E. M. Edghill, in *The Basic Works of Aristotle*, ed. Richard McKeon (New York: Random House, 1941), 17a4: "Yet every sentence is not a proposition; only such are propositions as have in them truth or falsity. Thus a prayer is a sentence, but is neither true nor false." The Latin from Aquinas's commentary on this passage uses *enunciativa* for "proposition" and *oratio* for "sentence."

40. Aquinas, *Commentary on Aristotle's De Interpretatione* Book 1, Lesson 3 and Lesson 7.

41. Ad primum ergo dicendum quod nec in Evangelio, nec in aliqua Scriptura canonica fas est opinari aliquod falsum *asseri*, nec quod scriptores earum mendacium dixerunt (emphasis added).

42. Et subiungit exemplum de figurativis locutionibus, in quibus fingitur quaedam res non ut *asseratur* ita esse, sed eam proponimus ut figuram alterius quod *asserere* volumus (emphasis added).

43. Ad primum ergo dicendum quod ille qui disputando falsum loquitur, quamvis scienter, non mentitur, *nisi asserendo dicat*; quia non ex sua persona falsum illud enuntiat, sed gerens personam veritatem negantis (S. Thomae Aquinatis, *Scriptum Super Sententiis*, vol. III, ed. R. P. Maria Fabianus Moos [Parisiis: P. Lethielleux, 1933], 1275; emphasis added).

44. Falsitatem tamen *proponere* in nullo casu licet alicui. . . . Non autem licet ei vel *falsitatem dicere* (emphasis added).

45. The etymology of the word is from the Latin *asserere*, which is *ad* (to) + *serere* (to join) (*OED*). This indicates that in making an assertion one is joining oneself or committing oneself to the claim that one makes. One is putting one's person behind the truth of what one speaks.

46. Christopher O. Tollefsen, *Lying and Christian Ethics* (New York: Cambridge University Press, 2014), 20.

47. As evidence of this, just ask a liar next time if he is making an assertion: Are you asserting that? If he really means to lie, then he will say yes. All liars (or at least those who wish to be successful in their lies and still to cover up the fact that they are lying) when pressed would insist that they are in fact asserting as true what they just spoke.

48. *Quaestiones de Quolibets* VIII, Q6, A4: est ibi inordinatio per abusum vocis (Sancti Thomae de Aquino, *Quaestiones de Quolibet*, in *Opera Omnia Iussu Leonis XIII P. M. Edita*, *Tomus* XXV, *Volumen* 1 [Roma: Commissio Leonina, 1996], 75–76).

49. *Commentary on NE* IV.7, *Lectio* 15: Ad hoc enim signa sunt instituta quod repraesentent res secundum quod sunt et ideo, si aliquis repraesentat rem aliter quam sit mentiendo, *inordinate agit* et vitiose, qui autem verum dicit, ordinate agit et virtuose (Sancti Thomae de Aquino, *Sententia Libri Ethicorum*, in *Opera Omnia Iussu Leonis XIII P. M. Edita*, *Tomus* XLVII, *Volumen* II (Romae: 1969), 252, 1127a28, lines 85–89; emphasis added).

50. *ST* II-II, Q110, A3, co.: cum enim voces sint signa naturaliter intellectuum, *innaturale est et indebitum* quod aliquis voce significet id quod non habet in mente (emphasis added).

51. Using the hands for the sake of walking is not disordered in itself. The hands are ordered towards movement. In using the hands for walking one is not engaging in an action

with its own end and at the same time deliberately frustrating that end from happening. Using a pencil to poke holes in the ground is not disordered in itself. In using a pencil to poke holes in the ground one is not engaging in an action with its own end while simultaneously frustrating that end from happening.

52. Janet E. Smith, "Why Tollefsen and Pruss Are Wrong about Lying": "Indeed, one could kill the Nazi or forcibly take his weapons from him to prevent him from killing Jews. Why is false signification morally impermissible in the same circumstances? The work that needs to be done now is to study why Aquinas thought it moral to kill in self-defense and to take what belongs to others when in dire need. What justifies those actions? Would that justification extend to false signification?"

53. *ST* I-II, Q1, A3, ad 3.

54. In *ST* I, Q19, A6, ad 1 Aquinas says, "Sicut hominem vivere est bonum, et *hominem occidi est malum, secundum absolutam considerationem*: sed si addatur circa aliquem hominem, quod sit homicida, vel vivens in periculum multitudinis, sic bonum est eum occidi, et malum est eum vivere" (Sancti Thomae de Aquino, *Summa Theologiae* [Rome: Editiones Paulinae, 1962], emphasis added). Aquinas is not here making a moral claim about the natural species of killing in itself. Presumably, what Aquinas means, rather, is that in the abstract nobody would choose killing for its own sake and so it is evil, as death is an evil for a human being. In *concreto*, however, it can become morally good due to a change in due circumstances of the action. The context here is that Aquinas is arguing that antecedently God wills all men to be saved, but consequently due to their sins he wills some to be damned. He is merely making a similar point with regard to killing and is not arguing that killing in its natural species is morally evil, but rather that in its natural species it involves an ontological evil and so in the abstract it is generally considered to be morally evil.

55. Here, however, an objector would press Aquinas. If killing in itself is not morally specified until one sees whether it is upon the innocent or guilty, then cannot the same be said for lying? Lying, it seems, should be morally specified depending upon whether the one to whom one is speaking is innocent or guilty. It is not possible to lie to plants or animals or someone who is incapable of understanding what you say. So it seems that the person to whom one is speaking should in some way enter into the *materia circa quam* of the act of lying. If the person enters into the *materia circa quam* of lying, then it seems probable that the guilt or innocence of the person spoken to should enter into the *materia circa quam* of the action and so morally specify lying as good or evil.

In reply to said objection I answer thus: the difficulty here is that a genus is not magically subdivided into its moral species based upon which species one wishes to say are good and which species one wishes to say are evil. At its worst, this would mean someone could divide the genus of killing the unborn into justified abortions and unjustified abortions simply because one wishes it to be so divided. My point here is that when Aquinas divides the genus of killing into its various species he does not do so presupposing without argument that some of these species are good and others evil. It is only *after* he has divided killing into its species that he then gives reasons why each of these species are good or evil. In other words, after dividing killing into killing of non-human living things and human beings does Aquinas argue that killing plants and animals can be licit. Only after dividing killing of human beings into its species of innocent and guilty does Aquinas argue that killing the guilty can be licit and that killing the innocent is never licit. Thus, it is simply improper methodology to divide lying into its species in order to, without argument, justify certain types of lies. The proper way to do this is first to divide lying into its species. Then to give arguments or an account as to why certain types of its species are licit and others are not. This proper methodology seems to be lacking in many of the authors cited earlier who wish to justify lying based upon an analogy with violence.

56. For more on this point see: Tollefsen, *Lying and Christian Ethics*, 150–151.

57. One could kill the person who is speaking an assertion or prevent him from so speaking it. Assertions indeed cease to be after spoken, but this is not to destroy them.

58. Cf. Edward Feser, "Smith, Tollefsen, and Pruss on Lying," *Edwardfeser.blogspot.com* (blog), January 5, 2012, http://edwardfeser.blogspot.com/2012/01/smith-tollefsen-and-pruss-on-lying.html (accessed January 17, 2015): "The problem with Smith's argument is that the cases of murder, stealing, and lying are simply not parallel in the way she supposes, certainly not from the point of view of the classical approach to natural law theory represented by Aquinas. For Aquinas and the classical natural law tradition that informed the thinking of the Scholastic manualists, deliberately telling a falsehood is *intrinsically* immoral, whether or not the listener has a right to know the truth, because it involves acting contrary to the natural end of our communicative faculties. It is in this respect like contraception, or deliberately vomiting up a meal so that one can gorge oneself indefinitely. Their argument is thus a species of what is known as a 'perverted faculty' argument. Murder and stealing do not involve the perversion of a faculty; they are immoral for other, more complex reasons. Hence the analogy Smith needs in order to make her case does not hold."

59. Ibid.

60. Tollefsen, *Lying and Christian Ethics*, 150: "A structural *disanalogy* between lying and killing dooms these arguments from the start. Unlike 'killing,' which can describe behaviors as causally, but not intentionally related to a person's death, 'lying' can only describe intentional actions, for an assertion is not something that can be done accidentally, or voluntarily but outside the intention of the speaker: to assert, one must intend to do so."

61. Cf. *ST* II-II, Q110, A1, co.: Sed tamen ratio mendacii sumitur a formali falsitate: ex hoc scilicet quod aliquis *voluntatem* falsum enuntiandi (emphasis added).

62. Cf. Augustine, *De Mendacio*, n. 11: "But if anyone thinks that a lie must be told to one person for the sake of another, so that the latter may live longer, or may not be harmed . . . there is no crime to which he may not be forced by the same reason" (Augustine, *Lying*, trans. Mary Sarah Muldowney, in *The Fathers of the Church: A New Translation*, vol. 16, ed. Roy J. Deferrari [Washington, DC: The Catholic University of America Press, 1952], 70). Augustine, *Contra Mendacium*, n. 38: "what is he saying who opposes me in pleading and defending the case for lying if he is not saying the truth? But, if he is to be heard because he is telling the truth, how can he in telling the truth want to make me a liar? How can lying claim truth as its advocate? Or does truth conquer for her adversary so as to be conquered by herself? Who can abide this absurdity? Therefore, let us not in any way hold that they who declare that sometimes we ought to lie are truthful in declaring so, lest—and this is most absurd and foolish to believe!—the truth teaches us to be liars. How is it that, while no one learns from chastity that he ought to commit adultery or from piety that he ought to harm his neighbor, we should learn from truth that we ought to lie?" (Augustine, *Against Lying*, trans. Harold B. Jaffee, in *The Fathers of the Church: A New Translation*, vol. 16, ed. Roy J. Deferrari [Washington, DC, The Catholic University of America Press, 1952], 174–175). See also *Contra Mendacium*, n. 1, n. 18–22, and n. 40 (ibid., 126, 143–151, 179 (the selection from n. 40 here is n. 41 in the newadvent.org translation).

Then and Now—A Thomistic Account of History

Timothy Kearns

Abstract: Thomists do not have a standard account of history as a discipline or of historical knowledge in general. Since Thomism is a tradition of thought derived in part from historical figures and their works, it is necessary for Thomists to be able to say how we know what we know about those figures and their works. In this paper, I analyze the notion of history both in its key contemporary senses and in how it was used by Aristotle and Aquinas. I show briefly how intellectual knowledge of the past is possible. Then, I argue that the Thomistic tradition implies a far wider notion of history than is generally recognized, history as study of the past in general, not a science in itself, but an aspect of other sciences. Finally, I indicate how this wider notion of history relates to the ordinary sense of history as an inquiry into the specifically human past and then how such an account fits within contemporary Thomism.

I

History and related disciplines have no clearly established place within the Thomistic framework.[1] There is evidence of this in the conflicting things Thomists say about history, particularly on the question of whether history is a science in the Aristotelian sense. Some Thomists (for example, Jacques Maritain, Charles De Koninck, and Glen Coughlin) argue that history is not a science because it treats of singulars which are unknowable.[2] Others (principally Benedict Ashley) claim that it is not a science but also that it can provide intellectual knowledge and a degree of certainty, although they offer no systematic account of how.[3] Still others (Charles De Koninck again—he changed his mind, seemingly—William Wallace, and Michael Buckley) argue that for various reasons history is a science, for example, because of the rational connections among acts (De Koninck), because of the necessity of the past (Wallace), or because of the influences of human beings on each other (Buckley).[4] Others (here we find most contemporary Thomists) refrain from addressing the question of whether or not history is a science in the Aristotelian sense but still treat history as a discipline producing intellectual knowledge and limited certainty.[5] The only one of these views with wide acceptance

© 2017, *Proceedings of the ACPA*, Vol. 90
doi: 10.5840/acpaproc20181369

today is the last one, that of most contemporary Thomists who draw on history but do not offer an account of it.

This state of Thomistic thinking on history is problematic for at least two reasons. First, since Thomism is based on the system of thought articulated in the thirteenth century by Thomas Aquinas, it is necessary that Thomists make coherent claims about how we can be said to know the past, about what it is that we can know about the past, and about why we might need inquiry into the past in the first place.[6] Second, if Thomism is to integrate the disciplines, as is often called for, it will be necessary for Thomists to have an account of those contemporary disciplines that are related to the study of the past. And, in order to carry out the integration of the disciplines more generally, Thomists must show how Thomism does a better job of explaining the disciplines and their subjects than the current theoretical underpinnings of the disciplines themselves do, which, as MacIntyre has argued, requires Thomists to give accounts of the past of the disciplines.[7] But to tell a history in the best way one must know what history and historical knowledge *are* and how they relate to other activities and kinds of knowledge. Unification of knowledge, however, also always implies a unification of the social groups that know, and so a further problem must be addressed within Thomism itself: the problem of the separation between Thomists who focus on Aquinas's work mainly as a part of intellectual history and those who study his work primarily for the problems it can solve in our time, that is, what he can teach us about the world. Can we in fact do one without the other, history divorced from addressing contemporary problems or addressing contemporary problems divorced from history? What is the relationship for Thomists between studying the history of a discipline and studying in the discipline itself? The daily practice of working Thomists requires an answer to these questions, one only an account of history can give.

My goal in this paper is to outline an account of history within the Thomistic tradition that will solve the first two problems, showing the possibility of historical knowledge and history's place in the Thomistic framework of disciplines, and through that to suggest an avenue of approach for solving the problem of the separation among those Thomists emphasizing history and those aiming to solve problems. Since most Thomists do seem to draw on history without claiming either that it is or is not a science, I will not primarily work through the various views on that question. Instead, I aim to provide an account of history that fits best with contemporary Thomistic practice, in the course of which I will show that history is not a science. To do that, I begin with an analysis of the notion of history.

II

The term "history" in English has at least three key senses: first, it refers to the past itself; second, to an account of the past; and, third, to a discipline of learning.[8] Let me take each in turn, considering first the sense in English and then the senses of the related terms used by Aristotle and Aquinas.

By "the past" I mean anything that has *been* in any sense before the present time, anything that has had being before now. So, anything that has ever been actual in any sense is part of the past. When Aristotle refers to the past, he does not use the Greek term ἱστορία; instead, he uses phrases like τόδε γέγονε (*Posterior Analytics* II.12). Aquinas sometimes refers to the past with the Latin term *historia*, for example, when he uses *ordo historiae* to mean the order of past events (e.g., at *Exposition of the Psalms*, Prologue); but he prefers the standard Latin word *praeteritum*.

In the second sense, history, as an account of the past, can be either the written or oral account of something in the past, or it can be the understanding that an inquirer has of something in the past and its causes. Since any written account of the past is derived from the inquirer's understanding of that past, history as the understanding of something in the past is prior to and more universal than history as a written account of that thing in the past. Aristotle refers to written accounts of the human past with the word ἱστορία when in *Poetics* (9) he discusses history as the genre of written or oral accounts of what has happened in the past. This is where he points out that poetry is more philosophical than history as a genre of writing, since a history treats of what has happened and a poem treats of what may happen, poetry therefore expressing what is more universal.[9] Aquinas too uses *historia* to refer to histories as written accounts of the human past (for example, at *Summa theologiae* II-II 2.7). Neither Aristotle nor Aquinas have occasion to refer specifically to the understanding of something in the past as opposed to the written account of it.

In the third sense, history is a discipline of learning. By "discipline," I mean anything that is learned as a habit and that involves truth in some way, like an art, science, practice, or skill; a discipline of learning seems to be one ordered to understanding. Now, when we talk about history as a discipline, we must mean something at least related to what is carried on in academic history departments by professional historians and also to what historians of philosophy and theology do. What historians do is inquire into the past in order to understand it. Within history departments particularly, history seems to be carried out as a discipline in two ways. First, history is carried out as an activity whereby one understands the past. This is the principal and defining activity of those who study the past. But, second, history is also carried out as the explanation and development of the methodology of understanding the past; this is what we usually call "historiography" or sometimes "historics."[10] Significantly, neither Aristotle nor Aquinas has any term for history either as a discipline of learning or as the study of the methodology of knowing the past.

We can now see an order among these different senses of the term "history." Since the activity of understanding the past is what produces accounts of the past, and since historiography is the explanation and justification of the activity of understanding the past, all of which lead to the description of the past itself as "history," every sense of the term "history" seems to derive from the activity of understanding the past.

So far, however, we have implicitly limited ourselves to considering history as restricted to the *human* past.[11] Do we ever refer to the non-human past or to an account of the non-human past or to a discipline that studies the non-human past as "history"? It is clear in each case that we do: we refer to the past of everything in the universe as "history" (called "big history" nowadays); we can study the geological history of our planet; we can produce accounts of the non-human past when we write a history of life; and we also do have certain sub-disciplines like paleontology that specifically study something non-human in the past, and these are certainly aimed at understanding that past, although we do not commonly call them "history." So, the term "history" is not properly restricted to the human past; instead, history seems to be inquiry into the past in general, of which inquiry into the human past is merely a special case. History in this general sense seems deeply related to the nature of inquiry itself.

And it is inquiry in general, not inquiry restricted to the past, that Aristotle and Aquinas know as ἱστορία in Greek and *historia* in Latin in their most general sense. It will be useful to look briefly at how Aristotle and Aquinas use these words in this sense. For Aristotle, ἱστορία means inquiry or research in general and has an important role to play in his understanding of science. In the *Prior Analytics* (I.30, 46a18–27), Aristotle says that experience gives the principles of any science, and if we have apprehended all the attributes of the thing under consideration, then we can make the demonstrations relevant to the science; then, he goes on (46a24–27), "For if nothing that truly belongs to the subjects has been left out of our collection of facts [κατὰ τὴν ἱστορίαν], then concerning every fact, if a demonstration for it exists, we will be able to find that demonstration and demonstrate it, while if it does not naturally have a demonstration, we will be able to make that evident."[12] He confirms this view in his scientific works too, for example, at *Historia Anima-lium* I.6. We see, then, that ἱστορία for Aristotle is something like general inquiry into the matters under study, the beginning of a science. It seems related to but higher than experience, since experience tends to be inchoate, unsystematic, and unreflected upon, and Aristotle indicates that a general understanding resulting from an inquiry should, in the ideal case, not omit any of the true attributes of the thing. For Aristotle, ἱστορία is a general inquiry that is in some sense part of and subordinate to a science.

Drawing on the Aristotelian tradition, Aquinas has nearly the same sense for the Latin word *historia*.[13] For example, in his commentary on the *De coelo* (III.1.547), Aquinas uses the term *historia naturalis* to refer in a general way to inquiry into natural things, coming quite close to the older English term "natural history"; here, Aquinas indicates that *historia naturalis* is a kind of *narratio*, i.e, account, of natural things. He elaborates a little more on what *historia* is when, in his commentary on the *De anima* (I.1.6), Aquinas says that Aristotle uses the term *historia* in the *De anima* to describe what he is doing in the work "because he is going to discuss the soul in a general way, without attempting in this treatise a thorough examination [*finalem inquisitionem*] of all its properties."[14] Aquinas also picks up on the more precise way Aristotle uses ἱστορία, namely as a stage in the movement toward scientific knowledge. In his commentary on the *Sentences of Peter Lombard* (II 11.2.3), Aquinas says that just as through *locutio* we do not acquire full knowledge of the subject being discussed, so too through *historia* we come to know something not known beforehand, but our intellect is not fully enlightened. *Historia*, then, in the key sense for Aquinas, is much like Aristotle's notion: an inquiry that results in knowledge of the subject in some sense but not knowledge of the highest kind.[15]

This reveals, it seems to me, a certain compatibility between history as inquiry into the past and Aristotelian ἱστορία as inquiry in general—respecting, of course, all the difference between what inquiry was for Aristotle and Aquinas and what it is for us. History as inquiry into the past can simply be taken as a special case of inquiry in the wide sense. Because this point has not, as far as I can tell, otherwise been noted, my discussion here is more general than earlier treatments of the nature of history, since those earlier treatments focused on history as the study of the *human* past.[16]

Having briefly surveyed the senses of the term, I propose a definition of history in the most general sense: history is inquiry that aims to understand things in the past and their causes. This definition raises at least two problems, as mentioned above: the possibility of historical knowledge and the place of history within a Thomistic system of the sciences. Let me start with the first.

III

Both of the problems related to history that I began with raise a corresponding question. The most general question that the possibility of the knowledge of the past raises is whether we can have intellectual knowledge of the past at all. There seems to be no reason to doubt that we can know the past in some sense. All human beings by nature desire to know themselves and others; a sign of this is the delight we have in conversation and in learning about remarkable acts and strange customs; indeed, friendship seems to be predicated on knowledge of others. In general, both self-knowledge and the knowledge of others imply knowledge of acts in the past; so, knowledge of the past seems to be possible for us—consider, for example, that tragedies like *Oedipus Rex* and novels like *Bleak House* depend for their very drama on coming to know about the past. Further, although Aristotle and Aquinas are nowhere concerned to address intellectual knowledge about the past directly, they both imply that it is possible when they discuss instances from the human past and treat them as if they can be known; at *Posterior Analytics* II.11, Aristotle and Aquinas both even treat of what they identify as a *propter quid* demonstration of the cause of a historical event, namely why Athens became involved in the Persian Wars.[17]

Both also imply that we can have knowledge of the past when they treat extensively of the history of the philosophical sciences. It is sometimes said that the history of a science is merely dialectical for Aristotle, but in fact it is not the history that is dialectical—Aristotle is not in any doubt that Socrates existed—it is the opinions that one considers that are dialectical with respect to the science. John of St. Thomas, Aquinas's great commentator, in his *Ars Logica* does explicitly address knowledge of things in the past and he concludes that we can know them, but only because something that we sense in the present represents past things to us in some intelligible way.[18] The wider Catholic tradition, of which Thomism is a part, also treats the past as knowable in some sense. To take the clearest recent example, in *Fides et Ratio*, John Paul II explicitly includes the discipline of history among those productive of knowledge and he confirms this in many places when he says or implies that we can know something from the study of history.[19] All this applies equally well, indeed more so, to the non-human past, since it seems clear that we can know some things about the past of living things or the past of stars and planets and so on. So, taking into account the usage of Aristotle and Aquinas as well as that of the wider tradition, it is clear that knowledge of both the human and non-human past is possible in some sense within the Thomistic tradition. But the key question for Thomists is this: since for Aristotle and Aquinas intellectual knowledge is of the universal and necessary, and things in the past seem to be material singulars, precisely how can we have intellectual knowledge about the past?

First, it should be noted that material singulars are not the only things or even the principal things that we seek to know about in the past. Focusing on the human past, consider the example of the office of the Pharaonic king of Egypt or feudalism in the Middle Ages or the genre of the novel in the nineteenth century. None of these are material singulars since all are attributable to more than one thing in whatever way historians do attribute them, but it is clear that things like these are what historians seek to understand; in fact, contemporary historians are more concerned with universal things like cultures and movements and genres than with particular details of which king did what, and, when they are concerned with details, it is almost exclusively for the sake of the more universal—as Aristotle was in his work on the Athenian constitution, a proto-institutional history. Likewise, those who study the non-human past do so mainly in order to know about things like stellar evolution or how salt and fresh water came to be differentiated, and such things are not singulars. Nor is the fact that such universals are in the past a bar to their being known. This is because things in the past possess their intelligibility from their forms, not from the fact that they are in the past, since that is accidental, as Aquinas says (*De veritate*, 10.3).[20]

But do not historians (and those who claim to know the non-human past) claim to know some material singulars, and is this not impossible for Aristotle and Aquinas? They do claim to know some material singulars, but this is not impossible. It is true that the intellect cannot know the singular *as such*, since that is the manner of knowing proper to the senses, but the intellect can know the singular indirectly, that is, in so far as it is intelligible, as Aquinas says when he asks explicitly whether the intellect knows the singular (*Summa theologiae* I 86.1).[21] To see why he says this, consider the two ways science treats of its subjects, which Aquinas outlines in his commentary on Boethius's *De trinitate* (5.2 ad 4). Principally and primarily, he says, intellectual knowledge is the knowledge of universal natures and their causes. Secondarily and by a kind of reflection, however, science includes knowledge of singulars because the intellect, using the sense powers, relates universal natures to the singulars that possess them. Of course, material singulars, being material, are not known scientifically in the strict sense, since they do not admit of the kind of certainty one has in science properly speaking; but singulars can be known scientifically in a lesser sense, as in natural or moral philosophy, although even here we would know the universal natures of material things better and more clearly than we could know a given singular.[22] Aristotle and Aquinas both insist that there is no science of the singular, not because we can know nothing about actually existing material things, which would be an odd thing for them to say, but because they are arguing against those who claim that intellectual knowledge comes directly through the senses.

We have seen, then, that both universal aspects of the past and material singulars in the past can be known by the intellect and we have also seen the sense in which we are said to have intellectual knowledge of them.[23] And on how things in the past can be known, John of St. Thomas makes the key point: we can only know the past by means of representations we have of it in the present. Given such a limitation, then, by what methods can we come to know about things in the past? Because the methods for knowing any subject are tied to the sciences that know that subject, before we can outline the methods of knowing the past by means of the present, we first need to lay out where knowledge of the past fits within the Thomistic framework of disciplines. This is to ask the question corresponding to the second problem I began with.

IV

History as defined above is the investigation both of something in the past and of things related causally to it. Since things in the past possess their intelligibility from their forms, as pointed out above, any given thing in the past is already the proper subject of some science, namely the science that knows that kind of thing in that respect. So, each thing in the past is studied by the science that knows that kind of thing; for example, the history of living things is part of biology, the history of the sun is part of astronomy, etc.—which is usually how such things are divvied up among contemporary researchers. This implies that we know the past through the present, not by a general method, but by means of the methods specific to a given science. History in the wide sense, then, is not a science of its own; it is an aspect of other sciences, and, in so far as it treats of material singulars, it seems to be the aspect of a science that knows secondarily and by way of reflection, as outlined above.[24]

In addition to investigations into the subjects of a science in the past, there are also investigations into the past related to the science itself, for example, how that science was discovered and articulated and how it has developed down to the present.[25] Since all intellectual teaching and learning begin from pre-existing knowledge and since our knowledge is almost never perfect or complete, it is clear that the more perfectly we come to know something in a given respect, the more we also come to know why our pre-existing knowledge was imperfect in the first place; if we did not come to know this in some way, then we could never know why we moved from our previous understanding to a more perfect one and we could therefore not even know whether our newly acquired knowledge was in fact more perfect than our pre-existing knowledge.[26] What we come to know here is the past of the given science, as it is in, and related to, us. In general, since much of our knowledge comes from what we have learned from those who have taught us, we must also come to understand the imperfections of such knowledge in order to come to a more perfect understanding of the subjects of the science; this implies moving beyond the limitations not just of particular teachers but also of the errors of those who taught our teachers, which includes things like the limitations due to cultural presuppositions.[27] In short, then, knowing the past of a science in at least some way is required in order to perfect our knowledge of the subjects of that science. And when we study the past of a science, we can only do so through our own understanding of the subjects of that science, since what determines the past of the science is that it is aimed at understanding those subjects. Thus, we cannot undertake to study the history of a science or its subjects without at the same time presupposing some scientific knowledge of those subjects.

So, we arrive at three key conclusions revealing the place of history in the wide sense within the Thomistic framework. First, inquiry into things in the past relevant to a given subject is part of the science that knows that subject in general. Second, the study of the past of a given science is part of that science too. Third, the study of the past of a science, far from being irrelevant, is in fact necessary for us because our very development toward perfected science implies knowing the past of the science in some way.

But what about history as the study of the human past? Is that not its own independent discipline? Since what historians study is human action and its circumstances in the past, the above considerations make clear that the study of the human past is part of the science that studies human action, namely moral philosophy.[28] To see this, one need only consult any attempt to justify why students should learn human history. Such attempts invariably rely on claims about human action and the good life, usually ending up by saying how knowing the past enables students to live for the best in the present. The same justification is used for all of what are called "the humanities," and this is a sign that all of the humanities, in so far as they are concerned with the study of the past, are in fact parts of moral philosophy; this is likewise true for those of the social sciences that study human action in the past (as opposed to those that focus on human nature more generally).[29] Of course, most universities today have these discipline as their own departments, and the story of how that came to be so is a long one. Suffice it to say here that history as the study of the human past was developed into a discipline in part for ethical and political reasons (even when it was claimed that historical facts could be discovered outside any theory)—one need only think of the ethical and political aims of Ranke and other early professionalizers of history.[30] In a similar way, the social sciences were developed to ground theories of human nature and action, as is clear from their history, beginning with Auguste Comte.[31] None of this should be taken to imply that the study of the human past is somehow illegitimate; indeed, my arguments above show why it is necessary. Nevertheless, we must be aware of history's place as part of moral philosophy in order to inquire into the human past in the best way.[32] And this is a point that Aristotle and Aquinas both make, although they are not as concerned to elaborate it as we are. Both Aristotle and Aquinas point out (in *Rhetoric* I.4 and *De regno* 98 respectively) that one must know the details of how one's community came to be the way it is in order to direct that community well, and so the knowledge of the past of a political community "belongs to politics," as Aristotle says there.[33] Likewise, customs and habits acquired from childhood determine in key part the choices that human beings make, as Aquinas says in *Summa contra gentiles* III.85, and so knowledge of customs and habits and their causes in the past are parts of moral philosophy. More generally, in the study of the human past, we aim to understand how aspects of the past of a given community or tradition relate causally to individual acts or to customs and habits or to conceptions of good or to other communities or traditions.[34] So, history as the study of the human past extends to all aspects of everything human beings have done in the past. Now, a Thomistic account of everything that human beings have done should begin with the central truth of Thomistic moral philosophy: human beings pursue happiness and perfection in political community in everything they do, and so in their communities they likewise pursue what they understand happiness to be. In so far as a community has a common life, its members will order that common life, not arbitrarily, but according to the conception of happiness that its members have (more or less); and so every community has a manner of realizing its members' idea of human happiness through an ordering of customs and habits. This is a Thomistic way of defining what culture is: a community's manner of realizing happiness through an ordering of customs and habits.[35] Cultures in this sense seem to be the highest subjects of the knowledge of the human past. This is for two reasons: first, cultures are the most intelligible and determinative aspects of the human past, being the most general; second, it is through a knowledge of specific cultures that such investigations contribute most to moral philosophy, since we need knowledge of our own culture in order to direct our community well—contemporary historians, then, are right to seek to understand cultures.[36] What has emerged from this account of inquiry into the human past are chiefly two points: first, that moral philosophy cannot be carried out without the knowledge of the human past; and, second, that the specialized study of that human past can only be carried out as part of and informed by moral philosophy.[37]

We have seen, then, at least an outline of history and where it fits among the disciplines. But what is the overall shape of this account in general, and how does it fit in with contemporary Thomistic projects? I turn to these in conclusion.[38]

V

One might first wish to know how this account relates to earlier Thomistic accounts of history. Let me just give a sketch, which is aimed more to show how I understand this account than to do justice to each view, for which I do not have the space here. Maritain and Coughlin are right, in my view, to insist that there is no knowledge of singulars as such, but my account develops theirs by making clear how indirect knowledge of singulars is possible. Benedict Ashley emphasizes that we can know things from history, and also that history is not a science, but he does not say much more than that; my account simply shows why what he says is right. Charles De Koninck's point that there are rational connections among individual acts captures well why the human past is knowable. Likewise, Wallace is right, in my view, to emphasize that such connections have necessity because they are in the past, which reveals why they possess the stability and determination to be known.

Buckley builds his account around the claim that human influences on one another do and can have generality, and, on my view, he is simply articulating part of the foundation for the role that the study of the human past has in moral philosophy; my work generalizes Buckley's. So, each of these Thomists was right in the main on what he wished to clarify and defend, and each of their points contributes to the whole of this account.

In general, my account shows that the various sciences, in so far as they treat of things in the past, are also the sciences that know those things in the past, and so history as inquiry into the past is always subordinate to the larger inquiries into the subjects, as is knowledge of the past of each science as a discipline. This reveals too that history poses no special problem for Thomists. Aristotle and Aquinas were always careful (within the limits of knowledge in their time) both to draw on the past as need be and also to build up their accounts with reference to the histories of the sciences—indeed, Aristotle seems to have been the first thinker to include systematic reflection on the past of a science within the science itself. And, precisely because what I have given here is an account of history, it can suggest an answer to the question of what the relationship is for Thomists between studying the history of a discipline and studying in the discipline itself. On this account of history, studying the past is always part of and subordinate to a larger inquiry, and inquiry makes progress in part by reflecting on its own past; so, Thomists who seek to solve contemporary problems need Thomists who study the history of philosophy and theology; but Thomists who study intellectual history cannot do so without an implicit theoretical account of the subjects of the science whose past they study, and so they need theorists focused on solving problems. In making that clear, I hope my work here can contribute to the Thomistic *resourcement*, not only by solving philosophical problems related to history, but also by proposing an account of history that can help to address this social problem within Thomism as a movement.

Legionaries of Christ, College of Humanities
Cheshire, CT

Notes

1. For their help (small or large) with aspects of the issues discussed in this paper (near or remote), I would like to thank David Appleby, Lucas Angioni, Michel Bastit, Brian Chrzastek OP, Therese Cory, Michael Dodds OP, Thérèse-Anne Druart, John McCarthy, Josef Froula, Jean De Groot, Alex Hall, Gyula Klima, Andreas Kramarz LC, Tony Lisska, Alasdair MacIntyre, Timothy Noone, Jean Rioux, John Rist, Michael Tkacz, and Brandon Zimmerman.

2. Jacques Maritain, *On the Philosophy of History* (New York: Charles Scribner's Sons, 1957); Charles De Koninck, "A Note on History" (unpublished manuscript; accessed on September 23rd, 2015 at http://www.charlesdekoninck.com/art-and-morality-with-a-note-on-history/); R. Glen Coughlin, "History and Liberal Education," *The Aquinas Review* 5.1 (1998): 1–40.

3. Benedict Ashley, *The Way toward Wisdom: An Intercultural and Interdisciplinary Approach to Metaphysics* (South Bend, IN: University of Notre Dame Press, 2006), 315–321.

4. Charles De Koninck, "The Nature of Man and His Historical Being," *Laval Théologique et Philosophique* 5.2 (1949): 271–277: narration of past events "may also reveal more or less rational connections that exist among [those events], and . . . the term 'history' also serves to designate the kind of knowledge ordained to the discovery of such connections. . . . History tends towards a certain universality and thus towards the estate of a 'science'" (271); Michael Buckley, "A Thomistic Philosophy of History," *New Scholasticism* 35.3 (1961): 342–362; William Wallace OP, *The Elements of Philosophy: A Compendium for Philosophers and Theologians* (Staten Island, NY: Alba House, 1977): 183–185, 268. The most recent Thomistic account of history is probably that of Thomas Joseph White in his *The Incarnate Lord: A Thomistic Study in Christology* (Washington, DC: The Catholic University of America Press, 2015), in his concluding chapter on why Christology is not a historical science (467–510). White's view seems to be closest to that of De Koninck and Wallace.

5. The most obvious example here is that of Alasdair MacIntyre, in particular in *After Virtue*, Third Edition (South Bend, IN: University of Notre Dame Press, 2007).

6. This is actually a general problem for contemporary theologians and philosophers who draw on historical work: most such historical work does not have a clear theoretical foundation for its results—and some of this work, of course, is used to argue against the claims of Thomists. In a similar way, contemporary Thomists are often seen as anachronizing by historians of thought, but those historians do not offer an account of history either or, if they do, it is only in the way of modern historiography, which is highly compartmentalized from the rest of philosophical inquiry. Both groups do, however, raise important problems for Thomists, and a strong account of history would allow Thomists to address those problems and respond to critics with clarity and depth. If my account here is successful, then Thomists will have both a robust metaphysical framework and also a robust historical framework, something no other contemporary school of thought has.

7. See in particular MacIntyre's *First Principle, Final Ends, and Contemporary Philosophical Issues* (Milwaukee, WI: Marquette University Press, 1990). One thing a reader of MacIntyre might be struck by is how seemingly un-Thomistic his work is at first glance. Part of my goal in this paper is to reveal in what ways historical work like his fits well within the Thomistic tradition on that tradition's own terms—although I make no claims about the details of MacIntyre's various theses that are controversial among Thomists. I have eschewed making points in broader sociological terms and have instead aimed to make related points within the Thomistic framework, from Thomistic authorities, and for the sake of what are recognizably Thomistic goals; although this will have less appeal to a wide audience, it will also ideally have more coherence and intelligibility and will be less liable to hidden errors introduced by a sociological language foreign to Aristotelian philosophy. This exposes me to criticism both from within the Thomistic tradition (have I read Aquinas rightly?) and from outside it (have I truly understood the historical situated-ness of human life in the relevant ways?). Both kinds of questions would raise important challenges to what I say here and are important directions in which this work should be developed.

8. This is a more general version of the set of distinctions Jorge Gracia makes in his *Philosophy and Its History: Issues in Philosophical Historiography* (Buffalo, NY: SUNY Press, 1988), 39–107. Wallace also begins with something like this distinction (*Elements of Philosophy*, 268).

9. But as an activity aimed at understanding the past (rather than at producing a genre of text), history is more philosophical than poetry, since history aims to discover truth and poetry does not.

10. Historiography is too ambiguous: it can mean the art of history writing, or historical methodology in general, or what was written at a given period, or even what has been written on a particular historical question. "Historics," although less common, seems a better term for the theory and method of the investigation and understanding of the human past. "Historiography" would seem to be best used to mean the writing about the past, the historiography of Ancient Greece would be, then, the historical writing of or about the Ancient Greeks, although some ambiguity is of course perfectly acceptable. History in general I define below.

11. It was a question of Michael Tkacz that helped me to see this important point.

12. Aristotle, *Prior Analytics*, translated with introduction, notes, and commentary by Robin Smith (Cambridge: Hackett Publishing Company, 1989), 49.

13. For a detailed account of this term in medieval philosophy in general, see Arno Seifert, "*Historia* im Mittelalter," *Archiv für Begriffsgeschichte* 21.2 (1977): 226–284.

14. Aquinas, *Commentary on Aristotle's* De anima, translated by K. Foster and S. Humphries, introduction by Ralph McInerny (Notre Dame, IN: Dumb Ox Books, 1994), 3.

15. Aquinas also has another general Latin word for inquiry, namely *inquisitio*; it seems that he prefers *historia* in those cases in which he is drawing directly on the translation of Aristotle, which tend to use *historia*. For example, the word *historia* in this more Greek sense does not appear in the *Summa theologiae*.

16. Consider the two main online encyclopedias of philosophy and their articles under "philosophy of history," Internet Encyclopedia of Philosophy (at http://www.iep.utm.edu/history/) and Stanford Encyclopedia of Philosophy (http://plato.stanford.edu/entries/history). Both say that history is the study of the past, but both fail to see that this claim is far wider than the human past: "History is the study of the past in all its forms" (Internet Encyclopedia); and "historians are interested in providing conceptualizations and factual descriptions of events and circumstances in the past" (*Stanford Encyclopedia*).

17. To take only two other examples like this one—Aquinas deploys history to support his case throughout the *Contra impugnantes* and, in his commentary on the *Nichomachean Ethics* (I.7 *lectio* 11), he refers to the fact that history teaches us that sciences can be completely forgotten.

18. John of St. Thomas addresses this in most detail in his *Ars Logica* (Second Part, Question 23, Article 2, "Utrum possit dari cognitio intuitiva de re physice absente sive in intellectu sive in sensu exteriori" in *Cursus Philosophicus Thomisticus* (Lyons, 1678), 289–293. John Deely translates one key passage this way (Jean Poinsot, *Tractatus de Signis: The Semiotics of Jean Poinsot*, edited and translated by John Deely (Berkeley, CA: University of California Press, 1985), 315: "For we say of a past thing that there can be a proper representation of the thing in itself, because it has already shown itself and so is able to terminate the representation of itself; but it cannot terminate through itself in the way required for an intuitive awareness, but in something produced by itself." John of St. Thomas is drawing on Aquinas's point that we can understand things outside of perception by means of their causes or effects that we can perceive (*Commentary on the* Sentences of Peter Lombard III.23, 1, 2, sol.).

19. John Paul II includes history among the disciplines that produce knowledge (5), and he confirms this when he says that we can know something from the study of history (4), that history reveals some truth (39, 48, 75, 77) or shows it (49, 96, 101), and in general when he implies that history gives knowledge (46, 56).

20. In various places, Aquinas makes the point that the memory is what knows the past (e.g., *Summa theologiae* II-II 48.1; *Commentary on Aristotle's* De interpretatione, *lectio* 14.19). Aquinas distinguishes taking memory in two ways, either as the power of retaining species or as a power including in some way its objects considered as past (*Summa theologiae* I 79.6). If we take memory as including a consideration of the past as past, then that means memory includes the past as here and now and thus is part of the senses. The question is complex and will involve a complete account of the memory and the cogitative power (as well as how both relate to the contemporary neuroscience), but it is clear that those seeking to know the past do not seek to know the past *as past*, which would be to know it through the sense powers. Historians, for example, are not seeking to re-experience the past, but to understand it; reenactors and historical fiction writers seem to be the ones concerned to re-experience the past.

21. For the full range of texts in Aquinas's corpus treating the issue, see George Klubertanz, "St. Thomas and the Knowledge of the Singular," *New Scholasticism* 26.2 (1952): 135–166. I would distinguish the indirect intellectual knowledge of singulars as in I 86.1 from "accidental knowledge," i.e, sophistical knowledge, which is how some commentators have understood Aquinas's account of how we know singulars and contingents. Accidental knowledge is the kind of "knowledge" we have when we can be said to "know" a singular just because we know the universal, in the way that I can be said to know Cardinal Richelieu's cats (he allegedly had fourteen!) for the simple reason that I know about cats.

22. Aquinas points out that we have a lesser degree of knowledge in natural and moral philosophy in many places; see especially, his *Commentary on Aristotle's* Posterior Analytics I.2 *lectio* 4.

23. Jean Rioux drew my attention to Pope Benedict XVI's claim that our knowledge of the past is hypothetical (in *Jesus von Nazareth: Erster Teil. Von der Taufe im Jordan bis zur Verklärung* (Freiburg: Verlag Herder, 2008). He says: "Sicher, es gibt Hypothesen vom hohem Gewissheitsgrad, aber insgesamt solten wir uns der Grenze unsere Gewissheiten bewusst bleiben" (xvi). And, for Thomists, this is certainly right: both that we can be said to have intellectual knowledge of the past and that such knowledge can only technically have a hypothetical degree of certainty, as much else in natural and moral philosophy. While it is doubtful that Benedict intended his point to be taken precisely as meaning that knowledge of the past can only have Aristotelian hypothetical certainty, what he says does seem to fit rather well with the position I outline in this paper. (As an aside, I should note that Jean Rioux referred me to Benedict as a way of objecting to my account of history.)

24. This might seem a bold claim. What about the experience of a material singular in the present? But our experience of singulars is only in the present analogously. All our knowledge of singulars must by definition, because dependent on the senses in some sense, be knowledge of singulars in the past. Light and sound take time to reach us; smell clearly does too, since the particles must move from the emitter to our nose; similarly, even touch and taste we are not instantaneously aware of. So, what we know about material singulars (etc.) is always knowledge of such things as they were in the past, near or remote.

25. The past of a science may be studied from any number of perspectives (ethics, politics, philosophical psychology, etc.), but what is most determinative about those human acts in the past related to the science is that they are aimed in some way at understanding the subjects of the science; such acts are most properly studied, then, as part of the science itself. The fact that one can study a science's past from many perspectives has led to things like feminist readings of modern science. On my account, such things are clearly not proper to the science itself as such; in so far they treat of either the politics or ethics involved in the past of the science, such studies are properly ethical or political and not part of the given science; in so far as such studies treat of ways in which the past of a science has been hindered by, for example, prejudices about femininity, such studies are (or at least can be) related to our own progress toward perfected science (science as it is in us). In this way, then, even things as seemingly un-Thomistic as gender studies can be integrated into a Thomistic framework.

26. The notion of perfected science I draw from Alasdair MacIntyre's Aquinas Lecture, *First Principles, Final Ends, and Contemporary Philosophical Issues* (cited above, note 7) and from his *Whose Justice? Which Rationality?* (Notre Dame, IN: University of Notre Dame Press, 1988).

27. Benedict Ashley observes (*Way toward Wisdom*, 318), "The best way to attain a degree of objectivity and freedom to think critically is to become aware of the limitations that our own personal and social histories ('narratives') impose on our thinking and that of others."

28. Two objections: 1. One commenter raised the objection here that the human past should be more generally studied by and part of philosophical anthropology within the philosophy of nature. I respond: understanding human acts is proper to natural philosophy only in so far as moral philosophy is itself part of natural philosophy. But understanding human acts requires that we understand what properly human action is, which is the province of moral philosophy. Of course, many historians think that it is obvious that we can come to know about this or that act without knowing what properly human action is, but this is false. Any account of this or that act implies a general picture of what human action is. And that is the province of moral philosophy. 2. Another commenter objected that if history were a part of moral philosophy, it would imply that history is part of the same discipline as meta-ethics; it seems strange to say that one inquires about the American Revolution in the same discipline as one inquires about theories like non-cognitivism. My response is that much of contemporary meta-ethics is not part of moral philosophy. For a Thomist, meta-ethics seems to be those parts of other disciplines that relate to and undergird moral philosophy, e.g., natural philosophy, psychology, etc. More generally, though, we do not seem able to come to know what courage is without having considered some acts (complete and therefore in the past) which we know to be courageous. And, even after theoretical reflection, our consideration of courageous acts in the past is one part of how we develop our understanding of courage.

29. To see this, consider one of the humanities, literature, for example: one can read literature to be formed (which is the end of the art); one can study literature to know how to make it (studying it as an art, i.e, what Aristotle and Aquinas call "poetics"); or one can study literature in order to understand key aspects of the society that produced that literature (studying it as part of moral science, which is what we usually mean when we include literature among the humanities). To elaborate on this last point, the genres of literature, for example, will be related to the social conditions of the given society; likewise, literature presents an account of something good, and that account is always related to the notion of

the good life as lived in that community, even if it is a negative response to that community's account of the good life; etc.

30. A good recent account of the social and intellectual history of history as a discipline, leading up to and including the German historicists, is F. Beiser's *The German Historicist Tradition* (Oxford: Oxford University Press, 2011), 19–23.

31. See *The Cambridge History of Science, Volume 7: The Modern Social Sciences*, ed. Theodore Porter (Cambridge: Cambridge University Press, 2003). The Catholic historian and intellectual Christopher Dawson argued that history is becoming the science of "the whole human cultural-process in so far as it can be studied by documentary evidence" ("Sociology as a Science," in *Dynamics of World History* [Wilmington, DE: ISI Books, 2002], 21); as such, in his view, it is indispensable for sociology and sociology for it. But, right as this is in one way, it is wrong in another: Dawson's view implies that the knowledge of the human past is divorced from and intelligible apart from moral philosophy; a proper understanding of the past and of inquiry into the past reveals that this is not so. In Dawson's defense, he seems to have understood moral philosophy in the modern sense (as focused on right and wrong, rules, duties, obligations, etc.) and he is certainly right that knowledge of the human past is more than and not only subject to morality thus understood; but in so far as we understand moral philosophy in a broadly Aristotelian way (as ordering everything human toward the *telos* of human life), we can see that there can in principle be nothing related to human action outside the domain of moral philosophy understood in this way; Dawson himself intimates something like this in at least a limited way when he observes that social life itself is by nature *artistic* ("Art and Society," in *Dynamics of World History*, 71–73). Dawson's work is also important because he proposes a relative ordering between history and sociology: in his view, sociology describes a culture in general, systematically, and (I would say) as to the ends of the institutions, customs, etc.; and the historian describes the genetic development of a culture—sociology outlines the form, Dawson suggests, history provides the content ("Sociology as a Science," 21).

32. The fact that the study of the human past is part of moral science can also be confirmed from the contemporary discipline of history itself. In the first place, history began with a clear focus on politics in authors like Herodotus and Thucydides and progressed slowly to widen out its purview to such an extent that among contemporary historians anything in the human past can be the subject of historical inquiry; its scope, then, slowly expanded from what is narrowly politics to what is broadly moral science; for the full story, the most comprehensive book in English is E. Breisach's *Historiography: Ancient, Medieval, and Modern*, 3rd edition (Chicago, IL: University of Chicago Press, 2007). Likewise, since history is part of moral science, one would expect to find in the study of the human past the kinds of disagreements that are common in ethics and politics; and this is just what we do find, as arguments over how to interpret the past reveal; for examples of this related to the study of antiquity, see Neville Morley, *Theories, Models, and Concepts in Ancient History* (New York: Routledge, 2004). Again as part of moral science, history should only be able to attain a limited and imperfect degree of certainty in its acts of understanding, and this too is what we find, since history does not admit of mathematical certainty and historians know this very well. Even in discussions, not of specific parts of the past, but of the historiographical method itself, the various approaches to the relevant questions divide along largely political and ethical lines; the book that brings this out most clearly is Michael Bentley, *Modern Historiography: An Introduction* (New York: Routledge, 1999).

33. Drawing on Avicenna, Aquinas outlines a distinction between those parts of a practical science that are close to practice and those that are remote from practice (*Commentary on Boethius's* De trinitate 5.1 ad 4). Intellectual knowledge of the past relevant to the founding of a community or the origins of habits and customs is in the more theoretical part of these practical sciences, rather than in the more practical part, since such knowledge is both necessary and also remote from practice.

34. It seems to be precisely this that the dogmatic constitution *Dei Verbum* seeks to call to the attention of the interpreter of revelation when it talks of literary forms and characteristic modes of thinking and feeling at the time of the sacred writer (12). By seeing that such things are subjects of moral philosophy, one can perhaps have a clear philosophical foundation for revealing the meaning that the scriptures had for their authors and successive audiences.

35. Tracey Rowland, in *Culture and the Thomist Tradition: After Vatican* II (New York: Routledge, 2003), takes a different view of culture, one that is articulated in less recognizably Thomistic terms, but has much to offer. I would only suggest that the definition I give here includes hers and shows clearly how accounts of culture like hers relate to Thomistic moral philosophy.

36. I would suggest that it is precisely in a shift of culture in this sense after Vatican II that we will find explanations for the marginalization of Thomism, both a shift in what the shared conception of happiness among Catholic philosophers and theologians was and a shift among such Catholics in the manner of realizing their shared conception of happiness, i.e, in Catholic intellectual culture. In so far as Thomists see the current intellectual culture among Catholics as problematic, we must aim to change it in part through being aware that we are aiming to change both the shared conception of happiness among Catholic intellectuals and the manner of realizing a shared conception of happiness—not that such things are simple in any sense. One has only to state this to realize that philosophy articles like mine are not enough. Thomists must become intellectual missionaries, with all that that implies about our shared social life, virtues, goods we pursue, etc., as well as our need for the interior conversion of self that is the heart of every mission: we are first missionaries to ourselves.

37. Nietzsche makes something like this point in his early *On the Advantage and Disadvantage of History for Life* (originally published 1874; I use the translation of Peter Preuss [Indianapolis, IN: Hackett Publishing, 1980]). His main claim is that history is necessary for living well, but among the weak history tends toward an excess of history which is destructive of life. He says: "that knowledge of the past is at all times only desired in the service of the future and the present, not to weaken the present, not to uproot a future strong with life: all of this is simple, as truth is simple, and immediately convinces even him who has not first been given a historical proof" (23). In Thomistic terms, we can agree that history is not for its own sake, and that excessive dwelling on history and an obsessive search to know the past (which one can see illustrated in the methods of some schools of psychology and psychiatry as well as among some contemporary historians) themselves are not conducive to happiness and human perfection. At the same time, a Thomistic account of history reveals why history is nevertheless necessary.

38. What I turn to in conclusion here is not mainly what a working historian would likely be interested in. Indeed, as David Appleby pointed out, what I present throughout the paper would seem to professional historians (perhaps Catholic ones especially) to be minimal as an account of history, with perhaps little of usefulness for examining sources, determining interpretive criteria, etc. I accept this point and agree that it is largely right. But providing yet more principles and criteria for historians is not my goal. What I hope

this account has done is show where the study of the past, in particular the human past, fits within the Thomistic system and thus provides a theoretical grounding for historical methodologies. From a historian's perspective, the way to read my paper is as an attempt, first, to provide an answer, in Thomistic terms, to the problems raised by postmodernism, as outlined in, e.g., Howell and Prevenier's *From Reliable Sources: An Introduction to Historical Method* (Ithaca, NY: Cornell University Press, 2001); and, second, as an attempt to show why the insights and results of historical work are important for Thomists, which in turn reveals that Thomists need to respect the relative autonomy of those who study the human past; history may be subordinate to theology, but it cannot be and is not subservient to it. Even though my goal here is quite general, having done some historical work myself, I am convinced that the Thomistic account of humankind, of our pursuit of goods we perceive, and of what culture is will prove to be useful for understanding the past.

Is Usury Still a Sin? Thomas Aquinas on the Justice and Injustice of Moneylending

Peter Karl Koritansky

Abstract: This paper examines Thomas Aquinas's condemnation of usury. In the first section, the details of Thomas's teaching are examined with special attention to the so-called "extrinsic titles" discussed in the Middle Ages as qualifications of the moral and legal strictures concerning moneylending. The reminder of the paper examines the particular extrinsic title of *Lucrum Cessans* (compensation for lost profit), which Thomas rejects, and attempts to square that rejection with other texts implying that compensation for lost profit is a requirement of justice when taken outside the context of moneylending. The paper concludes with some possible modern applications of Thomas's position.

Introduction: Aquinas's Condemnation of Usury

To my knowledge, the most thorough and consistent exponent of the classic condemnation of usury is St. Thomas. In the *Summa Theologiae*, he renders a teaching that goes considerably beyond the condemnations of both the Old Testament and of Aristotle. As he explains, the injustice of usury is impossible to understand without first understanding the nature of money. Among all goods that are bought and sold, we can draw a line between those whose value consist in their consumption and those whose value does not so consist. The best example of the first type of commodity is food and drink. As Aquinas explains, "in such things the use of the thing must not be considered apart from the thing itself, [and so] to lend things of this kind is to transfer the ownership." It would be absurd for me to lend someone food, charge him a monetary fee for the use of that food, and then to demand the food back as well. I would be, in Aquinas's language, "selling the same thing twice" or "selling what does not exist." Such is not the case with the other type of commodity. Aquinas's example is a house, which may be sold but also rented for a monetary amount that will not be returned. When the rental contract expires, the owner of the house keeps all of the money paid by the renter and receives back the house as well. This happens precisely because the house is a different kind

© 2017, *Proceedings of the ACPA*, Vol. 90
doi: 10.5840/acpaproc20169083

of commodity than the food. Its value does not consist in its consumption but rather in being used by the renter, a process through which the house endures.

Now the whole teaching on usury comes down to the following claim. Money should be considered more like food than like the house, and so the use of money must be thought of as consisting in its consumption. As Aquinas hearkens back to Aristotle's teaching in the *Politics*, this is evident upon examining the purpose for which money originally comes into being, namely, in order to facilitate the exchange of commodities and to establish a measure of each thing's market value. As Aristotle and Aquinas both know well, however, the introduction of money into human affairs, though extremely useful, opens the door to the desire for limitless gain. Once people make the mistake of thinking about money as a commodity unto itself, they soon realize that, considered as such, money is the only commodity of which one can never really have enough (as even the greediest of men can have enough servants, houses, or BMWs). The desire for money easily becomes a kind of fetish. To profit merely by lending money, which usury is always an attempt to do, is to misunderstand money at the most fundamental level. As a facilitator of exchange, it should always be "sunk in exchange."[1] Applying this concept to lending, the teaching is quite straightforward. If I lend a man $5000 and require $6000 in return as a fee for the use of the principal amount, there exists a disparity of $1000 in my favor that commutative justice requires me to return.

What makes Aquinas's remarks so interesting, however, is not his explanation of usury's injustice (something that had been explained many times over before), but his explanation of the so-called extrinsic titles which considerably qualify his teaching. Two well-known qualifications are especially important. The first is a distinction between a usurious contract and something that may appear usurious, but really is not. If, instead of lending the $5000 at 20 percent interest, I enter a business partnership (a *societas*) with someone, who invests my money along with his own and perhaps the investments of others, I will be entitled to receive a share in the profits that may equal or even exceed the amount of interest collected under the previous example. Receiving back the additional $1000, in this case, is not a fee for the use of the money, but my share in the profitable venture, which was never guaranteed, but which I receive from my willingness to take on the risk (*periculum*) of the venture itself. I am not, strictly speaking, lending money at all, but rather getting into the potato business, or the wine business, or whatever the case may be.[2] As Aquinas and nearly all other scholastics agreed, this kind of cooperative venture is not an attempt to make money reproduce itself. If any profit is gained it comes from the productivity of labor, and assuming that the commodity or commodities produced are sold at a just price, the requirements of commutative justice (the only kind of justice here at issue) are completely fulfilled.

A profitable *societas* in which an investor receives a 20 percent return is not, strictly speaking, an "extrinsic title," because there need not be any loan contract in the first place. Two or more parties are simply going into business together. Aquinas mentions it more as something that must be distinguished from usury as a transaction that, to an onlooker, may appear usurious, but really is not. Something more essentially tied to a loan contract is the extrinsic title that came to be known as *damnum emergens*, or the loss that may be endured by a lender precisely on account of the loan. According to Aquinas and many others, if I endure an identifiable loss in lending someone money, I may be entitled to receive back, not only the principal amount of the loan, but something in addition as compensation for that loss.[3] Let us return to the $5000 loan I made a moment ago. Imagine that I am the owner of a small business with a narrow margin between my profits and opportunity costs. A farmer needs $1000 to purchase a new plow without which his business will grind to a halt. If I loan him that money, however, I will be unable to pay the rent for the building in which I conduct my own business, thus incurring a late fee of $50 on my next installment. I am perfectly entitled, therefore, to require the borrower to pay me back the $1000 plus an additional $50 to compensate me for my additional loss. To do so, as Aquinas explains, "is not to sell the use of money, but to avoid [a] loss. It may also happen," Aquinas continues, "that the borrower avoids a greater loss than the lender incurs, whereby the borrower may repay the lender with what he has gained."

Questions about Aquinas's Teaching

If this were all Aquinas's teaching would be fairly straightforward but also incomplete. As he continues to explain, we must distinguish between the amount of money that a lender looses in making a loan and the fact that the money lent is no longer available to him to invest profitably. Whereas I may ask to be compensated for whatever losses I incur in lending, I may not require my debtor to compensate me for lost profits, an extrinsic title that came to be known as *lucrum cessans*, something clearly over and above the relatively uncontroversial *damnum emergens* already discussed. In Aquinas's own words, "the lender cannot enter an agreement for compensation, through the fact that he makes no profit out of his money: because he must not sell that which he has not yet and may be prevented in many ways from having."[4] To be sure, the line between *damnum emergens* and *lucrum cessans* may at times be difficult to see, but this does not take away from the clarity of the distinction made here by Aquinas. In many ways, Aquinas anticipates the objection of a modern day free market capitalist, who we may imagine arguing that, in some ways, making a loan always results in some kind of loss for which interest is necessary to make compensation. Should not a lender at least be permitted to charge a rate of interest equivalent to the most conservative return on the most stable investment? Aquinas's answer seems clear. To do so is to sell what one does not yet have, or to put it in terms of his original condemnation of usury, to sell what *does not exist*. The case would be otherwise, of course, if the justification for interest is something like inflation (a phenomenon that does not seem to factor into Aquinas's economic thought). If my money is actually worth less at the time of repayment than at the time of lending, one can imagine a Thomistic justification for an interest rate imposed for compensating the lender, but this of course would be justified under the rationale of *damnum emergens* rather than *lucrum cessans*, since inflation imposes a real and identifiable loss upon the lender that he endures precisely on account of the lending. *Lucrum cessans* is nevertheless ruled out because it involves compensation, not for a real loss, but for lost profits, which do not yet exist and therefore cannot *be lost* in any way that compensation would be due.

If this distinction holds, however, we must understand how to reconcile it with another remark that Aquinas makes, somewhat earlier in *Secunda Secundae*, in a more general discussion of commutative justice. In that text Aquinas asks the following question: Is a man bound to restore what he has not taken?[5] As Aquinas answers, we are always bound "to make restitution according to the loss [we] have brought upon another." This, however, can happen in one of two ways. Most straightforwardly, we must compensate the amount taken from what a person *actually* has, and so if I destroy my neighbor's house I must pay to have the house rebuilt. Secondly, I must also compensate what I take from my neighbor, not only for what he had actually, but for what he was "on the way" to having. Using Aquinas's own example, then, if I trample on someone else's field ruining his harvest, I must not only compensate him for what he *actually* had, namely, his seeds, but also for what he *virtually* had, namely, his crops. If I only repay him the value of the seeds, there still remains, Aquinas says, a kind of disparity in my favor. Aquinas is quick to add, of course, that I need not pay the full value of his estimated harvest. To have something virtually is, after all, to have it less than to have it actually. As he puts it, "a loss of this kind need not be made good in equivalent . . . and so were [my neighbor to receive] the thing actually, he would be paid, not the exact value taken from him, but more." Nevertheless, the crucial point is that Aquinas grants that compensation is due as a matter of commutative justice for something taken, yet not actually possessed by the one from whom it is taken.

What implications might this have for money-lending? Although Aquinas does not address the precise implications this teaching may have for his later condemnation of usury, we have at least a partial application to money in his reply to the second objection. There, the objector refers us to the example of a loan that is paid back late. "He who retains his creditor's money beyond the stated time," the objector explains, "would seem to occasion his loss of all his possible profits from that money, even though he does not really take them."[6] In his reply, Aquinas relies upon his answer to the question just given and reemphasizes the fact that takers of virtual wealth need not repay that virtual wealth in full. His very reliance upon the example of trampling the field, however, since he relies on that discussion to address the money-lending objection, gives us to understand that, for Aquinas, some compensation is due on account of paying back a loan after the agreed upon time. What, moreover, is the rationale for the additional charge? Nothing other than the compensation required for lost profits! In other words, when I borrow money from someone and fail to pay him back in the agreed upon time, I owe him more than the principal, not because of any actual loss I inflicted upon him, but because he was without the possession of that money which he may have used profitably. This, of course, seems to fly in the face of Aquinas's later assertion that one may never demand payment for lost profits, which are fully distinguishable from actual losses that may be compensated. To be sure, the examples are different. In one case, the borrower compensates the lender after having failed to pay the money back on time. In the other case, the borrower and lender agree in advance to compensation beyond the principal no matter when the loan is repaid. But in both cases, the compensation is being made, not for an actual loss, but for the loss of profits that the lender was on the way to getting. If compensation for lost profits, even within the context of a monetary loan, is not inherently unjust, Aquinas's rejection of *lucrum cessans*, and even perhaps the condemnation of usury itself, appears very much in question.

Possible Solutions

Several attempts to solve this problem must be examined. The first is that of John Finnis, who carefully analyses these very issues in chapter six of his study of Aquinas's moral, political, and legal thought. Finnis is keenly aware that Aquinas's rejection of *lucrum cessans* in 78.2 must be squared with his permission of compensating lenders for lost profits in 62.4. As he rightly points out, Aquinas allows for compensation of what someone was "on the way" to possessing, though not having possessed it actually. That Aquinas applies this to money-lending only within the context of late repayment on a loan, however, is practically ignored by Finnis, a dimension of Aquinas's teaching he apparently considers immaterial. Once it is granted that, as a matter of restitution, compensation is due for lost potential profits in addition to any actual losses suffered, the conclusion seems to follow that money-lenders may justly claim some percentage (certainly not the full amount, Finnis grants) of what they reasonably expected to gain whether the payment is late or on time. If I lost potential profits in lending, some compensation is due. A loss is a loss, Finnis might say, whether that loss is virtual or actual. The very moment that Aquinas acknowledges the legitimacy of virtual losses, the door to *lucrum cessans* is open and cannot be closed. Therefore, according to Finnis, "on the general theory which Aquinas's phrasing here unmistakably recalls, [lenders] should be entitled to claim not only for (a) the whole amount of their expenses and costs but also for (b) an amount proportionate to the gain (profit) their investible funds brought within their reach, not actually {actu}—nor merely by some bare, abstract, unquantifiable possibility—but at least potentially {virtute} and realistically {in via}."[7] What does Finnis make, then, of Aquinas's apparent denial of *lucrum cessans* in his discussion of usury? He continues,

> Aquinas seems to deny the last-mentioned type of compensation: the profit one might have made with the money one lends cannot, he says, be charged for, since one should not sell what one does not yet possess and may in many ways be prevented or impeded {impediri multipliciter} from getting. What he should have said, and perhaps did mean by his surely deliberate phrasing, is that any charge made for loss of profit from available alternative investment (manufacturing, trading, share-holding, etc.) of the funds loaned ought to be discounted to allow for the multiple uncertainties involved in such investment.

As Finnis goes on to say, because those uncertainties are largely removed in our contemporary economy through low risk investments like equities and bonds, Thomistic principles (apparently established both by what Aquinas said and what he should have said) are perfectly consistent with the modern market's allowance for interest rates on lending "correlated with the general rate of return on equities." To be sure, therefore, Aquinas's remark on which Finnis places the most emphasis is that lenders "must not sell that which he has not yet and may be prevented in many ways from having." According to Finnis's interpretation, it seems, there is a kind of correlative relationship between the likelihood of another profitable investment and one's claim to *lucrum cessans.* Of course, no investment is a guarantee and so no one is entitled to claim the full amount of an expected profit. But to the extent that, in a modern economy, certain investments are extremely secure, interest rates incorporating a consistent percentage of those expected returns are perfectly justifiable.

As an interpretation of Aquinas, Finnis seems to be ignoring some critical details. It is not simply a matter of choosing between Aquinas's rejection of *lucrum cessans* in one text and his allowance for it in another. As we have already seen, *ST* 62.4 does not address the principle of *lucrum cessans* directly, but only the related idea of compensation for lost profits in general (not necessarily in the context of money lending). In that text, however, Aquinas's examples are all those of what he calls involuntary or injurious commutations . . . the man who destroys another's house, the pedestrian who tramples on his neighbor's field, and the borrower who fails to pay back his lender on time. Finnis never considers the possibility that Aquinas's permitting the compensation of lost profits has some essential link with the injurious or involuntary nature of the commutation. In particular, the fact that he only mentions the compensation for lost profits in connection with an example of delayed payment on a loan "beyond the stated time" should lead us to consider this possibility, even though Aquinas himself does not explicitly say that lost profits may only be compensated in cases such as these. Where Aquinas does reject *lucrum cessans*, his words seem to be chosen carefully: "the lender cannot *enter an agreement* for compensation through the fact that he makes no profit out of his money." This would give all the more likelihood to the interpretation that the only conditions under which compensation for lost profit is permissible are those under which money is taken and kept beyond the terms of the agreement, such as precisely the case of a late repayment on a loan.

More faithful to the text of Aquinas is the interpretation of Cardinal Cajetan, and yet upon examination Cajetan ends up allowing for *lucrum cessans* in much the same way as Finnis.[8] As a theoretical point, however, Cajetan denies that the stability or safety of a potential investment warrants a claim to *lucrum cessans.* Even, in other words, if somehow I knew with 100 percent certainty that my $5000 could be invested with a 20 percent return over the next year, this fact by itself would not entitle me to one penny of interest based on the principle of *lucrum cessans.* This is precisely for the reasons Aquinas at least appears to provide when he allows for compensation on lost profits only within the context of an involuntary commutation, as when money is stolen or a loan is paid back late. Cajetan is aware, however, of the powerful objection to his position. How, really, and even under a Thomistic conception of commutative justice, can compensation for lost profit be required in the case of theft or delay, and not in the case of a voluntary loan contract? It would be wrong to consider the additional compensation for injurious commutations as a kind of penalty. That, while still belonging to commutative justice, is entirely something else in Aquinas's understanding.[9] Aquinas's position, on the contrary, appears to be that compensation is due in late repayment precisely on account of the profit that *could have been gained* with that money. But if compensation is due for this reason in the case of delay, that must mean that the borrower really takes something of value beyond the principal amount loaned, a value that must be returned to the lender. If this value exists in the case of delay, however, why doesn't it exist in the case of an ordinary loan? It should not matter that the lender has taken from a willing counterpart in one case and from an unwilling counterpart in the other. Casting aside whatever punitive damages we might award, *lucrum cessans* would appear either to be deserved in both cases or undeserved in both cases. One may respond that Aquinas is right to require compensation for *lucrum cessans* in the case of delay on the grounds that what is taken must be restored, and to forbid it in ordinary lending on the grounds that one cannot sell the use of one's money, but this would be to look past the single most relevant fact, namely, that if a lender's money has a value beyond its principal amount (which justifies its return), then that value would seem to be something that could be sold as well. To do so is not to sell the use of money, but simply to require compensation for that of which the lender is voluntarily deprived in making the loan.

Cajetan's response to this hypothetical objection is illuminating. As he explains, the differences between late repayment and a voluntary loan contract are not merely circumstantial. This is because, whereas money has an absolute value as a medium of exchange, it may have an added value in relation to some person, namely, its owner. More specifically, money that is being saved for investment actually has a higher value than the same amount of money that does not have this same potential, such as money that is lost, or stolen, or simply hidden under a rock and not intended for profit. When someone steals from me, or fails to pay me back, thus depriving me of a profitable venture, I deserve some percentage of the money in return and in addition to the principal amount in return for my lost opportunity. On the other hand, if I voluntarily loan my money to someone, the time our agreement requires me to be without that money should not be considered in calculating the amount I am ultimately owed. Why? Even though my money freely loaned is equally unable to profit me as the money stolen or kept beyond the agreed time, I am the one responsible for transferring my money to a less valuable position precisely by loaning it. By making the loan, in other words, my money actually loses value and *lucrum cessans* cannot be claimed without imputing to my loaned money a value it lost in the loan transfer itself. As Cajetan insists, therefore, Thomas Aquinas does not contradict himself in allowing compensation for lost profits in one case and not in the other.

Even Cajetan, however, adds qualifications to this teaching that considerably soften the restrictions on *lucrum cessans*. First, he says, because a lender loses his claim to *lucrum cessans* only in the voluntary transfer of his money, he who is compelled to make a loan may still claim it, since the voluntary nature of the loan is restricted. If, by a "compulsory loan," Cajetan meant physical compulsion or extreme duress, the loan would appear more like theft and *lucrum cessans* would be justified under the same principle as in the case of delay. But Cajetan does not mean only this. A compulsory loan may, for Cajetan, simply mean that the borrower is in need of the money and since my Christian duty is to help those in need, I am thus "compelled" to offer the loan but still entitled to *lucrum cessans*. Secondly, Cajetan states, *lucrum cessans* may be claimed when the money is lent precisely for a business venture, and for the following reason. Granted that money taken away from my own business plans loses some of its value, it immediately regains that value once it is transferred to, and becomes part of, the borrower's business plans. In fact, there was never really time that the money intended for lending, and later lent, was without its added value as potentially profitable. And so despite the voluntary transfer of the money, *lucrum cessans* may be rightly claimed. Cajetan's position is thus the paradoxical one that *lucrum cessans* is never permissible on a voluntary loan, except when that loan is made for either charitable or business purposes.

Conclusion

In the history of Christian teaching on money-lending, the attitude towards *lucrum cessans* appears pivotal. If compensation for lost profits may be required in loan contracts, the Church's relative silence on the issue of usury appears justified. If we exclude the large number, though low percentage, of creditors who gouge the poor with inordinately high interest rates, the majority of modern money-lending by legitimate banks falls well within what *lucrum cessans* would permit. Arguably, the situation improves as the capitalist ideal of economic equilibrium is approached and the price of money (as in the price of all commodities) is lowered to a point where only the lenders' opportunity costs are met. If compensation for lost profits is not permissible, however . . . if Aquinas's rejection of *lucrum cessans* is correct and not rendered completely insignificant by the qualifications laid upon it by the likes of Cajetan . . . we must then admit a striking incompatibility between Aquinas's theory of justice and a phenomenon that lies at the very core of our modern investment economy.

The University of Prince Edward Island
Charlottetown, PE, Canada

Notes

1. *Summa Theologiae* (*ST*), trans. Fathers of the English Dominican Province (Christian Classics, 1981), II-II, Q. 78, a. 1.

2. *ST* II-II, Q. 78, a. 2, ad 5.

3. *ST* II-II, Q. 78, a. 2, ad 1.

4. Ibid.

5. *ST* II-II, Q. 62, a. 4.

6. Ibid., obj. 2.

7. John Finnis, *Aquinas: Moral, Political, and Legal Theory* (Oxford: Oxford University Press, 1998), 209.

8. For my understanding of Cajetan's position, I am indebted to John Noonan's *The Scholastic Analysis of Usury* (Cambridge, MA: Harvard University Press, 1957), 250–255.

9. *ST* II-II, Q. 62, a. 6.

Obligation, Justice, and Law:
A Thomistic Reply to Anscombe

William Matthew Diem

Abstract: Anscombe argues in "Modern Moral Philosophy" that obligation and moral terms only have meaning in the context of a divine Lawgiver, whereas terms like 'unjust' have clear meaning without any such context and, in at least some cases, are incontrovertibly accurate descriptions. Because the context needed for moral-terms to have meaning does not generally obtain in modern moral philosophy, she argues that we should abandon the language of obligation, adopting instead the yet clear and meaningful language of injustice. She argues further that we should develop an account of human flourishing to answer the question why we need to be just. The essay contends that Aquinas has an account of obligation that requires neither a god nor an account of human flourishing, and that proceeds immediately from the common apprehension of justice Anscombe noted.

Elizabeth Anscombe closes "Modern Moral Philosophy" by "describing the advantages of using the word 'ought' in a non-emphatic fashion, rather than in a special 'moral' sense; of discarding the term 'wrong' in a 'moral' sense, and using such notions as 'unjust.'"[1] Aristotle, she contends, had no moral terms; they were introduced by Christianity "with its law conception of ethics,"[2] but, she asserts, "it is not possible to have such a conception unless you believe in God as a lawgiver."[3] Hence "the concepts of . . . *moral* obligation and *moral* duty . . . of what is *morally* right and wrong, and of the *moral* sense of 'ought,' . . . are survivals . . . from an earlier conception of ethics which no longer generally survives, and are only harmful without it."[4]

It is in light of this harmfulness of moral terms that she calls for the adoption of a non-emphatic 'ought' and of the use of terms like 'unjust' in their stead. These non-moral terms have clear and well-defined meanings. Whatever theoretical problems may plague attempts to exhaustively define 'justice,'[5] 'unjust' is, she holds, an uncontroversial description in at least some applications, in a way that moral terms are not: she writes, "we should no longer ask whether doing something was 'wrong,' . . . we should ask whether, e.g., it was unjust; and the answer would be clear at once."[6] "'Bilking,' 'theft' . . . , 'slander,' 'adultery,' 'punishment of the innocent'" are clear and incontrovertible examples of injustice.[7] Speaking of punishment of the innocent, she notes that neither circumstances nor expected consequences can change its injustice:

> Someone who attempted to dispute this would only be pretending to know what "unjust" means: for it is a paradigm case of injustice. And here we see the superiority of the term "unjust" over the terms "morally right" and "morally wrong."[8]

I am concerned in the present paper with the relation of three specific notions: Law, justice, and obligation. I will consider the relation of these three concepts in Aquinas, before attempting to formulate a Thomistic response to Anscombe's proposal.

Aquinas on Obligation, Law, and *Debitum*

All moral obligation is, Aquinas says, derived from law: "*virtutem obligandi . . . est proprium legis.*"[9] To be aware of a true law that applies to oneself is to be aware of moral obligation and vice versa. Moreover, law imposes obligation because it regards what is due. On the one hand, law has the *ratio* of due,[10] while on the other, what has the *ratio* of due therefore also has the *ratio* of law: "A precept imports the *ratio* of due. Therefore a thing has the *ratio* of due insofar as it falls under a precept."[11] Finally, it is this *ratio* of due that causes laws to impose obligation: "a precept of law, since it is of something obligatory, is of something which must be done [*quod fieri debet*]."[12] Similar expressions are scattered throughout Thomas's works.[13] Importantly, a thing has the *ratio* of law only because it regards what is due. Some laws (i.e., natural laws) have the *vim obligandi* because reason simply grasps what they command as due in itself, while other laws (i.e., positive laws) derive this power from their institution.[14] Yet even these positive laws only bind insofar as obedience is due to the lawgiver who institutes the law, and insofar as it is therefore just to obey the lawgiver.[15] That is, *debitum* is a cause before it is an effect of positive law.

I suggest, and will presently defend, that the *debitum* of the law, which causes it to be law, and in turn causes it to have the *vim obligandi*, is properly understood as something *owed to someone else*, a *debitum ad alium*. This is precisely the reason, Aquinas says, that the laws that are most evident to us, those most easily grasped, are those that regard another's good. Of the Decalogue he writes:

> The precepts of the decalogue are the first principles of the Law: and the natural reason assents to them at once, as to principles that are most evident. Now it is altogether evident that the notion of duty [*debitum*], which is essential to a precept, appears in justice, which is of one towards another. Because in those matters that relate to himself it would seem at a glance that man is master of himself, and that he may do as he likes: whereas in matters that refer to another it appears manifestly that a man

is under obligation to render to another that which is his due [*quod debet*]. Hence the precepts of the decalogue must needs pertain to justice.[16]

To tease this out, the Decalogue contains what is most manifest, i.e., the first principles of the law to which man assents at once. Because the notion of due [*debitum*] is required by the very notion of law, that which most manifestly has the *ratio* of law is that which most manifestly has the *ratio* of due. That which most manifestly has the *ratio* of due is, in turn, that which pertains to another, since it seems that man can do as he pleases regarding himself, but it is most manifest that man has a *debitum ad alium*. Therefore the Decalogue contains precepts of justice (since justice regards what is due to another).

This point—that the first principles of the law must pertain to justice because justice most manifestly regards what is due—is not isolated, it is found *explicitly* in *numerous* other passages in Aquinas.[17]

In short, the law must have the *ratio* of due, and it is due in the same sense in which we say that something is due to someone else, i.e., some sort of debt. This is simply to say that, for Aquinas, *debitum* encompasses both the notions of 'moral duty' and 'debt to another.' Consequently, law, by its nature, regards our duties to others and their corresponding rights.

It may appear that Aquinas is incorporating an accident of Latin into his account of obligation: *Debitum* can mean either something owed (i.e., a debt) or something that must be done (a duty). It is worth remembering that *debitum*—though most frequently used to mean due or debt—is just the passive participle of *debeo*, which can be used with moral signification to mean 'must.' Aquinas in his treatment of law and justice is taking *debitum* and cognate terms with both senses at once. He is essentially treating these two meanings of *debitum* not as two discrete meanings—which would render these passages equivocal—but as two interrelated, and mutually implicative concepts.

This identity of *debitum ad alium* with moral obligation or moral duty, as perceived by reason,[18] is the principal contention of the paper, so let us pause a moment to consider the plausibility of this point.

Consider, first, the distinction between "imprudent" and "immoral" in ordinary speech. Humans discussing free acts seem naturally to distinguish between that which is wrong (in the ethically normative sense) and that which is merely short-sighted or stupid (harming no one but the agent himself). Consider the act of dressing and behaving at a job interview in a manner that shows a want of education and breeding; most people would hesitate to say one has a moral obligation to present oneself in a way that would get oneself the job or to say that one is committing some moral wrong in presenting oneself in a slovenly, boorish, or vulgar manner. But most people would readily label such behavior imprudent, short-sighted, or stupid. Their analysis might change if they discovered that the candidate is the breadwinner for a family who must get the job to make rent, or if they consider that such action demonstrates disrespect to the hiring committee, or that such conduct would be wasting the organization's resources and depriving other candidates of an opportunity;

but note that in these cases a duty to others is introduced. Even if someone insists that a job-candidate does in fact have an obligation to present himself as well as possible—aside from anything's being owed to his family or interviewers or other candidates—it must be admitted that most people would hesitate to concur; hence the observation that people more easily grasp obligations when they regard another's rights—which is the point we are now considering—will stand.

The idea that moral obligation is most readily perceived as being toward another can be seen, again, in the distinction between the expressions 'owing something to someone else' and 'owing something to oneself.' If I say to someone, "you owe it to yourself to get your drinking under control," I am taken to be counseling him. If he acknowledged the truth of my advice and yet willfully ignored it, he would be judged foolish. On the other hand, if I said to the same man, "You owe it to your family to get your drinking under control," I would be understood to be making a very different sort of claim; a person who acknowledged the truth of this admonition but willfully disregarded it would be thought not foolish, but evil. What I voiced, and what he chose to ignore, was no mere counsel. It was a moral duty.

Consider, third, that in the moral tradition—both pagan and Judaeo-Christian—'just' and 'unjust' are used as synonyms for 'moral' and 'immoral,' and that this usage is both employed and positively defended by Aquinas.[19] Indeed, Charles Pigden asks as a rebuttal to Anscombe's contention that Aristotle had no word that captured the modern sense of 'morally wrong,' "Does not 'unjust' [for Aristotle] have much the same sense [as 'morally wrong'] when used as the opposite of the universal or legal 'just'?"[20] Indeed it seems so: Aristotle says of legal justice[21] that it is coextensive with all virtue, "not a part of virtue, but virtue entire," and moreover it is, as the name implies, essentially legal in character. To this general justice corresponds "unjust in the wide sense of 'contrary to the law'" or "unlawful."[22] (One will recall that this legal character is precisely what Anscombe thinks is distinctive of the Christian notion of 'morally right' and 'morally ought' which she advocates dropping in favor of Aristotelean moral language.)

Consider further that, for Aquinas as for Aristotle, justice is the moral virtue *par excellence*;[23] in a very real sense, it is the only strictly moral virtue, as it is the only virtue that directly governs moral acts as such; that is, it is the only cardinal moral virtue that informs the will directly. Hence—as we just saw—it encompasses all other virtues, and furthermore it encompasses the whole of the natural law insofar as the first precepts of the natural law (i.e., the Decalogue) are, according to Aquinas, all precepts of justice. Note also, that Aquinas elsewhere says that the golden rule[24] or the norm of charity[25] or the principle of not harming one's neighbor[26]—all precepts that pertain to the other—is each the sum of the natural law.

Finally, consider whether it is even conceivable to owe something to someone, without thereby having a duty to render it. Conversely, is it possible to have a duty or an obligation, without that duty being a duty to someone else? If a person owes something to himself alone, can he not dispense himself from that duty? Is it not a principle (explicitly defended by Aquinas[27] and sanctioned by near universal judgment) that *volenti non fit injuria*?

But if all obligation is nothing else than a *debitum ad alium*, then it would seem obligations regarding monastic virtues, those obligations that regard only our own good (e.g., temperance), are not only more difficult to grasp but impossible to grasp: Wouldn't the very notion of such obligations be oxymoronic? Certainly the virtue of temperance might be sometimes required in order for us to fulfill our obligations to others, for example, a father may owe it to his family not to drink to the point that it prevents him from keeping his job, but this would be a sort of accidental obligation to temperance. To whom, for example, does a man hopelessly stranded on a desert island have an obligation to conduct himself temperately?

The problem is made more acute when we consider that Aquinas holds that the natural law encompasses all virtue.[28] Even temperance, Aquinas holds, is the subject of law. Yet we just saw that Aquinas thinks the first principles of the natural law are necessarily precepts which regard our duty to another.

Succinctly, Aquinas explains elsewhere that, "Things referable to oneself are referable to another, especially in regard to the common good."[29] At greater length he explains,

> Justice . . . directs man in his relations with other men. Now this may happen in two ways: first as regards his relation with individuals, secondly as regards his relations with others in general, in so far as a man who serves a community, serves all those who are included in that community. Accordingly justice in its proper acceptation can be directed to another in both these senses. Now it is evident that all who are included in a community, stand in relation to that community as parts to a whole; while a part, as such, belongs to a whole, so that whatever is the good of a part can be directed to the good of the whole. It follows therefore that the good of any virtue, whether such virtue direct man in relation to himself, or in relation to certain other individual persons, is referable to the common good, to which justice directs: so that all acts of virtue can pertain to justice, in so far as it directs man to the common good. It is in this sense that justice is called a general virtue.[30]

All acts of virtue pertain to justice because man's own good is never just his own good, since man can be rightly viewed as belonging to another, namely, a community. From this perspective, harm to himself is harm not just to himself, but also the other that is the community. We see this idea—of man as belonging not just to himself—operative in Aquinas's discussion of whether it is possible to suffer injustice willingly. He explains that an individual can be considered in two ways: as an individual with duties *only* to other individuals, or as a part of some whole. And insofar as he is a part of some whole he is able to have duties to the whole with respect even to things that pertain to himself.[31] Aquinas explicitly uses the examples of suicide and fornication; by itself fornication doesn't seem to entail injustice, yet insofar as man is viewed not as an individual but as someone who belongs to God, it becomes clear that it is not the fornicator's body to do with as he pleases.

Again, in discussing merit and demerit, he says there is a twofold *retributio* owed when an individual helps or harms another, one from the individual helped or harmed and one from the society. He then continues,

> Whereas when a man does that which conduces to his own benefit or disadvantage, then again is retribution owed to him, in so far as this too affects the community, forasmuch as he is a part of society: although retribution is not due to him, in so far as it conduces to the good or harm of an individual, who is identical with the agent: unless, perchance, he owe retribution to himself, by a sort of resemblance, in so far as man is said to be just to himself.[32]

Thus, every action is meritorious or demeritorous according to retributive justice insofar as every action affects the good of the community. As he later puts it, "a man's good or evil actions, although not ordained to the good or evil of another individual, are nevertheless ordained to the good or evil of another, which is the community itself."[33]

There is no justice to oneself strictly speaking, but only "by a sort of resemblance," but one's own good is also the good of the community to whom one does owe something in justice. The distinction being noted in these passages is nothing else than the distinction between particular justice (which regulates relations between individuals) and general or legal justice (which regulates man as a member of a society, as belonging to another, and in relation to the common good of that community). It is this legal justice that subsumes all other virtues insofar as it directs them all to the last end, the common good.[34] And it is this legal justice that Pigden suggested expressed for Aristotle the sense of the modern 'morally right.'

While practical reason may concern itself with goodness generally, justice, law, and obligation are concerned with the good only to the extent it is due or owed to someone. This is why Aquinas says that every transgression, though materially a violation of particular virtues, is formally a violation of justice, since it belongs properly to legal justice to consider the binding character of a precept[35] insofar as legal justice regards "the good as due in respect of Divine or human law"[36] and so far as law, by definition, is directed to the common, not individual, good.[37] Further, since sin is nothing else than a violation of eternal law which directs to the common good of creation, every sin is, as such, a violation of legal justice.[38] Only when seen as belonging to another, i.e., as a part of the city or as a creature of God, does man's harming himself necessarily and always take on the aspect of injustice, i.e., of depriving another of his due.

We are then prepared to understand more deeply what Aquinas said earlier concerning the Decalogue's necessarily containing precepts of justice, viz., that we do not easily apprehend that we have obligations that regard our own good. The reason for this difficulty in apprehension of duty to ourselves is that before we can apprehend that we have obligations with regard to our own good, we must first recognize that our own good is not just our own—we must first realize, that in a very real and meaningful sense, we do not belong to ourselves but that we are in fact part of a whole and that we therefore belong to another; only then can we grasp that we owe it to someone else to act well in those things that seem only to affect ourselves. While we may easily perceive rights and duties of one individual to another, we must have a certain speculative understanding of our relation to the community and God before we can grasp that we have obligations not to harm ourselves.

Three Moments of Moral Awareness and I-II Q. 94, A. 2

With this notion of law and obligation in mind, we are faced with a difficulty in interpreting I-II, q. 94, a. 2. For in his explanation of how man discovers the first precepts of the natural law, there is no mention of the notions of *debitum* or justice or of any of the other related concepts that it has been argued are, for Aquinas, essential to the notion of obligation and law. Either the preceding observations are wrong, or q. 94, a. 2 is not actually a straightforward discussion of how man discovers moral obligation.

I believe this difficulty can be solved with a distinction implied in *ST* I-II, q. 100, a. 5, ad 1. There Thomas makes a perplexing set of claims.[39] He gives two apparently contradictory reasons why the Decalogue contains only precepts directing man with regard to God and neighbor, but none with regard to himself. The first reason is that the natural law retains its vigor concerning self-love even in fallen man, although the precepts of the natural law regarding love of God and neighbor were obscured on account of sin; consequently, man only needs instruction in love of God and neighbor.

The second reason he offers is that the Decalogue includes only those things that men can easily grasp. A precept, he holds, has the *ratio* of something owed (*debitum*); now while man easily grasps that he owes something to God and neighbor, it is not obvious that man owes something to himself. Indeed, it appears at first glance that man does not owe anything to himself but is free with regard to himself. Consequently, God left man's duty to himself to be explained to man by the wise. Hence Aquinas seems to say in one and the same reply that man's duty to himself is both too obvious and too obscure to require instruction.

This difficulty can be solved if we take the reply to say that what remains intact in fallen man is not his recognition of a *duty* to love himself, but the very *inclination* to love himself (which makes the explicit teaching of a *duty* unnecessary). Conversely, what is obscure to man in his present state is not his *inclination* to love himself, but his *duty* to love himself.

If such an interpretation should stand then we can discern in the passage three moments of moral awareness: First, an inclination to simple self-love (along it would seem, with a weakened inclination to love others, manifest in a tendency to friendliness[40]), second, an awareness of obligation towards others, and finally, a recognition that our obligation toward others includes also an obligation in those things that regard ourselves.

While I cannot claim to prove this interpretation conclusively, I think it has several notable virtues. First, it saves the short text from utter incoherence. Something must be said to reconcile a passage which, read literally, is a self-contradictory reply. I would suggest that this is among the simplest and most intuitive distinctions that can do the job.

Second, it fits elegantly—as we will presently discuss—with what has already been said about moral obligation, specifically the distinction between grasping an obligation regarding others' good and grasping an obligation with respect to one's own good. Simply put, the second and third moments here identified correspond perfectly to the distinction between particular and general justice.[41]

Third, it conforms also with various other passages in Aquinas. For example, that our inclination to love ourselves is prior to and differs from our inclination to love others can be seen in the fact that Aquinas holds that self-love is the "root and form" of love of another, as is clear from the very norm: "Do unto others as you would have them do unto you."[42] In other places Aquinas notes the causal priority of self-love to love of God and neighbor, noting that man needs no instruction in loving himself[43] and even says that it is psychologically impossible for man to cease loving himself entirely.[44] Likewise, that duty is seen more easily in those things that we owe others than in those things that regard ourselves is stated elsewhere.[45]

Fourth, and in one respect most importantly, it seems to accord with human experience. On the one hand, men do seem spontaneously to pursue that which they perceive as their own good. As Aquinas tells us, we naturally (and always) act for the sake of our ultimate good generically considered, i.e., happiness.[46] On the other hand, the most difficult precepts of the natural law to know, the parts that are most controversial or most often gotten wrong—at least presuming that Catholic ethics is right—all pertain principally to the individual's own good, for example: suicide, euthanasia, dueling, and non-reproductive, consensual, sexual acts.[47] And, as we mentioned earlier, people seem generally to distinguish the imprudent from the immoral, precisely according to whether the agent alone is harmed or whether someone else is harmed.

What we have, then, in q. 94 a. 2, appears to be a description of the first (strictly pre-moral) moment; that is, a description of how one begins to reason about achieving one's own good and a description of what constitutes one's own advantage or harm. If this is right, we would conclude that the gerundive of the first principle of practical reason (i.e., good is to be done and pursued; evil avoided) does not have the distinctive modal force of moral obligation but is nothing else than Anscombe's unemphatic ought. Indeed, if the 'good' is understood as 'what all things seek'—which Aquinas elsewhere explains means 'what calms desire'[48] or more generally 'what is desirable'[49]—then 'Good is to be pursued' says no more than 'If one seeks (or desires) something then one ought to pursue it.' This is little else than a generalized statement of the entailment of 'should' or 'ought' by 'wants' or 'needs.'[50]

This conclusion—that q. 94, a. 2 does not reach moral obligations but stops at describing the prior self-love—is only incongruous if we take q. 94, a. 2 to be a reasonably complete account of what moral obligation is or of how the natural law is derived, but, as recent authors have noted,[51] the text itself doesn't seem to warrant any such assumption, and other passages of Aquinas give us compelling reason to question the article's completeness as a description of moral reasoning.[52]

Thus, we can summarize the various sorts of precepts of which man is aware and the sorts of knowledge he must have to grasp them. Man is, first, naturally inclined to seek his own good. At the same time, he is naturally inclined also to love his neighbor, although this natural inclination to act as a friend to others is considerably weaker than his inclination to self-love and vanishes as the cost of friendliness appreciates. These are simple pre-moral inclinations, apprehended by reason but not yet constituting awareness of obligation, since they lack the notion of *debitum*. Second, man then readily grasps that he owes something to other individuals. This is the domain of particular justice, and with this he becomes aware of obligation. As far as I see, Aquinas does not discuss how man arrives at this apprehension, but he is clear that everyone does so easily. Obviously, this will require some knowledge of various facts, e.g., that there are other moral agents who are able to have rights, or that this or that activity would cause them harm. Finally, only once we have the speculative knowledge of ourselves as members of a community, and hence as belonging to another, do we reach an awareness of general or legal justice and thereby apprehend that we have obligations even in those matters that pertain principally to our own good. There are degrees of awareness here too: A human community can only make qualified claims on its members, whereas God has a claim on persons in all that they are and all that they have,[53] so those who do not believe in God, though they understand themselves as members of a human community, will not have access to some norms of general justice. Further, Aquinas notes[54] that it is especially easy for the believer—as opposed, e.g., to one with a deist understanding of a first cause—to understand that he owes something to God. This makes a good deal of sense in light, for example, of I Cor 6:18–20: "Fly fornication . . . Or do you not know . . . you are not your own? For you were bought at a great price."

There is at least one more important class of moral norms that require specific speculative knowledge to reach, namely those derived from nature itself, considered aside from reason. The "unnatural vices," Aquinas explains, are morally wrong insofar as violating the order of nature entails injury (i.e., injustice) to God, Who is the Author of nature.[55] These will clearly require both an understanding of the teleology of natural powers as well as an understanding of God as Author of nature. Since they presuppose a prior obligation to God, these do not, as some suggest,[56] appear paradigmatic of obligation generally.

A Reply to Anscombe

In fine, I believe that we find in Aquinas not just an account of what moral obligation is, but indeed a remarkably subtle account, an account that corresponds brilliantly to our actual experience of obligation, an account, moreover, that will be able to hold its own in the contemporary discussion of the nature of obligation and that can meet a number of contemporary objections.

And how might such a system provide an answer to Anscombe? Aquinas will readily concur with Anscombe that injustice is at least sometimes clear: Aquinas insists, much like Anscombe, that men do in fact easily perceive that theft and murder are wrong.[57] Yet the difference between Aquinas and Anscombe is seen clearly when she asserts, "If the divine law obliges us not to commit injustice by forbidding injustice, it really does add something to the description 'unjust' to say there is an obligation not to do it."[58] If the preceding interpretation of Aquinas is right, then he could never assent to this assertion for two reasons. First, for Aquinas, divine positive law is only seen to impose obligation (i.e., it is only seen *as law*) in light of a previously and independently recognized duty to God (a duty which belongs to natural, not positive, law). Second, for Aquinas, 'unjust' and 'obliged not' are mutually implicative concepts, and so there can in principle be no substantive "superiority of the term 'unjust' over the terms 'morally right' and 'morally wrong.'"[59] To recognize a thing as unjust is to have already recognized that something is due or owed; to apprehend that something is due or owed is to be obligated—bound by reason—to render it.

The system I ascribe to Aquinas may appear to assume its own conclusion. Simply stating that man grasps at the beginning of the moral life that he has moral duties to others seems to posit what needs to be proven. Is not showing that man ought not to harm other men the principal goal of ethics? Wouldn't Anscombe need to do serious philosophical work to show *why* injustice ought not to be done?

Said simply, no, at least not if humanity is as Aquinas sees it. Aquinas is clear that there are "first general principles" which "need no further promulgation after being once imprinted on the natural reason to which they are self-evident; as, for instance, that one should do evil to no man."[60] That one oughtn't do injustice is analytically true. Any system that suggests that we need to prove such an obligation before men can know it cannot claim to be Thomistic: "We do not err," he writes, "about first principles in practical matters, such as 'none is to be harmed,' 'nothing is to be done unjustly,' and the like, just as we do not err in first principles concerning speculative matters."[61]

Anscombe's real concern, however, seems to be not so much with obligation in itself but with providing a self-interested motive for virtuous behavior, that is, with showing that it is advantageous for agents to be concerned with being just, with making men *want* to be just.[62] "Can't it reasonably be asked," she wonders, "whether one might ever need to commit injustice . . . ? Of course it can. And the answers will be various."[63] This is why we need an account "above all of human 'flourishing.'"[64]

First, it seems to me that asking whether I owe it to someone to do or not do something is quite different from asking whether it will be to my advantage to do or not do something. In principle, it seems one must be able to recognize an obligation without necessarily seeing that fulfilling it will be to one's advantage: Justice is concerned with the other's due, not with the agent's advantage.

Second, Aquinas does explain how fulfilling obligation, or doing what is just, is—as it turns out—good even for the agent, and the explanation does not require recourse to divine law or to a philosophical account of human flourishing. In I-II q. 94, a. 3 he notes, "there is in every man a natural inclination to act according to reason: and this is to act according to virtue . . . each one's reason naturally dictates to him to act virtuously." Bear in mind that in the prior article Aquinas states that, "all those things to which man has a natural inclination, are naturally apprehended by reason as being good, and consequently as objects of pursuit." If reason establishes that something is unjust, then to do it is to deny another what is due, and this is to act contrary to reason, which in turn is to act against a natural inclination and is therefore naturally perceived as the agent's evil.

But why should one care about being reasonable? Because one cannot help but care. The very fact that one asks the question proves that he *does* care, for he is asking for nothing else than *a reason to act* in some way, and this alone shows that he recognizes the authority of reason in determining how to act. The privileged position of reason in the rational animal is inescapable; as Aquinas elsewhere explains, "this end [viz. "of each moral virtue" which "consists precisely in conformity with right reason"] is appointed to man according to natural reason, since natural reason dictates to each one that he should act according to reason."[65] This is not a case of circular logic—establishing the authority of reason by appeal to the authority of reason—; it is rather noting that reason itself just is the proximate norm of morality.[66] It is precisely this inescapable inclination to act in accord with reason that accounts for the eagerness of those who violate their consciences to rationalize their behavior.[67]

Indeed Anscombe uses exactly such reasoning in what is perhaps the most famous line from "Modern Moral Philosophy": "if someone thinks, *in advance*, that it is open to question whether such an action as procuring the judicial execution of the innocent should be quite excluded from consideration—I do not want argue with him; he shows a corrupt mind."[68] Here she moves immediately from the common apprehension of 'unjust' to a law-like, absolute, categorical verdict of what *should or should not* be done. As a justification for this move, she offers only that anyone who fails so to reason demonstrates a fundamental and irremediable defect in moral reasoning.

Although we may still—as she notes—have plenty of philosophical work to do in explaining human flourishing, *if* Aquinas is right in his description of the natural law, or what is the same, *if* Aquinas is right in his factual claims about what moral truths men do and do not universally apprehend, then in principle we must not need such an account to apprehend at least some obligations with their full moral force, in the modern sense of 'moral.' Neither do we need a concept of a divine law or even of a god. For Aquinas, obligation is not a *terminus ad quem* but a *terminus a quo*, not a conclusion to be proven to the English moral philosophers since Sidgwick, but a brute fact of universal human experience.

University of St. Thomas
Houston, Texas

Notes

1. G. E. M. Anscombe, "Modern Moral Philosophy," *Philosophy* 33 (1958): 1–19, at 15.

2. Anscombe, "Modern Moral Philosophy," 5.

3. Anscombe, "Modern Moral Philosophy," 6.

4. Anscombe, "Modern Moral Philosophy," 1.

5. Anscombe, "Modern Moral Philosophy," 4.

6. Anscombe, "Modern Moral Philosophy," 9.

7. Anscombe, "Modern Moral Philosophy," 4.

8. Anscombe, "Modern Moral Philosophy," 16.

9. Thomas Aquinas, *Summa theologiae* [*ST*], *prima secundae partis*, q. 90, a. 4, co., "Unde ad hoc quod lex virtutem obligandi obtineat, quod est proprium legis, oportet quod applicetur hominibus qui secundum eam regulari debent."

10. *ST* I-II, q. 100, a. 5, ad 1: "Praeceptum autem habet rationem debiti."

11. *ST* II-II, q. 44, a. 1, co. English translation that of the Fathers of the English Dominican Province, 2nd ed. 1920, throughout.

12. *ST* I-II, q. 99, a. 1, co., "praeceptum legis, cum sit obligatorium, est de aliquo quod fieri debet."

13. *ST* II-II, q. 122, a. 1, *ST* II-II, q. 56, a. 1, ad 1.

14. *ST* I-II, q. 104, a. 1, co.

15. *ST* I-II, q. 100, a. 2, ad 1.

16. *ST* II-II, q. 122, a. 1, co.

17. *ST* I-II, q. 99, a. 5, ad 1; *ST* I-II, q. 100, a. 5, ad 1; *ST* II-II, q. 56, a. 1, ad 1 and a. 2, co.; *ST* II-II, q. 140, a. 1, ad 3.

18. Which is to say, the question the present section is concerned with is how people in fact perceive obligation. The section is not asking whether there ever is an obligation to oneself. The two questions are intimately related but not identical.

19. E.g., *ST* I-II, q. 100, a. 12. Aquinas quotes Cicero's explanation of this usage favorably, *ST* II-II, q. 123, a. 12, sc. 1.

20. Charles Pigden, "Anscombe on 'Ought,'" *Philosophical Quarterly* 38.1 (1988): 20–41, at 33.

21. *Nichomachean Ethics*, 1130a.

22. *Nichomachean Ethics*, 1130a–b.

23. *ST* II-II, q. 58, a. 12.

24. *ST* I-II, q. 99, a. 1, ad 2 and ad 3.

25. *ST* I-II, q. 100, a. 11, co. and ad 1.

26. *ST* I-II, q. 100, a. 3, co.

27. *ST* II-II, q. 59, a. 3, co., "Dicendum est ergo quod iniustum, per se et formaliter loquendo, nullus potest facere nisi volens, nec pati nisi nolens." and ad 2; cf. *ST* I-II, q. 21, aa. 3–4.

28. *ST* I-II, q. 94, a. 3.

29. *ST* II-II, q. 58, a. 5, ad 3.

30. *ST* II-II, q. 58, a. 5.

31. *ST* II-II, q. 59, a. 3, ad 2.: "Ad secundum dicendum quod aliqua persona singularis dupliciter potest considerari. Uno modo, secundum se. Et sic, si sibi aliquod nocumentum inferat, potest quidem habere rationem alterius peccati, puta intemperantiae vel imprudentiae, non tamen rationem iniustitiae, quia sicut iustitia semper est ad alterum, ita et iniustitia. Alio modo potest considerari aliquis homo inquantum est aliquid civitatis, scilicet pars; vel inquantum est aliquid Dei, scilicet creatura et imago. Et sic qui occidit seipsum iniuriam quidem facit non sibi, sed civitati et Deo. Et ideo punitur tam secundum legem divinam quam secundum legem humanam, sicut et de fornicatore apostolus dicit, *si quis templum Dei violaverit, disperdet ipsum Deus.*" Cf. *ST* I-II, q. 21, aa. 3–4.

32. *ST* I-II, q. 21, a. 3, co, "Cum vero aliquis agit quod in bonum proprium vel malum vergit, etiam debetur ei retributio, inquantum etiam hoc vergit in commune secundum quod ipse est pars collegii, licet non debeatur ei retributio inquantum est bonum vel malum singularis personae, quae est eadem agenti, nisi forte a seipso secundum quandam similitudinem, prout est iustitia hominis ad seipsum."

33. *ST* I-II, q. 21, a. 3, ad 1.

34. *ST* II-II, q. 58, a. 6, ad 4.

35. *ST* II-II, q. 79, a. 2.

36. *ST* II-II, q. 79, a. 1.

37. *ST* I-II, q. 90, a. 2.

38. *ST* I-II, q. 71, a. 6, ad 4.

39. *ST* I-II, q. 100, a. 5, ad 1: "Ad primum ergo potest responderi dupliciter. Primo quidem, quia praecepta Decalogi referuntur ad praecepta dilectionis. Fuit autem dandum praeceptum homini de dilectione Dei et proximi, quia quantum ad hoc lex naturalis obscurata erat propter peccatum, non autem quantum ad dilectionem sui ipsius, quia quantum ad hoc lex naturalis vigebat. Vel quia etiam dilectio sui ipsius includitur in dilectione Dei et proximi, in hoc enim homo vere se diligit, quod se ordinat in Deum. Et ideo etiam in praeceptis Decalogi ponuntur solum praecepta pertinentia ad proximum et ad Deum. Aliter potest dici quod praecepta Decalogi sunt illa quae immediate populus recepit a Deo, unde dicitur Deut. X, *scripsit in tabulis, iuxta id quod prius scripserat, verba decem, quae locutus est ad vos dominus.* Unde oportet praecepta Decalogi talia esse quae statim in mente populi cadere possunt. Praeceptum autem habet rationem debiti. Quod autem homo ex necessitate debeat aliquid Deo vel proximo, hoc de facili cadit in conceptione hominis, et praecipue fidelis. Sed quod aliquid ex necessitate sit debitum homini de his quae pertinent ad seipsum et non ad alium, hoc non ita in promptu apparet, videtur enim primo aspectu quod quilibet sit liber in his quae ad ipsum pertinent. Et ideo praecepta quibus prohibentur inordinationes hominis ad seipsum, perveniunt ad populum mediante instructione sapientum. Unde non pertinent ad Decalogum."

40. This is a fourth permutation (the *inclination*, rather than duty, to *another's*, rather than one's own, good), and—as a basic inclination—it seems to be yet present in man from the start (in the first moment) alongside his natural inclination to self-love, cf., *ST* II-II, q. 114, a. 1, ad 2 and *Sententia libri ethicorum VIII*, lec. 1, n. 5 "laudamus *philanthropos*, idest amatores hominum, quasi implentes id quod est homini naturale, ut manifeste apparet in erroribus viarum." It seems to me this tendency is principally at the level of an emotional urge to cooperate and be helpful—why does everyone give the time of day or directions to a complete stranger who asks?—though, as Aquinas here says, this natural inclination toward

friendliness is weakened in fallen man. Our spontaneous willingness to help others is clearest when the cost to ourselves is trivial. As soon as the cost of cooperation becomes appreciable, we begin to show selfish tendencies. Is this weakened natural inclination to love others the same as the inclination mentioned in q. 94, a. 2 to have good relations with those among whom one must live? I am inclined to think that this latter inclination refers by synecdoche to the whole of the active life and thus to the whole of moral virtue (a thesis I defend in an as yet unpublished paper), whereas the first is an inclination specifically to the good of *philia*.

41. *ST* II-II, q. 79, a. 1, co.: "ad iustitiam specialem pertinet facere bonum sub ratione debiti in comparatione ad proximum, et vitare malum oppositum, scilicet quod est nocivum proximo. Ad iustitiam vero generalem pertinet facere bonum debitum in ordine ad communitatem vel ad Deum, et vitare malum oppositum."

42. *ST* II-II, q. 25, a. 4. Cf. *ST* I-II, q. 99, a. 1, ad 2, where he reduces the twofold love of God and neighbor to love of neighbor.

43. *ST* II-II, q. 44, a. 3, ad 1.

44. *ST* II-II, q. 126, a. 1, co.

45. *ST* II-II, q. 122, a. 1: "Manifestissime autem ratio debiti, quae requiritur ad praeceptum, apparet in iustitia, quae est ad alterum, quia in his quae spectant ad seipsum, videtur primo aspectui quod homo sit sui dominus, et quod liceat ei facere quodlibet; sed in his quae sunt ad alterum, manifeste apparet quod homo est alteri obligatus ad reddendum ei quod debet."

46. *ST* I-II, q. 1, a. 6.

47. The obvious apparent exception to this today would be abortion, but it seems to me that for many—though admittedly not all—advocates of abortion, the key question is whether the foetus is a human with rights at all, i.e., it is a question of fact more often than a question of principle. Even those who do not dispute that the foetus is human—e.g., Judith Jarvis Thompson, in "A Defense of Abortion," *Philosophy and Public Affairs* 1 (1971): 47–66—support it not because they deny the foetus has a right, but because they deny that its right can trump certain rights of the mother.

48. *ST* I-II, q. 27, a. 1, ad 3.

49. *ST* I, q. 5, a. 1.

50. Cf. Alastair MacIntyre, "Hume on 'Is' and 'Ought,'" *Philosophical Review* 68 (1959): 451–468 at 462–463 and Max Black, "The Gap Between 'Is' and 'Should,'" *Philosophical Review* 73 (1964): 165–181.

51. For a brief discussion cf. Jean Porter, "Does the Natural Law Provide a Universally Valid Morality?" in *Intractable Disputes about the Natural Law*, ed. Lawrence Cunningham (Notre Dame: Notre Dame University Press, 2009), 53–95, at 61–62.

52. The strongest objection to this argument seems to me to be that Aquinas explicitly calls the first principle of practical reason a *praeceptum legis*. If duty to another is essential to the *ratio* of both duty and law, and if *ST* I-II, q. 94, a. 2 does not reach the point of considering the other, then how can Aquinas call this a precept of law? There are two possible replies to this. First Aquinas conceives of a metaphorical justice that obtains between the various powers of man, as he explains in *ST* II-II q. 58, a. 4, such that a command of reason is in some sense a precept. Second, Aquinas conceives of natural inclinations themselves (even in irrational creatures) as having the nature of law (i.e., physical law) when viewed in

light of the creating God's providential plan and wise design (eternal law), as explained in, e.g., *ST* I-II, q. 93, aa. 5–6 and q. 91, a. 2. Hence, these pre-moral, natural apprehensions can have the nature of law (at least in an analogous or metaphorical sense) while not being consciously grasped by the subject as either law or duty. Based on the purpose of the tract on law in which q. 94, a. 2 is situated, I think the latter of these options the more plausible.

53. *ST* I-II, q. 21, a. 4, ad 3. Although contrast with I-II, q. 96, a. 4, co.

54. *ST* I-II, q. 100, a. 5 ad 1.

55. *ST* II-II, q. 154 a. 12 ad 1 and ad 2.

56. E.g., Steven J. Jensen, *Knowing the Natural Law: From Precepts and Inclinations to Deriving Oughts* (Washington, DC: The Catholic University of America Press, 2015), 85–107.

57. *ST* I-II, q. 100, a. 1, co., "Quaedam enim sunt quae statim per se ratio naturalis cuiuslibet hominis diiudicat esse facienda vel non facienda, sicut . . . *non occides, non furtum facies*."

58. Anscombe, "Modern Moral Philosophy," 18.

59. Anscombe, "Modern Moral Philosophy," 16.

60. *ST* I-II, q. 100, a. 3, co., cf. *ST* I-II, q. 100, a. 5 ad 4.

61. *Sentencia De anima*, III, lect. 15, n. 9, "Non enim erramus circa prima principia in operabilibus, cuiusmodi sunt, nulli nocendum esse, non esse aliquid iniuste agendum, et similia; sicut nec erramus circa prima principia in speculativis." Translation mine.

62. Anscombe, "Modern Moral Philosophy," 4, "Naturally the consideration [that an act is unjust] will not have any effect on my actions unless I want to commit or avoid acts of injustice."

63. Anscombe, "Modern Moral Philosophy," 18.

64. Anscombe, "Modern Moral Philosophy," 18.

65. *ST* II-II, q. 47, a. 7, co.

66. *ST* I-II, q. 71, a. 6, co., "Regula autem voluntatis humanae est duplex, una propinqua et homogenea, scilicet ipsa humana ratio; alia vero est prima regula, scilicet lex aeterna, quae est quasi ratio Dei," and *ST* I-II, q. 21, a. 1, co.; for the relation between these two rules cf. *ST* I-II, q. 73, a. 7, ad 3, "aversionem a regula rationis, sequitur aversio a Deo, cui debet homo per rectam rationem coniungi," and *ST* I-II, q. 71, a. 6, ad 5.

67. Joseph Rickaby gives a memorable description of the logic: "'You *ought* not break your word, . . . *if* you don't want to do violence to that nature which is yours as a reasonable being.' . . . Here it seems the chain [of hypothetical oughts] is made fast to a staple in the wall. If a person goes on to ask, 'Well, what if I do contradict my rational self?'—we can only tell him that he is a fool for his question" (*Moral Philosophy: Or Ethics and Natural Law*, 4th edition [London: Longmans, Green, and Co., 1905], 115–116). Compare this with Immanuel Kant: "In any transgression of duty . . . What we really intend is . . . that [our maxim's] opposite should remain a law generally; we only take the liberty of making an *exception* to it, for ourselves . . . Consequently if we weighed it all up from one and the same perspective—that of reason—we should find a contradiction in our own will, the contradiction that a certain principle should be objectively necessary as a universal law and yet subjectively should not hold universally but should admit of exceptions" (*Groundwork of the Metaphysics of Morals*, trans. Arnulf Zweig, ed. A. Zweig and Thomas E. Hill Jr. [Oxford: Oxford University Press,

2002], 225, chap. 2, no. 29). The similarity between Rickaby's staple in the wall and Kant's categorical imperative was not lost on Rickaby; on the following page he identifies the two: "the *ought* wherein [our illustration] terminated, [Kant] calls the *categorical imperative*, an alternative being such as no rational man can accept, and therefore no alternative at all. . . . This doctrine of the Categorical Imperative is correct and valuable so far as it goes," Rickaby, *Moral Philosophy*, 116.

68. Anscombe, "Modern Moral Philosophy," 17.

Goods and Groups:
Thomistic Social Action and Metaphysics

James Dominic Rooney, OP

Abstract: Hans Bernhard Schmid has argued that contemporary theories of collective action and social metaphysics unnecessarily reject the concept of a "shared intentional state." I will argue that three neo-Thomist philosophers, Jacques Maritain, Charles de Koninck, and Yves Simon, all seem to agree that the goals of certain kinds of collective agency cannot be analyzed merely in terms of intentional states of individuals. This was prompted by a controversy over the nature of the "common good," in response to a perceived threat from "personalist" theories of political life. Common goods, as these three authors analyze them, ground our collective action in pursuit of certain kinds of goals which are immanent to social activity itself. Their analysis can support an alternate position to "intentional individualism," providing an account of collective practical reasoning and social metaphysics based on shared intentional states, but without involving implausible "group minds."

Hans Bernhard Schmid and Annette Baier contend that most contemporary analyses of collective intentionality hold a version of "intentional individualism."[1] Schmid has defined intentional individualism as the position that "Any interpretation of an individual's behavior has to be given in terms of *individual* [intentional] states."[2] Both Baier and Schmid have argued that there are good reasons for thinking that collective action and our metaphysics of groups can only really be grounded in shared, rather than individual, intentional states. Some twentieth-century Thomists have, I will argue, offered an analysis of what these "shared intentions" in group agency would look like.[3] This was prompted by a controversy over the nature of the "common good," in response to a perceived threat from more individualist (as opposed to communitarian) theories of political life. Three prominent neo-Thomist philosophers, Jacques Maritain, Charles de Koninck, and Yves Simon, all seem to agree that the goals of certain kinds of collective agency cannot be analyzed merely in terms of intentional states of individuals. Common goods, if truly "common" to all members of a group, are intended communally and not individually. This analysis seems to support the

© 2017, *Proceedings of the ACPA*, Vol. 90
doi: 10.5840/acpaproc201822879

plausibility of an alternate position to "intentional individualism" in collective agency and social metaphysics.

The debate between the Thomist philosophers in question concerned, at least initially, the goal(s) of political society. All three—Maritain, de Koninck, and Simon—held that society, or political life generally speaking, exists to achieve some goal. The debate concerned specifically how we ought to construe that collective goal. Does political life exist to achieve the average maximal well-being of all individuals who compose society—something akin to maximizing "utility" in the group? This kind of position might be termed a "utilitarian" view of society, but was unacceptable to any of the Thomists in this debate, given their philosophical commitments.[4] Granting that societal well-being was not a matter of maximizing some standard of utility, a more difficult question for their classical Thomist position concerned how we should understand the role of individual persons in political life, given that European liberal politics was then emphasizing individual autonomy and freedom in the horrific aftermath of totalitarian government. Fundamentally, the Thomists were aligned with the classical intuition that society exists to "make men good" and promote virtue, but this position is perhaps intuitively more aligned to monarchical theories of government rather than democratic political life. This posed a problem in adapting the classical intuition to the modern situation.

Charles de Koninck started the discussion, initially attacking a position that society exists to achieve the good of every individual person in some "maximal" sense. This position was termed "personalism," because it was influenced by a trend in philosophy to see individual "persons" as the primary ends of society. While all three seemingly agreed in rejecting the personalist position as presented by de Koninck, each offered distinct but complimentary accounts of communal life and action. While they often presented their views as commentaries on texts from Thomas Aquinas, I will instead highlight what I see as each of their distinct perspectives on the matter.

Charles de Koninck focused on the social aspects of human nature to argue that each human person can never be considered as a goal "in itself" apart from the way in which each person at least potentially functions in society. Personalism seems plausible because society cannot have, conceivably, the goal of anything other than achieving something for the individuals which compose it; it would be strange if our political life existed to benefit, for example, the paper on which our laws were written. But this does not necessitate that society only achieves *individual* goals. That perspective ignores that there really are both common goals of groups of individuals and the more basic fact that human beings are social animals.

If we think there are objective facts about what it means for human beings to live well (as de Koninck did and the Thomist tradition as a whole affirmed), and humans are social by nature, then there are some unique kinds of social goods. It seems obvious that human beings are, by nature, social animals; speech, group planning, and rational communications are natural human activities.[5] Aquinas himself held that social life is connatural to human beings, so that, even in a world without sin, there would be leadership and government.[6] But, then, living well *together* is distinct from questions about individual well-being. Both Jacques Maritain and Yves

Simon, consequently, had to clarify the nature of collective intention and action in order to adequately avoid the charge of being a "personalist." Each had to base their analysis on some uniquely social goods in light of which individuals flourish socially rather than merely individually.

Charles de Koninck makes much of the fact that Aquinas follows Aristotle in (counter-intuitively) affirming that human society is naturally prior to individual human beings as a whole is prior to a part.[7] While individual people might exist before human society in time, every human being comes into existence as an inherently social animal, so that human society is essential to being human. Society is "naturally" prior to individuals in the same way that human nature is logically prior to any individual human instance. Social well-being is, consequently, not contrary to the well-being of individual members. The common good of a group, as in the case of society as a whole, would require that there is some way in which the well-being of each member of the group is included under a higher perspective; achieving individual well-being happens in light of how this well-being is achieved by the group. The good of family life, for instance, is the well-being of each person in the family, but includes those people within a higher common goal of living together well.[8] By contrast, if the well-being of the group somehow existed without reference to the well-being of the members, it would only accidentally achieve the well-being of any member, as it was essentially the well-being of no concrete member.

But, if de Koninck is right about the existence of distinct "collective" kinds of well-being which follow from the social nature of human beings, the implication is that social well-being can only be caused or exist in a uniquely social or collective way. Jacques Maritain noted this contrast between what we might call "public goods" and "common goods."[9] The former are goods that need distribution but are not themselves shared by all members of a group, but the latter are goods that can be enjoyed simultaneously by each member. There are public goods, for example, in bee hives (e.g., honey being parceled out to each member) so that each bee both contributes to the common task and receives some benefit from the collective activity of the hive. But a "common" good would be a uniquely social good in a different way. While we need not get deeply involved in the psychological situation of bees, it would seem that the bees use social coordination to achieve their end, but would not be affected if they could achieve the end without social interaction (e.g., with miniature mechanized help). Their coordination of tasks is not an end in itself, but a means to the production and rationing of honey. Further, the end is unsharable in a public goods scenario. The same individual ration of honey cannot be eaten by two bees simultaneously.

By contrast, Maritain thinks "common" goods are those that are uniquely social or communicative, even when they might involve an external task. Without such goods, it would be hard to say what constituted social well-being in a way that was uniquely social. Population health, for example, might require coordination among members and might only be maintained when everyone cooperates in achieving it, but it is fundamentally only the health of each member. Public health is thus a public good, but not "common" or shared; there is not a separate "health of society" over and above health of each member. However, common goods are distinctly "social goods" and only *exist* as "shared," such as relationships between persons, truth, or friendship. In human society writ large, some uniquely social goods are the rule of law, a civic conscience, traditions, justice, heroism, and culture. Maritain's language is that common goods are thus "immanent" rather than transitive products of social interaction—the process of their production has some non-instrumental value.[10] While there may be some concrete task at issue (e.g., we paint the fence together or we fight for justice for John), in cases of social goods, there is always some *immanent* product integral to the activity being truly collective or social. Maritain thinks this implies that common goods can only be achieved by rational agents who can communicate and engage in higher-level social relationships, but we might bracket whether some higher animals can engage in similar activities; it might be plausible that some higher animals can achieve truly non-instrumental social goods.

A corollary of Maritain's view is that one cannot be "mistaken" about achieving some kinds of common goods in collective action. Some common goods are either identical with or something closely connected to a relational or social activity (e.g., either be the activity itself or a disposition intimate to the activity, such as "being in a relationship with . . ."). While illusions remain possible (of a sort), it would be unusual for someone to think he is enjoying family life or another type of common good and not actually be doing so. A radical mistake in these cases is not *really* possible. A person might have the odd false belief that she is living as a member of a family, for example, but she would not really be "living family life" if she were not actually a member of the social circle in question.[11] Relational activity is built into the notion of these common goods; they "depend on the existence of more than one person to share them."[12] "Justice," for example, would be inconceivable except as founded on relations between persons.[13] For these reasons, common goods of social life have "externalist" conditions because they are social activities and only exist with a minimum of at least two people.

The third element to complete the picture comes in Yves Simon's *Philosophy of Democratic Government*. de Koninck provided the thought that human beings are social in essence, implying that there are distinct aspects of social well-being which are "common goods"; Maritain argued that common goods are either social activities or "immanent" products of social activities; and Yves Simon contributes to this discussion by highlighting elements of the practical reasoning proper to groups. He distinguishes between "partnerships" and social groups ("societies" in Simon's terminology) on the basis of different intentional relationships to the goods intended by each member. Partnerships are contractual agreements to achieve some aim together, but entail no truly joint agency, given that there is no deep commonality or sociality. Each member is merely achieving their own individual good by reference to the intentions of the others (Searle's example of selfish businessmen who think their own individual pursuit of money will benefit society comes to mind[14]). Simon gives an example of a moneylender and handicrafts man, where the one loans money to the other for the purposes of business. They are engaged only in a contractual relationship seeking their individual private goals, even if coordinated.[15]

These groups would seem to be constituted by jointly intending public goods, at most, and not common goods.

A social group (a society) is constituted, for Simon, when each member jointly intends a distinct kind of goal: they seek to achieve some truly "common" good. This is apparent when three conditions are fulfilled: "some transitive actions are traceable not to any particular individual but to the team,"[16] "the transitive actions of a community are prepared and intrinsically conditioned by immanent actions of knowledge and desire in which members commune," and "communion-causing communications" aim to produce in the members a similar set of cognitions and emotions.[17] Some of his examples are a football team, a team of workers, and an army. There is a collective intention in any of these cases because they are essentially social activities. They require a shared intention among all members. The reason the team needs communication is because part of the goal of the activity is "team-building." The goal sought is at least partly the process itself. A game is another similar case: playing the game is as much a part of the goal as winning might be. Without this notion of a common good intended by each, one would destroy the critical feature of true sociality and commonality in shared intentions.[18]

As Simon sees it, common goods are "causal" for the formation of groups because they provide the basic aim and reason for which this set of people are co-ordinating their actions. This contrasts subtly with John Finnis, for example, who sees the common good as "the factor or set of factors which, as considerations in someone's practical reasoning, would make sense or give reason for his collaboration with others."[19] Instead, Simon thinks a group does not exist to the extent that they *lack* one and the same goal or intentional attitude toward it. Members do not merely coordinate inter-locking personal goals.[20]

There are parallels to this in contemporary theory of collective agency. Raimo Tuomela has analyzed "we-reasons" or "we-goals" as the kind of reasons sufficient to motivate group action. These differ from the kinds of reasons for first-personal private actions ("I-reasons/goals").[21] We can act in pursuit of our private goals "to-gether," but it is not a "we-goal" that we pursue, even if the individual goals are the same. "We-goals" of the right type seem to be central to a group's formation and persistence, giving the reason for collective action. Similarly, Philip Pettit has argued that a "discursive dilemma" (aggregating judgments in collective cases can result in contradictions) requires that there is a separate kind of rational unity among social groups; there is a different perspective on what it means to achieve unity, who de-cides, etc., so that individuals in group situations are "forced to collectivize reason."[22]

Simon seems to hold that this requires a shared intentional state, differing in this respect from many contemporary authors. Simon here follows Thomas Aquinas, who claims that a group can have "here and now" one and the same intentional goal (as armies have one goal).[23] Following this insight, Simon affirms that a group can have the same goal because there is communication which facilitates a collective intention. In both the army and the football team there is a constant interchange of signs and symbols to help everyone in the group be "on the same page" with their goals and purposes. Partnerships, as Simon notes, only need to share information relative to planning for the achievement of their individual goals (even if inter-dependent). It is a mark of weakness in a community (such as a poorly disciplined army) when its members do not clearly understand the common goal or desire it strongly; their possession of the group intention is qualitatively weaker and can even lead to the dissolution of the group when it passes a minimum threshold.[24]

Simon's goal was to affirm the "natural" character of authority in groups. Authority is not an imposition of outside force to maintain order, merely mitigating or coordinating personal goals of each member in a group, but instead is required to facilitate the very process of collective practical reasoning. Simon argued that common goods thus *necessitate* authority structures. His thought experiment is to suppose that we have a perfectly united group who share relevantly similar attitudes or volitional states toward their collective action (e.g, they all intend to act together for the good of the state). Additionally, they have perfect common knowledge of each others' beliefs and understand what is required for human society to flourish in general. But all of this will *not* lead to a unanimous decision to act. Simon contends that there is no possibility of a purely rationally convincing reason to act in one way rather than another; there is no absolutely "best" possible course of action rationally apparent to each member.[25] Because there is no individual rational means to decide how to act, there needs to be some agreed upon collective authority which "breaks the tie."

Every case of collective action properly so called requires an authority because there needs to be a shared intentional state—a shared conception and intention of the goal.[26] Even in cases of unanimity where no overt authority structure is present,[27] the implicit authority is the norms of the community—these are inherent in the context of the activity. We do not need an umpire for a game of "pick-up" baseball, because common knowledge of the activity's performance normativity acts as an authority structure to help guide collective intention. Acceptance of certain authoritative norms for decision making (that govern the collective action) follow from the common good intended; a conception of the group goal entails norms. Becoming part of an army involves a "public" conception (perhaps minimal) of how to act as a member. Rather than a problem for individual autonomy, these norms are required for agency in large groups; they facilitate (without subsuming) the participants' agency.[28]

This same problem appears in contemporary theories of collective agency. Caroline Arruda argues that current construals of the "common knowledge" conditions in theories of collective intentionality make the mistake of "over-rationalizing." Group members need to understand others as having justifying reasons for acting as they do. This is because the parties to a collective act cannot individually seem to settle the decision to act, so they need to perceive a common reason which incites collective action.[29] But this presents the same problem Simon highlighted: there is no rationally compelling option or reason that would command assent from all parties (independent of some norm, like Simon's authority).

Thus, as Arruda points out, some theories of collective agency might have difficulty explaining how we actually settle on intending to "take the next step" in joint activity. Michael Bratman, for instance, arguably runs into this problem. If our intentions are perfectly egalitarian in Bratman's preferred "modest sociality" cases, then we each intend to do *J* only if the other has the same intention, and by means of the others' intention. But I cannot unilaterally decide that we *will J*, and I cannot "jointly" decide it without you, and neither can you without me.[30] The question of asymmetric collective intention is not brought up by Bratman, but would be interesting in the context of this problem. Similarly, Margaret Gilbert has been critiqued that joint commitments seems to require some kind of communication of "joint readiness" to act and a tacit agreement to act prior to the action itself. But, naturally, "if individuals already have to be jointly committed in some way in order to enter into a joint commitment . . . either a vicious circle or an infinite regress seems to ensue."[31]

If Simon is correct, we have a picture of how collective agency happens. There are some external norms that are the basis for developing a collective intention from the individual goals or intentions of each member. The structure is not just instrumental, but constitutive of the common good intended by each.[32] Authoritative structures, norms, or standards of action are, at least in part, "constitutive" of the group goal and how the group achieves it because it would not be a *group* goal if we did not conceive of our project in the same way. Authoritative norms thus help facilitate a shared intention. Problems in coordinating 'public goods,' for instance, do not just require public knowledge of the intentions of others, but the knowledge of certain collective judgments and norms in order for us to facilitate collective action and decision-making.[33]

Collective action requires not just having the same intended task in mind, or a commitment to the other members, but also an expectation that other people sharing the same goal will pursue a similar course of action.[34] As Schmid notes: "just as the relation of individual agents to themselves cannot be limited to cognitive expectations, the relations *between* agents acting in pursuit of shared goals have to include a normative element, too. They have to expect each other to choose the suitable means *normatively.*"[35] Simon's intuition that authority and collective intention facilitates individual agency is reinforced by Schmid's argument that acting on the intentions or even attitudes of others is normal, not an exception. We *often* act on the attitudes of others (empathetic action, courtesy in opening doors, etc.), as opposed to our entire agency revolving around only our own attitudes.[36] There are thus some clear parallels between the Thomist position of Simon and contemporary positions like Schmid which reject intentional individualism.

Finally, though none of the three Thomists treat very extensively the question of the ontology of groups, Yves Simon gives hints to how we might construe it. As we saw, he seems to think a true social group is nothing other than a certain shared "common life of desire and action"—it is a shared activity, according to certain norms of behavior and a shared conception of what the activity entails. This is conceived as existing on the basis of the intentional state shared among the members—that is the whole reason Simon emphasized "communication" as the basis for the persistence of a social group. The group's existence seems to supervene upon the intentional state. Further, the shared intention itself is part of the very social character of the activity, just as the dispositions or relations involved constitute its sociality. While one can share a conception of the activity without engaging in it, one cannot seem to have the intention for collective agency without being part of it and vice-versa. My intention to be friends with someone is part of what it means to be their friend and engage in relationship with them. This seems to be the implication of Maritain's insistence on the "immanent" nature of social relationships. The intention itself is part of what it means to engage in the right kind of social activity that constitutes pursuit/enjoyment of a "common" good. Our jointly intending to be part of the book club is essential to pursuit and enjoyment of our love of reading together.

Contemporary social metaphysicians might fear that a shared intentional state would require a group mind, which, as many authors point out, seems metaphysically excessive or "spooky."[37] Maritain, de Koninck, and Simon are in agreement with many contemporary metaphysicians that individual persons are the only things that really exist as substances in a group; there is no group mind or will in anything more than a figurative sense in purely human societies. They did not seem to think that a shared intentional state required a "group mind," but do affirm that "common goods" can only exist as shared.[38] There is, however, an analogy from Thomas Aquinas's writings on our relationship with God that seems to constitute a distinct kind of ontological state, shared among individuals. In discussing how God dwells in the hearts and minds of believers (the "divine indwelling"), Thomas notes that this is possible because there are unique ways that human beings can have God present to them. Beyond "spatial" presence, which would be impossible, human beings can know and love God, and thus have God present as the object of their knowing and loving.[39] Love, in particular, implies a unique relationship because the person loved is somehow in the lover. This is because love involves something akin to intentional states. The union between lover and beloved is not a product or result aside from the activity of loving the other person; instead "love itself is [the] union or bond."[40]

Friendship, of which the virtue of love of God (*caritas*) is an instance,[41] is founded on a commonality intrinsic to both parties in the relations between them; "if there were no communication, it would not be possible to be friends."[42] Further, there is only one intentional state among all believers who truly love God, which unites them as the Church.[43] The shared intentional state required to pursue or enjoy any common good is a species of friendship and so follows the same pattern. Thus, these groups have the very unity of their activity as part of what they intend in acting together. The life of the community itself is constituted by our collective intentionality, and it forms the goal of the political life for Aquinas.[44] Groups come into existence on the basis of common goods intended through collective action, and they exist insofar as the group shares an intentional state of the sort that intends a common good among its members. Like a "friendship," a social group exists in the relations between individuals, and so involves supervenient and emergent properties which do not exist merely internally in one of the members. Without requiring a group mind, Maritain, de Koninck, and Simon seem to point the way toward a promising account of the metaphysics of groups which is perhaps more robust than some contemporary theories.

If we find plausible the criticism of "intentional individualism" in contemporary theories of collective intention, there are resources in the Thomist tradition for supporting the idea of a shared intentional state. This tradition also enunciates how such an intentional state structures our collective practical reasoning and that it need not require a "group mind." The distinctive Thomist perspective which begins with the analysis of uniquely social goods—"common goods"—can help clarify what it means for us to act and live together.

Saint Louis University
St. Louis, MO

Notes

1. Annette Baier, "Doing Things With Others: The Mental Commons," in *Commonality and Particularity in Ethics*, ed. L. Alanen, S. Heinämaa, and T. Wallgren (New York: St. Martin's Press, 1997), 15–44; Hans Bernhard Schmid, *Wir-Intentionalität. Kritik des ontologischen Individualismus und Rekonstruktion der Gemeinschaft* (Freiburg: Alber, 2005).

2. Hans Bernard Schmid, "Plural Action," *Philosophy of the Social Sciences* 30.1 (Mar. 2008): 48.

3. I bracket the question whether St. Thomas Aquinas himself affirms something akin to "shared intentional states." I will only address interpretation of the position of the aforementioned later Thomist philosophers.

4. Leslie Armour, "Charles de Koninck, the Common Good, and the Human Environment," *Laval theologique et philosophique* 43.1 (1987): 70.

5. Thomas Aquinas, *Sententia Libri Politicorum*, 36–38.

6. Thomas Aquinas, *Summa Theologiae* [Henceforth: *ST*], I, q. 96, a. 4, resp.

7. Thomas Aquinas, *Sententia Libri Politicorum*, 38–39.

8. Charles de Koninck, "The Primacy of the Common Good," in *The Writings of Charles de Koninck*, vol. 2, ed. and trans. Ralph McInerny (Notre Dame, IN: University of Notre Dame Press, 1999), 75.

9. Jacques Maritain, *The Person and the Common Good*, trans. J. Fitzgerald (New York: Charles Scribner's Sons, 1947), 37–42.

10. Ibid., 40–43.

11. This has some parallel to how Meijers responds to Searle's "internalism" along the lines of saying a collective intention or action requires the existence of other agents. He critiques Bratman on that count as well. Cf. Anthonie Meijers, "Can Collective Intentions be Individualized?" *The American Journal of Economics and Sociology* 62.1 (Jan. 2003): 179.

12. Maritain views social goods as common because they only exist *as shared*; this is a distinction which De Koninck might not share. But this insight is at least valid for *social* common goods of the kinds relevant to group action. In fact, all of those related to collective

action in social life (like the good of political flourishing) seem to be such that they are *per se* communicable but also don't exist apart from the communication which makes them possible. Cf., De Koninck, "The Primacy of the Common Good," 75.

13. *ST* II-II, q. 58, a. 2. See also Sullivan, 927.

14. Cf., John Searle, "Collective Intentions and Actions," in *Intentions in Communication* (Cambridge, MA: MIT Press, 1990), 401–415.

15. Yves R. Simon, "The Volition of the Common Good," in *Philosophy of Democratic Government* (Notre Dame, IN: University of Notre Dame Press, 1993), https://www3.nd.edu/~maritain/jmc/etext/pdg-1d.htm (accessed November 10, 2015).

16. Ibid.

17. Ibid.

18. De Koninck, "The Primacy of the Common Good," 105.

19. John Finnis, *Natural Law and Natural Rights* (Oxford: Clarendon Press, 1980), 154–155.

20. Simon, "Volition of the Common Good," ibid.

21. Raimo Tuomela, "Collective Intentionality and Group Reasons," in *Concepts of Sharedness: Essays on Collective Intentionality*, ed. H. Schmid (Berlin and New York: Walter de Gruyter, 2008), 5.

22. Philip Pettit, *A Theory of Freedom: From the Psychology to the Politics of Agency* (New York: Oxford University Press. 2001), 110.

23. Thomas Aquinas, *Sentencia Libri Metaphysicae*, Bk. VIII, lect. 7, n. 1303.

24. There are minimal conditions for what it means to share the same intention, which entail some common understanding of the common good or goal, but Simon implies this would permit variation in our understanding of that content. It would take more work but, for example, we can both intend the same joint action without having exactly the same conception of what the act entails, like we can intend to play football together despite you being a pro and myself a novice with correspondingly different conceptions of the sport. But we both need to know the meaning of "to play football," at minimum. Similarly, we commonly use terms indicating that, while having the same intention, one person might be "more committed" to the group intention than others.

25. Simon, "Authority as Cause of United Action," in *Philosophy of Democratic Government*, n15.

26. Ibid.

27. Schmid, "Plural Action," 36.

28. Ibid., 45. We might also note the ways in which individual sub-goals can be validly derived from group goals. See Wilfrid Sellars, "Imperatives, Intentions, and the Logic of 'Ought,'" in *Morality and the Language of Conduct*, ed. G. Nakhnikian and H.-N. Castaneda (Detroit: Wayne State University Press: 1963); *Science and Metaphysics*; "On Reasoning about Values," *American Philosophical Quarterly* 17.2 (1980): 81–101.

29. Caroline Arruda, "Shared Intention and Reasons for Action," *Philosophy of the Social Sciences* 45.6 (2015): 612.

30. Ibid., 603–623.

31. Hans Bernard Schmid and David Schweikard, "Collective Intentionality," in *The Stanford Encyclopedia of Philosophy* (Summer 2013 Edition), ed. Edward N. Zalta, https://plato.stanford.edu/entries/collective-intentionality/.

32. Mark Murphy, "Consent, Custom, and the Common Good in Aquinas's Account of Political Authority," *The Review of Politics* 59.2 (Spring 1997): 340.

33. Naturally, what we need are *signs* of those judgments. See Kai Spiekerman, "Translucency, Assortation, and Information Pooling," *Politics, Philosophy, and Economics* 6.3 (2007): 285–306, esp. 301–303.

34. Hans Bernhard Schmid, *Plural Action* (Netherlands: Springer Netherlands, 2009), 243.

35. Ibid.

36. Ibid., 42.

37. Cf., John Searle, "Social Ontology and the Philosophy of Society," *Analyse and Kritik* 20 (1998): 150; Raimo Tuomela, *The Importance of Us: A Study of Basic Social Notions* (Stanford: Stanford University Press, 1995), ix, 5, 353, 367.

38. The only exception is noteworthy: Jacques Maritain claimed that the Church is a special group which possesses a group personality *above that of the human members* because it is constituted by God. It is a unique instance of a "group mind." The Church can have a corporate or group personality, as opposed to other collectives, only because God sustains her with a special kind of intentionality. Thus, the Holy Spirit, which causes the life of grace, is both a person in His own right and causes the identical intentional state in each member by indwelling (i.e., love of God). It seems appropriately "spooky" to concede this unique role of group mind to the Holy Ghost. Cf., *On the Church of Christ*, trans. J. Evans (Notre Dame: Univ. of Notre Dame Press, 1973), III.

39. *ST* I, a. 43, a. 3, resp.

40. *ST* II-II, q. 28, a. 1, resp.

41. *ST* II-II, q. 23, a. 2.

42. Thomas Aquinas, *Sententia Libri Ethicorum*, bk. VIII, lec. 9 [*si nulla esset communicatio non posset esse amicitia.*]

43. Thomas Aquinas, *Expositio in Symbolum Apostolorum*, art. 9 ["*ex unitate caritatis, quia omnes connectuntur in amore Dei, et ad invicem in amore mutuo*"]

44. Clarke Cochran, "Yves Simon and 'The Common Good," *Ethics* 88.3 (1978): 237. Cf., Murphy, "Consent, Custom, and the Common Good," 237.

American Catholic Philosophical Association Ninetieth Annual Meeting

Minutes of the 2016 Executive Council Meeting

Westin Saint Francis Hotel
November 3, 2016, 6 p.m. to 11 p.m.

1. Dinner in Cambridge room, 6 to 7:30 p.m. Meeting in Victorian room, 7:30 to 11 p.m.

2. *Present*: Kevin Flannery, SJ (President), Thomas Hibbs (Vice-President), Jorge Garcia (Past President), Mirela Oliva (Secretary), Steven Jensen (Treasurer), Jon McGinnis, Michael Rota, Jennifer Hart Weed, Therese Cory, Gloria Frost, W. Matthews Grant, Catherine Jack Deavel, Marc Gossiaux, Eileen Sweeney, Kevin White

3. *Secretary's Report*: Presented by Mirela Oliva, with copies for members. Discussion on the increasing cost of the annual meeting. Possible measures: disclose the conference rooms only on the printed program, available upon registration; require membership for satellite sessions; require a fee for satellite sessions.

4. *Treasurer's Report*: Presented by Steven Jensen.

5. ACPQ *Report*: presented by David Clemenson. Proposal: a special issue on Aquinas' *Quodlibetal Questions*.
   Vote: Approved unanimously.

6. *Request of the ACPA Committee on Priestly Formation (David Foster)*. The grant proposal of this committee must be approved by the ACPA president. ACPA will manage the grant submission and the grant administration. The members of the committee must be approved by the ACPA president, and their term must be clarified. It is recommended that the committee informs regularly all ACPA members about their activity.
   Vote: Approved unanimously.

7. *Aquinas Medalist 2016*: Linda Zagzebski named Aquinas Medalist for 2017.

8. *Election of the new Executive Committee*: Therese Cory, Gloria Frost.

© 2017, *Proceedings of the ACPA*, Vol. 90
Doi: 10.5840/acpaproc20169084

9. Vote on new ACPA members.

> Vote: Approved unanimously.

10. *Discussion on ACPA spending limits.* The council asks the finance committee to make a proposal about setting the guidelines for spending and a benchmark for endowment.

> Vote: Approved (1 opposed, 1 abstention).

11. *Proposal on diversity (Jorge Garcia).* ACPA will sponsor a regular session at Rutgers University's annual Summer Institute for Diversity in Philosophy. ACPA will provide the speaker with standard travel expenses (airfare, room, board) and honorarium not to exceed $1000.

> Vote: Approved unanimously.

12. *Proposals of the planning committee:*

   a) Outreach. It is proposed that ACPA gives $12,000 distributed between international and local outreach. An Outreach Committee should be created.

> Vote: Approved (1 abstention).

   b) Graduate Student Help. Proposal: variable rates for graduate students for registration, banquet, and women's luncheon.

> Vote: Approved (1 abstention).

   c) ACPA Planning Committee could organize a special session on Job Search.

> Vote: Approved (1 abstention).

   d) Presence at Professional Meetings. It is recommended that ACPA be represented as a group in group sessions at Professional Meetings such as APA.

> Vote: Approved (1 abstention).

13. It is recommended that the paper acceptance rate for annual meeting be published each year in Proceedings.

> Vote: Approved unanimously.

14. *Proposal for new financial conditions for the hosting university:* $8000 for small universities and $15,000 big universities. These conditions might be too difficult for many universities. They should be indicated as orientative, not mandatory.

> Vote: Approved unanimously.

15. Meeting adjourned at 11 p.m.

Respectfully submitted,
Mirela Oliva
National Secretary of ACPA

American Catholic Philosophical Association

Secretary's Report (2016)

I. 2016 Meeting

1. We had 78 submissions and 38 satellite sessions. We have an increasingly high number of satellite sessions which keeps the food and beverage minimum high as compensation for conference room rentals.

2. We created a Facebook page for room sharing for graduate students.

II. Future Annual Meetings

2017: Dallas, Host: Baylor University/University of Dallas
Local contact: Thomas Hibbs, Chad Engelland

We had a proposal from Wake Forest University (Patrick Toner), but the executive committee rejected it because of the transportation problem.

2018: University of San Diego, host Turner Nevitt (undecided)
2019: University of St Thomas, MN, host Matthews Grant (undecided)

III. Statement of the ACPA Executive Committee on Mount St. Mary's —February 13, 2016

IV. Amendment to the Constitution

The ACPA Executive Committee has voted (October 4, 2016) to propose Steven Jensen's amendment to Constitution at the Business Meeting 2016.

Article IV (OFFICERS AND GOVERNMENT), section C, currently reads as follows:

C. The Vice-President (President-Elect) and the members of the Council shall be elected by a plurality of signed postal ballots cast by Constituent members of the Association.

© 2017, *Proceedings of the ACPA*, Vol. 90
doi: 10.5840/acpaproc20169085

The executive committee proposes that this section be amended to read as follows:

C. The Vice-President (President-Elect) and the members of the Council shall be elected by a plurality of ballots cast by Constituent members of the Association.

The only change is that the two words "signed postal" have been deleted. This would allow for balloting by other means, either by paper ballots at the meeting, or by electronic voting. It seems that given the current state of technology the requirement of signed postal ballots is now obsolete. Furthermore, the option of other means of voting may prove helpful in a variety of ways. First, if we allow for electronic voting, more people might vote than is the case currently with mail voting. Second, money can be saved by eliminating mailings with envelopes (currently, we spend hundreds of dollars sending out ballots and envelopes to all of our members).

If you wish to vote on this amendment, then you must show up to the business meeting at the annual meeting, which will be at 11:15 a.m. on Saturday, November 5.

V. ACPA Elections

The complete results of this year's elections (concluded April 1, 2016) are as follows:

Vice-President/President Elect:
    Francis Beckwith (Baylor University)

Executive Council Members
    Thomas Cavanaugh (University of San Francisco)
    Karen Chan (St. Patrick's Seminary & University)
    Heidi Giebel (University of St. Thomas, MN)
    Michael Pakaluk (Ave Maria University)
    Christopher Tollefsen (University of South Carolina)

On behalf of the ACPA, I would like to thank these newly-elected scholars, and to thank all who were willing to stand for election.

VI. ACPA Membership

Membership Category	For 2016 Meeting / Active in 2015	For 2015 Meeting / Active in 2014	For 2014 Meeting / Active in 2013	For 2013 Meeting / Active in 2012	For 2012 Meeting / Active in 2011	For 2011 Meeting / Active in 2010	For 2010 Meeting / Active in 2009
Professor	133	142	140	125	133	153	159
Associate Professor	113	104	135	117	113	126	120
Assistant Professor	144	186	155	133	144	201	222
Instructor	0	0	0	0	0	0	0
Lecturer	0	0	0	0	0	0	0
Student	181	215	256	225	181	250	235
Emeritus	100	89	93	89	100	106	110
Associate	74	118	99	84	74	80	78

Membership Category	For 2016 Meeting Active in 2015	For 2015 Meeting Active in 2014	For 2014 Meeting Active in 2013	For 2013 Meeting Active in 2012	For 2012 Meeting Active in 2011	For 2011 Meeting Active in 2010	For 2010 Meeting Active in 2009
Institutional	59	66	67	63	59	78	76
Library	0	0	0	0	0	0	0
Index/Exchange	21	19	19	20	21	22	0
Life	71	73	73	73	71	68	77
Totals	896	1012	1037	929	896	1084	1077

A clearer idea of trends perhaps can be gathered from the following chart, which tracks membership from the year the person first became a member of the ACPA. B4 counts dues paying members whose first membership year has not been able to be traced.

Old Members	2015	2014	2013	2012	2011	2010	2009
B4	82	95	105	105	113	118	135
1941	0	0	0	0	0	0	0
1942	0	0	0	0	0	0	0
1946	0	0	0	1	1	1	1
1948	0	0	0	0	0	1	1
1949	0	0	0	0	0	0	0
1950	1	1	1	1	1	1	1
1952	0	1	1	1	1	1	2
1953	0	0	0	0	0	0	1
1954	1	2	3	3	3	3	3
1955	0	0	0	0	0	1	3
1956	1	1	1	1	1	1	1
1957	2	3	3	3	3	3	3
1958	1	3	3	3	4	4	4
1959	1	1	1	1	2	1	3
1960	4	5	5	5	5	8	10
1961	1	1	1	1	2	3	3
1962	0	1	1	1	1	2	2
1963	3	5	5	5	5	5	6
1964	2	4	4	4	4	5	6
1965	2	3	3	3	4	4	4
1966	2	3	3	3	4	4	5
1967	1	3	3	3	5	6	6
1968	3	4	4	4	5	6	6
1969	4	4	4	4	4	6	6
1970	5	6	6	6	7	9	10
1971	2	2	2	2	2	2	2
1972	3	3	4	4	4	4	4
1973	2	2	2	2	2	2	2
1974	10	10	10	10	10	11	11
1975	5	6	7	7	8	8	8

Old Members	2015	2014	2013	2012	2011	2010	2009
1976	3	4	4	4	6	6	6
1977	5	5	5	5	5	5	5
1978	4	6	6	6	6	7	7
1979	1	1	1	1	1	1	2
1980	9	9	9	9	9	9	10
1981	2	1	2	2	2	2	1
1982	2	3	3	3	3	3	4
1983	4	4	4	3	3	3	3
1984	1	1	1	1	1	1	2
1985	5	5	5	5	5	5	5
1986	1	1	1	1	2	2	2
1987	9	9	8	8	8	7	7
1988	3	4	4	4	4	4	3
1989	4	6	6	6	6	6	6
1990	5	7	7	7	7	8	11
1991	5	6	6	5	7	9	11
1992	12	13	12	13	13	14	14
1993	34	40	44	44	46	61	63
1994	7	12	15	14	16	19	19
1995	9	10	13	12	13	13	13
1996	4	9	10	9	9	10	16
1997	11	15	15	15	19	22	25
1998	6	8	8	7	8	12	11
1999	25	26	27	28	33	37	42
2000	18	23	23	23	25	31	37
2001	29	31	30	27	32	40	46
2002	15	21	21	19	23	33	37
2003	12	16	18	18	20	22	25
2004	9	12	14	12	14	19	22
2005	22	24	26	24	28	40	45
2006	21	22	23	22	31	43	49
2007	23	32	33	30	35	47	61
2008	18	36	43	41	44	64	96
2009	22	32	40	36	44	85	92
2010	22	32	37	36	40	54	53
2011	37	61	77	77	127	120	
2012	23	41	78	81	0		
2013	43	86	86	88			
2014	47	87	90				
2015	85	82					
2016	93						
Totals	**848**	**1012**	**1037**	**929**	**896**	**1084**	**1100**

VII. ACPA Publications

A. ACPQ

Distribution Type	2015	2014	2013	2012	2011	2010	2009	2008	2007	2006
ACPA Members	828	993	1048	909	875	1062	1077	1151	1161	1166
Subscribers	444	409	470	438	456	452	485	487	453	488
Index/Exchange	32	29	30	33	34	36	36	37	34	49
Totals	1304	1434	1518	1380	1365	1550	1598	1675	1648	1703

B. Proceedings

Distribution Type	2014	2014	2013	2012	2011	2010	2009	2008	2007	2006
ACPA Members	828	993	1018	909	875	1062	1077	1151	1161	1166
Subscribers	42	124	165	109	174	131	88	133	148	129
Exchanges	23	19	19	24	25	32	27	27	27	42
Totals	892	1136	1202	1042	1074	1225	1192	1311	1336	1337

VIII. Thanks and Acknowledgments

On behalf of the ACPA, I would first like to thank my graduate assistant Andrew Grimes for his dedicated work through the year 2015-2016. I would also like to thank Joseph Grossheim and Catherine Peters for their work at the 2016 meeting. Finally, I would like to thank the University of St. Thomas (Houston, TX) for its financial and institutional support of the National Office of the ACPA.

Respectfully submitted,
Mirela Oliva
National Secretary of ACPA

Associate Professor of Philosophy
Center for Thomistic Studies
University of St. Thomas, Houston

November 3, 2016

American Catholic Philosophical Association

Treasurer's Report (2015)

I. Financial Statement

The Financial Statement shows that 2015 was a negative year for the ACPA. In 2015, the ACPA's total net gain of revenues over losses was –$41,139 (compared to $34,356 in 2014). The Financial Statement shows that at the end of 2015, the Association's total liabilities and net assets were $680,614 (compared to $720,496 in 2014). Of this amount, $676,809 represents net (unrestricted) assets (compared to $717,948 in unrestricted assets in 2014). In 2015, therefore, the ACPA's net assets decreased by $41,139.

	2015	2014
Total Assets	$680,614	$720,496
Liabilities	–$3,805	–$2,548
Net Assets	$676,809	$717,948
Gain or Loss from Previous Year	–$41,139	$34,356

II. Annual Revenues and Expenses

Between 2015 and 2014, total annual revenues decreased by $58,118 (total revenues in 2015 were $75,369, while in 2014 they were $133,487), and total annual expenses increased by $17,377 (total expenses in 2015 were $116,508, while in 2014 they were $99,131).

	2015	2014
Annual Revenues	$75,369	$133,487
Change in Revenues	–$58,118	–$28,160
Annual Expenses	$116,508	$99,131
Change in Expenses	$17,377	$32,401

© 2017, *Proceedings of the ACPA*, Vol. 90
doi: 10.5840/acpaproc20169086

III. Annual Meeting

A summary of revenues and expenses in connection with the 2015 Annual Meeting is attached. The Association is very grateful to the local host institution —Boston College—for its direct donations of $15,000 in connection with the meeting. The attached financial statements show that the 2015 Annual Meeting resulted in a $47,814 deficit of expenses over revenues (compared to a deficit of $36,592 in 2014).

	2015	2014
Annual Meeting Earnings or Losses	-$47,814	-$36,592

IV. Assets and Investments—Total: $680,614

The Statement of Financial Position lists our assets on December 31, 2015, as follows:

A. Cash and Cash Equivalents: $42,281

On December 31, 2015, the Association held $42,281 in Chase Manhattan checking and savings accounts and the University of St. Thomas accounts.

	2015
Chase accounts	$41,252
UST accounts	$1,029
Total Cash	$42,281

B. Inventory and Supplies: $495

C. Non-cash Investments: $626,125

On December 31, 2015, the Association's non-cash investment holdings with TIAA-CREF were valued at $626,125.

D. Accounts Receivable: $11,713

On December 31, 2015, the Association had $11,713 earned in 2015 but not yet received until 2016.

V. Liabilities—Total: $3,805

Account Payable: $2,548

The amount of $3,805 represents expenses incurred by the ACPA in 2015 (such as fees attributable to work performed in 2015), but not yet paid for until after December 31, 2015, i.e., after the closing date for 2015 statements from the ACPA's bank and investment manager. Accordingly, the ACPA carried these not-yet-paid expenses as a liability.

VI. Reminder

The Association depends for revenue on membership dues and subscription payments. Therefore, the National Office reminds members to be prompt in paying their dues and/or subscription charges.

VII. Donations

As always, the Association welcomes donations. Since the ACPA is a tax-exempt organization under section 501(c)(3) of the Internal Revenue Code, all donations to the Association are tax-deductible to the full extent allowed by law.

VIII. Acknowledgements

On behalf of the Association, the Treasurer would like to thank the University of St. Thomas in Houston for its generous financial support of the Association throughout 2015. In 2015, the Association received $9,000 in cash donations and $19,100 in in-kind donations from the University of St. Thomas, for a total of $28,100.

American Catholic Philosophical Association
Financial Statements

Years Ended December 31, 2015 and 2014

© 2017, *Proceedings of the ACPA*, Vol. 90
doi: 10.5840/acpaproc20169087

pp. 311–320

American Catholic Philosophical Association
Accountants' Compilation Report

Years Ended December 31, 2015 and 2014

TABLE OF CONTENTS

American Catholic Philosophical Association
Independent Accountants' Compilation Report

Years Ended December 31, 2015 and 2014

To the Board of Directors
American Catholic Philosophical Association
Houston, Texas

Management is responsible for the accompanying financial statements of American Catholic Philosophical Association, which comprise the financial position as of December 31, 2015 and 2014, and the related statements of activities and changes in net assets and cash flows for the years then ended, in accordance with accounting principles generally accepted in the United States of America. We have performed a compilation engagement in accordance with Statements on Standards for Accounting and Review Services promulgated by the Accounting and Review Services Committee of the American Institute of Certified Public Accountants. We did not audit or review the financial statements nor were we required to perform any procedures to verify the accuracy or completeness of the information provided by management. Accordingly, we do not express an opinion, conclusion, nor provide any form of assurance on these financial statements.

The supplementary information contained in Schedule I is presented only for supplementary analysis purposes. Such information has been compiled from information that is the representation of management, without audit or review. Accordingly, we do not express an opinion, conclusion, nor provide any other form of assurance on the supplementary information.

Management has elected to omit substantially all of the disclosures and the statement of cash flows required by accounting principles generally accepted in the United States of America. If the omitted disclosures and statement of cash flows were included in the financial statements, they might influence the user's conclusions about the Company's financial position, results of operations, and cash flows. Accordingly, the financial statements are not designed for those who are not informed about such matters.

Hutchinson and Bloodgood LLP

May 4, 2016

American Catholic Philosophical Association
Statements of Financial Position

Years Ended December 31, 2015 and 2014

ASSETS	2015	2014
Current assets		
Cash—checking and savings	$ 42,281	$ 67,283
Accounts receivable	11,713	9,636
Prepaid expense	—	2,500
Inventory and supplies	495	534
Investments, at market value	626,125	640,543
Total assets	680,614	$ 720,496

LIABILITIES AND NET ASSETS		
Current liabilities		
Accounts payable and accrued expenses	$ 3,805	$ 2,548
Unrestricted net assets	676,809	717,948
Total liabilities and net assets	680,614	$ 720,496

See independent accountants' compilation report.

American Catholic Philosophical Association
Statements of Activities and Changes in Net Assets

Years Ended December 31, 2015 and 2014

SUPPORT AND REVENUES	2015	2014
Annual meeting	$ 34,345	$ 30,936
Royalties	29,836	31,290
Donations from University of St. Thomas	25,600	21,500
Interest and dividends	7,504	9,247
Net realized and unrealized gain in investments	(21,916)	40,514
Total support and revenues	75,369	133,487
EXPENSES		
Annual meeting	82,159	67,528
Rising scholar award	3,000	—
Salaries and wages	19,100	15,208
Insurance	1,523	1,474
Accounting services	3,900	3,900
Web service charges	209	113
Office equipment	949	—
Travel stipend	5,668	10,908
Total expenses	116,508	99,131
Increase in unrestricted net assets	(41,139)	34,356
NET ASSETS, BEGINNING OF YEAR	717,948	683,592
NET ASSETS, END OF YEAR	676,809	$ 717,948

See independent accountants' compilation report.

American Catholic Philosophical Association
Statements of Cash Flows

Years Ended December 31, 2015 and 2014

CASH FLOWS FROM OPERATING ACTIVITIES	2015	2014
Increase in unrestricted net assets	$ (41,139)	$ 34,356
Adjustments to reconcile increase in unrestricted net assets to net cash provided by operating activities		
Net realized and unrealized loss (gain) in investments	21,916	(40,514)
Net change in:		
Accounts receivable	(2,077)	17,489
Inventory and supplies	39	38
Prepaid expense	2,500	(2,500)
Accounts payable and accrued expenses	1,257	(2,463)
Net cash provided by operating activities	(17,503)	6,406

CASH FLOWS FROM INVESTING ACTIVITIES		
Net purchases in investments	(7,498)	(34,224)
Net increase (decrease) in cash	(25,002)	(27,818)
CASH, beginning of year	67,283	95,101
CASH, end of year	42,281	$ 67,283

See independent accountants' compilation report.

American Catholic Philosophical Association
Supplementary Information

Years Ended December 31, 2015 and 2014

American Catholic Philosophical Association
Schedule I: Revenues and Expenses of Annual Meeting

Years Ended December 31, 2015 and 2014

REVENUES	2015	2014
Registration and banquet	$ 19,345	$ 23,136
Donations:		
The Catholic University of America	—	6,000
Boston University	15,000	1,800
	34,345	30,936
EXPENSES		
Banquet expenses	58,384	55,669
Honorarium expenses	5,000	1,800
Young scholar award	250	1,000
Aquinas medal and engraving	39	68
Meeting registration services	4,887	976
Printing and duplicating expenses	4,757	3,309
Postage	810	509
Travel	8,032	4,197
	82,159	67,528
Shortage of revenues over expenses	(47,814)	$ (36,592)

See independent accountants' compilation report.

American Catholic Philosophical Association

ACPQ Editor's Report (2016)

I. Summary of ACPQ-Related Activities,
October 1, 2015–September 30, 2016

1. Rising Scholar Essay Contest: We received 13 submissions this year, down from last year's 32. (We were less aggressive about advertising this year, believing [apparently mistakenly] that by the fourth year of the contest the word must be out. We'll advertise earlier and more widely next year.)

2. Our total submissions rose slightly to 109 this year (from 103 last year).

3. We published one special issue this year: on Elizabeth Anscombe, edited by John Haldane; it has received numerous compliments.

4. Our acceptance rate was 24.7%: up slightly from 22.4% in 2015. We attribute this phenomenon primarily to the high quality of submissions we have received lately.

5. Our turn-around time averaged 38 days, down significantly from 74 days in 2014 and 57 in 2015.

Requests to the Executive Council

1. Approve proposed upcoming special issue (see below).

2. Encourage (good) submissions so we can keep quality high and acceptance rates low.

© 2017, *Proceedings of the ACPA*, Vol. 90
doi: 10.5840/acpaproc20169088

Schedule of Upcoming *ACPQ* Special Issues

Submission Deadline	Topic	Guest Editor(s)	Scheduled Issue	Editorial Office Deadline for Manuscripts	PDC Deadline for Edited Manuscripts
9/2016	Dietrich von Hildebrand	Crosby	91:4 Fall 2017	4/1/2017	8/1/2017
6/2017	Religious Epistemology	Dougherty	92:3 Summer 2018	1/1/2018	5/1/2018
3/2018	Baroque Scholasticism	Dvorak and Schmutz	93:2 Spring 2019	10/1/2018	2/1/2019
12/2018	John Henry Newman*	Pakaluk	94:1 Winter 2020	7/1/2019	11/1/2019
9/2019	Aquinas's Quodlibetal Questions**	Nevitt and Davies	94:4 Fall 2020	i4/1/2020	8/1/2020
6/2020	TBA	TBA	95:3 Summer 2021	1/1/2021	5/1/2021

*Rescheduled from 91:1 Winter 2017.
**Pending EC approval.

ACPQ Article Submissions *Received*: 2009–2016

Year	Submissions Received	Numerical Change	Percent Change
2009	90	NA	NA
2010	95	+5	+5.5%
2011	87	-8	-8.4%
2012	107	+20	+23.0%
2013	148	+41	+38.3%
2014	97	-51	-34.4%
2015	103	+6	+6.2%
2016	109	+6	+5.8%
Total 2009–2015	727	NA	NA

ACPQ Articles *Decided* October 1, 2015 through September 30, 2016

Category	Number	Percent of Total Reviewed
Rejected	72	50.7%
Revise and Resubmit	35	24.6%
Withdrawn by Author	0	0%
Subtotal: Articles Not Accepted	107	75.3%
Accepted	15	10.6%
Conditionally accepted	20	14.1%
Subtotal: Articles Accepted[1]	35	24.7%
Total: Articles Reviewed	142	100.0%

ACPQ Submission Turn-Around Times
October 1, 2015 through September 30, 2016

Category	Average Weeks from Receipt to Determination
Accepted or conditionally accepted	6.9
Rejected or R&R	4.6
All articles	5.3

ACPQ Submission Turn-Around Times 2009–2016

Year	Average Weeks from Receipt to Acceptance	Average Weeks from Receipt to Rejection
2009	13.6	12.7
2010	11.7	8.0
2011	16.2	8.0
2012	4.7	6.2
2013	9.5	11.0
2014	11.6	10.2
2015	10.7	7.0
2016	6.9	4.6

Notes

1. Does not include articles published in special issues, for which we do not have acceptance rate statistics.

Necrology (2016–June 2017)

Jan Aertsen, Universitaet zu Koeln (2016)

Doug Benscoter, (student) Holy Apostles College (2016)

Dr. Joseph Boyle, St Michael's College (2016)

Rev. Vincent Cooke, Canisius College (2017)

Sr. Mary Bernard Curran, St Cecilia Convent (2017)

Louis Decourty (2017)

Kenneth T. Gallagher, Fordham Univeristy (2017)

Hugh McCann, Texas A&M University (2016)

Roland Teske, SJ, Marquette University (2015)

Requiescant in pace.

© 2017, *Proceedings of the ACPA*, Vol. 90
doi: 10.5840/acpaproc20169089

Available Back Issues of the *Proceedings*

Volumes

Please send orders to:

Philosophy Documentation Center
P.O. Box 7147
Charlottesville, VA 22906-7147
Web: www.pdcnet.org

800-444-2419 (U.S. & Canada) or
434-220-3300
Fax: 434-220-3301
E-mail: order@pdcnet.org

All back issues of the *Proceedings* are $50 each, plus shipping per volume outside the US. Make checks payable to the Philosophy Documentation Center. Please send checks in U.S. dollars only. Visa, MasterCard, American Express, and Discover are accepted for your convenience.

© 2017, *Proceedings of the ACPA*, Vol. 90
doi: 10.5840/acpaproc20169090